ONE WOMAN ARMY

The Life of Claire Culhane

Mick Lowe

Macmillan Canada
Toronto

Quote from *Dreams of Equality* by Joan Sangster used by permission of the Canadian Publishers, McClelland & Stewart, Toronto.

Quote from *A Hard Man to Beat* by Howard White used by permission of Pulp Press, Vancouver.

For information regarding dramatic, film, foreign, and other related rights please contact Aurora Artists, 3 Charles St. W., Suite 207, Toronto, Ontario, Canada M4Y 1R4, (416) 929-2042.

Canadian Cataloguing in Publication Data

Lowe, Mick, 1947–
    One Woman Army: the life of Claire Culhane

Includes index.
ISBN 0-7715-9182-9

1. Culhane, Claire, 1918– . 2. Social action—
Canada.   3. Corrections—Canada.   4. Social
reformers—Canada—Biography.   5. Political
activists—Canada—Biography.   I. title

HN103.5.L69 1992   324'.4'092   C92–094309–8

Macmillan Canada wishes to thank the Canada Council for supporting its publishing program.

1 2 3 4 5   GP   96 95 94 93 92

*Cover photo: Claire outside the gates of the B.C. Penitentiary observing the first Prison Justice Day, August 10, 1976. Prison Justice Day, which Claire helped co-found, is still observed annually as a day of fasting by Canadian prisoners and their families to commemorate the hundreds of men and women who have died of unnatural causes while in custody. (*Vancouver Sun *photo)*

Macmillan Canada
A Division of Canada Publishing Corporation
Toronto, Ontario, Canada

Printed in Canada

For Grace Ellenwood Lowe, 1911-1982, who taught me

*"That the salvation of the state
is the watchfulness of its citizens."*

Contents

Foreword

I first heard someone talk about the elusive nature of goodness about ten years ago when Sister Mary Jo Leddy was granted the Ida Nudel Humanitarian Award. In her acceptance speech, given in a high-ceilinged room in the Ontario Legislature building at Queen's Park, this magnificent and modest nun of the Sisters of Sion mused about altruism. She said that we don't understand much about the inclination some people have to take responsibility for the well-being of others. We pay considerable attention to the nature of evil, she said, but the motivation for selfless acts of kindness is a mystery on which we rarely speculate.

Like Socrates, she made no attempt to answer the questions she raised, but the enigma she left hanging in the air has stayed with me. Some years later it was my good fortune to enter into a friendship with Mary Jo. One day I asked her, "Why are you a good person?" She grinned and replied, "Because my parents were good people."

That's a start, the healthiest, most promising start possible, but it doesn't entirely explain why Mary Jo is continually breaking her heart and exhausting all her resources, except the spiritual ones, in her efforts to help refugees. And it doesn't explain Claire Culhane, who rises at five in the morning in her tiny apartment, which is jammed on every side with filing cabinets and stacks of correspondence, in order to front-load a day that will be spent sending letters to politicians, the media, and bureaucrats on behalf of men and women who are suffering in Canadian prisons.

I wrote about Claire Culhane in April 1989, in the *Globe and Mail*, observing, "She fights tenaciously and without compromise because she's a Montreal radical from the 1930s and she doesn't know any other way to live her life except to assail the manifest evils Gandhi described as 'injustice, untruth, and humbug.'"

On perusal of the column, I note there is no analysis in it of why Claire Culhane doesn't know any other way to live her life. Loads of people in their seventies manage to get through an entire day without writing more than a dozen warm, encouraging letters to people serving life sentences and five tightly documented, tautly written, enraged broadsides to solicitors-general.

In February 1991 Paul Reed of Statistics Canada headed a colloquium in Ottawa to discuss the Civic Sector. His concern was similar to that of Mary Jo Leddy. He said that Statistics Canada wasn't able to quantify the amount of goodness, which he called civic responsibility, existing in this country so perhaps an attempt should be made to qualify the term. He was looking for the connections, the way people contribute to the common good. The glue in communities, he explained, is its composition of people who care what happens to others—even if they don't know them. The work of volunteers in Canada is estimated at $13.5 billion dollars a year, not a penny of which is recognized in the economy. Volunteers spoon-feed helpless people in geriatric wards; they rock babies in a centre for teenaged mothers; they take downtown children to a horse ranch; they collect eyeglasses for the Third World; they canvas, picket, petition, go on walk-a-thons, sit on committees concerned for the environment. Who are these people, and why do they do what they do?

The participants at the colloquium—lawyers, clergy, journalists, foundation heads, sociologists—talked all day in both official languages, but no one could answer the question.

Claire Culhane doesn't know either. When pressed, she formulates something about prison conditions being a metaphor for every kind of oppression in society. She might add that prison conditions represent the most conspicious, and most appalling example, of institutionalized abuse against helpless people.

Her reply casts no light on the why of her. Lots of people are aware that Canadian prisons are inhumane and it outrages their sensibilities to think about it, but they confine their indignation to short bursts of activity. As this wonderful book by the superb journalist Mick Lowe amply illustrates, Claire Culhane has always responded to whatever is unfair or degrading to another human being with all the passion, intellect, and strategy at her command, even at the risk of her health (many times) and her life (a few). It's a simple reflex for her—like breathing.

Goodness, for me, is not the absence of evil. That's too passive a concept. Goodness marches out and performs deeds that spring from empathy with the human condition. Goodness is the vigorous expression of human divinity; it is religion in motion.

Claire Culhane is chock-full of goodness. Like Mary Jo Leddy, like Stats Canada, I don't know what makes the invincible Claire Culhane care so much, but I do know that all Canadians are fortunate that she does. She does us proud; she gives us all hope for ourselves.

Acknowledgements

I first met Claire Culhane in Vancouver, in June of 1970. I was a twenty-year-old draft dodger newly arrived from the United States and dating Dara Culhane, who had told me much (laudatory and otherwise) about her mother. Good or bad, there was a certain tone of grudging admiration when Dara spoke of Claire, and I was anxious to meet her.

We were late for the appointment at our Kitsalano apartment, I remember, and the door was locked. I first saw Claire sitting imperturbably on a curb between two parked cars on West Seventh Avenue. She carries a bag of correspondence the way that many older women carry a bag of knitting, and it was beside her on the pavement even then as she sat, oblivious to the traffic, intent on that day's incoming mail. She was dressed like the Viet Cong—baggy black pants, rubber-tire soled sandals, and a loose fitting top. I saw her instantly as the diametric opposite of my ex mother-in-law in Nebraska, a "charm school instructor" who was anorexic, fashionable, and uptight.

I'm not sure exactly when I realized that I wanted to tell her life story. It may have been that night, or it may have been a night two years later, in Calgary, when I first read her description of the Tet Offensive in her book *Why Is Canada in Vietnam?* It was early on, anyway, and I am delighted, though not really surprised, that I haven't been "scooped" by some other story-teller. Suffice it to say, I've had my eye on this particular story for a long, long time.

Few readers appreciate, I believe, the extent to which a work of non-fiction is a truly collaborative effort. A multitude of collaborators and supporters have crossed the stage from the moment I first knew that I wanted to tell Claire's story to the release of the book you are reading now. My long-standing desire received concrete impetus in the summer of 1986 when Claire's daughters Roisin and Dara founded the Claire Culhane Life History Project. The Project's goal was to have Claire's life story told in book form, and some two hundred of Claire's friends and supporters were contacted to this end.

Next the family invited applications from writers and, in the spring of 1987, I was fortunate enough to be selected for the task. My first interview with Claire was in Ottawa on June 1, 1987, and our interviews have continued intermittently, and in a variety of locations, until the date of this writing. After Dara and Roisin, who conceived of this project, I must thank Claire herself; she has unstintingly offered her time, and brought to the telling of her life story the same energy, wit, and keen memory that she has deployed for so many causes over half a century.

I must also acknowledge the dozens of champions of the Claire Culhane Life History Project who took the time to jot down their reminiscences of Claire or to send tapes, clippings, correspondence, and other memorabilia. And a special thank you must go to Joanne Drummond, a long-time friend and supporter of Claire, who prepared the index for this volume, and who provided an invaluable first reading and criticism of the original manuscript in draft.

Research for this book has taken me literally from coast to coast, and along the way I was assisted by a small host of librarians and archivists. Among them: Dale Huston, reference librarian of the Cote St. Luc Public Library, Montreal; Ronald Finegold of the Montreal Jewish Public Library; Donna MacHutchin, librarian for the Montreal *Gazette*; David Fraser of the National Archives of Canada in Ottawa; Ashley Thompson of the Laurentian University Library in Sudbury; Kay Turner and Joyce Milne of the Protestant School Board of Greater Montreal; Anastasia Bolovis of Outremont Secondary School, Montreal; Margaret Henricks of the Ottawa Civic Hospital; Alexander Wright, Archivist at the MacLennan Library at McGill University; Nola O'Brien of the Moncton, New Brunswick, *Times-Transcript*; and Gwen Whissell and Lynn Imbeau of the Valley East, Ontario, Public Library. I must especially thank George Brandak and the staff of the University of British Columbia Library's Special Collections, which houses Claire's papers from 1975 to the present, and Charlotte Stewart of the Archives Research Collection at McMaster University in Hamilton, where Claire's Vietnam war-era papers have been collected.

A number of people across Canada were generous with their time and recollections of Claire through interviews for this book. They include: Raymond Boyer, Ken Andrews, Edith Josephson, Julius Briskin, and Lea Roback in Montreal; Harry and Jonnie Rankin, Liz Elliott, Sylvia Friedman, Hank Rosenthal, Trudy Harkness, and Dr. Alje Vennema in Vancouver; Art Solomon in Sudbury; Charlotte MacEwan and Gil Rhodes in Ottawa; and Muriel Duckworth in Halifax.

Several of my friends and colleagues very kindly shared their own research materials and thoughts on the diverse subjects that affected Claire's life. Mercedes Steedman, Christine Ball, and Terry Pender in Sudbury, Bob Sarti in Vancouver, and Sandra Lythe at CSC Headquarters in Ottawa all provided invaluable input. I must especially thank Larry Hannant of Vancouver in this regard. It was Larry who guided Claire through the labyrinthe process of Freedom of Information and Privacy Act applications that produced the priceless yield of five decades of documents that the Canadian government has accumulated on Claire's personal and public life.

There are always, thank God, individuals and institutions wise (or foolish) enough to financially support the inherently risky business of book writing. Chief among these, of course, was Macmillan Canada, but I must also acknowledge the contributions of the Canada Council; the Ontario Arts Council; Doug Yeo, Ron Andrews, Rita Chiasson, and the staff of the Sudbury Regional Credit Union; and Gerry Wrigley and the staff of the Kent Credit Union in New Minas, Nova Scotia.

Another, tighter circle of collaborators played an almost daily role over the two years required to complete the writing of this book. Denise Schon, the publisher of Macmillan Canada, never waivered in her commitment to the chancy publishing proposition of bringing Claire's story to the Canadian public. Jackie Rothstein, also of Macmillan, laboured long and hard over the manuscript, as did my friend, editor, and soul mate, Sheldon Fischer, who once again shared, and improved upon, my vision. And my agent Janine Cheeseman, of Aurora Artists in Toronto, has always been there when I needed her.

Finally, as always, I must once again thank my most intimate collaborators: my wife Ruth Reyno, and my daughters Julia and Melanie Lowe. Ruth for her belief in me, for sharing my conviction in the importance of Claire's story, and for her unflagging willingness to provide moral and financial support in the telling of it. And Julia and Melanie for respecting the invisible yet essential creative bubble within which all writers must spend a good part of their waking hours.

I am deeply grateful for the cooperation and support of all those mentioned above. Any errors or omissions in the finished product are, however, my own.

M.L.
August 1992
Onwatin Lake, Ontario

This Movie Is Not Over
(for Claire Culhane)

Now we begin
riding the hump of night
the gulf over the planet
this is the world
this is the world we live in

now we are tickled by flowers
the same colour as flags
On cue
the soldiers fling their arms upwards
bare in short-sleeved tropical uniforms
their disembodied
arms

Now we are watching
released prisoners
inching along the floor
he has perfected a system:
the hand crosses to the ankle
moves the leg forward
then the other.
this is still happening.

walking the streets of Quang Ngai
after six years absence
I am suddenly
embraced by strangers.
they were young girls
   who have married
   had children, and grown
   unrecognizably old.

this too is happening:
they are eating bark.

Now people are hurrying
for their coats
leaving the room
refusing to witness
now we are reaching
for logic, for comfort
rebuilding our headless capitals

even the film projector
refuses to witness:
it goes beserk, breaks the film
but we are still
faced with this
tired incorruptible woman,
witness

Not one of us here really
understanding what it is to be
unbought, uncomforted
the continual pull at the guts
the planet's heaviness

This movie is not over.
this witness takes
down her posters
petitions, our intentions
broken as the night rides
in through the open door

Pat Lowther
November 1974

Prologue

Quang Ngai, Central Vietnam, 1968

The shock of the incoming artillery lifted her bodily from the bed, and she awoke only after hitting the floor. It was dark in the room (*had she been dreaming?*), and it took a moment to regain her senses.

Her wristwatch told her that it was one minute after four in the morning. She remembered, gradually, that it was January 31, 1968, the cusp of the Vietnamese lunar new year.

Claire's first conscious thought was of the hospital and its patients—*her* patients. She was concerned for their safety in the horrific battle that had just begun outside her room.

Nocturnal assaults by the National Liberation Front were nothing new; the South Vietnamese Army and the Americans held Quang Ngai—tenuously—by day, and by night both Quang Ngai City and Quang Ngai province became a free-fire zone. But she could tell by the intensity of the barrage beyond her window that this was no ordinary firefight.

Still on the floor, listening, stunned, she remembered that afternoon on the patio, how the American major had watched, and counted, the armoured personnel carriers zipping through the dusty streets of the provincial capital and into the surrounding countryside. As he counted she had listened idly. Finally the major's count reached twelve, and then he got excited. They only had eighteen APCs on the base, he muttered, and normally kept at least half that number in for the night—just in case. Something really must be up. Half an hour later a captain roared up in a jeep. He came running onto the patio, shouting breathlessly that the American base was on "100 percent red alert." The major gulped the rest of his drink down his tanned, confident American throat and then scurried off in the captain's jeep.

Claire recalled, too, how a Vietnamese soldier had warned her earlier in the day, in whispered French, "VC come tonight." She had, at the time, discounted the prediction, which she had heard so many times before.

But now as her eyes adjusted to the light from the flares outside, she wondered . . . Then her thoughts returned urgently to the hospital. There were perhaps forty Vietnamese patients that night in the Canadian Anti-Tuberculosis Hospital in Quang Ngai, and the ward was on the second floor, precariously exposed to the surrounding battle. The patients must be terrified.

She quickly dressed and ran out the door of her room on to the patio. Louise Piché, a Canadian nurse, and Chau, their Vietnamese interpreter, met her in the hallway. They hurriedly discussed the situation. The residence was undamaged—evidently not a target. They glanced at the wing where the Canadian men slept—Dr. Michel Jutras, the head of the delegation, Dr. Harold Jerema, and X-ray technician Arthur Ludwick—but there was no sound, and no one emerged from their door. It was impossible that anyone could sleep through such a night as this! Clearly, whatever would be done was to be left up to the women.

Only Pauline Trudel, another Canadian nurse, was on duty in the hospital, Claire reminded Louise.

But it would be far too dangerous to walk to the hospital, a kilometre away, Louise responded. Pauline and their patients would have to fend for themselves.

Claire looked once more at the men's door, but saw no sign of movement.

Louise and Chau returned to their rooms, but Claire, unable to sleep, remained on the patio, watching the flares, listening to the artillery and mortar barrage as it echoed through the countryside.

At 4:30 a.m. a jeep passed by from the direction of the hospital, which told her that at least the road to the hospital was still open. There was no doubt what she must do.

Before departing the relative security of the house Claire paused: should she take her bike? She decided against it; she might have to dive for cover in the ditch at any moment, and her bicycle, whatever it might gain her in speed, could prove a dangerous encumbrance. Taking a deep breath, Claire Culhane emerged into the middle of the Tet Offensive.

The road was deserted. By day, it would be teeming with life, crowded with peasants going to and from the local market, bicycles, jeeps. As a Canadian, one of her most enduring impressions of Vietnam would always be of its sheer human density—nearly fifty million people crammed into a country less than one-quarter the size of her native Quebec. Normally, even at this hour, there would be some reminder of human habitation—roosters crowing, dogs barking.

But now there was not a soul, not a sound, save the rattle of machine-gun fire and the steady thud of artillery somewhere in the distance. The apparent emptiness of the ramshackle dwellings that lined the roadway (the Americans called them "hooches") was positively eerie, and would forever remain for Claire the clearest memory of the most extraordinary walk of her life.

As she peered into the darkness up the road, looking anxiously for the sentry point that guarded the approach to the hospital, she imagined that the roadside inhabitants were, like the Canadian doctors, cowering in their beds, praying for the morning light.

But she was wrong. Her passing was watched in silence by hundreds of wondering eyes. *They* and their ancestors had survived nights like these, had watched men toting weapons—Americans, French, Japanese, Chinese—stalk this very road. For a thousand years, dating back to the fall of the T'ang dynasty, men armed with weapons and ideology, fighting for territory, for power, had come from distant lands to contend for this narrow strip of land beside the South China Sea.

But this was truly remarkable: a woman, dressed in white, with no weapon and no apparent ideology, walking through this deadly night alone, leaving the safety of the Canadian place to reach the hospital where their own people lay suffering.

Clearly, she was not one of them. *So who was this woman, and why had she come?*

CHAPTER ONE

Now We Begin

*All persons of this birth date are strong mentally and
physically, with great persistence and willpower.
They are not easily discouraged, and will accomplish
whatever plans they start out to do.*
        —Horoscope, *Montreal Daily Star*, September 2, 1918

There is no history, only biography.
                              —Ralph Waldo Emerson

A be Eglin cursed to himself in Yiddish before glancing anxiously at his
wife, Rose. She was obviously in pain, and Abe began to sweat in the
damp heat that still lingered at the end of another muggy Montreal summer.
He looked again through the windshield of the Model T, but the sight before
them was the same as before. St. Catherine Street was hopelessly congested,
blocked off by police barricades. St. Catherine Street, of all places!

Why on earth, on this Monday, a holiday—and then he groaned
inwardly. Of course, it was Labour Day, and he had driven them squarely
into the route of the city's Labour Day parade. The irony wouldn't hit him
until later, and then the story would enter family lore.

Abe was no expert, but he feared his Rose was already in hard labour on
the car seat beside him, and this was no ordinary birth. The severity of the
contractions was frightening, and so soon! This was nothing like the birth
of Jack, their first child, five years before. He had to get to that hospital!

He swung the Ford right, off St. Catherine, and headed north in the
general direction of Montreal Maternity Hospital, unwittingly driving into
the heart of the parade.

Thirty thousand working men and women formed the procession
through the streets of Montreal that day, with Médéric Martin, the city's
mercurial mayor, walking proudly at their head. He'd once been a working
man himself, a member of Cigarmakers' Union Local 58, no small factor

in his populist appeal. Behind him, stretching for many blocks, thronged cutters, patternmakers, and seamstresses from the sweatshops along the Main; longshoremen, teamsters, and shipbuilders from the city's water-front; and machinists, boilermakers, and engineers from the CPR's sprawling Angus Works, the largest railway shop in the world.[1]

There were men who cut hair, shod horses, served beer made by other men farther back in the line; women who toiled as clerks, dressmakers, and city employees; and the men who had built Canada's most magnificent city: carpenters and joiners, asbestos workers, tile layers, plasterers, stone and granite cutters, masons, bricklayers, and the ironworkers who erected the structural steel for Montreal's finest buildings.[2]

Led by a mounted police escort and accompanied by no fewer than twenty-one brass bands, the procession had turned right onto St. Lawrence. Like Abe and Rose Eglin, they were headed north. Abe raced the parade, hoping to get ahead of and around it, but at Ontario Street Eglin discovered that even the way north was blocked. He was almost surrounded on three sides by the parade. Abe Eglin had nothing against labour, but why, at this hour, did they seem to be keeping him and his Rose from safety?

He doubled back then and turned east, away from the hospital, back toward the family flat far to the east in Hochelaga. Then north, then west again, finally arriving at the emergency entrance to Montreal Maternity Hospital, at the corner of St. Urbain and Prince Arthur. The doctors rushed Rose directly into the delivery room, and a baby girl was born within minutes of their arrival, "just in time for lunch," which, everyone in the family later agreed, was in keeping with the baby's prodigious appetite.

As Abe had feared, it had not been a normal delivery, but a difficult breech birth. Even though she was only twenty-three, his beloved Rose would never have another child.

The speed of the birth, the nature of her first brush with history in the Labour Day parade, and the fact that she had literally kicked her way out of her mother's womb, all perfectly foreshadowed the singular life that was to follow. "You see?" Claire Culhane would say years later, with a certain impish satisfaction, "I put my foot in it right from the start."

"Nineteen eighteen," Abraham Eglin would tell his grandchildren with a flourish and a mock sigh. "The year they ended one war in Europe, and another started in my house."

The baby's name had been decided before her birth, determined by Jewish folklore. Even before Rose had known she was pregnant, a vision of her recently deceased aunt Kayla had appeared to her in a dream. Aunt Kayla was restless, unable to settle in her coffin, and kept muttering that she wouldn't pass happily into the next world until someone was named after her. Following the Jewish belief that the sooner and the more children who are named after the deceased the happier the departed will be, Rose vowed to name her next child Kayla. Rose and Abe kept the promise. The new baby was named Claire, the Canadian equivalent of Kayla, but was given no middle name, thus providing Claire with one of her earliest grievances against the world. Her brother Jack had received two names—Moses Jack Eglin—while her parents, whether by design or oversight, had given her only one.

Her paternal grandparents, being very much of the Old World, always called her Kayla. Samuel (Sholem) and Fanny (Fagel) Eglin had emigrated to Canada from a *shtetl* near Vilnius (then part of Poland, now the capital of Lithuania) in 1907. Sholem was an itinerant tinker who repaired brass pots and pans, a trade he pursued both in the Old World and the New. Fagel was a tough, laconic matriarch who ran a small store to augment Sholem's income. A large man, Sholem Eglin was a gifted storyteller, fond of wine and cherry brandy, which he brewed at home.

Rose Eglin's parents, Abraham and Toba Briskin, had come to Canada from Kiev, the capital of Ukraine, in 1905. Rose's mother, it was said, had been a great beauty in her youth in Kiev, who had become betrothed to a man she loved deeply. Unfortunately for the young couple, her fiancé had been observed one day wearing a watch chain on the sabbath. Such adornment was forbidden by the strictures of Orthodox Judaism, and Toba was forced to break off her engagement. Her parents matched her instead with Abraham Briskin, whom she detested from the first day they met. But she had dutifully submitted to the marriage—she had had no choice.

Toba and Abraham Briskin fled the Ukraine to escape religious persecution in the notorious pogroms of 1905. As Russia teetered on the brink of revolution, a wave of anti-Semitism swept through the country, encouraged by Czar Nicholas the Second, who hoped to divert popular discontent with his own regime by unleashing anti-Jewish sentiment. In Ukraine, attacks by the Cossacks, the fierce cavalry troops of the czar, became legendary throughout the Jewish world. One of Claire's aunts by marriage would hold the younger generation spellbound by recounting the decapitation of her own parents at the hands of anti-Semites, a scene the horrified girl witnessed while hiding behind a couch. The Briskins had narrowly escaped Russia themselves. Abraham and his two oldest sons, Morris and Louis had gone into hiding, in fear for their lives, while Toba emigrated to America with the six younger children.[3]

Rose Briskin, who was born in 1894, had became the victim of a peculiar tragedy as a girl of eight. As part of a childish prank one of her older brothers tied her to the branch of a tree and hung her upside down and then, unaccountably, forgot about her. When someone finally discovered Rose's plight so much blood had rushed to her head that she was completely blind. She was taken to a specialist in Moscow and for the next few years Rose lived in the doctor's home while undergoing treatment. But her blindness remained, and her eyes were kept bandaged, while special herbs were applied, for three long years. When the bandages were finally removed the first thing she remembered seeing, Rose Eglin would tell her own children many years later, was the doll with which she'd been playing all that time.

She returned to her parents' home just in time for the pogrom of 1905. While her father and older brothers went into hiding, Rose and the five younger children sailed for America with their mother. Rose was carried aboard the ship on a stretcher, suffering from pneumonia, and there were doubts whether she would survive the voyage. But while her brothers and sisters became seasick, Rose got stronger, revived by the sea air.

When Toba Briskin and her brood arrived in the New World they were penniless and spoke no English or French. The family settled in Montreal—where they were later joined by Abe, Morris, and Louis—and the children went to work almost at once. Rose's first job, when she was just thirteen, was in a cigar-factory sweatshop. The pay was two dollars for a twelve-hour, six-day week, but since she was unable to work on Saturdays because of the Jewish sabbath, Rose was docked twenty-five cents a week. Illness and menstrual cramps received precious little consideration from the factory owners. Workers were expected to stay at their posts until they dropped, which they sometimes did—passing out in the sweltering summer heat. But work would carry on as if nothing had happened.

Abraham Eglin was born in 1891, the second child but eldest son in a family that would eventually number five. As a boy Abe would sometimes accompany his tinker father on his travels. At the end of the day they would have enough money to buy a fare home—but only for one—on the three-horse Russian sleigh that was the main conveyance in winter in that part of Poland. While Sholem Eglin rode in the troika young Abraham trotted alongside, often arriving home hours later, or even the next day.

Abe was sixteen when his family emigrated to Canada in 1907, part of a great wave of Jewish immigration to Canada in the first two decades of the twentieth century. Sixty-eight thousand Jews arrived in Canada between 1901 and 1911, and like the Briskins and Eglins most of them came from eastern Europe.[4] Montreal was a favoured destination for many; the city was home to more than one-third of all Jews in Canada throughout the first half of the century, and the city's Jewish community would eventually become, after London, the largest Jewish community in the Commonwealth, and the eighth largest in the world.[5]

Like the families of Rose Briskin and Abraham Eglin, most of the newcomers were extremely poor. But they were also survivors—sturdy, determined, and hard-working. Many prospered in the New World, and some, in less than a generation, would become wealthy. One of Rose's brothers would become a stockbroker, another the owner of a sizeable dress factory. But such rapid success would carry a price. Even though they were themselves a minority in the province, an Anglo-Canadian élite controlled most of the Quebec, indeed the Canadian, economy. From their baronial mansions in Westmount and on the Mountain overlooking the city, families like the Molsons, the Redpaths, and the Ogilvies ruled the commanding heights of the Dominion's commerce—its financial, transportation, industrial, and retail sectors. French Canadians found themselves either toiling for these anglophone masters or contenting themselves with upward mobility through the so-called "soft professions"—law, medicine, or the priesthood. If they succeeded in gaining a toe-hold in business, it was often in small, labour-intensive operations like the needle trades or retailing. To the perennial resentment of native-born Canadians against more successful immigrants was added the fact that French Canadians often found themselves competing against Jewish businessmen in the few economic pursuits open to both.[6] The resulting anti-Semitism would have a lasting impact on the young Claire Eglin.

Abraham Eglin and Rose Briskin were married on December 12, 1912. Jack was born just over one year later, on December 26, 1913. As the first-born grandson of Sholem and Fagel Eglin, Jack's birth was an occasion for joyful celebration. The birth of a son was always considered a sign of good fortune in the Jewish community, and the fact that he was also the first grandson—and the first born in the New World—seemed an especially happy augury that made the new baby the subject of added adoration, a special adulation that was notably lacking when Jack's baby sister was born almost five years later.

But the family's joy very nearly proved to be short-lived. Unsafe water, impure milk, and the relative absence of smallpox and diphtheria vaccinations made Montreal "the most dangerous city in the civilized world to be born in," and the city's atrocious infant mortality rate (double that of New York City and better than only one other major city in the world—Calcutta)[7] almost claimed Claire's older brother. In 1915, some time before his second birthday, the infant contracted a raging fever, perhaps diphtheria. The doctor who visited the family flat mistook the youngster's delirium for insanity, and recommended that he be moved to the asylum for the

insane at Verdun. As the distraught Rose awaited the ambulance attendants Baba Eglin happened to drop by, and she immediately took charge.

"Ice!" she ordered—they must apply ice to the child's forehead. The
women set about at once furiously chipping ice from the block that provided the family's only refrigeration. As soon as the ice was applied to
Jack's head it seemed to turn to steam with a hiss, rather than melting, so
high was his fever. When the block from Rose's icebox was exhausted the
women scrambled to obtain more from the neighbours. Finally the fever
abated, and Jack recognized his mother. To the overwhelming relief of
everyone present, it became apparent that the child's delirium had been
caused by the fever, not insanity.

But just at that moment a knock was heard at the front door of the Eglin
flat. The door was thrown open and there, at the top of the stairs, were two
men in white suits, one of them carrying a rolled-up stretcher. Once again,
Baba Eglin took charge. She grabbed a broom and began swinging it
furiously at the ambulance attendants, knocking both of them down the
two flights of stairs that led to the Eglin's third-storey apartment. Then
Baba Eglin slammed the door and put the broom back in its place.
Throughout the confrontation she never said a word. To Claire, this piece
of the family legend would precisely describe her father's mother: stern,
unforgiving, fiercely protective of her children and grandchildren, and
almost unbelievably tight-lipped.[8]

The first centre of young Claire's universe was the kitchen in the flat on
St. Catherine Street, and, more specifically, the kitchen table. From that
table in the centre of the room seemed to emanate all of the best, and
worst, things in life. Although blessed with an otherwise healthy consti-
tution, Claire suffered from a chronic infection of the eardrum, and in
her early years its treatment became a dreaded annual event. Family
members would hold the child down on the table while chloroform was
applied to keep her from squirming. Then a doctor would puncture and
drain the abscess.

The kitchen table was also the venue of physical punishment, which, by
today's standards, could often be quite brutal. Claire would be spread-
eagled on the table for strapping or spanking, but this was mild beside
some of the other punishments meted out to recalcitrant children. She
could remember once having seen an uncle literally break a chair over the
head of one of her cousins. It wasn't that her parents were sadistic or cruel,
she thought later, but more a reflection of their own harsh upbringings.
Claire's father recalled that Zayde Eglin had punished him by simply
picking him up by the scruff of the neck and then dropping him. As Sholem
Eglin was a big man, the impact was frightfully jarring. Zayde Eglin never

lost his temper at such times—it was simply the way children were disciplined.

But the table was also the focus of some of Claire's fondest childhood memories, especially of cooking and food. The latter was always present in abundance in the Eglins' kosher household, although the routine was unvarying. You could tell the day of the week by what you had for dinner—Wednesday was bean soup, Friday was fish, Saturday was chicken (or, in later years for a special Saturday-night treat, Cokes and smoked meat sandwiches from Schwartz's), and Sunday was steak or roast—if you were lucky. Since work, including cooking, was forbidden on the Jewish sabbath (sundown Friday to sundown Saturday), Friday was also baking day. More than once the young Claire, whose appetite was always healthy, found it impossible to resist the week's supply of cakes and pies her mother left to cool on the kitchen table, thereby provoking more parental scolding.

The kitchen was also the focal point of another hated family ritual—Saturday-night baths. Since the flat had only cold running water, daily baths were out of the question, which suited the youthful Claire just fine. But every Saturday a bath was *de rigueur*. The big metal basin that served as a bathtub was hauled out to the middle of the kitchen floor, water was heated in buckets on the coal- and wood-burning cooking stove, and the kicking and screaming would begin.

Once, Claire discovered that one of her neighbourhood playmates had no mother.

"Boy, is she lucky," Claire announced enviously to her own mother.

"Why would you say that?"

"Because she doesn't have a mother to make her take baths on Saturday night!"

By the time Claire was five her father had become a modest success in business. Abraham Eglin's ladies' ready-to-wear shop on the street level beneath the family flat was prospering sufficiently that he was able to contemplate opening another store. But the shop's location at the corner of St. Catherine and Bourbonnière, deep in the east end of Montreal, meant that Jack and Claire Eglin were growing up far from the city's Jewish ghetto, a five-street slice of central Montreal bordered by Park Avenue on the west and St. Lawrence Boulevard ("The Main") on the east. As a result, virtually all Claire's neighbourhood playmates were French, and she quickly absorbed *joual*, the elided French slang of working-class Montreal. Her schooling, however, was in English. Like most Jewish children in the city, Claire and her brother attended schools run by the Protestant School Board of Greater Montreal where English was the primary language of instruction, and where religious teaching was minimal, at least compared to the church-ridden institutions of the Catholic school system where the primary language of instruction was French. It was a diverse linguistic and cultural mix for a small child—French and Catholic in the neighbourhood, English and Protestant in school, Yiddish and Jewish at home.

Claire began her formal education at Maisonneuve School, far enough from home that she and Jack had to ride the streetcars to and from school each day. The daily rides on the Montreal street railway system provided her with her first ambition in life—to become a motorman. With the appreciative eye of a five-year-old she watched the trammers chew tobacco; she was especially taken with the practiced way they had with the cud. From their peak-seat at the front of the car they could open the doors—just a crack, no more—and spit sideways with unerring aim through the narrow gap. It seemed to her the most wonderful talent in the world, and she began to practise at home, from the third-floor balcony overlooking St. Catherine Street. As her aim improved she sought moving targets—the fedoras and chapeaux of pedestrians on the sidewalk below. Her spit found its mark on more than one occasion, landing Claire back on the kitchen table for still more parental discipline.

Montreal was an exciting place for a little girl—Canada's greatest city, with more than half a million people, spread out around her in every direction with its profusion of cultures, its babble of languages, the clip-clop of horse-drawn wagons, the rumble of the trams with their clanging bells, the ceaseless flow of motorized traffic, and the endless stream of people on St. Catherine, the city's main street, right outside the window. And life at home was equally colourful.

The social world revolved around the family, and frequent visits provided ample opportunity for a child to study adult character. And such characters! There were eleven aunts and uncles in all, and an equal number by marriage. On the Briskin side there was Uncle Morris, by now a successful Montreal stockbroker, who never tired of reminding the children how he had made his start as a young immigrant *boychik* washing dirty glassware in a bottling plant. Uncle Louis was the owner of a dress factory, and he was already becoming a big wheel in the Montreal Jewish community. Then there was Uncle Eddy, a furrier, who had been "bitten by the barbotte bug." Eddy's addiction to gambling (barbotte is a dice game similar to craps) would eventually cost him a fortune and leave him a ruined man. Aunt Annie, Rose Briskin's older sister, had, it was said, married a first cousin and given birth to a son who was "strange," and about whom little was spoken. Brash and fast-talking Uncle Charley, also a furrier, had moved to the United States to set up shop in Pittsburgh. Next came Aunt Sophie, a member of the wealthier wing of the Briskin clan. The youngest was Aunt Pearl, a strong-willed character like Claire's mother, Rose. She had nearly disappointed the family by marrying a violinist, when everyone knew that a musician's hours were irregular, his life was irregular, and, worst of all, his pay was irregular. In the end, Pearl had yielded to parental pressure and married someone more acceptable, but in the family her name had become synonymous with independence and fierce determination bordering, it was understood, on the irrational.

On the Eglin side there was Aunt Edith, one of whose two daughters would make family history by marrying "the first Jewish fireman in Montreal." Aunt Sally married and left Montreal eventually, moving to New York City, as did Aunt Julia, who worked for a time in Claire's father's store. Finally, there was Abe's only brother, Moe, a man of considerable mystery. Uncle Moe, the elders agreed in hushed tones, was "the bad one." There were rumours of scrapes with the law, but all Claire could see was that Uncle Moe was away a lot, and when he returned he liked to flash his diamond rings and, to the children's delight, buy them treats with money peeled from his thick bankroll.

As endlessly varied and wonderful as life could be in the home and on the streets outside, it could also be cruel to a little girl, and Claire was to learn two harsh lessons about her place in the world before she turned seven. The first originated with Jessie, the family's pet bulldog. Claire and Jack would often fight to see who would get to take Jessie to bed to keep their feet warm. Jack would kiss Jessie goodnight, but he would never kiss Claire. It became a family joke, and Abe Eglin would bet his daughter a nickel that she couldn't get her brother to kiss her. But to Claire, who desperately craved her older brother's affection, it was no laughing matter, and she often cried herself to sleep, heartbroken, because Jack appeared to care more for the dog than he did for her.

"It was the first big tragedy in my life, and I mean tragedy," she would say years later. What started as a boyish prank cast a pall over the sibling relationship that was never resolved, and Claire and Jack would never be close. Jack's attitude toward his sister was illustrated by another family tale that always occasioned much laughter. As Rose and Abe had prepared to leave for the hospital that Labour Day Monday in 1918, Jack had admonished his mother to give birth to a baby boy. "If it's a baby sister," the four-year-old was reported to have said half-jokingly, "I'll throw her out the window." "And I should have done it, too," Jack would say in later years when the old story was retold. Again, the tone was half-joking. But Claire always wondered: if these remarks were half in jest, what was the other half?

The second great lesson occurred one day when Claire and her brother had gone to synagogue with Zayde and Baba Eglin. Fairmount Synagogue was one of the more Orthodox synagogues in Montreal, and women and men were strictly segregated during services, as they are in the Orthodox faith to this day. Claire sat upstairs with Baba Eglin, while Jack and Zayde Eglin sat downstairs with the men. Baba Eglin excused herself early to go home and make lunch, and she whispered to Claire to bring Jack and Sholem home when the service was over. When the service ended Claire ventured downstairs to meet her brother and grandfather. She watched as the Torah, in its sacred blue-and-gold satin wrappings, was carried down the aisle to the back of the sanctuary by the rabbi. As it passed, the men and boys bent forward to kiss the holy scroll, and Claire prepared to do the same. As the Torah reached her Claire was just bending over, about to bestow the reverential kiss, when a terrific blow hit her across the shoulders from behind. If the stroke had caught her on the neck, she was convinced, it would have decapitated her, just like Aunt Nellie's parents back in the Ukraine. Startled, mortified, and in genuine pain, Claire ran home to Baba Eglin, howling all the way. Through her tears she told her grandmother what had happened, and she would never forget the response. Instead of comforting her granddaughter, the stern matriarch offered only a stinging reproof.

"Good for you. Serves you right. Girls aren't supposed to kiss the Torah. They'd have had to throw it out if you'd have touched it."

"But if God made my brother," Claire sobbed, "didn't He make me, too?"

The arguments of a six-year-old girl carried no weight against the teachings of two thousand years of patriarchal Jewish orthodoxy. The same woman who had batted furiously at the ambulance attendants who threatened to carry off her grandson ten years before was not about to defend this rebellious granddaughter. This was different; everyone knew that women were unclean, and that was all there was to it.

If being a girl was turning out to have distinct drawbacks at home and in the Jewish faith, it was also proving to be no picnic to be a Jew of either gender on the streets of Montreal. There was little overt anti-Semitism among Claire's French playmates in the neighbourhood, or so it seemed. It wasn't until she was ten that she learned that *un maudit juif* (a goddamned Jew) was a pejorative reference. Claire had heard the term so often—and it was not always spoken viciously or with malice—that she described herself that way until the day she heard someone refer to *un juif*. She corrected the speaker—surely he meant *un maudit juif*—and the significance of the modifier was finally explained to her.

Claire and her brother were the only Jewish children at Maisonneuve

School, which also presented some problems. It felt strange to say the Lord's Prayer every day in school, when they never heard it spoken at home. Holidays were another issue. School holidays like Christmas and Easter had nothing to do with them, and their family's holidays—Yom Kippur, Rosh Hashanah, and Passover—had no meaning to the other children. Easter was always the worst. Across Montreal students were reminded by their teachers that the Jews had crucified Christ. Catholic and Protestant students would temporarily put aside their own robust linguistic and religious enmities to unite, for a brief ecumenical moment, in a sudden upsurge of Jew hating. You had to be prepared to run home after school through a hail of stones as Easter approached.

The great wave of fascism and anti-Semitism that was to break over Quebec in the 1930s was still approaching, but its symptoms were already visible. Claire would never forget seeing a huge billboard posted on a nearby beach at Saint Jacques. *Pas de chiens pas de juifs* (No dogs or Jews allowed) it proclaimed. On another occasion she remembered returning from a school trip to the Laurentians on the train with her brother, Jack. A handful of Jewish boys was being taunted by a crowd of other students. A feeling of shame washed over Claire. Why didn't they fight back?

"If they talk back they'll get beaten up," Jack explained. "Do you want that?"

She had to admit it was a terrible choice.

Still, being part of a persecuted minority afforded her, even as a young child, great insights into the politics of racism and exclusion. It made her people chippy, aggressive, often bringing out the worst in them, too. A poor school mark was often rationalized with a ready-made excuse: the teacher was anti-Semitic. But in later years, when a minority group pressing for its rights was criticized for being "too aggressive," she could understand full well where such aggressiveness sprang from.

Sometimes, when her family had visitors, she would listen to the adults discussing the *goyim*, dismissing their Québecois neighbours and customers as *gollechems* (priest-lovers) and blacks as *schvartzes* (niggers). It was clear from the contempt with which these words were spoken that these were not complimentary references.

"You don't like it when people call us kikes and *maudits juifs*. Why are you calling these people names?" she would ask the grown-ups.

Usually she'd get a cuff across the mouth and be sent to her room for such impertinence.

When would this *maidel* of Abe's finally learn some respect for the wisdom of her elders?

*　*　*

By the 1920s a clearly defined socioeconomic ladder had emerged within Montreal's Jewish community, and one of the factors that determined a family's status was where it spent its summers. The poorest resigned themselves to spending the season in the stifling heat and cramped quarters of the Jewish ghetto around the Main, their only relief via a streetcar to the Mountain, where they could sit out the hottest nights on Fletcher's Field, on Park Avenue. But the upper and middle classes managed to escape the city for the summer. The really well-to-do, and some of the Briskin clan was soon among this number, went to Old Orchard Beach, in Maine. The middle class travelled to the Laurentians, north of Montreal, where two or three families often combined resources to rent a farmhouse for the summer. The French-Canadian farmer moved his family into the barn for the season, gaining additional income from the city folk who occupied his home. The Eglins, now ensconced on the middle rungs of the socioeconomic ladder, returned each summer to the Laurentians, staying at farms or villages from Piedmont to La Macaza, two hundred or so kilometres north of Montreal. Claire spent every summer of her childhood there, and these times became the source of many of her happiest memories. It was here she formed friendships with her cousins, engaged in her first girlish flirtations, and began a relationship with an extraordinary young man that would last, off and on, for the next forty years.

The summers were a truly idyllic time. The children were given greater freedom than they had in the city and they roamed the fields and woods, and swam in the rivers and lakes. On hot days Claire practically lived in the water, and she developed a lifelong love of swimming. She always clamoured to ride the farm horses, which drove her mother to distraction. Rose was convinced that her daughter would be thrown from a horse and seriously injured. Claire was equally convinced that her mother was neurotic about the state of her children's health. ("You didn't dare show her a scratch, or there'd be three doctors at the house within five minutes," Claire recalls with only slight exaggeration.) Her father took a more equable position: "If she falls off and breaks a leg, she won't go again, and if she doesn't, then you're worrying for nothing." In the end the adventuresome child would go horseback riding, and she would be thrown, but never seriously injured.

The Eglin cousins formed their own little cliques, complete with games and their own delicious secrets. The daily life of a working farm went on all around them, providing the children with experiences they could never have had in the city. Young Claire was given a "job" that paid a nickel a day—holding the cow's tail to keep it out of the farmer's face at milking time—though she could never remember actually getting paid.

Claire's curiosity was irrepressible, and one of her earliest memories—she couldn't have been more than six or seven—was of the great excitement that surrounded the impending birth of a litter of pigs. Everyone was aware of the event as the big day approached, and it was necessary to have a number of hands present at the birth so the piglets could be removed to safety before the sow rolled over and inadvertently smothered them. On this occasion the birth began at night, and her brother and a few older cousins assembled in the barn with the farmer. Claire was deemed to be too young and was sent to bed. But she was determined to see for herself what was about to happen in the barn. She climbed out of her bedroom window and returned to the barn. Again, she was sent back to bed, and again she escaped. Seeing her determination and sensing the futility of trying to keep this unruly child away, the farmer relented. He gave her what seemed at the time to be a big and very heavy lantern, and told her to stand at the sow's head and watch its mouth carefully, as that was where the baby pigs would come from. Only when the litter was complete and laid out on the floor did Claire realize she had been duped, and she was furious.

Even on the farm, though, there were some children's games from which girls were excluded, to Claire's intense irritation. One such game was "Fireman." Whenever a new boy would arrive on the farm, he would be subjected to an initiation rite by all the other boys, who told her flatly, "Girls can't play this game," a rebuff which Claire, characteristically, refused to accept. She observed that at the start of Fireman all the boys would drink copious quantities of water and then retire behind the barn. Once, as the game was getting started, she hid inside the barn, peeking through a knothole to learn for herself what was going on.

The newcomer, she discovered, was made to stand in the centre of a circle formed by the other boys.

"Church on fire, church on fire," he had to cry out.

"Piss on it, piss on it!" the other boys chanted, fishing out their penises and peeing on the initiate.

Even though she was only eight or nine, Claire had already adopted a resolution in response to the favouritism shown boys: you simply had to find a way to prove there wasn't anything you couldn't do just because you were a girl. But for once she was stumped. She walked away from the barn that day having to admit that here was a game a girl really couldn't play.

Another enduring memory of summers in the Laurentians stemmed from the year that Aunt Pearl came to visit. She had long since renounced her violinist love and settled down, in Pittsburgh, with a man more acceptable to the family, and she returned one summer with her own children.

Aunt Pearl always seemed to prefer the company of teenagers—Jack's crowd—and after the younger children had been sent to bed she'd sit up with the adolescents, laughing and talking in the long twilight of midsummer evenings. It was all quite innocent, but Claire was scandalized. It was disgusting. Didn't she realize how old she was? (In fact, Aunt Pearl was then about twenty-five.) And here she was, mixing with teenagers, trying to pretend she was young. Years later, when Claire herself was in her fifties and she had become a kind of guru and role model to a fresh generation of young Canadian women and men, her secret disdain of Aunt Pearl that summer would return to haunt her, for fear she might be viewed in the same light by this next generation.

But Claire's sweetest memory of the Laurentians was the summer of 1926 when she joined the Reel Fren's Club. Named after the Reel Fren's Inn, a small guest hotel in the village of La Macaza owned by the Rabinovitch family, the club was led by its eighteen-year-old founder, Reuben "Rube" Rabinovitch. His family, who had emigrated from Russia, were most unusual among Jewish immigrants to Canada in that they settled in the country to farm, and they had in fact pioneered in La Macaza. Rube (pronounced "Ruby") was eighteen that summer, and he was taking correspondence courses to prepare for a degree in law. A childhood in the bush had made him fluent in French, and he had learned Russian and Yiddish at home. He was on his way to New York City, to attend university, but he returned in the summers to help his parents with the hotel and the farm. Part of his contribution was the club, a recreational organization for the children of families holidaying in the area. Rube would take them swimming, boating, and fishing, and organize day outings and field trips. Claire was just one of many children in the club that year, and all she really felt for Rube then was that wherever he went, things happened. He was an organizer, an instigator who knew how to make people laugh, how to make the long and sometimes boring days of summer come alive.

The next time Claire saw Rube was during the Christmas holidays in 1928. The Eglins decided to go up to La Macaza for a winter vacation, and Rube was there, home from his studies at New York University. He joined the family for skiing, tobogganing, and snowshoeing. Claire was ten then and Rube twenty, and there was still nothing extraordinary about their relationship. He was more like a big brother and she a little sister. But a bond was forming, and a relationship was germinating that would survive war, life underground, imprisonment, and long periods of separation.

She didn't know it then, but that Christmas holiday in the snows of La Macaza marked the end of something for Claire. The next fall, seven weeks after her eleventh birthday, the stock market crashed in New York City, and the long descent into the Great Depression began. The Eglin family fortunes suffered a similar decline. One by one Abe Eglin would lose each of the three east-end Montreal dress shops he had worked so hard to open, and by the late 1930s the family would be on the verge of bankruptcy.

Paradoxically, the eve of the depression was also the time that the family began a series of moves to more "respectable" neighbourhoods within the city. The first was to the Esplanade and Fairmount Avenue area, just north of the Jewish ghetto and a few blocks east of Outremont. Claire and Jack attended Fairmount School, which was right across the street from their new flat. The move uprooted Claire from the only home she had ever known, the apartment at Bourbonnière and St. Catherine, and she would never again live in such close proximity to the city's French-Canadian population. On the other hand there were far more Jewish students at Fairmount School, so that in school, at least, anti-Semitism became less of a factor in their everyday lives.

But anti-Semitism was still abroad in the great city. Claire would always remember apartment hunting with her mother and having the door slammed abruptly in their faces more than once when the landlady inquired if they were Jewish. In 1928 the Eglins moved once again, this time to Champagneur Avenue in Outremont, where Claire attended Guy Drummond School from grades five to seven. It was at Guy Drummond that Claire received her first enduring school instruction in character, from a teacher named Miss O'Brien. While she wore both her hair and her skirts short in the fashion of the day, Miss O'Brien seemed ancient to Claire, though she was probably no older than forty. Each day Miss O'Brien would tell the class stories about something that had happened to her on the way to school. The moral of the stories was always the same: "I learned something," Miss O'Brien concluded. "And you know, if you learn something every day you never get old." The homily would stay with Claire the rest of her life.

When their daughter was thirteen the Eglins moved yet again, to a duplex far to the west, in the solidly middle-class Anglo-Jewish enclave of Notre Dame de Grace (NDG). It says a great deal about how far the Eglins had come from their cold-water flat in the east end that one of their new neighbours owned a private tennis court, where Claire was able to add tennis to her growing list of athletic accomplishments. She entered secondary school in NDG at West Hill High, where she played on the girls' basketball team, though in 1934-35 she commuted to Strathcona Academy back in Outremont for her final year of high school.

In their moves the Eglin family was conforming to the classic demographic trend of upwardly mobile immigrant Jewish families in Montreal:

northward, up the Main, the traditional dividing line between the French- and English-speaking populations of Montreal; then west around the shoulders of Mount Royal through Outremont; settling finally in the new and predominantly English-speaking suburbs of Côte des Neiges, Snowdon, NDG, and Hampstead.[9]

When she was fifteen two events occurred in Claire's life that were typical of the sea changes among immigrant families to North America. The first was the death of Zayde Eglin. The family knew he was dying, and Claire went to visit him one afternoon. He was lying in bed, and he greeted her with a hug and a big smile. She sat there as he drifted off to sleep. Eventually, her grandfather simply stopped breathing. She reached over, kissed him and removed his ring, and then called out to one of her uncles, who summoned the doctor. There was nothing scary or traumatic about it, she would remember; it just seemed very natural and peaceful. The funeral was another matter. The Old World belief still held that the more people who prayed over the deceased, the more successful they would be in warding off evil, and so the house soon filled with professional mourners, people who were paid to loudly commiserate over the body of Zayde Eglin. It all seemed quite horrible to Claire and Jack, and it was reflective of the assimilation that was already taking place among the Canadian-born generation of Eglins that they did their best to clear the mourners, who seemed little more than beggars, from the house. The funeral was the only time she could ever remember seeing her father cry.

The second big event that year was strictly New World and middle class—Claire learned to drive the family car. Jack had obtained his licence (a simple matter: you just sent in a dollar and your licence arrived in the mail) when he was fifteen, and she'd made a mental note of that at the time. When Claire turned fifteen in the fall of 1933 she demanded equal treatment, but no one would teach her. Jack grudgingly agreed, but imposed conditions of his own: one lesson, only one lesson, and where and when he decided. They drove to Parc Lafontaine in east-end Montreal, and Jack stopped the car with its front wheels just inches from the lake at the centre of the big park. The lesson took ten seconds as he deftly shifted the gears: "First, second, third, reverse; if you're nervous go home," and then he relinquished the driver's seat. Somehow, Claire managed to back the car away from the water's edge, and that was how she learned to drive.

Claire had just turned sixteen when she entered Strathcona Academy in September 1934. If her parents' frequent moves had had any negative impact on her, school records don't show it—she was in the top half of her class throughout the school year, finishing tenth in a class of twenty-three. Her top marks were in History, French and English Composition, her lowest in Latin (Cicero and Virgil) and in Elementary Algebra. The teacher who inspired Claire most that year was Julia E. Bradshaw, the head of Strathcona's history department. Miss Bradshaw encouraged Claire to enter the school public speaking contest with the topic "Women's Political Status in the Province of Quebec." It was Miss Bradshaw, too, who suggested that Claire interview Strathcona's principal, W. Allan Walsh, on the subject.

When Claire asked her principal for research material on her topic he replied with a broad laugh that "Women have no political status in the province of Quebec," and in this assessment he was not far wrong. Although they had been enfranchised in federal elections since 1918, and in every other province since 1922 (Newfoundland, then a separate Dominion, followed suit in 1925), women were not even close to being allowed to vote in Quebec provincial elections in 1934. A cabal of politicians, journalists (notably Henri Bourassa), and the Roman Catholic clergy steadfastly opposed all attempts to enfranchise the women of Quebec. The province's Civil Code, a body of laws unique to Quebec among the Canadian provinces, was blatantly discriminatory against women. A wife's earnings had been considered the property of her husband until the Code was amended in 1931, but women were still barred from entering into legal agreements without their husband's permission. One especially noxious provision of the Civil Code stipulated that his wife's infidelity was grounds for marital separation for a husband, but a wife could seek legal separation from an adulterous husband only if he "keeps his concubine in their common habitation." The Dorion Commission, which had been appointed to review the Code vis-à-vis women, recommended against changing the adultery article in 1930 because "everyone knows that, in fact, the wound to the heart of the wife [when the husband commits adultery] is not generally as severe as the wound to the husband who has been deceived by his wife."[10]

Since it was clear that her prize pupil was going to receive little assistance from the school's principal, Miss Bradshaw made another suggestion: Claire should talk to Madame Thérèse Casgrain. A cofounder in 1929 of Quebec's Ligue des droits de la femme (League of Women's Rights), and its first president, Casgrain had come to embody the feminist movement in the province.[11] Claire made an appointment with Casgrain, and the meeting had a lasting impact on the young schoolgirl. She found the forty-year-old Casgrain to be a beautiful woman, handsomely dressed, with the bearing of an aristocrat, which indeed she was. Her father was Rodolphe Forget, a wealthy Montreal stockbroker and one of a handful of French Canadians who could lay claim to equality with the Anglo-Canadian business élite. Casgrain's husband, Pierre, was a long-time Liberal MP, who would become Speaker of the House of Commons in 1936. Here was a woman of charm, warmth, and evident sincerity who, despite her privileged background, was totally committed to bluntly challenging the province's male establishment, even though its members were her social peers.

Claire was also impressed with Casgrain's determination. The older woman had made her first trip to Quebec City to lobby for women's rights in 1922. Liberal premier Louis Taschereau had declared that, while women might some day get the vote, it would never happen while he was the Premier of Quebec. So far, the suffragist question was proving to be one instance of a politician actually making good on a promise.[12] Since 1927 Casgrain and a handful of women had conducted annual lobbying "pilgrimages" to Quebec's Legislative Assembly to support private members' bills granting women the right to vote. Each bill was decisively defeated, but each winter the women returned, even though they were often exposed to ridicule and boorish behaviour by the province's male lawmakers. (During the 1932 debate one J. Filion of Laval offered "to lend his pants to [suffrage leader] Idola Saint Jean any time she wanted them.")[13]

Claire was inspired as she departed Casgrain's home that day in the winter of 1934-35, her heart thrilling at the older woman's graciousness and courage, and her hands full of feminist literature. Neither of them could have foreseen that on another autumn day more than thirty years later they would make common cause once again, and this time gain entrance to the highest political office in the land.

And so it was that on the afternoon of Monday, February 11, 1935, Claire rose in Strathcona Academy's Memorial Assembly Hall to compete for the J. D. Hudson Cup in the school's sixteenth annual public speaking contest. In some ways her presentation coincided with the nadir of the Quebec suffragist struggle. Just three weeks earlier the Quebec Legislative Assembly had debated a bill which offered a stunning solution to unemployment in the province: Liberal MLA J.-A. Francoeur proposed that women should be banned from the workforce (except in farming, cooking, and domestic service) in order to provide more jobs for men. Even Premier Taschereau found the measure draconian, stating that he "was not ready to refuse [women] the right to make their living," and he led the opposition to the resolution. In the end it was voted down forty-seven to sixteen, but the fact that such a proposal could be the subject of serious debate and actually receive the support of sixteen members of the Assembly was a sobering reflection on the status of women in the province.[14]

Claire gave a *tour d'horizon* of women's political predicament: without the right to vote, with no control over matrimonial property, unable even to have a medical operation without their spouse's signature, women basically had but a single right in the province—to decide where they wanted to be buried. But her impassioned and exhaustively researched oration found no favour with the judges. Grade ten student George Flower won the cup for his speech, "Personality."[15]

Five weeks later Quebec suffragists, led by Thérèse Casgrain and Idola Saint Jean, made yet another pilgrimage to the Legislative Assembly. The level of debate that year was particularly odious, with MLA Robert Bachand observing, to the general merriment of the assembled lawmakers, that "since cigarettes and cocktails are no longer masculine prerogatives, the least the ladies can do is leave politics to the gentlemen."[16] On March 21, 1935, the enfranchisement of women in Quebec was decisively defeated by the Legislative Assembly for the ninth time in as many years.[17]

But Claire carried on with her competitive public speaking, and ten days after the debacle in the Quebec legislature her persistence was rewarded. On April 1, she and her grade eleven partners won the Charles P. Tucker Cup over the grade ten debaters by upholding the negative side of the proposition that "Preparedness for War is the Best Guarantee of Peace."[18]

Claire graduated from Strathcona Academy later that spring. That she had made an impact on the school during her brief time there was revealed in the 1935 edition of the Strathcona yearbook, *The Oracle*. Her prototype, the editors wrote, was British suffragette Emmeline Pankhurst. Her favourite quotation was "He is great who can alter my state of mind." Her favourite expression was "Open the windows," her pet aversion "Waiting," and her favourite occupation "Prompting with the wrong answers." Her destiny, the editors declared with truly oracular foresight, was to be "a helper to Atlas," the mythic Greek Titan upon whose shoulders the world was said to rest.

A photograph of Claire taken at about that time is equally revealing of her character. She looks almost coquettishly over her left shoulder at the camera. Her dark eyes retain a strong hint of girlish mischief, of adventure. Her head is held high, the set of her lips is determined, with the faintest hint of a smile playing about the corners. She was not a great beauty in a classical sense, perhaps, but men would be drawn to her all the same. Life was sweet and full of promise for Claire Eglin that spring of 1935. She was not yet ready to take the world upon her shoulders, but she was certainly prepared to take it by storm.

CHAPTER TWO

This Is the World We Live In

*"Spain is a scar on my heart . . . a scar that can never
heal. The pain will be with me always, reminding me of
the things I have seen."*
—Norman Bethune in a letter to his wife, January 1938

H er ambition that spring of 1935 was to become a doctor because she
regarded the profession as a way of helping people by relieving
suffering, but it quickly became apparent that here even Claire's reach
exceeded her grasp. The dream foundered on three immediate and ineluct-
able shoals—her birth order, her gender, and her ethnicity.

Jack was already attending McGill's School of Dentistry, and Claire was
told that the family could not afford to support another lengthy course of
university study. Once again, she felt short-changed. Her brother, because
he came first, and because he was male, got the best of everything. Then
too, the family's attitude may have been a reflection of sentiments in
Quebec society in general: medicine was a males-only profession.

Apart from industrial sweatshops, domestic service, and low-paying
and menial work in the clerical and service sectors, female participation in
the Quebec labour force was strictly limited. Women would be prohibited
by law from admission to the Quebec bar until 1941, from becoming notary
publics until 1956.[1] Female physicians, engineers, and architects were a
rarity, and most of them had attended professional schools outside the
province. There were, in fact, only three vocations open to a young Québécoise who desired to continue her education: one of the Catholic religious
orders, teaching, or nursing.

The first option was clearly out of the question in Claire's case, and the second held little attraction, not least because of the appallingly poor salaries and low social esteem afforded female teachers in Quebec; it has been estimated that women teachers earned slightly more than half the annual salary of male janitors in the province's urban schools.[2] And so Claire chose to become a nurse, but here she encountered yet another obstacle—bright, well educated and ambitious though she was.

Since her family had moved from east-end Montreal in 1928, Claire had been largely buffered from the alarming rise of anti-Semitism in Quebec. From her days at Fairmount School through to her graduation from Strathcona, she had attended schools with a predominantly Jewish enrolment. She was not, therefore, emotionally prepared for the obstacles that bigotry would put in her way. But she had experienced the anguish of anti-Semitism at one remove, through Rube.

The two of them had spent some time together in the Laurentians in the summer of 1934. Their friendship was deepening, and he was beginning to treat Claire more as a grown-up. Rube had graduated with a B.A. from New York University that spring, and had already begun reading law. But he felt that law exploited, rather than relieved, human misery, and instead turned his attention toward medicine. He had approached McGill's Faculty of Medicine for admission and been summarily rejected. Rube's high marks, his fluency in four languages, his obvious brilliance, counted for nothing. All that mattered was his ethnic origin, and McGill's 20 percent quota for Jewish students had already been filled. It was a terrible humiliation. "It's like fighting with your hands tied behind your back," Rube agonized to Claire. "How can you defeat that?"

In the end, Rube discovered that he could study medicine at the University of Paris, where institutionalized anti-Semitism was not as rampant, and where the tuition was so inexpensive he could afford to return to La Macaza each summer to work on the family farm. Rube's decision to leave Quebec for his studies may also have been influenced by an incident that occurred that year in June within Montreal's medical profession. When news of a Jewish intern's appointment to a Catholic hospital reached the medical staff it sparked a walkout of the other interns. The strike soon spread to five other hospitals in the city and, when the nursing staff of all six hospitals threatened to join the protest, the young intern reluctantly resigned his position.[3]

It was into this miasma that Claire strode when she entered the office of the Director of Admissions for the School of Nursing at Montreal General Hospital in the spring of 1935. She was young (in fact, too young: she would turn seventeen only in September, and the minimum age for acceptance was eighteen, but the Eglin family doctor had agreed to falsify a document stating her age) and "she was beautiful," Lea Roback, a long-time friend would recall of the teenaged Claire many years later. "She wanted to be something, she had it all there bubbling in her, and it had to be received somewhere. She had to give, not just to one, but to many."[4]

Claire selected the Montreal General for her training because it was the city's largest hospital, and she may have hoped that in a Protestant institution she might encounter less overt anti-Semitism. But after filling out an application and writing an admission exam she was quickly disabused of any such notion.

"I suppose I have to accept you," sniffed the head nurse, "because under the charter of the hospital we must accept one person of each nationality. I don't think Jewish girls make good nurses, but if you want to come and do your probation period I guess I can't stop you." Claire knew what that meant. After completing her probationary studies she would have to appear before a review board, whose members would determine if she had the qualifications to be a good nurse. The panel could base its decision on any criteria it chose, and its decision was final.

Such blatant discrimination might have crushed the aspirations of many another young woman, but Claire was not to be denied. "She really wanted [an education in nursing], and so she stuck to her guns," Roback remembers. Several of Claire's Jewish classmates had applied successfully to the Civic Hospital School of Nursing in Ottawa, and she talked with them. They had encountered no similar anti-Semitism there, they assured her. Perhaps mindful of Rube's example, Claire decided to leave the province for her post-secondary education.

*   *   *

She entered Ottawa Civic on September 5, 1935, one of forty-six students beginning the three-year progam. It was to prove a difficult world for a spirited young woman just turned seventeen. Claire quickly learned that nursing school was a harshly regimented, top-down hierarchy organized along quasi-military lines. The male doctors were at the top of the pyramid, with the female teaching staff just below. There followed, in descending order, the third-year or senior students, the second-year or intermediate students, the first-year or junior students, and, at the bottom of the heap, the probationary students, or "probies." All students were expected to stand when an instructor, nursing supervisor, doctor, patient, or visitor entered a room. Intermediates stood for seniors, juniors stood for intermediates and seniors, and probies stood for everyone. The same order applied when entering crowded elevators, with the added dictum that, when members of the same class were waiting, students boarded in alphabetical order by last name.[5]

The doyenne of the Ottawa Civic Hospital School of Nursing was Gertrude Bennett. Miss Bennett was the school's founder and superintendent, a position considered to be the top post open to a woman in Ottawa at that time. Miss Bennett was fifty-six the year Claire entered the school, and her regime, which had begun when the Civic opened its doors in December 1924, would last until 1946. During her twenty-two-year tenure, Gertrude Bennett left an indelible stamp upon the institution she founded. Although she was a gifted administrator with absolute devotion to her profession, Bennett's "innate authoritarianism" was legendary. In 1929 Bennett had cancelled the school yearbook because she disapproved of student nurses selling advertising. A few years later she refused to allow an orchestra performing at a school dance to use the saxophone because she considered the sound of the instrument too suggestive. Edna Osborne, one of the Civic's most distinguished alumni, recalled a half-century after her 1934 graduation that "It took me years to be myself and to express myself after those years of discipline and authoritarian rule." The young Claire Eglin, however, had no lack of self-awareness or capacity for strong-willed self-expression, traits that would lock her onto an unintentional collision course with the Bennett regime from her earliest days at the Civic.

The first great organizing precept of the school was that you never talked back. Like a foot soldier in an army at war, you were to accept and follow orders without thinking and without question. If a student nurse suspected that following an order might prove injurious to a patient, she was to obey nonetheless because, she was assured, one of two things would happen: either subsequent investigations would reveal that the authorities had been wrong, in which case the student would be vindicated; or the student would be wrong, and her fears would be proved groundless.

The uniform Claire was required to wear upon entering the school was as constricting as the regimen. Mandatory attire included a lined skirt and blouse with long sleeves and starched cuffs and collar, a billowing apron, long black stockings, and black shoes. Following the probationary period a starched bib, linen cap, and collar pin were added. The whole affair was colour coded; a blue-and-white striped dress for probies and juniors, pink for intermediates and seniors, and all-white for graduates, so that one's place in the pecking order was visible at a glance.

"I was in trouble every week," Claire would say of her ill-fated nursing-school career, and one of her first confrontations with authority was caused by the uniform itself. She quickly fell into the habit of removing every bit of unnecessary clothing beneath the visible garments for comfort in the oppressive end-of-summer heat, and she had done so on the day she was assigned to a routine bed-changing demonstration under a supervisor's watchful eye. Claire assumed that the supervisor, who was scribbling notes, was writing a letter to someone, until the next day in class.

The teacher was Miss E. Bell Rogers, the senior staff instructor and a graduate of McGill and the Royal Victoria Hospital School of Nursing in Montreal. Ottawa Civic alumni remember her as being a fine teacher who was greatly respected by the students, but Claire describes her as being "haughty as a queen."

"Before the class leaves will you wait just a moment, please? Miss Eglin, will you step up to the front of the class?"

Claire stepped forward.

"I would like to ask, do you wear a slip when you're on duty?"

"No, Miss Rogers."

"Do you wear a girdle?"

"No, Miss Rogers."

"How do you keep your stockings up so?"

Claire lifted her skirt to reveal the tops of her rolled stockings.

"Are you wearing a bra?"

"No, Miss Rogers."

"Well," said the grande dame of the teaching staff, heaving an indignant sigh. "I hesitate to ask any further!"

"She might as well have," Claire would recall with a grin, "because I had absolutely nothing on other than what you saw."[6]

The average probationary period lasted six months, but for the young probationer it must have felt like six years. The school day began with a 6:00 a.m. wake-up call and lasted until 9:30 at night, six days a week. The probie began her nursing-school training by learning to strip and make a bed in five minutes, to assemble gauze sponges from scratch, and to make eye pads, peripads, oakum pads, and square compresses. She learned to stack linen "with geometric exactness" and to clean supply-room and nursing-station cupboards with equal precision. The probationer

> then progressed to more complicated tasks: administering a cleans-ing enema; applying dry heat by means of a hot-water bottle or a baker (a solid walled metal cage, with anywhere from ten to twelve light bulbs); applying linseed and starch poultices, lead and opium fomentations, all of which she had made herself; giving a sitz bath and a local antiseptic bath; and providing post mortem care, with the assistance of another nurse or orderly. All told, she would be required to master some forty different procedures before the end of her preliminary term.[7]

Work on the wards took priority over classroom instruction because the Ottawa Civic, like most other hospitals of the day, used its student nurses as cheap labour. Nursing schools thus became a financial asset rather than a liability, a symbiotic relationship which encouraged hospitals to attach nursing schools to their institutions.[8]

It was "an inviolable rule . . . that every probationer should demonstrate a procedure to her instructor in the demonstration room and then carry it out under supervision on the ward before performing it unaided on a patient," and it was in the breach of this "inviolable rule" that Claire learned her first sobering lesson about individual responsibility versus blind obedience to authority.[9]

She was working the wards on a Sunday, and a supervising nurse ordered Claire to perform an extended enema, known as a colonic irrigation, on a patient who was scheduled for surgery the next morning. Claire cautioned that although she had performed the procedure in the classroom, she had never done so unsupervised on an actual patient.

"Oh, never mind," the nurse replied. "Just go and do it."

Claire obeyed. She knew the purpose of the procedure was to void the intestine of all fecal matter so that an involuntary bowel movement wouldn't occur when the patient's muscles were relaxed by anesthetic on the operating table. She knew, too, that the sign that all impacted feces had been removed from the intestinal tract was a return of clear water that had been pumped into the colon. But try as she might Claire couldn't get the clear return. She knew that was wrong, and she told the senior nurse so. But it was Sunday, the ward was short-staffed, and the nursing supervisor shrugged off Claire's concern.

The next morning both Claire and the nurse happened to be on duty when Dr. Evans, still in his surgical gown, stormed onto the floor.

"I want to see the nurse who did that colonic!" he thundered.

Claire was called onto the carpet, and she waited expectantly for the anticipated vindication, for the admission that the system had been in error. But the nursing supervisor said nothing.

What was a lowly probie to do? Claire hesitated to speak up, for fear of later recriminations from the nurse. But to say nothing guaranteed humiliation. She chose the latter course, and received a thorough dressing down.

"There were days when you went back to your room and you just crawled, for the humiliation," Claire remembers. "But I was determined I was going to finish, and in those days it was a rare thing to go through a whole three years without some problems."

As with her violation of the dress code, some of Claire's disciplinary infractions seemed so trivial as to be humorous, were it not for the fact that each of them was earning her another unfavourable notice from Miss Bennett. Such an incident occurred the day Claire was working on the hospital's uppermost floor. An emergency developed, and Claire was ordered to fetch a stretcher immediately. The stretchers were stored in the hospital's basement, and Claire knew the quickest way down the Civic's six floors was a side-straddle ride down the banisters. She was just completing her exhilarating descent when she zoomed straight into a doctor.

"Well," said the doctor, picking himself up off the floor, "it's been a long time since I've had my breath taken away by such a young lady."

Claire relished this courtly response, but she could see a nursing supervisor standing behind the doctor, and it was clear from her glowering expression that Claire had just earned another black mark in Miss Bennett's unforgiving books.

Although it would end in heartbreak, Claire's time at Ottawa Civic was a crucially formative period, and several of her experiences there can rightly be described as turning points in her life.

High on a probie's curriculum was a ten-hour course in Principles of Ethics. The subject even had its own textbook, which defined one of a nurse's great guiding principles: "Never sacrifice the soul of your work for the technique." Claire took this precept very much to heart, and believed she'd found an opportunity to apply it the day that she was working on Second Floor East, the Civic's public ward. The sixteen beds were full of indigent male patients, and there was always a chronic shortage of clean bed linen. It was doled out once a day, early in the morning, and there was never enough for more than one change every twenty-four hours. Claire had made the available supply go as far as she could that morning, but around three o'clock in the afternoon one of her patients vomited on himself and his bed. It was unthinkable that he and his fellow patients should eat and sleep in such a stench, and Claire suddenly remembered having seen a well-stocked linen closet on one of the private wards on the hospital's fourth floor.

Congratulating herself on her initiative, Claire was leaving the fourth floor with an armful of clean linen when she was accosted by a nurse.

"Where do you think you're going with that?"

"Oh, it's all right, I'm just taking it down to Second East." She wasn't stealing it, after all.

"You can't do that! This is Four West!"

This time Claire chose to stand her ground. She explained that there was a patient lying in his own vomit two floors down, but there was no clean linen. Surely it made no sense to have an overabundance of fresh bedding on one floor when it was so desperately needed on another. Wasn't it all one hospital? She argued at length, but her efforts were as unavailing as they had been with Baba Eglin over the question of kissing the Torah ten years before.

For Claire, who had been sheltered by her middle-class family from the worst effects of the Great Depression, it was truly a revelation that poor people should be treated so differently from people with money. It was also the seminal event in her growing awareness that Canada was, in fact, a class society.

Despite all her difficulties with the administration, Claire performed well on her written exams, finishing third in the class after the probationary period and eighth after the junior term, so no one could fault her on the academic front. But her disciplinary infractions continued. When she asked, in all earnestness, why she was in constant difficulty with her supervisors, the answer was always the same: she was too impulsive. Her final confrontation with Miss Bennett was nearing.

As the nursing students moved up through the hierarchy their responsibilities on the wards increased, as did the level of care they were allowed to provide. About halfway through her intermediate year Claire, who was assigned to work on the post-partum ward, took a special interest in a six-week-old baby suffering from such a severe case of intestinal intoxication that he had been placed on the danger list and wasn't expected to live. Sitting in a chair at the foot of his crib, Claire gave the baby his bottle with exquisite slowness, literally drop by drop, so the formula seeped in almost by osmosis. The process took hours and required absolute stillness and rapt concentration, but after two or three days the infant had actually gained an ounce, and was taken off the danger list. Claire was thrilled. It was, to her, the essence of nursing: prolonging a human life and even, occasionally, saving one.

Claire was sitting with the tiny bundle in her arms on the fourth or fifth day of her treatment when the head nurse returned from her holidays. As she entered the room everyone stood, except for Claire. She figured to hell with it. The head nurse should have read the charts, and would know why she wasn't standing. And surely a human life came before protocol.

The head nurse surveyed the room. Her imperious eyes fastened on Claire, the only person in the room who wasn't standing. She didn't say anything, and neither did Claire.

Half an hour later she received a message: "Miss Bennett would like to see you in her office."

"Miss Eglin, what are we going to do with you?" the imposing matron inquired with a withering glance. "How are you ever going to be a nurse? You haven't even enough discipline to stand up when your superior comes into the room!"

Claire began to explain herself, about the baby and the need for absolute stillness, about the weight gain—and then she snapped. Claire would never be able to recall what she actually said next, but she never forgot the deep purple that coloured the face of one of the most powerful women in all of Ottawa.

There was a note waiting for Claire when she returned to her room in the residence. It contained but a single word: "Pack!" She had been suspended for six months.

Claire couldn't bear to face her parents, so she stayed in Ottawa for a few days with a cousin. When her trunk arrived in Montreal without her, Abe and Rose didn't know what to make of it. "We thought maybe your body was inside," Abe quipped later, when they were able to laugh about it.

But for the moment Claire was heartbroken, believing that she was an absolute disgrace to her family, and that her ambitions for a nursing career were dashed forever. Even though she'd only been suspended and not dismissed outright, Claire knew she could never return to the Civic.

But while she had been living the almost cloistered life of a nursing student, momentous events had been occurring in western Europe and in Quebec, and they were about to overtake her.

$$* \quad * \quad *$$

The first political convulsion that would have a direct impact on Claire's life had occurred on the night of July 17, 1936, at about the time she and her classmates were receiving their pink uniforms. Military commanders in the North African Spanish colony of Morocco, led by General Francisco Franco, launched an armed rebellion against the democratically elected, if deeply divided, Republican government of Spain. By the time Claire returned to Montreal early in 1937, the rebellion had widened into a six-month-old civil war that engulfed most of the country. On one side of the conflict were arrayed Spain's large landowners, monarchists, fascists, and the Catholic church. They were opposed by the Loyalist or Republican forces, which included trade unions and workers, anarchists, and members of the Spanish Communist and Socialist parties. More ominous, from a global standpoint, were the military alliances that had coalesced around the Spanish struggle: Italy, under strongman Benito Mussolini, and Germany, led by Adolf Hitler, had quickly rallied to the Francoist cause, providing loans, planes, artillery, troops, and pilots; the Soviet Union, led by Joseph Stalin, countered with military aid of its own in support of the Republican side. The western democracies, meanwhile, did nothing to aid their sister government in Spain. Following the lead of British prime minister Stanley Baldwin, France, the United States, and Canada proclaimed policies of non-intervention, and agreed to place an arms embargo on Spain. The fear of another general war in Europe was allowed to outweigh the defence of democracy, with tragic consequences for Spain and for the entire world.

The second historical event that would have a direct bearing on Claire's life had occurred in the Quebec provincial elections of August 1936. L'Union Nationale, led by Maurice Duplessis, had swept to power, ending thirty-nine years of Liberal rule. While promising reform, Duplessis's government was poised to usher in one of the most repressive periods in Quebec's history.

Having been immersed in her nursing studies for the previous sixteen months, Claire was largely oblivious to the portentous events unfolding around her. Now eighteen, she was, in any case, preoccupied with a more pressing personal quandary: what was she to do with the rest of her life?

She decided to take a short business course in Montreal, after which she accepted a job as a stenographer-bookkeeper at the Reliable Dress Company, her Uncle Louis's factory. Louis Briskin had always been held up as a model to Claire, especially by her mother, as one of the immigrant family's signal success stories. Rose's brother was wealthy, influential, and a noted Jewish philanthropist. (His name can still be found on a plaque listing benefactors of the Montreal headquarters of the Young Men's and Women's Hebrew Associations.) Claire was also aware of her mother's less-than-subtle desire that her husband might emulate Uncle Louis in his own business dealings, a pressure to which the easy-going Abe was not inclined to submit. As she began working at Uncle Louis's factory in the Jacobs Building on St. Catherine Street West in downtown Montreal, Claire was utterly shocked at the conditions she found there. Things weren't so bad in the office, but the shop floor was another matter.

"It was a real cheap line," Lea Roback recalls of Reliable Dress, "and they were not nice bosses." French-Canadian and immigrant Greek, Italian, and Jewish women laboured up to seventy hours a week in squalid conditions for ten cents an hour, a situation typical of the Montreal needle trades as a whole. The Jacobs Building itself was "dirty, and the workers would sit at lunchtime and eat their sandwiches amidst the cockroaches and they had to work—turn belts and so on—right during their lunch hour," according to Roback, who was then organizing the International Ladies' Garment Workers Union (ILGWU) among the city's dressmakers. The lighting was poor, and the shops were freezing in winter and suffocating in summer, conditions altogether reminiscent of the cigarmakers' sweatshops that Rose Briskin had worked in as a child in Montreal a quarter-century before. Claire found herself thinking of life on the public wards back at the Ottawa Civic.

For the first time in her life Claire now began to grapple with the misery she was seeing firsthand, and through after-work activities she started to analyze the world around her in a systematic way. Several of her high school friends were attending McGill, and they invited her to join them at meetings of the university's Student Christian Movement. The SCM held discussions about the great issues of the day: unemployment, the rise of fascism, and the Spanish civil war, and the progressive views espoused by many of the group's members made perfect sense to Claire. Through the SCM she learned of the Young Communist League or YCL, the youth wing of the Communist Party of Canada, and Claire began to attend its meetings, too.

The YCL study sessions were frequently held at the home of Sam Wolofsky and his sister Miriam, on St. Catherine Road. Their father was the well-respected editor of the *Forward*, Montreal's conservative Jewish newspaper, but when Sam and Miriam's parents were in Florida on extended vacations, the comfortable Walsh home became a kind of centre for the YCL. (After changing his surname to Walsh, Sam Wolofsky would later become the long-time head of the Quebec wing of the Communist Party of Canada.) Claire found the incessant meetings, with their discussions of Marxist theory, somewhat tedious, and the arcane economist jargon often went right over her head, no matter how hard she tried to grasp its meaning. But the broad strokes of what these Communists were saying she understood instinctively, in her gut. Of course there shouldn't be poor people, of course people shouldn't be dying in Spain, of course fascism was a threat to democratic people everywhere. Yet the conditions she had seen at the Ottawa Civic and in Uncle Louis's dress shop were real enough and totally unconscionable; the Communist cry for the overthrow of capitalism made perfect sense.

It was a unique time and place for a political coming of age. Never before in Canada had the gulf between rich and poor been so wide, or so painfully apparent, never before had the division between left and right been so clear, the alignment of forces so electric, so dangerous. "Never before was Montreal as it was in the thirties and it will never be like that again," wrote Hugh MacLennan in *The Watch that Ends the Night*, his evocative novel of the period.

The unemployed used to flow in two rivers along St. Catherine Street, and I used to see eddies of them stopping in front of shop windows to stare at the goods they could not buy. There was a restaurant that used to roast chickens in its window over electrically-operated spits, and there were always slavering men outside staring at the crinkling skin of the chickens and the sputtering fat. I remember how silent the unemployed were when they emerged after a snowfall to clean the streets, often without mittens on their hands, and how pitiful their cheap worn shoes looked as the snow wet them and turned the unpolished leather gray.

With the energy of youth and the ardour of the newly converted, Claire threw herself into political work, often attending three and four meetings a night, keeping rendezvous with her boyfriends at midnight, while still managing to put in a full shift at Reliable Dress during the day. She was present on April 15, 1937, when the denizens of Montreal's sweatshops, including her Uncle Louis's, rose at long last to strike back against their miserable working conditions. Four thousand workers, most of them women, walked out that Thursday morning, led by militants from the ILGWU, Lea Roback among them. Montreal's entire garment district, from Peel Street to Bleury and down the length of St. Catherine, was out on strike. As an office worker, Claire was ineligible to join the union, but she heartily approved of the strike and did what she could to help out, occasionally conveying confidential information about management to the strikers.

The strike was in its twelfth day when word reached Canada of an alarming new development in Spain. On the afternoon of Monday, April 26, Franco's air force conducted bombing raids on the Basque market town of Guernica in northern Spain. Although the community of seven thousand was a symbol of Basque independence, it had little strategic importance. It was nevertheless pulverized in the first mass aerial bombing of a civilian population in the history of warfare. The world was stunned at the news of this fascist atrocity, a reaction which today seems almost naive in the wake of the London Blitz, Hiroshima and Nagasaki, the carpet bombing of Hanoi, the Israeli air raids of West Beirut, and the American bombing of Baghdad. But Guernica quickly became a galvanizing symbol of humanity's potential for evil.[10]

Claire found herself in the middle of an almost Manichaean struggle on the streets of Montreal. In the city of her youth there now emerged a microcosm of the global contention of good versus evil, and all the struggles of her own eighteen years now seemed universalized, thrown into stark relief. For Claire, the forces of darkness were embodied by Adrien Arcand and His Eminence Jean-Marie Cardinal Rodrigue Villeneuve.

Tall, erudite, and a gifted demagogue, Arcand was proving adept at distilling historic French-Canadian nationalism, with its isolationism, Catholicism, and latent anti-Semitism, into a potent witches' brew of fascism that crystallized in the *achat chez nous* ("Buy Quebec") movement. Since "Jews were foreigners," the movement maintained, loyal Quebeckers should patronize only French-Canadian-owned shops, boycotting those of their Jewish neighbours. Arcand's National Socialist

Christian Party had enjoyed the support of some powerful, and surprising, political benefactors along the way, including Pierre-Edouard Blondin, the Conservative Speaker of the Senate, and J. E. Laforce, the president of the St. Jean Baptiste Society. Indeed, so powerful were Arcand's admirers within the Tory party that he was appointed the Conservatives' director of publicity for Quebec in the October 1935 general elections.[11]

From his palace in Quebec City Archbishop Villeneuve presided over a church that was both fiercely nationalistic in Quebec, and staunchly reactionary throughout the world. Under Pope Pius XI the Vatican had early embraced the rise of European fascism, signing concordats with Mussolini in 1929 and with Hitler in 1933. In Quebec Villeneuve's church had become a haven for French-Canadian ultra-nationalism, including the movement's then-current eminence Abbé Lionel Groulx. Unlike his nationalist predecessor Henri Bourassa, whose vision was of a bilingual, binational Canada with Quebec as a full and equal partner, Groulx had become an early exponent of Quebec separatism. In January 1934 he penned a column extolling the "happy peoples who have found dictators." Groulx's new publication *L'Action nationale* suggested not only cutting off the flow of Jewish immigrants to Canada from Nazi Germany, but also stripping all Jewish Canadians of their rights, including the right to vote.[12]

Cardinal Villeneuve did nothing to dampen the forces of reaction within his Church. Indeed, on Sunday morning, May 18, 1937, a letter was read from Catholic pulpits across Montreal "demanding that the government arrest and deport 'foreign agents' and 'Communists'" who were responsible for the general strike in the city's garment industry. The letter's authors claimed to have the support of their cardinal, and doubtless they had.[13]

Like the garment worker's strike, the Spanish civil war was also polarizing Quebec society. The Church, which had seen its role in Spain sharply curtailed by the Republican government, stood foursquare on the side of Franco's rebels. Further solidifying Claire's instinctive awareness of which side she was on was the Church's attitude towards women. Cardinal Villeneuve was a determined opponent of female suffrage in Quebec and, when the measure was at long last on the eve of adoption by the Legislative Assembly in March 1940, Villeneuve would make one last-ditch, and unsuccessful, effort to prevent its passage.[14]

On the other hand, one of the best-known Republican leaders was a woman, a fact not lost on Claire. Her name was Dolores Gomez Ibarruri, but she would be known to history as La Pasionaria (The Passion Flower) for the flaming quality of her oratory. The widow of an Asturian miner, Ibarruri had helped found the Communist Party of Spain, and she had become a member of its Central Committee in 1930. As a member of the Cortes (the Spanish parliament) at the outbreak of the civil war, she had, in one brilliant speech, coined two phrases that would enter the lexicon of the century. *"No pasarán"* ("They shall not pass"), she said of Franco's legions in North Africa, adding, "It is better to die on your feet than to live on your knees." La Pasionaria joined Thérèse Casgrain in Claire's pantheon of heroines, and a leatherbound copy of the Spanish leader's speeches—a birthday gift from a boyfriend—soon became one of her most cherished possessions.

Claire joined the Young Communist League in the spring of 1937. While her status as a non-union employee had prevented her from taking an active role in the garment workers' strike, there was no such proscription when it came to the Spanish war, and she threw herself into the conflict on the Canadian home front, where the battle was distinctly one-sided. Arcand's fascists and Groulx's young ultra-nationalist disciples did everything they could to prevent public displays of pro-Republican sentiment on the streets of Montreal, physically disrupting meetings if they were unable to prevent them from being held in the first place.

While the Canadian government of Liberal prime minister Mackenzie King persisted in its policy of strict neutrality in the conflict, the Duplessis government was openly hostile to supporters of the Republic. Duplessis was only too happy to label Republican sympathizers as Communists, and in March 1937 the Duplessis government passed the draconian Padlock Law, empowering the "Red squad" of the Sûreté du Québec (the provincial police force) to padlock any home, school, or building used for Communist meetings, and to imprison anyone disseminating "Bolshevik" or "Communist" propaganda, neither of which the act actually bothered to define.

Still, Canadian supporters of a democratic Spain persevered. Led by the Communist Party of Canada and individual members of the CCF (the party as a whole was sharply divided between the pacifist sentiments of its leader J. S. Woodsworth and advocates of a more militant role in the fight against fascism) they founded the Committee to Aid Spanish Democracy, which had as its goal the involvement of Canadians in moral, financial, and political support of the Spanish Republic. On May 20, 1937, a second organization was formed, mainly by members of the Communist party; it was called the Friends of the Mackenzie-Papineau Battalion. Named after William Lyon Mackenzie and Louis-Joseph Papineau, the two best-remembered heroes of the Rebellion of 1837, the battalion was made up entirely of Canadian volunteers.

Claire joined the Montreal branch of the Friends of the Mac-Paps soon after its founding, and through its work determined her next ambition in life: she would go to Spain. The Friends of the Mac-Paps worked to provide direct material support for Canadians wishing to join volunteers from around the world who were travelling to Spain to fight in the Republican cause as members of the Fifteenth International Brigade. The most famous of these volunteers was Montreal surgeon Norman Bethune, but many of the twelve hundred or so other Canadians who served in Spain became members of the Mackenzie-Papineau Battalion.

The King government took a dim view of Canadian citizens volunteering for a war in which it was trying to maintain strict neutrality, and on April 10 the House of Commons passed the Foreign Enlistment Act, which imposed fines and jail terms for Canadian citizens who served "in the armed forces of any foreign state at war with a friendly state." The act did not yet apply specifically to the Spanish war, however, and Claire continued her planning to join the conflict. She obtained her passport and the other requisite papers, eager to lend her student nursing expertise to the Republican cause. If it came to that, she could always drive an ambulance, thanks to her brother Jack's grudging driving lesson in Parc Lafontaine. Claire's youth, her new-found political commitment, the undeniable romance of the Spanish cause, and the example of Norman Bethune's pioneering mobile blood transfusion unit, which was already beginning to make headlines around the world, overcame any fear she may have had about the danger she would face. She did, however, harbour one serious misgiving: the effect of her enlistment on her parents. For the first time in her life she was embarking on a course of action which she knew would be unalterably opposed by Abe and Rose. But, like many an eighteen-year-old before and since, Claire was certain she knew what was best for herself.

It was during this heady period in the spring of 1937 that she phoned Rube's father one day to inquire for news of her old friend.

"As it happens, Rube is arriving from Paris tomorrow," Mr. Rabinovitch told her. "Why don't you go down and meet him?"

The next day found her at quayside, eagerly scanning the observation decks as the big liner was nudged into its moorings.

High above, Rube was leaning over the railing, lost in thought. He was daydreaming about the Reel Fren's Club, wondering what had become of its members, wondering what had become of Claire Eglin when he suddenly saw her, waving at him.

They both laughed when he told her of this coincidence, and it enhanced the joy of their reunion. They had both been bruised by life: Rube by the sudden death of his young wife, Claire by her suspension from her nursing course.

They became lovers, spending time together at La Macaza off and on throughout the summer of 1937, while Claire awaited her own departure for Europe. It was an idyllic summer, but they were seriously at loggerheads over Claire's plan to go to Spain. They discussed it repeatedly, and Rube was adamant on the question. In addition to being concerned for her physical safety, Rube was also a staunch anti-Communist. Why should she go out of her way to fight on the side of the Soviet Union, which was even then persecuting its own Jews? Claire, still in her true believer stage, denied that there was anti-Semitism under Stalin. Besides, she argued, surely Rube believed in democracy and had to agree that the Republican government was the legitimate, democratically elected government of Spain?

One morning she started awake to discover Rube sitting on the side of the bed, looking down at her.

"What's the matter?" she asked with alarm.

His face darkened. "Spain!" was all he said.

A few days later they were speeding down a bumpy country road in the Rabinovitch's battered pick-up truck, on their way to meet some new guests arriving at the train station, and Claire was at the wheel.

"Stop!" Rube roared.

"What's wrong?" Claire asked after bringing the truck to a halt.

"Get out of there," he ordered.

"What's the matter?" Claire asked as Rube climbed into the driver's seat.

He glared at her. "You're just practising for driving an ambulance in Spain, aren't you?"

Between visits to La Macaza Claire continued her work with the Friends of the Mac-Paps, who were then organizing, along with the Committee to Aid Spanish Democracy, a continent-wide speaking tour for Dr. Norman Bethune. Claire was in attendance at Bethune's first public appearance in North America, a triumphant rally at Montreal's Mount Royal Arena, on the night of June 16, 1937. Despite the opposition of the Catholic Church, the Quebec press, the ultra-nationalists, and the persecution of the Duplessis government, nearly fifteen thousand people packed the arena that Wednesday night to hear Bethune recount firsthand his experiences in Spain. Claire listened spellbound as the Montreal surgeon condemned the embargo against Spain and excoriated the western powers for their policies of non-intervention in the civil war.

"The Soviet Union and Mexico, by according the Spanish government its legal rights, are aiding the government elected and supported by the people themselves," Bethune told his audience. "The Western powers, by embargoing the Loyalists and shutting their eyes to the flow of arms and armies from Italy and Germany to Franco, are supporting the choice of Hitler, Mussolini, and the clique of Spanish financiers and feudalists who mint their wealth out of the poverty of the people . . . Spain can be the tomb of fascism. History will some day take full revenge on those who fail her."[15]

Claire joined in the thunderous standing ovation that followed Bethune's prophetic conclusion. His words redoubled her determination to get to Spain, no matter what Rube or her parents might say.

But Bethune's passion, and the thousands who flocked to cheer him across Canada, left the King government unmoved. On July 31 Ottawa applied the Foreign Enlistment Act to the Spanish war. It was now a federal crime for any Canadian citizen to enlist in the Republican cause, and there was considerable doubt whether those who did so would be readmitted to the country once hostilities ended. Claire was a scant two weeks from departing for Spain when the Non-Intervention Pact was signed, forcing all foreign volunteers to withdraw. She reluctantly abandoned her dream of volunteering for the Spanish cause. But her experience with the Foreign Enlistment Act would serve her well thirty years later, when the Canadian government was once again maintaining a public posture of neutrality in a foreign war, and when Ottawa would adopt a much different attitude towards Canadian volunteers.

Still, Claire knew, there was work to be done on the home front, and she performed it with alacrity. One tactic in the effort to arouse public sympathy for the Republic centred on public demonstrations which, in Montreal at least, became a kind of ritual between militants and the police. The demonstrators would quietly converge on Phillips Square in downtown Montreal, placards carefully concealed beneath their coats. In unison they would pull out their Hands Off Spain picket signs and begin to march in overt violation of Duplessis's Padlock Law, which forbade public demonstrations in favour of, among other things, democracy in Spain. The marchers usually had time to parade just once around the square before the police descended, throwing them into paddy wagons. Claire was hauled off in this way at least half a dozen times, marking the first of many occasions when she would be jailed, at least temporarily, for acting on her political beliefs.

Claire saw Rube off to Paris to resume his studies at the end of that summer, and she returned to life with Abe and Rose who were now living on St. Urbain Street. But the fall of 1937 was not a happy time for the Eglin family. Jack had moved to California and Rose missed her son terribly, and Abe's business had hit rock bottom. It may be that he was a victim of Arcand's *achat chez nous* movement (his stores were in primarily French-Canadian neighbourhoods), or his difficulties may simply have been the result of general business conditions during the depression. Whatever the cause, Abe had now lost each of his three clothing stores, and the Eglins had been forced into bankruptcy. Abe was depressed by his business failure, and Rose was angry, more often than not venting her frustration on her husband, blaming him for what had happened, or so it seemed to Claire.

As if to start afresh, Rose and Abe decided to move to California. Jack reported promising prospects in the greater Los Angeles area, and, of course, they wanted Claire to come with them to keep the family together. Because they were Russian-born it would take Abe and Rose longer to obtain their American visas, but they encouraged Claire to apply for hers and precede them to California.

It took four days and nights to reach Los Angeles from Montreal by bus, with comfort stops (aptly named, as in-coach toilets had not yet been invented) every three hours. At Pittsburgh a young black man took the seat next to her and they began to chat. He was a student at Carnegie Tech where one of Claire's Pittsburgh cousins also attended school. Their talk helped speed the miles by, and Claire failed to notice when they crossed the Mason-Dixon line. But at the next stop she received her first introduction to Jim Crow America. As she emerged from the rest room Claire scanned the diner for her new friend, and at first couldn't see him. She looked again and spotted him sitting in a corner marked Coloreds Only. He didn't even look like the same person. It was like suddenly finding an old friend crippled by some wasting, terminal disease.

Her first urge was to say, "To hell with it," and join him, but she caught herself. Perhaps it would embarrass him, or cause him more trouble. Instead she refused to order anything, and returned to the bus. Once he boarded she tried to revive their earlier conversation, but it proved impossible. He just wasn't the same person. Something inside him seemed missing. Twenty years later, as the civil rights movement was hitting full stride and young militants, both black and white, were being murdered as they attempted to end segregation forever, Claire would recall that day on the bus. Many people would cluck their tongues and deplore the fact that the civil rights struggle had led to such violence, but not Claire. Her young friend, she always believed, would have been happier dying fighting segregation than sitting the way he'd sat in that Jim Crow diner.

After settling in at Jack's and finding work in a medical lab Claire quickly located the local branch of the Young Communist League of the Communist Party U.S.A. The comparison with the YCL back home was striking. The Roosevelt administration took a benign view towards American communism, or so it seemed relative to life under Duplessis. Here, the party was completely above ground, and the YCL actually held some of its meetings at the beach! In Quebec, by contrast, the Communist party was being driven ever farther underground. In November 1937 the party's French-language newspaper, *Clarté*, one of the few Quebec papers which supported Republican Spain, had been shut down under the Padlock Law. Yet, without the official repression, and the resulting intrigue and sense of danger, party life just seemed less exciting, and her sense of not quite belonging was continually exacerbated by Americans' appalling ignorance of Canada.

As much as she liked her new friends and even though she and the newly married Jack were living together amicably for once, Claire decided she simply didn't want to be an American. She was a Canadian. She had just purchased a bus ticket home when a call came for her from Ben Dobbs, the California secretary of the YCL, summoning her to the party's state head-quarters in San Francisco. Because of her youth and lack of experience Claire was astonished when Dobbs told her she had been hand-picked to attend party school, that the position came with a nominal stipend of ten dollars per week, and that eventually the party wanted to make her a full-time functionary.

It was a flattering offer, and a big temptation to become part of the much larger and better-financed Communist Party U.S.A. But then she remembered the ticket in her purse, and Montreal. She thanked Dobbs, and boarded the bus for the long ride home a few days later.

*   *   *

Even though she was now only nineteen, the habits Claire would bring to a lifetime of political work were already forming. Whatever the task, she brought energy, intelligence, and a thoroughgoing commitment to the project, and these qualities, which doubtless commended her to the American party, were soon recognized by the Quebec wing of the Canadian party, as well. Upon her return to Montreal Claire moved in with her parents, who were still awaiting their visas, landed a job with the Reardon Paint Company in Old Montreal, and was soon helping to organize the Office Workers' Union (part of the American Federation of Labor).

Claire discovered that little had changed in Montreal's political scene during her California sojourn and she slipped comfortably back into her old routine . . . work by day, endless rounds of meetings at night, social life squeezed in whenever time would allow. But in western Europe, 1938 was to prove a decisive and difficult year. The news from Spain was bleak for supporters of the Republic. The Mac-Paps had taken part in a number of bloody battles, casualties were heavy, and the fascist superiority in munitions and air power, combined with the crippling effects of the embargo, was beginning to tell.

In Canada, meanwhile, the country's flirtation with fascism was continuing—on both sides of the Ottawa River. Prime Minister Mackenzie King had visited Hitler in the summer of 1937. Although horrified at the Nazi leader's treatment of Jews, King wrote that he found Hitler to be "a man of deep sincerity and a genuine patriot . . ."[16] The King government also ignored the repeated entreaties of world Jewish leaders that Canada grant asylum to the more than one million Jews fleeing Europe before the onrushing Nazi tide—fewer than four thousand would find refuge in Canada.[17]

A year later Henri Bourassa, the old warhorse of Quebec nationalism, would tour the Third Reich and write favourably of Germany under Hitler, much as Mackenzie King had done the summer before. While Bourassa had publicly deplored the rise of anti-Semitism in his beloved Quebec, he was blinded by his admiration of Hitler's own brand of nationalism. In a series of articles in *Le Devoir* he wrote an apologia for the impending Nazi assault on Czechoslovakia, arguing that Hitler had the right to take over the Slavic states because the German füehrer was imposing order on chaos, and that France and Britain had no right to stop him.[18]

Only with Hitler's overrunning of Austria in March of 1938 did Ottawa and the Canadian public awake at last to the Nazi menace—something the Canadian left had been decrying for years. The *Anschluss* with Austria precipitated a break between Hitler and the Vatican, thus splitting Arcand's fascist movement in Quebec. The Roman Catholic clergy began to oppose Hitler, driving a wedge into Arcand's *mélange* of ultra-nationalists, Catholics, and anti-Semites.

As awareness of the fascist threat grew during 1937 and 1938, the Communist Party of Canada enjoyed tremendous growth. From a total national membership of fewer than two thousand in 1931, the party would grow to boast nearly eighteen thousand members by 1939.[19] The party's work in organizing the unemployed during the Dirty Thirties, its agitation in favour of unemployment insurance, its leading role in organizing the industrial unions that were about to come to the fore in the early 1940s, and, most of all, its staunch opposition to fascism around the world earned it considerable prestige, and Claire was an energetic contributor to the party's growth.

It was during this period that Claire began to meet other comrades who would, like herself, play a significant role in Canadian political life over the next half-century. Some, like Kent Rowley and Madeline Parent, were her own age, while others, like Lea Roback and Emery Samuel, were older. She was particularly in awe of Samuel. A working-class French Canadian from the Gaspé, Samuel, who had been selected by the party to spend a lengthy period at the International Lenin School in Moscow studying Marxist theory, unintentionally provided Claire with her first doubts about the

Communist party. They were attending a meeting in somebody's living room ("Because the party was illegal in Quebec we'd always hold our meetings in private homes, and you didn't tell your mother you were going to a YCL meeting—you just said you were going to meet some friends") and Claire was seated beside Samuel on the couch. On her other side was a wealthy Jewish party member who had just returned from a winter holiday in Florida. "He was all tanned and well dressed, and he and Emery were talking across me, and calling each other 'comrade.' I was thinking 'Hey, there's something wrong here. I knew Emery and his wife were so poor that their kids didn't go to school in the winter because they didn't have boots and they used flour sacks for sheets. 'This guy's living one way and this guy's living the other, and if he's your comrade wouldn't you want to help him?'"

Claire didn't know what the answers were, and if she had ever raised the point in party circles she was certain the response would have been "What are you talking about? A person's supposed to take money out of their pocket and give it to someone else just because you're both Communists? That's not what it's all about." But the longer she remained in the movement the more she came to believe that "That *is* what it's all about. If you believe in something, you *live* that life-style. You can't believe in being concerned about the working class and struggle and still have your sights set on a big home and a trip to Hawaii and having not just a car but the best car; in other words, where money has a different value than it does for people who are just surviving on it."

She corresponded with Rube throughout the winter of 1937-38, and he sent her postcards from Paris with beautiful reproductions of Van Goghs on the front, which she pinned up on the wall of her bedroom. Claire was there to meet his ship when he returned in the summer of 1938 as she had been the year before, and their love affair continued, this time without the irritant of her dream of going to Spain. She continued her support work with the Friends of the Mac-Paps, and her heart leapt on July 25 when news reached Montreal that the Republican army had launched a massive counter-offensive across the Ebro River. The Mac-Paps were part of this attack, but the initial advance soon faltered beneath the weight of brutal fascist artillery and aerial bombardments.

The Ebro was to be the last major offensive of Republican Spain and, on September 22, 1938, just as Claire was seeing Rube off for Paris once again, the Republican government announced that it was sending the members of the Fifteenth International Brigade home. The decision to withdraw foreign volunteers meant still more work for the Friends of the Mac-Paps—raising money for return travel, negotiating with the King government to have the

Canadians readmitted to the country despite the Foreign Enlistment Act, taking steps to ease the soldiers back into civilian life.

The first group of war-weary veterans arrived in Halifax on February 3, 1939, and the overall statistics of the Canadian effort in Spain told a grim tale. Of the more than twelve hundred Canadians who volunteered for the war, fully half were killed, missing in action and presumed dead, or refused readmission to Canada.[20] The *Toronto Star*, one of the few Canadian dailies that supported the Republic, dispatched reporter Greg Clark to Halifax to board the train carrying the veterans back to their homes across Canada. "I don't recollect ever seeing soldiers who inspired in me so strange a mingling of reverence and humiliation and embarrassment at meeting their gaze," Clark reported.

But the bitter truth was that with the fall of Madrid on March 31, fascism ruled in Spain.

The summer of 1939 was remembered by those who survived the coming slaughter as one of the sunniest and most brilliant on record throughout the capitals of Europe. In Montreal's extreme heat and humidity "the garbage smelled high in back alleys, tenement dwellers gasped for breath on their steps and porches after sunset; even the calls from the belfries rang like dull bronze in the dead air," wrote Hugh MacLennan.

Claire had one last summer with Rube in the Laurentians, listening longingly to his stories of Paris, but as her twenty-first birthday approached the world took its last downward spiral toward war. On August 24, Vyacheslav Molotov, Stalin's foreign minister, signed a non-aggression treaty with Adolph Hitler's foreign minister, Joachim von Ribbentrop. The deal, which stunned the world, included the partition of Poland and ceded the Baltic states to the Soviet Union. The pact would also have drastic consequences for Communist parties around the world, including Claire's own. On the eve of Claire's birthday Hitler's panzers rolled into Poland, and on the day after Claire turned twenty-one Great Britain declared war on Germany. Canada followed suit one week later.

She urged Rube to let her return to France with him, but he refused, uncertain whether he himself would make it back to Paris for his final year of medical school. Their parting at dockside that autumn was the most poignant yet, each fearing for the safety of the other, both of them filled with the premonition that their relationship would be irrevocably altered by the war. All but the darkest of their personal forebodings were about to come true; neither their world nor their relationship would ever be quite the same again.

CHAPTER THREE

Underground

"There were three disasters in 1912: the Titanic *sank, I got married, and your father was born."*
—Abe Eglin to his granddaughters Roisin and Dara

N ews of Hitler's attack on Poland created deep consternation within the ranks of the Communist Party of Canada, whose members were still reeling from the implications of the non-aggression pact, which the party leadership had elected to support just the week before. Suddenly the Canadian political party that had led the fight against fascism found itself sanctioning a deal with Hitler. This apparent sell-out created a serious rift within party ranks, and the effect was both disturbing and demoralizing.[1]

But confusion degenerated into downright chaos with the invasion of Poland on September first. In a series of all-night meetings in and around Toronto the party leadership agonized over the correct line on the European war. Should they join the call for war against Hitler, abandoning their support for the non-aggression pact and reverting to the familiar (and popular) stance of fighting fascism? Or should they follow the neutralist lead of the Soviet Union, and the isolationist positions of the Communist Party U.S.A. and President Roosevelt and call for the Canadian government to stay out of the impending European war? The Canadian politburo decided to pass a resolution declaring the fight against Hitler to be just another imperialist conflict, similar to the First World War.

But events in Europe were fast outpacing the ad hoc resolutions of the Canadian Communist leadership. Within hours of their decision to urge Canadian neutrality, news reached Toronto that Great Britian had declared war against Germany. Realizing that the Canadian government was now certain to follow the British lead and join the war against Hitler, the party leadership decided to meet once again and reconsider the question. It was clear that if war was declared by the King government the Canadian working class, the very working class that the party had spent the previous half-decade trying to rally against fascism, would support its government, leaving the party hopelessly isolated. But support for the war would put the Canadian party at odds with its political masters in the Soviet Union, as well as its sister organization in the United States.

At the second all-night meeting in three days the politburo arrived at a new conclusion, one that was diametrically opposed to the position reached just twenty-four hours earlier: Canada should press for an all-out war against Hitler and oppose any suggestion of neutrality.

This new party line had no sooner been determined than some of the politburo members began to have second thoughts. Perhaps this outspoken support for the war (and the break with Soviet policy) was too "adventurist." Perhaps the leadership should reconsider. Yet a third emergency meeting was called, and in the end the party leadership decided there was only one position they could unequivocally defend: that the war against Hitler was an imperialist war, and that Canada should remain neutral.[2]

The party's vacillation and its unwillingness to break with Moscow would cost the organization dearly. The decision to urge neutrality after war was declared would, as its leaders had feared, subject the party to official suppression by the Canadian government, and isolate it from the Canadian working class. The flip-flop on the war in its early stages and its apparently slavish devotion to Soviet policy later would inflict serious damage on the prestige and credibility of the Communist Party of Canada.

None of this was immediately apparent to Claire in Montreal, although she would participate in the rise and fall of party fortunes over the next decade. Ardent anti-Fascist though she was, Claire accepted at face value the party's rationale for its support of the non-aggression pact. If the interests of world socialism were best served by building socialism in a single country (that is, the Soviet Union), then so be it. And if socialist interests were further served by abruptly compromising (at least temporarily) with fascism instead of fighting it, she was willing to accept that, too. Her faith in the party leadership remained unwavering, although she could see for herself the immense confusion the twists and turns of party policy were causing for the rank and file.

One example of this uncertainty occurred the morning Claire arrived for work at the Office Workers' Union headquarters on St. Catherine Street to find Kent Rowley already there, proudly wearing the uniform of a soldier in the Royal Montreal Regiment. Rowley, who would later become a legendary figure in the nationalist Canadian trade union movement, was then the full-time organizer of the Office Workers' Union, and Claire, because of her business-school training, was its secretary. She remembers that Kent, who was from an anglo working-class family in Montreal which had been hard hit by the depression, was particularly proud of his boots. "They were big heavy boots, the first ones he'd ever had in his life. And the uniform and the shirt—this is what most of them joined the army for—the first three meals a day and first set of new clothes they'd had since the depression started."

In joining up to fight fascism Rowley, who at twenty-one was already a trade union veteran, had doubtless made a political commitment as well. But it soon became apparent that within party circles, by volunteering for a "phoney, imperialist war," as it was then deemed by the party leadership, Kent had committed a grievous political error. "He had done the right thing," Claire recalls, "but he had just done it too fast. Within a week or ten days he was damn near expelled from the party." In Rowley's absence the party asked Claire to assume his role as organizer for the Office Workers' Union. "I sure didn't have much experience or ability, but I suppose they didn't have anyone else, so I took over."

The Office Workers' Union for which Claire was now responsible shared its modest premises with the Retail Clerks' Union, and it was about this time that she became aware of the president of the latter organization, a dashing young Irish-Canadian Communist named Garry Culhane. Six-foot-two and lantern-jawed, with wavy hair and blue eyes, the twenty-seven-year-old Culhane was a brilliant orator with a keen mind and quick-witted (and often acid) tongue. He made an immediate impression wherever he went, especially among the female comrades. "Charming" is the description used over and over again by people who knew him in the 1940s, and there is little doubt that Culhane possessed in abundance that magnetic but enigmatic quality that a later political generation would describe as "charisma."

In addition to his impressive appearance and intellectual attributes, young Garry Culhane claimed an impeccable political pedigree that both intrigued and attracted Claire Eglin. His full name was Gerard Joseph Sheehy-Culhane, and he was descended from a long and distinguished line of Irish patriots and intellectuals. His mother, Margaret Sheehy, was the daughter of David Sheehy and Elizabeth (Bessie) McCoy. Sheehy had been a member of Parnell's Irish Nationalist Party Home Rule cabinet and had served several terms as a member of the British parliament, and Bessie shared her husband's dream of a free and united Ireland. Indeed, as Conor Cruise O'Brien, the noted Irish essayist and political pundit and Garry's first cousin, would observe of their grandmother, Bessie "intended quite consciously, I believe, to preside over the birth of a new ruling class: those who would run the country when Home Rule was won."[3]

Margaret Sheehy was the second oldest in a family that included three other daughters, Hanna, Mary, and Kathleen, and two sons, Eugene and David. All six enjoyed a charmed and privileged childhood. Their comfortable house on Dublin's Belvedere Place became the venue of a Sunday-night salon where the children could hear discussions among some of the best young minds of their generation. Chief among the participants was James Joyce, who, it was said, was secretly in love for many years with Margaret's younger sister Mary. Other Sunday-night visitors included Tom Kettle, Cruise O'Brien, and Francis Skeffington, each of whom would marry one of Margaret's sisters.

Tall and statuesque, Margaret was considered the most handsome of the four girls (though Mary was the prettiest), and she developed an early and abiding passion for the theatre. The second oldest of the Sheehy daughters often organized the theatrical portions of the Sunday-night soirées, and she achieved minor celebrity when one of her plays was performed in a café on Grafton Street. She also acted in the production, and Joyce played the role of the villain.[4] Margaret would later go on to perform with the famed Abbey Street Theatre, and she would pass her dramatic flair and her love for the theatre on to her son.

In 1907 Margaret married John Francis ("Frank") Culhane, the son of a Belfast feather merchant. Bessie Sheehy reportedly looked askance at the union because her daughter's new in-laws were "in trade" rather than from her own more patrician, intellectual circles. Still, despite the parental misgivings, the marriage was a success. Frank was a likeable young solicitor who would rise to become Taxing Master to the King's Bench in Dublin City. The couple had four children: Patricia, Garry, born on February 24, 1912, Peggy, and Frank, Jr.

By 1916 it must have seemed that Bessie's ambitions for her family were on the brink of realization. Thanks to British attempts to impose conscription on Ireland, nationalist sentiment had reached a fever pitch, and Home Rule appeared, at long last, just within reach. Each of her four daughters had made successful, in some cases brilliant marriages, and each had already had at least one child, ensuring that yet another generation of Sheehys would play a leading role in the new Ireland about to be born. But during one devastating week in April Bessie's dreams were shattered forever.

Garry Culhane had just turned four by Easter Sunday of 1916, but he would later claim to have almost surreal memories of that nightmarish weekend in Irish history, when a full-scale insurrection by the Irish Republican Army was brutally suppressed by British troops. Within four days much of central Dublin, the dream of an Irish Republic, and the prospects of the Sheehy family had been reduced to rubble beneath the pounding of British artillery.

The most immediate blow to the Sheehys was the murder of Hanna's husband, Francis Sheehy-Skeffington, by a British army firing squad on the Wednesday morning of the Rising. A militant pacifist, feminist, and editor of the *Irish Citizen* newspaper, Francis had been attempting to control looting at the time of his arrest, and his death caused a sensation in Ireland. The British officer who ordered the execution was later court-martialled and convicted of murder, though the court also ruled that he was insane at the time the act was committed. Sheehy-Skeffington's martyrdom was a grievous blow to the Sheehy family and to the future of the Irish Republic.

By the end of the year, two more of the Sheehy sisters had lost their husbands. Thomas Kettle, Mary's husband, had been killed at the Battle of the Somme, and Garry's father, Frank, had died of natural causes in Dublin. By the end of 1916 three of David and Bessie's daughters had become widows, six of their grandchildren had been left without fathers, and not one of their children had yet turned forty. Moreover, an entire generation of Republican leadership, including Francis Sheehy-Skeffington, had been wiped out in the wake of the Rising through wholesale executions by British firing squads. As quickly as it had appeared within reach, the Republican dream now seemed to recede into the distant future, and though he was not yet five, the events of that bloody year would leave an indelible impact on the character of the man with whom Claire Eglin was about to fall in love.

Five years after her husband's death Margaret Sheehy began an affair with Michael Thomas Casey, a twenty-one-year-old poet. A liaison between a forty-year-old widow who was now a mother of four and a man Casey's age must have sorely tested even the Sheehys' liberal sensibilities and when in 1921 she became pregnant out of wedlock with Casey's child, it was too much. The deeply religious Culhanes, upon whom Margaret had relied for financial support, took an even dimmer view and it was time for her, in Garry's words, "to get the hell out of the country."[5] In 1922 she left her three other children with the Culhanes and, with Garry, now ten, and her new husband Casey, Margaret emigrated to Montreal. Shortly after their arrival Garry's half-brother, Ronan Casey, was born.

Alone in a new country and cut off from the Culhane largesse, it soon became apparent that neither Margaret's connections to Ireland's intelligentsia nor Casey's abilities as a poet would enable the couple to actually earn a living. Although Michael eventually landed a good job as the

Harbour Master of Montreal, Margaret would never enjoy the prominence her family had in Ireland. She did, however, manage to gain a social foothold in the city's Irish theatre and intellectual circles, and she counted a young Eugene Forsey among her friends. Margaret was also at pains to maintain appearances, and, with her six-foot frame wrapped in a flowing cape, she cut quite a flamboyant figure on the streets of Montreal.

She was a frequent guest at banquets and celebrations among the Irish community. At the end of the festivities she more than once gathered the leftover food in a tablecloth, bringing it home to feed her sons. She considered it beneath her high-born station in life to stand in line at a bus stop, an indignity she avoided by standing in the street and hailing a bus with outstretched arms whenever she needed one. Margaret lived her life as if 1916 had never happened, as if the Sheehy sisters and their husbands were still on the verge of becoming a new Irish ruling class.[6]

At the age of sixteen Garry Culhane quit school and began to work on the Montreal waterfront to help support his family. He held a variety of labouring jobs over the next decade, working as a longshoreman, a seaman (he worked his way across the Atlantic twice), and as a structural steelworker. He apparently joined the Communist party (or the Young Communist League) around 1930, and he was active in a number of party causes in Montreal, including campaigns for tenants' rights, slum clearances, public works projects, and unemployment insurance benefits throughout the 1930s.[7]

Garry's political and intellectual background, which he was never shy about discussing, gave him a certain cachet within some party circles, and his stories about the Sheehys seemed tremendously romantic to Claire. Their love affair began during that eventful fall of 1939, even though Claire was aware that she was violating her own code about relationships. Her personal guidelines were simple enough: you didn't cheat on your lover, and you didn't take anyone away from anyone else. It was on the second point that Claire had misgivings, because Garry was by now a married man. He had married Nora Brunton, a member of Montreal's upwardly mobile "lace curtain Irish" community in 1927, and he was the father of two children, Garry Og (Og is Gaelic for junior) and Patricia. But Garry assured Claire that the marriage had fallen apart, and that his life with Nora was over.

However disparate their backgrounds, Claire and Garry made a handsome couple. They were young, confident, articulate, both committed members of a social movement and a political party that would, they were certain, change the world. In the first delicious flush of getting to know one another they talked endlessly, of politics, the world, and of their families and friends. Claire especially loved to hear Garry's stories about his aunt,

Hanna Sheehy-Skeffington, and her martyred husband, Francis. Both Hanna and Francis had been dedicated proponents of suffrage for Irish women, pacifism, and Irish Home Rule. Both had spent time in Irish jails, and both had underscored their status as political prisoners by refusing to wear standard prison garb and by engaging in hunger strikes.

After Francis's assassination British prime minister Herbert Asquith offered Hanna compensation for her husband's murder. She refused to accept the money, instead demanding a full public inquiry. Her father-in-law in particular urged her to reconsider and, as a penniless widow, to at least think of the welfare of her son, Owen. "Maybe he wouldn't think you were so bright." "Yes," Hanna replied, "I've thought of that. But if Owen should ever think that, then he wouldn't have been worth accepting the bribe for in the first place."[8]

She went on to become a noted Irish political activist, writer, editor, and lecturer, commanding sizeable audiences wherever she spoke. (She had completed her fourth lecture tour of North America the year before the war broke out.) But it was Garry's descriptions of Hanna's personal character—fiery, indomitable, and committed to direct action—that most impressed Claire. In her youth Hanna had disrupted political meetings, smashed the windows of public buildings, and personally confronted politicians in her struggle to win the vote for Irish women. When militant Irish suffragists adopted the tactic of dumping thick black ink into mailboxes as a form of protest, Hanna observed that "Desperate diseases need desperate remedies, and if the vote is wrested from Government by methods of terrorism when five and forty years of sweet and quiet reason produced only seven talked-out or tricked-out suffrage bills, why, who can say it wasn't worth a mutilated letter, a cut wire, a Premier's wracked nerves?"[9]

Throughout her long political career Hanna remained a pacifist, as well as a staunch proponent of attacks on property as a valid form of political protest. To those who regarded her tactics as contradictory to her ideals, she replied that war destroyed life in order to protect property, while militant pacifists destroyed property in order to enhance the value of life. "The stone and the shillelagh need no apologia: they have an honoured place in the armoury of argument."[10]

Although they never met, Garry's aunt Hanna made a deep impression on Claire, and the fiery Irishwoman's influence on Claire would later be reflected in her own political tactics, and in the naming of her second-born daughter.

For her part, Claire told Garry grim stories about the struggles of her own hard-working immigrant family, and he found one anecdote, the story of how Claire was named for her great-aunt, particularly striking. Perhaps because the name had an almost Gaelic lilt, her new lover soon dubbed her

Kayla, instead of Claire, and she would always be known in the Vancouver circles she moved through with Garry by her aunt's name (and by her original Yiddish name). It was also, as Claire came to realize only when it was much too late, Garry's way of obliterating Claire Eglin and her personal past.

The wartime repression feared by leaders of the Canadian Communist party was not long in coming, with drastic consequences for both Claire and Garry. On September 3, 1939, Ottawa proclaimed the Defence of Canada Regulations, which "represented the most serious restrictions upon the civil liberties of Canadians since Confederation," in the judgement of one Canadian historian.[11] Overnight Canada's citizens were deprived of freedom of speech and of the press by a system of state-controlled censorship. The ancient rights of habeas corpus, access to legal representation, and normal trial procedures were swept aside, replaced by "preventive detention," which allowed for indefinite incarceration without trial. Simply voicing sentiments which "would or might be prejudicial to the safety of the state or the efficient prosecution of the war" could result in an indeterminate jail term. Freedom of association was similarly restricted. Before the war was over the regulations would be invoked to intern Japanese, German, and Italian Canadians, domestic fascists, (including Adrien Arcand), Jehovah's Witnesses, Quebec anti-conscriptionists (most notably Camillien Houde, the mayor of Montreal), and members of the Canadian Communist party. In all, the federal government would intern 2,423 of its citizens, as well as the entire Japanese population of British Columbia.[12]

But there is ample evidence that, even though Canada was now officially at war with fascism, police and government authorities regarded Communists like Claire and Garry as the most dangerous enemies on the home front. "We are of the opinion that there is more to fear from acts of espionage and sabotage on the part of the Communist party than from Nazi or Fascist organizations and adherents," the RCMP Intelligence Bulletin, a secret publication circulated privately to cabinet ministers and senior civil servants, noted in October 1939.[13] "It is not the Nazi nor the Fascist, but the radical who constitutes our most troublesome problem," RCMP Commissioner S.T. Wood agreed in 1941.[14]

While Claire Eglin and Garry Culhane could hardly be classified as prime candidates for either spying or sabotage, they and fellow militants like Lea Roback and Kent Rowley were seen as a threat to the interests of the Canadian establishment in another sense—through their union-organizing activities. Across Canada in the steel, auto, manufacturing, and mining industries, as well as the textile, office, and retail shops of

Montreal, hundreds of Communists were playing a leading role in bringing a militant brand of industrial unionism to Canada. To the extent that these organizing drives were successful in raising wages and introducing job security and safety standards, they might also, employers feared, erode profit levels and reduce management control of the workplace. In some quarters a pseudopatriotic wartime Red scare was also a convenient way of suppressing trade unions.

The suppression of the Communist party by the King government tightened. In November 1939 the party's English-language newspaper, the *Clarion*, was banned. Like other party members in Quebec, where Red squad raids on homes and offices had long since become commonplace under the Padlock Law, Claire and Garry already considered themselves old hands at playing cat and mouse with the police. The first such visit by Duplessis's police to Claire's home had so frightened Abe and Rose, (still awaiting their coveted American visas and fearful of having their applications denied because of their daughter's political activities) that they destroyed all of Claire's papers and books, including, to her bitter dismay, her prized leatherbound edition of La Pasionaria's speeches.

But far more serious persecution was imminent. Indeed, the first entry in Claire's voluminous RCMP file was made during this period. Dated March 11, 1940, and addressed to the RCMP commissioner in Ottawa from "C" Division, Montreal detachment, the single page notes the presence of Claire Eglin at a meeting of unemployed workers in Verdun the previous evening. While so heavily censored by government officials (in 1989) as to be nearly indecipherable, the document is nevertheless significant as the earliest surviving record in a dossier that runs to many hundreds of pages. Wherever she went, whatever she did, said, or wrote, Claire would remain a target of more or less continuous state surveillance for the next fifty years.[15]

By 1940 Nora and the children were living with Nora's mother in the Laurentians, and Claire was spending more and more time away from her parents to be with Garry. Both of them used as explanations the parlous circumstances facing Communists during the period, but the fact was that they were beginning to live together. Abe and Rose were at last on the eve of their departure for the United States, which was something of a relief to Claire, who had been at pains to separate her romantic and family lives. Knowing full well her parents' dreams for her—that she should marry a nice young Jewish doctor or lawyer and settle down—Claire had carefully avoided introducing Garry to them.

But Garry had other ideas. He grew ever more insistent that Claire should introduce him before her parents emigrated. Whether motivated by a sincere curiosity to meet Claire's parents or whether he was seeking an earnest of Claire's own commitment to him is unclear, but at last Claire relented. The meeting, when it came, proved even more disastrous than she had feared. To Claire's everlasting regret, she chose the tactless course of absolute honesty in making the introduction. Garry was, she proclaimed, the man she loved. He was also a married man with two children, a Communist who was about to become a fugitive, a lapsed Catholic, he was unemployed and—the greatest sin of all in her parents' eyes, she noted wryly later—he was penniless. Abe had only one question of Garry: "Don't you think you should finish with one before starting up with another?" But Quebec divorce laws, as Abe himself must have realized, made any prospect of an early legal separation from Nora an impossibility.

Claire knew when they left her parents' flat that the meeting had not gone well, but only when she returned to visit them three days later did she grasp the full gravity of their reaction. She found her parents still sitting in the same chairs, dressed in the same clothes, with the mirrors covered. They were sitting *shivah*, the Jewish ritual of mourning the dead. Claire realized with a shock that they were mourning her, that, in her parents' eyes, she might as well have been dead. She had passed the test of her commitment to Garry (if that's what it was) with flying colours, but she had lost her parents in the process. The wound thus opened would gradually close, but it would never entirely heal.

* * *

In October 1939, in a badly timed provincial election, Duplessis's Union Nationale government was decisively defeated by the Liberals, due, to a large extent, to the federal Liberals' promise not to introduce conscription for overseas military service. Adélard Godbout, Quebec's new Liberal premier, wasted little time making good one of his campaign promises. When the new legislative session opened on February 20, the speech from the throne included a provision for women's suffrage, and on the afternoon of April 25, 1940, Thérèse Casgrain and her fellow lobbyists were in the visitors' gallery for the third and final reading of Bill number 18, an act giving women the dual rights of voting and holding office in the province of Quebec. Although the measure passed by a vote of thirteen to five, veteran suffrage opponents like Médéric Martin (the former mayor of Montreal who had led the Labour Day parade that so frustrated Abe Eglin on the day of his daughter's birth) and Sir Thomas Chapais could not resist a few parting shots. Eyeing the visitors' gallery, Chapais was heard to observe: "Well, before the ladies sit here with us, I hope a new style of hats will have been introduced." But even such insufferable chauvinist gibes could not hold back the clock. Shortly after six in the evening Casgrain and her fellow suffragists could finally celebrate. Their fourteenth annual pilgrimage to Quebec City would be their last: the women of Quebec now had the right to vote.[16]

But Claire's satisfaction in the triumph of a cause that she had supported since her high school days was to prove short-lived. While the Quebec government was at last acknowledging hard-won rights, Ottawa was about to take others away. Just twenty-eight days after Quebec granted women the right to vote, the King cabinet, acting by Order in Council, declared the Communist Party of Canada illegal.

Garry and Claire quietly prepared for life underground. Like dozens of other party members across Canada who would quit their jobs and slip unobtrusively away from their residences, they were determined to evade the authorities and the indeterminate prison sentences imposed by the Defence of Canada Regulations any way they could. They decided that Garry, as the higher-profile and senior party member of the pair, should quit his job, while Claire retained hers. She was now earning twelve dollars a week as a secretary. Seven dollars went to help support Nora and her two children, by then settled into her mother's small boarding house in the Laurentians. On the remaining five dollars they struggled to pay rent and feed themselves.

"I've never been so hungry in my life as I was in that time," Claire would recall of her months underground. "There were times I was so hungry that I'd bump into friends and they'd say, 'Oh, come over for supper with us,' and I wouldn't go because I knew I'd be such a pig. A whole tableful of food, and I was afraid I wouldn't be able to keep my hands off it."

Her parents were slowly reconciling themselves with their daughter, if not with Garry, and Claire was now at least able to return home twice a week for dinner, after which Rose would look the other way as her daughter filled a shopping bag with the canned goods and other food that was sometimes the only nourishment that stood between Garry and Claire and hunger.

They stayed in a succession of dreary rented rooms in downtown Montreal in an atmosphere of paranoia as well as privation. "Living underground meant you rented a room and as soon as someone moved in next door without luggage, you moved out." But then, as now, Claire was sanguine about the hardships of life underground. "You lived through it. You were young, and in love, and it all went with the territory."

The news from Europe that spring of 1940 was grim. In late May the British Expeditionary Force had been evacuated from Dunkirk, in mid-June the German army rolled into Paris, and the next day France surrendered.

The loss of Paris and the French surrender shocked Quebec. The "phoney war" no longer seemed so phoney now that Britain was the last bulwark against complete Nazi domination of western Europe. Mackenzie King seized on the situation to take a giant step toward conscription while clamping even tighter controls on Canada's civilian population. On June 21, the House of Commons passed the National Resources Mobilization Act, which imposed conscription for males in a domestic militia, but carefully refrained from requiring citizens to serve in the Canadian forces outside the country. The Mobilization Act also stipulated that every resident of Canada over the age of sixteen must obtain a registration card which had to be carried at all times. Claire and Garry feared that as soon as Garry, in particular, presented himself for registration he would be detained. But the police had already announced their intentions of establishing spot checks on city streets across the country to enforce the regulation. "You'd go to a movie, and all of a sudden there'd be someone standing at the wicket. Or you could be stopped crossing a bridge. You could be spot-checked any time." To be caught without a registration card would arouse suspicion; it was also a serious offence. The new regulations appeared to present the young couple with an insoluble dilemma, but the ever-resourceful Claire found a solution.

August 19 through 21 was declared the week of national registration. Claire decided to register with her parents, as a family unit, in the hope that she would make herself less conspicuous. They went together to the neighbourhood school where the registration process was under way. It was all a bit like an election—tables were set out in the gymnasium, behind which sat government clerks who handed out the registration forms, and then checked over the completed papers. After filling out her own form Claire adopted her best schoolgirl demeanour and approached one of the overworked women behind the desk.

"Is there anything I can do to help?"

"Oh, yes, thank you. If you could just help people fill these in. But I have to sign them."

She cheerfully drew up a chair beside the clerk and began to busy herself with paperwork. When no one was looking Claire deftly pocketed a handful of the blank registration forms. Garry's problems of evading internment were solved—at least temporarily.

They had devised an early warning system for use against the police. Reasoning that her parents' flat was the first place the police would come looking for her, Claire gave her mother the phone number of a friend to use if and when the police arrived with an order for her detention.

Their evasions were successful until the fall of 1941. Montreal had been selected as the site for the founding convention of the Commonwealth Cooperative Youth Movement, the youth wing of the CCF. David Lewis and Grace MacInnis were present, and Claire attended the meeting along with Madeline Parent. Both Claire and Parent (who would, like Claire, go on to a lifetime of social activism) played a prominent-enough role in the conference that they were picked to head a special committee on the problems of poverty and unemployment. As part of their work on the committee Claire and Madeline organized an anti-poverty meeting at the Monument National in downtown Montreal. About forty people attended, and Claire could tell at a glance that half of them were policemen. "In those days you could always tell who the infiltrators were, because if you were poor you couldn't afford to dress very well. Anybody in a three-piece suit had to be a cop. At least half of the people at the meeting were wearing suits, so it was a pretty well-attended meeting."

The next evening the friend who was acting as Claire's go-between with her parents phoned in a message. "Your mother called this morning. She said to tell you not to go to work tomorrow." A few days later Claire went to visit her parents, slipping in the back way. The police had arrived at their door, detention order for Claire in hand, the morning after the meeting at the Monument National, Rose and Abe told her. They had entered the flat and ransacked the place, apparently searching for incriminating evidence. Claire's parents had finally received their entry visas from the United States government, and they departed for California shortly after the police raid. Abe and Rose must have been greatly relieved that Claire's politics had not prevented their own emigration. It was the last time that Claire and her parents would live in the same city or even in the same country.

Now neither Claire nor Garry dared work. They talked the situation over, and Garry emphatically refused to let Claire risk detention by going back to her job. Instead, he decided to apply for a job, and to plan for the inevitable imprisonment that would follow. He made the rounds of his mother's influential friends in Montreal, including Eugene Forsey, Father X. Bryant of Loyola College, and Robert Calder, Montreal's foremost civil liberties lawyer. Remembering the tactics employed by his Irish forebears, Garry announced his intention of going on hunger strike to protest his apprehension until charges were laid in open court.

Then, just when it seemed that matters couldn't get much worse for the young couple, Claire discovered that she was pregnant. However much she would have loved to have a baby, Claire realized that becoming a mother was out of the question given the precarious nature of their life underground. She managed to locate a doctor who performed illegal abortions, but he told her it would cost fifty dollars. Even when she had been able to work, the amount equalled a full month's pay—now such a sum represented a small fortune. In desperation, she phoned California and asked her brother, Jack, for the money, hinting that it was for the bus fare down. Her brother came to her support and sent her the money.

At least the illegal abortionist was an M.D. But he also took advantage, it seemed to Claire, fondling and petting unnecessarily while giving her the physical examination. But what could she do? If she protested, she desperately feared he would refuse to perform the abortion, and reporting him was clearly impossible—she was as implicated as he in the illegal procedure. She was quite literally at his mercy. Fortunately, he was at least competent. The doctor told her to come back on the date of her third post-conception period, when the risk of miscarriage is highest, and he simply inserted a sterile tube into her vagina. After that, he told her to go home and wait.

She returned to their shabby room, changed the sheets, and got into bed. Within a few hours her labour began. It turned out to be four or five hours of hard labour, harder even than she would later experience when giving birth at full term. The walls in the rooming house were paper thin and the landlady lived right next door, so Claire stuffed a pillow in her mouth to ensure that her screams wouldn't be heard, while Garry nervously paced the floor. When it was finally over, and before Garry disposed of the fetus, she couldn't help asking if it was a girl or a boy. It was a boy.

There was little time for depression or remorse. Christmas was approaching and Garry decided to visit Nora and the children at her mother's in the Laurentians. Before starting the trip he went to see Nora's sister in the city, to ask whether she wanted him to take anything up on the train. In hindsight, Garry and Claire concluded that the sister or her husband (a professor at McGill) phoned the police. Claire had checked on the train and bus schedules and found that the bus would be more convenient, so at the last minute Garry took the bus instead. Not having found Garry at the train station, the police arrived at Nora's mother's house half an hour after Garry arrived from the bus depot on the day before Christmas Eve. Garry had a half-dozen of the registration cards that Claire had stolen in his pocket, and when on the pretext of changing clothes the police allowed him to go unaccompanied into a bedroom, he quickly disposed of the incriminating cards, which would have netted him a ten-year prison sentence. He also asked Nora to call a mutual friend in Montreal to tell him that he wasn't returning to the city the same way he'd left. It had been prearranged that such a message from Nora would be immediately relayed to Claire.

Knowing full well what the message meant, Claire acted quickly. She phoned Nora and urged her to come to the city. Nora did so. After outlining Garry's preparations, Claire suggested Nora make the rounds of the prominent Montrealers with whom Garry had already spoken, to inform them that he had finally been detained. They also fired off a telegram to his mother in Dublin to alert her that her son was in Bordeaux Prison, and on hunger strike.

Margaret and her sisters Hanna and Mary (Kathleen had died three years before) evidently wasted little time in wielding their political influence in the Irish capital, because Nora soon received a cable from Eamon de Valera, the prime minister of Ireland, promising to investigate Garry's detention. Thanks to de Valera's intervention and Garry's hunger strike events began to unfold in Ottawa with almost breakneck speed. John J. Hearne, the Irish high commissioner, discussed Garry's case with O. D. Skelton, Canada's under secretary of state for external affairs, and on December 10, 1941, he underscored his concern in an urgent letter to Skelton.

Hearne was careful to establish Garry's family connections, adding that he knew Margaret and Garry's late stepfather, Michael Casey, personally. "Garry Culhane's father was a Taxing Master in the Four Courts. Mrs. Casey, the former Mrs. Culhane, is a daughter of the late David Sheehy MP, a well-known member of the Irish Parliamentary party. She is a sister of Circuit Court Judge Sheehy. She and her first husband were intimate friends of the late Joe Devlin MP."

Skelton was the leading civil servant of his time and Mackenzie King's most trusted adviser, and what happened next can only be described as illustrative of the importance of having influence in high places. On Monday, December 13, Skelton wrote to the head of the RCMP, Commissioner S.T. Wood, politely but quite firmly asking for information about the case, particularly about Garry's health.

Three days later Skelton drafted a carefully worded reply to Hearne. An order for Culhane's internment had been issued "as the result of his activities with the Communist Party of Canada," Skelton informed the high commissioner. But because Culhane's health had proved bad during a medical examination, and because he "had not attained any important position in the Communist Party," Culhane had been released on December 28 "on compassionate grounds."[17]

This remarkable exchange of memos and the swift decision to release Garry showed the celerity with which the Ottawa mandarinate could act upon learning that it had detained the scion of an influential family. But the latter memo is also remarkable for what can charitably be described as blatant dissembling, skirting mention of the hunger strike to protest violation of basic civil rights by references to "bad health." Similarly the intimation that Garry had been released because of his relative unimportance in the party can probably be ascribed to the need for face-saving in

Ottawa—the RCMP must have known Garry's party history before his detention. And the statement that he had been released on December 28 appears to be a blatant falsehood. Claire was at the train station in Montreal to meet Garry on his return from Bordeaux "twelve or thirteen days" after his internment, or the fourth or fifth of January. Whether Skelton deliberately minimized the length of Garry's internment to the Irish government or whether he was himself misinformed by the RCMP will probably never be known. In any case the spectre of the diplomatic row that was bound to ensue if the son of a well-known Irish family starved himself to death in a Canadian prison evidently outweighed Garry's perceived threat to Canadian security, as Garry himself had cagily banked that it would. So, while dozens of other members of the Communist Party of Canada languished in internment camps throughout the first half of the war, Garry Culhane remained a free man. But this situation in itself would soon create a new problem for Claire and Garry.

While Garry Culhane's quick release from detention was a triumph in a tactical sense, it also provoked a contrary reaction in party circles: word began to circulate among party members in Montreal that Garry had been released because he was a police informer. Garry and Claire had always known that some members of the party were less than completely enamoured with Garry because of his patrician background, and the party was not, of course, privy to Skelton's private correspondence. On the face of it, the evidence appeared damning: Garry was released after only two weeks in jail, while many of his comrades, including several members of his own party branch, or cell, were to spend months, even years, in prison under the Defence of Canada Regulations.

Because the entire Communist party was now underground Garry and Claire were unable to phone, visit, or correspond with any of their comrades to explain Garry's precipitate release. Any chance encounter with a party friend always resulted in the comrade crossing the street to avoid the couple entirely. At least Garry was now able to hold a job legally, if he could keep one—the RCMP were not at all above visiting one's new employers to inform them that they had just hired a Red. With a detention order still outstanding for her, Claire agreed to maintain a low profile and not seek work. Garry found a job for a while, in Lachine, at the south end of Montreal Island, but the financial situation remained tight. Even on two incomes it had been hard to make ends meet because of the necessity to contribute to the support of Nora and Garry's two children. To save rent they spent the summer of 1941 camping out in a tent near Lachine. They were there in late June when the war, party policy, and their lives took yet another abrupt turn.

On the morning of Sunday, June 22, the German army attacked the Soviet Union along a fourteen-hundred-kilometre front extending from the Baltic in the north to the Black Sea in the south. Code named Operation Barbarossa, the offensive was the largest mechanized assault in the annals of warfare, and within a few weeks German panzer divisions had advanced deep into the Soviet Union. By Christmas, they would be on the outskirts of Moscow and Leningrad.

Just as it had when the non-aggression pact was signed twenty-one months earlier, the Communist Party of Canada performed a sharp *volte-face* in its line on the war now that the Soviet Union was in peril. Where the conflict had earlier been a "phoney imperialist" war, now it was suddenly viewed as a righteous, anti-Fascist struggle. Where Communist party organizers within the trade union movement had seized on the war as an opportunity to win wage gains and organize thousands of non-union workers, using strikes if necessary, they now urged all-out support for the war, complete with no-strike pledges for the duration. As one anti-Communist Canadian trade union leader noted sardonically, but prophetically, the Communists were likely to "become too patriotic . . . so that those of us who have assumed that our country needs our services will be portrayed in the light of traitors because we are not pushing the war on a 'proletarian' basis sufficient enough to save Russian Christianity and Russian Democracy . . . The Communists may develop into such ardent patriots that we shall pale into fifth columnists by comparison."[18]

As winter approached, Claire and Garry took stock of their situation. Quebec's divorce laws, the most repressive in the country, meant that Garry had little chance of ever obtaining a divorce from Nora and marrying Claire, which both Garry and Claire desired. Hitler's attack on the Soviet Union and the party's new line on the war lent a sense of urgency for a return to political work, but Garry remained under a cloud of suspicion in the Quebec wing of the party. They decided that he would go to the opposite end of the country, to British Columbia, to search for work. If he was successful, Claire would follow, and they would try to reassemble the pieces of their war-shattered lives.

CHAPTER FOUR

Kayla

*In 1945 Canada was fourth among the ship-owning
nations of the world with over 500 ships employing at
least 20,000 men. In 1948 she was down to 145 vessels
employing 6,000 men. By 1955 she was down to 15 dry
cargo vessels. By 1963 she was down to one ship, a
10,000 tonner with the completely ridiculous name
SS Federal Pioneer.*
> —Former Boilermakers' Union president Bill White on
> the rise and fall of Canada's maritime industry

The Second World War galvanized Canada. Almost overnight the country was transformed, the torpor of the depression sloughed off. Stimulated by the adrenalin of war, the pace of life quickened, and the making of a genuine industrial miracle began. Once again huge convoys of ships swung at anchor in Halifax's Bedford Basin, their holds bearing the bounty of a continent—munitions, vehicles, spare parts, food, clothing, lumber. Around the Great Lakes Canada's steel mills belched fiery rivers of metal night and day. On the Laurentian Shield hard rock mines returned to three-shift, around-the-clock production, in a furious race to extract the nickel, copper, lead, zinc, iron, and gold necessary to feed the insatiable industrial maw. On the Prairies, even Mother Nature smiled—by 1944 the wheat yield more than doubled the production of the drought year 1937— and the Lakehead became the largest grain-shipping terminal in the world.

The spiral of numbers was dizzying. In the first ten months of 1940 unemployment fell from 13.8 percent to 4.0 percent, the greatest employment increase in the history of the Dominion. Whole integrated industries sprang up out of nowhere. Canada's aircraft industry, which had employed only 1,000 workers before the war would, by 1943, employ 55,000 people capable of turning out eighty planes per week. Steel production had nearly doubled by 1944, making Canada the fourth-largest steel maker among the Allies. The auto industry, retooled for wartime production exclusively, would produce 550,000 military vehicles through the first five years of the war.[1]

Fifty years later, with the de-industrialization of the country in full flight, Canada's wartime industrial achievements are nearly forgotten, but they were real enough, and Claire and Garry were about to find themselves in the middle of the miracle. By 1944 Canada, with a population of 11.5 million, had suddenly become one of the world's foremost industrial powers. No country produced more nickel, asbestos, platinum, radium, or newsprint. Canada was the world's second-largest producer of aluminum, wood pulp, hydroelectric power, and cargo ships. The Royal Canadian Navy, which had had fifteen ships at the outbreak of war, now boasted more than eight hundred, making it the third-largest naval power among the Allies. The RCAF was the fourth-largest air force on the Allied side.[2]

Driven by war, and by government spending—the national debt nearly tripled between 1939 and 1944—Canada was at last able to provide what its citizens had lacked in peacetime: full employment, living wages, and a modicum of security.

Garry Culhane arrived on the west coast in early October 1941, and he could not have picked a more propitious time to seek employment or to resume work in the party. German U-boats were taking a severe toll on Allied shipping in the North Atlantic, sinking eight hundred thousand tons in 1939, four million tons the following year. Suddenly the successful outcome of the war hinged on building enough cargo ships to resupply Great Britain and the Soviet Union, and British Columbia's shipbuilding industry was entering the greatest boom in its history.[3]

The tremendous growth in the workforce that resulted from Canada's explosive industrial expansion created a new upsurge in the trade union movement. Whole industries were organized into new unions, old locals reported exponential growth in membership, and the Communist party, despite its illegal status, played a major role in trade union leadership. Nowhere was this clearer than in British Columbia. In the province's logging camps and sawmills the International Woodworkers of America were a powerful force. The president of the IWA, Harold Pritchett, was a party man, and the union's secretary-treasurer under him, Nigel Morgan, would eventually become the Communist party chairman in British Columbia. In the hard rock mining industry, the International Union of Mine, Mill and Smelter Workers held sway, led by long-time party member Harvey Murphy. On the waterfront, in the Vancouver shipyards that were beginning to teem with activity, the Party quickly gained a foothold in the Boilermakers' and Iron Shipbuilders' Union. In September 1939 the Boilermakers' Union had been struggling to stay alive, with a membership of only two hundred. Two years later its membership rolls had soared to over thirteen thousand, making it the largest union within the Canadian Congress of Labour or CCL, the forerunner of the Canadian Labour Congress. Garry Culhane became a member of the Boilermakers when he landed a job at the Burrard shipyards soon after his arrival in Vancouver, and for the next five years the shipyard trade union movement would be the focus of his political work as it would be, to a lesser extent, for Claire.

She took the train from Montreal to Vancouver, arriving in early November. Like all trains in those days the cars had been packed with servicemen, and Claire had passed the time on the four-day-and-night journey by talking with the young sailors and soldiers. About a month after her arrival Claire was baffled when Garry came home from work clearly furious with her, but unwilling to discuss the problem. A week later the story came spilling out: apparently a new hire at the shipyard had mentioned that he'd come from Montreal or Toronto on the same train Claire had taken. What a time they'd had, with women and smoking and booze. There were about eighteen cars on the train, but Claire couldn't convince Garry that she'd had nothing to do with the festivities. She'd never been a drinker, so there's no reason she would have joined the party, but she did sit and talk with the guys. It was a foreshadowing of things to come in the relationship. Garry's resentment of Claire's lovers before him bred suspicion that she was less than faithful now. The suspicions were destined to deepen into paranoia, a manic possessiveness, and, finally, dangerous rage. But that was in the future. For now, despite her fidelity, Claire was still trying to puzzle out what she had done to excite Garry's jealousy.

Like Garry, Claire had little difficulty finding work in British Columbia's booming wartime economy. By March 1942 she was employed at the Sauder Lumber Company in False Creek, next to the Sweeney Cooperage, as a stenographer-bookkeeper, and the young couple settled into rooms on lower Cardero Street, near what is now the Bayshore Inn. Despite Garry's occasional flashes of intense jealousy, their relationship was still a happy one. They went for long walks on the shores of Coal Harbour, which was then still undeveloped and a mooring for part of the British Columbia fishing fleet. They often paused at the foot of Cardero Street so that Garry could watch the fishing boats and dream of the day when he could own his own boat and live near the water. Sometimes they would talk late into the night about their dreams and ambitions. Garry's goal was to eventually win election to the provincial executive of the British Columbia Communist Party, and Claire assured him that she didn't mind being the breadwinner to allow him the freedom to do more full-time party work. "No," Garry answered, "even if I do get elected to the Central Committee, it's you who will make your mark some day, and it will be far more important than anything I ever do." Although she pooh-poohed the remark at the time, she never forgot it, not least because Garry was so sparing of his compliments.

Their stay in Vancouver was brief. In the summer of 1942 Garry was offered a better job in the Yarrows shipyards at Victoria and they were on the move once again, across the Strait of Georgia to the provincial capital. By early August Claire had begun working in the chief treasury office of the Esquimalt Naval Dockyards in Victoria.

As part of its wartime counter-espionage precautions Ottawa had instituted a system of security screening for all government employees, and by November the Mounties were at pains to ascertain whether the Claire Eglin who had applied for a civil service job in Victoria was the same young woman about whom they had files in Montreal. On November 27 a constable in the Montreal detachment was able to report "that through discreet inquiries . . . it has definitely been ascertained that Claire EGLIN of . . . Victoria B.C., the applicant in this case, is identical with the subject of our fyle [sic] No. [censored]." A check with her former Montreal employers had confirmed Claire's references on her Victoria application; "however very little faith can be placed in these recommendations as it is evident that Claire EGLIN was very active in the radical movement whilst she stayed in Montreal, P.Q."[4]

The Mounties forwarded their reports to the Civil Service Commission in Ottawa, but Claire was allowed to keep her job as a Grade 2 clerk in the treasury office at His Majesty's Canadian dockyard Esquimalt.

Shortly after their arrival in Victoria the opportunity to buy a boat presented itself, thanks to Rose and Abe. Claire's parents had taken out an insurance policy for her when she was born, a not uncommon practice of the time, and in 1942 it reached maturity. Claire and Garry unexpectedly found themselves the recipients of the handsome sum of three hundred dollars. They agreed to spend the windfall on a boat, and the *RLR*, a ten-metre gill-netter, became their home for the next eighteen months. They tied her up at the government dock at the foot of Johnson Street in downtown Victoria, where there were no moorage fees, and they became part of a floating community of fishermen, many of them natives. They soon met the couple in the next boat over, the *Muriel D.* They were the Dalys, John and Pixie, and the four of them became fast friends. John was a lifelong fisherman, a strong union man and CCFer, and an avid reader with a quick sense of humour. "Like so many others, he considered Garry brilliant and hung on his every word, politically, et cetera, and as usual, too, it didn't take Garry long to borrow money from John, who took the magnanimous attitude 'No one has ever reneged on paying me back—and if they have, then they just needed it more than me, I guess.'" Claire was beginning to learn that it was always a struggle to get Garry to repay his debts "as he operated on the theory that it's the creditor who has to worry, not the debtor . . ."[5] Forty-five years later John Daly would become the subject of a book-length portrait by his second wife, *New Yorker* writer Edith Iglauer, and Claire would comment favourably when she happened across an evocative magazine excerpt from the book.[6] "It certainly captured the 'fishing fever' we were all infected with once we got out on to the water . . . and while there was much that I griped about, must admit I did glory in the sunrises, sunsets, rocking of the boat at bedtime, salt smells, moonlight on the water. This brings it all back."[7]

But such romantic moments were rare. The more quotidian reality was of life tied up at the wharf: the incessant smell of rotting fish, the inescapable dampness of life on the water in a British Columbia winter, the bucket that served as a toilet, and the single wash basin pressed into service for washing dishes, clothes, and, worst of all, for sponge baths. But they did find an escape, though to a most unlikely haven. After supper Garry and Claire dressed respectably, gathered up their reading and writing materials, and walked to the nearby Empress Hotel. "We had located a lovely corner of the ground floor lounge, with all its fashionable furnishings, deep rugs, and heavy drapes, and best of all LOVELY AND WARM . . . and we would spend our evenings there. In fact whenever anyone came over from Vancouver or elsewhere to visit, that is where we would entertain them—it became our unofficial residence. No one ever bothered us. We just became part of the scene. It was marvellous."[8]

The one thing the welcoming lobby of the Empress could not provide, however, was a hot bath. For this Claire turned to Kitty Mitchell, whose physician husband was serving in Malta. They had met Kitty through John Daly, and she soon proffered Claire and Garry a standing Saturday-night dinner invitation. Claire waited until about ten o'clock, when she knew Garry and Kitty, a staunch CCFer, would get into a spirited political argument, before quietly excusing herself and slipping upstairs for a bath. She soon reached the point where she could escape, bathe, and return to the dining room in about eight minutes flat—before anyone noticed her absence. That winter on the boat in Victoria gave Claire a lifelong appreciation of the pleasures of the bath, and her idea of the ultimate in hospitality would, forever after, be to ask house guests if they wanted to take a bath. She would liken just seeing a bathroom with a bathtub to the "feeling an alcoholic must experience when dropping in to a liquor store—wow!"[9]

Despite its discomforts, the *RLR*, and their two steady paycheques, allowed Garry and Claire to honour a pledge they had made before leaving

Montreal. As soon as they were settled out west, they had agreed, they would send for Nora and the children. Because of his job at the shipyard Garry was entitled to one unit of wartime housing in Victoria, and that allowed Nora, who was still legally his wife, and the two children to move to the Island. Garry's paycheque always went to support Nora, Garry Og, and Paddy while Garry and Claire lived on her earnings. It still wasn't easy making ends meet on a single income, but the effort, as Claire would admit later, went some way toward assuaging her guilt that she had come between Nora and her husband, notwithstanding Garry's insistence that his relationship with Nora had been over before Claire entered the picture.

They were all just achieving some semblance of normalcy, the first, really, in her three years with Garry, when Claire realized in November 1942, that she was pregnant again. But Garry was adamantly opposed to becoming a father for a third time, and once again Claire was forced to admit that their living conditions, aboard the *RLR*, were hardly suitable for the care of a newborn.

Reluctantly Claire began to search for another abortionist, but this time there was a complication. She knew hardly anyone in Victoria, certainly no one she could approach about the delicate subject of obtaining an illegal abortion. Her mother had been urging her to come to California for a visit, so, in late November, Claire obtained an extended leave without pay from the dockyard and travelled down to Los Angeles.

As she had hoped, her mother agreed to help her find a doctor, but this time the experience was truly a nightmare. The doctor demanded five hundred dollars instead of fifty, an extortionate figure when one remembers that three hundred dollars bought an entire fishing boat, but somehow Rose came up with the money. Then there were the visits to his office. It was underground, in a basement, and she had to pass through three locked doors before reaching the actual operating room.

Claire told the doctor that she had already had one abortion, how it was done, and would he please do it that way again? She was already in her third month.

But the doctor said no, he had concocted a special ointment which, when injected into the cervix, invariably produced a miscarriage. He performed the insertion and Claire went home. Nothing happened. The procedure was repeated, and still nothing. She was now entering her fourth month, and her concerns were mounting. The doctor professed amazement: even if she merely stubbed her toe the miscarriage should occur, after what he'd pumped into her.

Once again she begged him to just repeat the Montreal procedure, and this time he agreed. As she lay back on the table, appropriately draped so she couldn't see what was happening, for one horrible instant she was certain she felt a penis penetrating her vagina. She jumped in terror, but the doctor just looked at her blandly and said, "What's the matter?"

What could she say? She could never be sure, in later years, whether she had been assaulted, or whether she was so nervous it was just her imagination.

This time, in any event, the procedure worked. Rose sent Abe off to a movie as Claire went into labour shortly after her return home. Once again it was a boy, but this time Claire had Rose clean and wrap him, so that she could cuddle the fetus the rest of the night. She wanted that baby.

The war in Europe had entered its fourth year, and the Soviet Union had been doing most of the fighting. The Red Army stiffened, and then held, just outside Leningrad. On the southern front, on the banks of the Volga River, the world watched and held its breath as a huge battle was joined in September 1942 for control of the Russian city of Stalingrad.

In Canada, meanwhile, the Communist Party of Canada languished in a kind of legal limbo as Ottawa maintained the dubious distinction of being the only major Allied government to have imprisoned its Communists during the war.[10] At the same time, the Liberal government was in desperate need of every ounce of pro-war sentiment it could muster. The problem, once again, was Quebec. In its throne speech of January 1942, the King government called for a plebiscite on conscription, provoking the anti-conscription furies of Quebec, who rightly regarded the plebiscite as the harbinger of a military draft for overseas service.

The vote was held on April 27 and the results provided renewed evidence of the irreconcilable gulf that separated Canada's French and English nations: while Quebec voted 72 percent against conscription, the rest of Canada voted 80 percent in favour. The Communist Party of Canada had given a ringing endorsement to the "yes" side in the plebiscite and in the summer of 1942, on a boat on the Ottawa River, a curious and historic secret meeting was held. The Canadian government, represented by an up-and-coming diplomat named Lester Pearson, met with the Communist Party of Canada, represented by Fred Rose, one of the party's most prominent Quebec leaders. The two struck a deal, a saw-off in the best tradition of Canadian politics: if the Communist party continued its all-out support for the war effort, it would be allowed to emerge from underground. In order to save political face for the King government (especially in Quebec, where anti-Communist hysteria was still exceeded only by anti-conscription sentiment), the party leaders would pledge not to function as the Communist Party of Canada, and the official ban on the party would remain in place. But the party would be free to throw its not inconsiderable weight, especially in trade union ranks, into all-out industrial production for the war effort. In practical terms, this would often translate into support for the King government itself. And so, one of the most bizarre alliances in Canadian political history was born.[11]

On January 31, 1943, the Germans surrendered at Stalingrad, ending what many military historians consider the single most pivotal land battle of the Second World War. Here, at long last, was concrete evidence that the Nazi military machine could indeed be defeated. The Red Army, the Soviet people, and their leader, Joseph Stalin, were suddenly the toast of the free world. Three weeks after the German defeat at Stalingrad Mackenzie King rose in the House to praise the Red Army, which had given "all the free peoples who have been resisting Nazi aggression so much cause for encouragement and thanksgiving," and in the spring the first Soviet embassy was opened in Ottawa, marking a thaw in the chilly diplomatic relations that had existed between Canada and the Soviet Union since the Bolshevik revolution of 1918.[12]

The Canadian Communist party, meanwhile, re-emerged as a legal political entity in August 1943 as the Labour Progressive Party. Propelled by Canadian admiration for the Soviet Union's heroism during the war, and by LPP calls for all-out prosecution of the fight against Nazism, the prestige of the party had reached a new high-water mark. In the Cartier by-election of August 1943, Fred Rose became the first Communist elected to Parliament in Canadian history. In Ontario the LPP elected two members to the provincial legislature, as well as city councillors across the country. But the party's growing popularity, especially within the trade union movement, was anathema to the social democrats of the CCF. The most disgraceful chapter in the history of Canadian labour was about to be written, and Garry and Claire would be in the thick of the fight.

*   *   *

The Cold War in Canada began, not as is commonly believed, at the end of the Second World War, but a full two years before, in 1943. Canada's first and most vociferous cold warriors were to be found, not in the ranks of the RCMP, on the right wing of the political spectrum, or even on Bay Street, but on the left, among the leadership of the country's social democratic party. In hindsight, the bitter struggle which erupted between the CCF and the Communist party is not surprising. Both parties were vying for the same prize—the hearts and minds of the Canadian working class—and thanks to the war effort it had become an immense prize, indeed. The immediate battleground was the trade union movement, whose membership had nearly doubled by 1943.[13] At stake were millions of dues dollars, control over union offices and staff, and influence over the commanding heights of the Canadian economy and on the political life of the nation.

The opening salvo in the battle was aimed at Garry's union, the Boiler-makers. Thanks to U-boat activity in the North Atlantic the Boilermakers had suddenly become the largest union in the CCL, and by 1942 its dues contributions to the Congress was greater than all of the international unions combined.[14] In December 1942 party members Bill Stewart and Malcolm MacLeod were elected president and secretary, respectively, of Boilermakers Local 1 in Vancouver, the largest single local in the CCL. The Boilermakers, CCF supporters in the Congress leadership decided, was far too important to be allowed to fall into party hands, even though Stewart and MacLeod had been democratically elected by the membership. The Congress executive in Ottawa intervened, overturned the election results, and appointed a new executive composed entirely of the defeated candi-dates. The pro-party faction within the Boilermakers ignored the Congress and swore Stewart and MacLeod into office, touching off an ugly year-long court battle that ended in complete vindication for the party. The British Columbia Supreme Court ruled that Stewart's slate had been "legally elected . . . with complete control over union property and funds." The Congress leadership, humiliated and discredited, was forced to reinstate Stewart and his executive and to relinquish control over union funds.[15]

Garry Culhane's own political stock had been rising steadily, mean-while, both in Boilermakers Local 2 at the Yarrows shipyard in Victoria where he was elected president in 1943, and within the ranks of the British Columbia Communist Party. On January 15, 1944, delegates representing more than twenty thousand shipyard workers in ten local unions met in Vancouver for the founding convention of the British Columbia Federation of Shipyard Workers. The new federation, comprised of the Dockyards Workers' Union and smaller CCL-affiliated shipbuilding unions as well as the Boilermakers, had been one of the surrender terms in the CCL's disas-trous attempt to oust the Communists from Local 1, and it was to provide Garry with his entrée into the senior circles of both Communist party leadership in British Columbia and Canada's national trade union leader-ship. Malcolm MacLeod, secretary of Boilermakers Local 1 was elected president, and Garry became the federation's first secretary-treasurer. The new organization adopted the Boilermakers' newspaper, the *Main Deck*, as its official publication and set up shop in the Boilermakers Hall at 339 West Pender in Vancouver. (The building, now popularly known as The Pender Auditorium, still stands.)

For Claire, Garry's new position had a dual significance: it meant moving back to Vancouver, and it meant that Garry had a steady income for at least a year. She quit her job at Esquimalt in late February and in March they moved into a boarding house on Barkley Street in Vancouver's west end. It was only a single room, but it was large enough and comfortable, and they were able to live cheaply—one hundred dollars a month for room and board.

Once they were settled, Claire was seized by a yearning that preoccupied her until it became an obsession: she wanted to have a baby. At times the urge to have children was overpowering. Once, on a crowded bus, she found herself sitting across from a mother with her young child, and Claire's sense of desire, envy, bereavement—she wasn't sure which—became so overwhelming that she felt physically ill and had to get off the bus at the next stop. They were no longer wanted by the police, the rooming house had indoor plumbing, and Garry was guaranteed a regular salary. Garry was opposed, but Claire became more determined than ever to become a mother. She would nurse the baby for the first year to save on formula, they would at least qualify for the new family allowance of five dollars per month (Canada's first universal welfare scheme had been legislated by the King government in 1944), and she could always take in typing to earn a little extra money.

Garry, however, was adamant in his opposition. His career had taken flight since his election to the number-two position in the Shipyard General Workers Union (SGWU). His articles, always well-crafted and closely reasoned, began to appear regularly in the *Main Deck*, often accompanied by a picture of the wavy-haired, clear-eyed rising star of the British Columbia labour movement. The paper was a powerful platform—by the spring of 1944 its circulation had risen to 25,000 in shipyards up and down the coast. Through the federation Garry also had access to a larger public across the lower mainland via radio, and on at least one occasion his talk was transcribed and circulated as a leaflet. Since the SGWU was an affiliate of the Canadian Congress of Labour it was entitled to a seat on the CCL executive, which elevated Garry and the federation into the leadership of the trade movement at the national level. His role in the SGWU would also help Garry reach the goal he had set his sights on when they arrived on the coast two years earlier: he was elected to the Central Committee of the British Columbia Communist Party (or LPP).

Claire was soon hired as the secretary to Boilermakers president Bill Stewart, a job she would hold until the end of the war. Later, Claire would be self-deprecating about her own political practice during this period ("I wasn't too active . . . I never had the time for reading and studying, it was more bluff than anything else, when I think back on it. I don't know how I had the nerve . . . "), but the RCMP record shows otherwise. Over the next three years the Intelligence Branch would report her variously as the educational director of the west-end branch of the Labour Progressive Party, as a member of the executive of the Workers' Educational Association, as the only female speaker in a series of LPP weekly forums (alongside such party luminaries as Fergus McKean, British Columbia chairman of the LPP, Harold Pritchett of the IWA, and "Boilermaker Bill" Stewart), and, in October 1945 as a newly elected member of the LPP Provincial Committee.

Claire also became chair of the party's British Columbia Women's Commission, in which capacity she toured the province, and she somehow found the time to write the occasional article for party publications (often on women's issues), as well as her first letters to the editor.

The latter activity would, in later years, become a favourite means of reaching the public, and the earliest surviving example of her epistolary style was published in the *Worker*, the New York-based newspaper of the Communist Party U.S.A., on September 3, 1944. Addressed to a "Woman Brakeman" who had published an article the previous month, the letter tackled head-on what is still, for too many, a vexing question: should women receive equal pay and seniority for heavy industrial work even if they lack the physical strength of some men? Claire's answer was an emphatic yes.

> The thought occurred to me—"Are all the Brothers Supermen?" Surely there must be a few who are physically unable, as well as technically inferior, to do any and every job on the railroad! Is their seniority immediately challenged? Are they automatically reclassified on the seniority list? Is there any clause in your [union] Constitution which qualifies the type of work necessary before seniority is granted? . . .
>
> There can and must be some consideration shown for the future mothers of our country, even if they are railroad employees. It is quite consistent, to say the least, for a trade union to make such allowances . . .
>
> With further reference to your own feelings on the subject— "that there is something humiliating in admitting we can't do the work"—I would say that you too are forgetting that our limitations in one field are more than compensated for in our contribution towards producing the next generation of trade unionists. So, where- fore the humiliation? . . .
>
> Examining the human side, the possible resentment that there may be some women workers who will take unfair advantage of their "frailty" while cashing in on the benefits accrued, I would say, has any one sex a corner on slackers? Seems to me they come in all sizes, colours and sexes . . .

Here is a strong intimation of the mature Claire to come: the serviceable, direct prose, the common sense capable of slashing through a thicket of dogma, jargon, and cant, and, in the final paragraph's dismissal of the notion that any one gender, race, or type had a predisposition for a particular form of behaviour, the lifelong intolerance for what she would come to call "groupism."

Still, there was no doubt that Claire's political work was overshadowed by Garry, who would be preoccupied for the next three years in fighting two vital but, in hindsight, rearguard actions. The first was an attempt to ensure that Canada's preeminent role in shipbuilding and the merchant marine would be preserved after the war, thus protecting the jobs (and the flow of dues dollars) in two of the unionized industries where party influence was greatest—the shipyards and the Canadian Seamen's Union.

By the fall of 1944 an end to the European war seemed near. The lifting of the siege of Leningrad in January, the Normandy landings in June, and American successes in the Pacific made an Allied victory no longer a question of "if" but simply "when." In Canada there were already signs of a slowdown in the industrial war effort. All the gains made during the war—for working women like Claire's "Woman Brakeman," for trade unions, and for the Canadian economy as a whole—now hung in the balance. Garry turned his attention to this outlook in a long article in the September second issue of the *Main Deck*. "Our wartime shipbuilding program is a great achievement," he noted. "It is essentially an achievement of the Canadian people, financed from the public purse, organized, promoted, supplied with its materials, its plans and its specifications, and guided through its early difficulties by the government through a crown company, made efficient and highly productive through the insistence of organized labour."

The war had made Canada "a great world trader," Garry continued, and the country was in a favourable position to compete in the post-war years. But the shipyard owners were already planning a considerable downsizing, and there had been no consultation with labour. In a cry that would be repeated, with ever-growing urgency, over the next two years, the union urged Ottawa to convene a conference of government, owner, and union representatives to begin planning for the industry's future after the war.

Garry's words, even fifty years later, remain masterful for their breadth of scope and stirring vision: through the continuation of state intervention Canada would remain a great maritime power—Canadian goods would be shipped to rebuild the war-ravaged economies of Europe and Asia in Canadian bottoms operated by Canadian crews. Post-war recovery would further strengthen demand for Canadian exports and the resulting domestic employment and increasing standard of living would in turn stimulate Canadian demand for imports. "We want, and we can have, if we work and fight for it, an economy of abundance and full employment."

But if Garry's head proved to be in the clouds in his vision of post-war

Canada, his boots were planted firmly in the political mud. His second great preoccupation was beating back CCF attempts to oust the party from the Canadian Congress of Labour. The issue came to a head over the CCL's national Political Action Committee, of which Garry was a member. Although the link between Canadian labour and the NDP now seems a fixity in the country's political universe, no such tie bound the trade union movement until 1943. The Cooperative Commonwealth Federation, led by its national secretary, David Lewis, was anxious to affiliate organized labour to the federation. This was vociferously opposed by the Communist party, which saw itself as the genuine party of labour, and therefore argued that the Congress should not endorse any single political party.

Lewis personally attended a Congress convention in 1943 to engineer the passage, over strenuous party objections, of a resolution declaring the CCF "the political arm of labour in Canada." Garry and the party fought back in 1944 when they, joined by other allies in the Congress, passed a counter-resolution proclaiming the CCL's Political Action Committee "wholly independent of any political party." But Garry had no sooner returned to Vancouver, to applause at achieving the non-party policy, than Lewis and CCL president (and Ontario CCF MPP) Charles Millard rammed through yet a third resolution endorsing the CCF. Garry, who was not present at the meeting, was understandably outraged, and blasted the sudden reversal in policy as "a betrayal" in the *Main Deck*.

What was more, Garry added, even before the pro-CCF resolution was passed, Millard and PAC director Eamon Park had pledged the support of the PAC and the entire Canadian Congress of Labour to the CCF candidate in a forthcoming federal by-election in the Ontario riding of Grey North.[16] The Grey North by-election of February 1945, considered "one of the most publicized political battles in Canadian history," was intended to elect General A. G. L. McNaughton, the newly appointed minister of national defence in the King cabinet, to a safe Liberal seat.[17] McNaughton had at first opposed conscription for overseas service, until it had become clear that Canada could not properly reinforce its troops in Europe without it. The Tories, on the other hand, had long been railing against the "zombies" who served in the domestic force under the National Resources Mobilization Act but who refused to volunteer for the fighting in Europe. As usual, Quebeckers, rightly or wrongly, bore the brunt of these attacks against "slackers," which in turn fuelled anti-war and anti-English sentiments in Quebec. The Conservatives intended to exploit the Grey North by-election as an opportunity to defeat McNaughton and embarrass the King government, even if it meant reopening Canada's eternal binational wounds. They accused the general of being soft on Quebec, of undercutting Canada's war effort, and even of being under the influence of the

Church of Rome because his wife was a Catholic. On January 5, 1945, one Dr. T.T. Shields of Toronto travelled to Grey North to speak on behalf of the Canadian Protestant League and the Tory candidate. He charged that the Catholic hierarchy was "determined to keep *its* followers at home, to breed their kind, while *our* men are allowed to go overseas to be killed or wounded, so that the balance of the population will be more speedily adjusted."[18]

The LPP, meanwhile, had decided that the high road in such a campaign was to support McNaughton, who stood for reason, moderation, and national unity, and it urged the CCF to do the same. Instead, the CCF fielded its own candidate, retired Air Vice-Marshal Earl Godfrey. Given the divisive nature of the Grey North campaign, Garry's outrage with unauthorized CCL-PAC support of Godfrey makes considerable sense: the party feared that the CCF presence in a campaign it had no hope of winning would take enough votes from McNaughton in the heavily rural and Protestant riding to reward the Tory Quebec-bashing with success. In the event, on polling day, February 5, 1945, that is precisely what happened. Tory Garfield Case received 7,333 votes to McNaughton's 6,097.

The CCF's Godfrey, with 3,118, lost his deposit, but not before, in all probability, diverting enough anti-Tory votes away from McNaughton to cost him the election.[19]

In his memoirs David Lewis pointed to Grey North as "the first major instance of the Liberal-LPP partnership in the period . . . the illicit honeymoon between the Liberal Party and Canadian communists was displayed openly . . . " While castigating LPP union leaders for taking out a full-page newspaper ad supporting McNaughton two days before the election, Lewis omitted the vote totals, and any reference to Millard's precipitate support for Godfrey.[20]

The LPP responded in kind, coyly noting in the *Main Deck* that Earl Godfrey, the CCF candidate in the election, was a director of the Permeller & Bullock Rivet Company of Gananoque, Ontario. The firm was owned by Mr. Godfrey's father-in-law, and it had been, until the former air vice-marshal's nomination by the CCF, a non-union shop. The union certified at Permeller & Bullock was none other than the United Steelworkers, led by Charlie Millard.[21]

The split in Canadian union ranks soon spilled over in public. Garry repeated his claim of betrayal in the *Vancouver Sun*. "The Millard group has run off on a tangent of extreme danger to the whole Canadian labour movement, which threatens to shatter our unity and destroy the progress achieved by labour during the course of the war," he told a reporter.[22] The gloves were coming off in an intra-union battle that was degenerating into a vitriolic no-holds-barred struggle.

Nor was Claire herself immune to bashing the CCF. She had managed to take a swipe at the federation in the *Province* when she deplored Duplessis's August 1944 return to power, and the RCMP reported on November 7 that "The policies of the CCF Party were attacked on four public platforms on Sunday night in Vancouver . . . The four meetings held by the LPP . . . brought out a total of about 1,100 . . . " Kayla Culhane, the memo noted, had been a featured speaker at the Swedish Community Hall meeting.

It is, in hindsight, difficult to take up a brief for either side in the internecine feuds that now began to preoccupy Garry and Claire, the union movement, and the left in Canada, to the exclusion of much else. That the Communists were not guiltless Garry learned for himself in December 1944, when he discovered that comrades Bill Stewart and Malcolm MacLeod had indulged in a crude attempt at ballot-box stuffing to ensure their re-election to the leadership of the Boilermakers Local 1. The vote against them was so overwhelming that they were defeated despite the vote rigging, although a few of the lesser party officers were "re-elected." ("We were just making a wee bit sure," Claire remembers MacLeod confiding.) She insists that Garry knew nothing of the attempt beforehand, and that he was outraged by it. Stewart was disciplined by the party, barred from holding union office for two years, and ordered back to a rank and file job in the yard. But Bill White, who had joined the party and would soon succeed Stewart as Boilermakers president, believes "the party was madder at (Stewart) for losing the election than slugging the ballots. The guys who held onto their seats weren't disciplined in any way."[23]

Throughout Garry's emergence as a trade union leader in the late fall and early winter of 1944–45 and despite her own increasing prominence in British Columbia party circles, Claire held fast to her own private goal: she wanted to start a family. She had suppressed this desire during the party's underground years at the start of the war, had endured two heartrending abortions, had helped Garry launch an apparently successful career as a party and union functionary. But by late 1944 she could resist no longer. Garry, she knew, was still opposed, so she presented her demand in the form of an ultimatum: either they start a family immediately or she would leave him.

That she meant to carry through on her threat Garry did not doubt. Due to leave on yet another of his all-important union trips back east, he tried to temporize: at least she could wait until he got back.

"No way. If we do that, you'll claim it's not yours," she answered stubbornly, knowing Garry's obsessive suspicions.

By early 1945 her persistence had paid off. She was pregnant. At the age of twenty-six, she could finally feel stirring within her the life of a baby that she was actually going to be able to keep.

Their lives changed little during most of her pregnancy. Claire kept her secretarial job in the Boilermakers Hall, and Garry was now, more than ever, caught up in the cut-and-thrust of union and party politics. His new prominence in British Columbia affairs had also made him a target in the CCF-LLP struggle, and for the first nine months of 1945 it seemed that his name was in the papers almost daily. In one eventful month, February, Garry was in court over a charge by the secretary-treasurer of his old local in Victoria that he had wrongfully taken the local's membership lists the previous August; was embroiled in a controversy over an audit of the union's books in Vancouver's Local 1; and was in the public eye, and on the defensive once again, when a minor scuffle broke out in the Boilermakers Hall involving Myron Kuzych, a right-wing and essentially anti-union member of the Boilermakers whose lawsuits would bedevil the union for years.

In April Garry became part of Canadian labour history when he, along with George Harris of the United Electrical Workers, Harold Pritchett of the IWA, and George Burt of the Auto Workers quit the Political Action Committee of the CCL over its decision to endorse the CCF. The withdrawal of LPP loyalists left the field to the CCF, which was now free to solidify its alliance with organized labour. For better or worse, the Canadian trade union movement was becoming inextricably linked with a single political party, and for the next half-century and beyond, labour's alliance with social democracy would become a permanent fixture of the Canadian political landscape.

In April, too, Garry put on another political hat, becoming the LPP candidate for the House of Commons in the riding of Victoria. It had been five years since Canadians last went to the polls in a federal election, and on April 16, 1945, the nineteenth Parliament was dissolved and elections were called for June 11. Although the war in Europe would not be officially over until May 8, Allied forces had crossed the Rhine and the Red Army had fought its way to the suburbs of Berlin when Mackenzie King at last decided to attempt renewal of his government's mandate.

Still smarting from the perceived CCF-PAC double-cross in Grey North and believing the Tories to be a serious threat to national unity, the LPP elected to continue its strange alliance with the Liberals, to the intense displeasure of the CCF. Fearing a Liberal-Tory coalition government, or even a Tory minority (early election polls predicted that no party would win a clear majority), the LPP proposed a coalition of Liberal, CCF, and LPP forces. The LPP argued that the three left-of-centre parties should decline to run candidates against one another in ridings where one of them actually had a chance to win. The CCF spurned the partnership.

In Victoria Garry handed out a leaflet hammering the CCF for its refusal to join in the Liberal-Labour coalition, and campaigned on a platform of strong state intervention to create jobs and raise living standards to prevent a return to pre-war depression conditions. He emphasized the need for labour unity to defeat the Tories nationally. But as the campaign drew to a close the sniping between the CCF and the LPP grew more pronounced. Two days before the election the Victoria and District Trades and Labour Council tore a page from the LPP book in Grey North by taking out an ad in the *Victoria Daily Times*. "The So-Called 'Labour Progressive Party' Is NOT The Labour Party," the headline proclaimed. "The Communist Party of Canada has (for obvious reasons) adopted the name 'Labour Progressive Party' but it does not, in any way represent Organized Labor, and the Trades and Labor Council of Victoria does NOT endorse its policies or candidates." The Victoria TLC had not endorsed any party in the election, the ad concluded.[24]

What impact this last-minute disavowal had on election day is difficult to judge, but Garry was soundly defeated, finishing a distant fourth in a field of five with 997 votes. (The Social Credit candidate finished dead last.) The Tory candidate won the riding by a narrow 80-vote margin over the Liberals, and the CCF finished a strong third, 1,300 votes behind.

Still, Garry was able to pronounce himself well satisfied with the overall results, as the King Liberals had been returned to power in Ottawa with a slim majority. Despite its decision to contest only 101 seats, the LPP finished with 116,000 votes, and Fred Rose was re-elected in Montreal Cartier. The CCF received 832,000 votes, and its seat total trebled, from eight to twenty-eight, but CCF leaders were deeply disappointed by their party's failure to win support east of Manitoba.[25] The CCF decision to oust Communists from the labour movement and to shun political coalitions with them was proving costly in the short run, but over the longer term the 1945 federal election would turn out to be the zenith of Communist party electoral fortunes in Canada.

In the early months of her pregnancy Claire carried on with her own political work, much of it concerned with the role of women in post-war Canada. In January 1945 she attended a day-long conference on "The Future of Women in Employment" sponsored by the Vancouver Women's School for Citizenship. The conference had been called in response to what was already a growing crisis even four months before the war's end: the large-scale layoffs of women from war industries in British Columbia, "and the difficulties of these women in finding other satisfactory employment . . ."[26]

As they had during the First World War, Canadian women had responded with alacrity to the war effort. By June 1941 there had been 630,000 female wage earners in Canada, and by June 1944, the number had soared to one million. One out of every three workers in Canada was a woman, though in British Columbia the ratio was one in five. Because of the wartime labour shortage women were welcomed into industrial jobs that had previously been all-male preserves: steel mills, smelters, shipyards, and aircraft and munitions factories. Their dedication and ability proved beyond reproach but what, conference delegates asked themselves, would happen to working women after the war? Already, they were told, there were only 1,400 available jobs for the 2,300 women seeking work in British Columbia.[27]

The women attending the conference struggled to address issues that remain unresolved to this day, and forty-five years later their concerns, and even the language employed, remain astonishingly contemporary. Wage disparities between men and women performing the same work, the ease with which employers could dodge laws forbidding on-the-job gender discrimination and the Female Minimum Wage Act, and the legal exclusion of domestic workers from all workplace regulations were the focal points of discussion.

Speaking as a representative of the Office Workers' Union, Claire adopted the LPP's economist approach to the question of employment for women after the war, urging a buildup of secondary industries in British Columbia to process and primary materials which were being shipped out in a raw state. She also advocated public ownership of the province's hydroelectric system to provide cheaper power to industry. Both of her recommendations were adopted as resolutions.[28]

Claire continued her secretarial job with the Boilermakers until two months before her September due date, and Garry was busier than ever attempting to suppress the brush fires that now flared hotter than ever as the CCF-LPP rivalry intensified. Claire entered labour on September 4, while Garry was in Victoria on union business. He returned to Vancouver just in time to take Claire to the hospital, scant hours before the birth of a healthy baby girl. She called the baby Sandra Roisin Sheehy-Culhane, after selecting the name from a list of Gaelic names sent from Ireland by Garry's mother.

If Roisin's birth did little to bring Claire and Garry closer together as parents (he was preoccupied with union and party politics, and for three days during Claire's hospital confinement disappeared altogether), it did bring reconciliation on another front: Abe and Rose were delighted at the birth of their granddaughter, and began to forgive Claire for her choice of partners. They started to visit their new granddaughter in Vancouver at least once a year, always arriving laden with presents for Claire's family, and three generations of Eglin-Sheehy-Culhanes celebrated Christmas under one roof in 1945.

By late winter Claire was ready to resume her own political work. She helped to organize the International Women's Day celebration in Vancouver on March 8. The *Pacific Tribune*, the British Columbia party newspaper, gave full-page play to articles "by Kayla Culhane" recounting the history of International Women's Day, and praising leading radical women from around the world including La Pasionaria from Spain, Gini Bianchi and Camilla Ravera from Italy, Ella Reeve "Mother" Bloor and Elizabeth Gurley Flynn from the United States, and Annie Buller and Beckie Buhay, the legendary organizers from the Communist Party of Canada.[29]

Even today, the party's support of women and of activities like International Women's Day looks impressive. But in Claire's recollections the practice of party men often fell far short of the progressive theory. "When it came to baby-sitting, when it came to who would go to a conference, men always had the upper hand. Garry was a great speaker, and he'd be out giving some very impressive speech about women's rights, and it would sound good, but meanwhile I'd be the one at home with the kids!"

In her study of women on the Canadian left between 1920 and 1950 Joan Sangster found that both the CCF and the Communist Party of Canada tended to treat women as second-class citizens, despite official party espousals of equality.

> Women made inordinate contributions to electioneering, fund-raising, and social convening, and were sometimes [like Claire] visible in educational and cultural work. But they were rarely represented as theoreticians, union organizers, or national policy-makers . . . Aside from a few brave calls from Communists for shared work in the households, consistent stress was not placed on the collectivization of domestic work or on sharing it equally with men. The transformation of family life, an end to women's unpaid labour in the home, challenges to the sexual division of labour, and women's reproductive freedom were either largely ignored by CCFers or assigned to the never-never land of "after the revolution" by the Communists.[30]

The party tended to regard women as workers to be unionized or as members of the working class, but it did not define them along latter-day feminist lines, as a discrete group facing issues and struggles of its own. Nor did Claire, publicly at least, challenge this outlook. In her International

Women's Day article she honoured women as militant anti-Fascists or as union and party organizers, but not as leaders of other women. The party leadership, especially the national Central Committee in Toronto, remained resolutely all-male, despite the presence of proven female leaders like Annie Buller or Saskatchewan LPP MP Dorise Nielsen, and such male domination was bound to influence party policy vis-à-vis women. Most telling of all, there was very little attempt to incorporate the theory of gender equality into practical terms in one's private life. In Claire's case liberation, when it came, would occur despite Garry and the party, and not because of them.

April brought news from Ireland of the passing of one of Claire's exemplars who had successfully combined thoroughgoing feminism with a lifetime of labour and nationalist struggle. Hanna Sheehy-Skeffington had died in Dublin, at the age of sixty-eight. Even on her deathbed Garry's aunt had maintained the fierce devotion to the beliefs that she had fought for all her life. When a priest had attempted to enter her house to administer the last rites, Hanna's son, Owen, turned him away at the door. When he told his mother what he had done Hanna thanked him. "'I always feared I might be one of those death-bed converts back to religion.' And she died quite happily 'an unrepentant pagan' in Hanna's exact words . . . until the very end," Claire noted later with evident satisfaction.[31]

✳   ✳   ✳

Canada, that spring of 1946, stood at a historic crossroads. The country had emerged from the Second World War a preeminent industrial power. But what would happen after?

Both the LPP and the CCF urged Ottawa to retain its Crown corporations, expand foreign sales, and continue its hands-on management of the national economy, as Garry Culhane and the shipyard federation had been urging in the shipbuilding industry since 1944. But the King government, and especially its minister for reconstruction, C.D. Howe, had other ideas. A small-c conservative at heart, Howe had every confidence in the private sector to manage the Canadian economy after the war, and so began the country's first great experiment in privatization. Howe insisted on dismantling many of the Crown corporations, selling off their assets to private enterprise, and he had little concern whether the buyers were Canadian or American.

The impact of Howe's policy was clearly visible to Garry Culhane in October 1946 as he looked out at the floor of the annual convention of the British Columbia Shipyard General Workers' Federation. Where previous conventions had drawn hundreds of delegates, there were now only thirty, reflective of the precipitous decline in shipbuilding on the Pacific Coast after the war. The Canadian shipbuilding industry contracted in 1945–46 as quickly as it had expanded in 1940–41, and the post-war years would be remembered in the industry as the time of "the shrinkage." Where once the federation had represented more than twenty thousand workers, it now had only four thousand members. The meeting was held at the Knights of Pythias Hall in Victoria, and Garry used the setting in the capital to score the provincial government "for its abject failure to fight for this industry."[32] The Victoria papers gave good coverage to Garry's attack on the government, but it was to be one of his last hurrahs.

Ottawa dismantled Wartime Merchant Shipping Limited, the Crown corporation established to coordinate Canada's wartime shipbulding effort, and the owners of the nation's shipyards were content to think small. Almost forty years later Bill White, the former president of the Boilermakers' Union, reflected bitterly on the shrinkage:

> Today [1983] I don't think there is an average of one ship a year
> launched on the west coast, and when one is, they get royalty out to
> christen it. But during the war, west coast yards put out 349 ships
> inside of four years. It's almost impossible to imagine the scale of
> the work that was undertaken . . . By the peak there they were pop-
> ping 10,000-ton ships out in sixty days . . . Meanwhile employment
> in the shipbuilding industry in B.C. has fallen from 31,200 at the
> peak to less than 1,000 today. The skill and ability they assured us
> would never be wasted is not only lost, it's forgotten we ever had it.[33]

Along with the decline in shipbuilding, Canada's overall role as a maritime power also went a'glimmering, as the country's great merchant and military navies were quietly allowed to gather rust.

The shrinkage guaranteed a greatly diminished role for the Communist party within the Canadian Congress of Labour. The Boilermakers' and shipyard federation was no longer a force to be reckoned with; similarly, the once-formidable Canadian Seamen's Union withered under a series of vicious raids by the Seamen's International Union, led by a mob-connected American named Hal Banks.

The handwriting was on the wall for Garry, too. Its declining membership meant that the shipyard federation could no longer afford paid staff, and the very future of the organization was now in jeopardy. The party clung desperately to its last power bases in British Columbia labour, the Mine, Mill, and Smelter Workers, and the IWA, but in November 1947 its final nemesis arrived on the west coast.

His name was William Mahoney, an up-and-coming Steelworker organizer from Sault Ste. Marie, and he had been dispatched to British Columbia by the CCL in Ottawa to accomplish one straightforward task: to rid the province's union movement of its Communist leadership. Given two years to complete the job, he was to meet his deadline almost to the day.[34]

Mahoney began his campaign by wresting control of the Vancouver Labour Council away from the Communists at its annual executive elections in January 1948 using the tactics that had once worked so well for the Communists—caucusing well before the vote to ensure that every local not dominated by the party sent delegates to "pack" the crucial meeting.

One by one he went on to roll up the other preserves of party power in the province—the British Columbia Federation of Labour, the Union of Mine, Mill, and Smelter Workers, even the powerful IWA. Mahoney's techniques weren't pretty, but they worked. Before it was all over, "families split, friendships were shattered, and in some cases open warfare broke out."[35] Through a public campaign of innuendo, Red baiting, and character assassination Mahoney destroyed reputations, ruined careers, and ended the livelihoods of many of the old-line British Columbia labour leaders and their supporters.

One of Mahoney's chief allies was an ambitious rookie reporter for the *Vancouver Sun* named Jack Webster. The two had met just months before aboard ship when the latter emigrated from Scotland, and Webster immediately began to support the anti-Communist drive in the *Sun*. "I led the witch-hunt in print," Webster would say simply forty-five years later. "The *Sun*'s management was happy with my work, partly because McCarthyism was rearing its ugly head and my reporting echoed the tenor of the times. I once described Harvey Murphy as 'a Communist, real name Chernikovsky, trained in Moscow.' It was pretty sleazy character assassination." Webster later claimed to regret his role in the CCL campaign to oust the Communists. "Would I do it again? Probably not. I consider myself a reasonably fair reporter except for the way I treated the Communists in the early days."[36] But that was long after he and Mahoney had used one another to springboard into brilliant careers, Webster as British Columbia's best-known open-line host and Mahoney as the Canadian director of the United Steelworkers of America.

Mahoney's successful tactics were employed over and over again across Canada by the CCL and their CCF allies. If they were unable to defeat Communist leaders by democratic means, they purged entire unions from the Congress. Criticism of either the CCL or CCF in union newspapers was regarded as apostasy, especially criticism from the left, and dissent was ruthlessly suppressed. "The fact that Communists were never very concerned with civil liberties in their own unions or even elsewhere does not excuse the same lack of concern by men who were championing 'democracy' against 'totalitarianism,'" concluded one labour historian who was not unsympathetic to either the Congress or CCF leadership. "The reasons given for the expulsion of the left-wing unions were spurious and almost fatuous. At any other period and against any other unions they would have been dismissed out of hand. The entire Communist purge was not one of the Congress's finer achievements."[37]

Claire had a ringside seat for the final rounds of the CCF-LPP battle in the British Columbia union movement. By 1947 it was clear the shipyard federation was on its last legs and that Garry would soon be out of a job. So after Roisin's second birthday that fall, Claire arranged for day care and returned full time to her secretarial position at the Boilermakers' Union. But the union's heyday, when thousands of its members crammed the North Van ferry at shift change to ride to work at the Burrard shipyards, were long since over. Times were changing inside the party, too. Bill White, still the president of the Vancouver Boilermakers and once again Claire's boss, described the period as a time of cannibalism.

> They say if you take a bunch of rats and subject them to enough harassment they will turn on each other—the mothers will eat the young, the followers will cannibalize the leaders and they will appear to lose all sense. If you take a political movement and smash it like they did the left in the Cold War, you can see the same thing happen. Everybody gets suspicious of everybody else, the leaders lose their sense of direction and cannibalism becomes commonplace.[38]

It wasn't long before Claire and Garry began to feel the cannibalism. It was no surprise when Garry lost his position as secretary of the shipyard federation because of the shrinkage; they had both seen that coming for a long time. But it was still difficult for Garry. Apart from the loss in income, it wasn't easy to adjust to being unemployed, especially after the heady federation days. He was no longer sought after by reporters, his picture no longer appeared in the daily papers or the *Main Deck*, there were no more radio broadcasts, no more leaflet transcriptions of those broadcasts, printed and distributed by the thousands at the bustling shipyard gates.

And, having lost his powerful political platform in the federation, Garry's star started to lose some of its lustre in the party, too. He had made some formidable enemies within the party, and the knives began to come out. His outspokenness, his intellectual background, and, curiously, his abstinence from drink had set him apart from other party leaders like Harvey Murphy, Bill Stewart, Malcolm MacLeod, and Bill White, all of whom were heavy drinkers.

Although he always got on well with Claire, in his memoirs Bill White was characteristically blunt in his assessment of Garry: "He was one of the phoniest bastards ever to come down the pike." White accused Garry and the federation of wasting money, and even of angling for his own position as president of the Boilermakers' Union after the federation folded. Garry, White concludes, "was a prick of the first water."[39]

Whatever Garry's shortcomings, Claire has always been quick to come to his defence when she believes he is wrongfully accused, and she still considers his politics while part of the British Columbia Communist scene to have been above reproach. She flatly denies he had designs on White's job, that the federation squandered large amounts of the members' money, or that Garry was overly ambitious in terms of his own advancement within the party.

Their break with the party came gradually. In May 1948 Garry was still prominent enough to be named as parade marshal and secretary of the Vancouver Labour Council's May Day parade. But the party's growing dogmatism, its increasing tendency towards internal "trials" and expulsions, behaviour which was the product of a siege mentality, were wearing on both Garry and Claire. "I didn't leave one church just to join another!" Garry protested privately to Claire with ever-growing frequency.

For a time it seemed that all of this—Garry's loss of his job, the growing disillusionment with the party, the presence of Roisin—brought them closer together as a family. They certainly looked the part when a sidewalk photographer snapped their picture on West Hastings Street in February 1948, Claire and Garry well dressed, still a handsome couple smiling confidently into the camera, each of them holding Roisin's hand, their daughter, two-and-a-half now, looking distractedly away, her head a mop of curly blonde ringlets.

Certainly, too, Claire had enough confidence in the future of the relationship to marry Garry that fall, when Nora, who had fallen in love with someone else, finally sought a divorce. It was a simple civil ceremony at the Vancouver Courthouse on September 7, 1948, just five days after Claire's thirtieth birthday.

But there were growing problems in the marriage. Garry was having difficulty adapting to life after the shipyard federation—the job market had little demand for an unemployed Communist trade union leader. And Garry was proving to be his mother's son, after all. The darker side of his intellectual brilliance and assertiveness was an overweening pride in his background, and a steely arrogance. He never suffered fools gladly, and Garry's attempts to find and hold a steady job were usually abortive affairs that ended when he had a falling-out with a boss or his co-workers. Rather than remembering her father going to work each morning Roisin remembers "a constant ending of jobs," with Garry being fired or quitting.

With more time on his hands Garry became increasingly moody and morose. Roisin believes that he was haunted by the ghosts of 1916 and the dream of prominence that should have been his birthright. Clearly, like his mother before him, Garry was unable to come to grips with a workaday existence, or his responsibilities as a parent. All of this meant that the family was dependent, more often than not, on Claire's income, which, while steady, was not large. Chronic poverty was becoming a way of life.

In 1949 Claire happened to bump into Emery Samuel, her *beau idéal* in Montreal days, in downtown Vancouver. She knew of his expulsion from the party two years earlier, for his advocacy of a nationalist line on Quebec, but she was still shocked at the change in the man who had been, in her eyes, the very embodiment of a Communist. Where once Samuel had seemed absolutely scintillating and vivacious, he was now a beaten man.

They went for a coffee, and Samuel explained that he had moved out west with his wife, Nancy, who was from Vancouver, after the purge of the party's Quebec francophone leadership in 1947. Claire's sympathies went out to her old comrade, and they agreed that they must get together for dinner some time soon. She was also revolted that the party, her party, could behave in such heartless fashion toward a member whose whole life had been lived for the party and its ideals. More than anything else, the party's ruthlessness toward Samuel precipitated Claire's own growing disillusionment with the Communist party.

But when she arrived home she was shocked at Garry's reaction when she told him that she'd invited Emery and Nancy to dinner.

"Oh, no," Garry demurred, mindful of his own precarious standing in the party. "We can't have them over here." Claire was absolutely stunned at Garry's attitude, and for the first time she began to wonder to herself just how much of a Communist Garry really was.

In retrospect, Garry needn't have worried about conforming to the latest party orthodoxy when it came to a choice of dinner companions; the following year it was his turn for expulsion. The official pretext was that his party dues were more than two months in arrears, and the end came with more of a whimper than a bang—rather than confront him face-to-face, the party notified Garry by mail that he was no longer a member in good standing.

Claire left the party with Garry, and for the first time in thirteen years she was no longer an activist in the Communist Party of Canada. But they were both sick of the dogma and the cannibalism and besides, Claire had other worries. Chief among them was supporting her family, a task that was about to grow more complicated—she was pregnant again.

Claire put off telling Garry about her condition in the spring of 1950. She feared his reaction would not be altogether positive, and he was under a great deal of pressure in any event, directing a play for the UJPO Drama Workshop. The United Jewish People's Order was a left-wing Jewish cultural group which had been expelled from the Canadian Jewish Congress over its pro-Communist leanings.

The Order had founded the drama workshop to present amateur theatricals, usually with a progressive political bent, and it had hired Garry as the group's director. The pay was minimal, but Garry had also been given a sales job by Sydney Sarken, a Vancouver clothier and UJPO supporter, to augment his income. Doubtless because of his mother, the theatre was in Garry's blood, and he was a natural for the job. "He was very charismatic," recalls Sylvia Friedman, who appeared in several UJPO productions. "The girls had crushes on him. He knew how to charm anything out of the actors. He was good-looking, tall, and imposing, a little like [Canadian prime minister] Mulroney with the chin. You could love him and you could hate him."

The workshop had already staged three one-act plays under Garry's direction, memorable today only because a young Dave Broadfoot, who would later earn renown as a founding member of the Royal Canadian Air Farce, appeared in one of them. The production in rehearsal when Claire became pregnant was a full-length effort, *It's Hard to be a Jew*, by Sholom Aleichem. ("You think it's hard to be a Jew, let me tell you it's harder to be a director," Friedman remembers Garry wisecracking.)

Garry had trouble filling the cast for the Aleichem play, and so had recruited a reluctant Claire for the part of Betty, the teenaged sister of one of the main characters. Claire felt a little silly playing a teenager at the age of thirty-two, and Friedman recalls that Garry, in his directorial role, "was hard on her, because he expected too much. She wasn't trained as an actor."

For Claire, the play represented the kind of double and even triple work shift that was becoming all too familiar. Besides being six weeks pregnant, she had a full-time job, and all of the responsibilities for Roisin and the housework. A typical day would find her rushing to get Roisin up and dressed, and dropping her off at nursery school before arriving at her own job. After work she'd pick up Roisin, do the grocery shopping, go home and cook dinner, put Roisin to bed, and then hurry out for an evening rehearsal. Still, she considered it was Garry who was under pressure.

The play opened for its brief run on Sunday, April 23, 1950, at the York

Theatre (since renamed the New York Theatre) on Commercial Drive between Hastings and Venables in Vancouver's east end. All 449 of the York's seats were sold out for the production, which received critical praise, at least from the reviewer for the party's *Pacific Tribune*. (The review was carefully extracted and preserved for posterity, classified "Secret," in Claire's file at RCMP headquarters.)[40]

When the play closed Claire broke the news of her pregnancy to Garry, whose jealous obsession had only grown with the insecurity and endless financial worries brought about by his long periods of unemployment. He angrily denied that the baby was his, and accused her of having an affair.

Claire pointed out her exhausting schedule of the past few months and asked Garry how in the world she could have found the time for an extra-marital love affair.

"Over your lunch hour," Garry replied.

Claire gave birth to a healthy baby girl on December 16, 1950, and they named her Hanna (in honour of Hanna Sheehy-Skeffington) Dara ("second" in Gaelic) Sheehy-Culhane, although she would always be known as Dara.

In August 1949 the Soviet Union tested its first atom bomb, almost four years to the day after the United States had dropped the first A-bomb on Hiroshima. To the Cold War were now added the nuclear arms race, the balance of terror, mutually assured destruction—there were many names for the phenomenon that would hold the world in thrall for the next forty years.

The prospect of obliterating the human species with the push of a button represented an unprecedented global threat, and the international progressive community reacted quickly to the arms race. By 1950 disarmament groups had sprung up throughout the Western world, and British Columbia was no exception. The Communist party played a key role in the founding of the British Columbia Peace Council and Claire and Garry remained involved in the province's burgeoning peace movement even after they left the party. "We rallied, we lobbied every single MLA and MP, we put on big concerts every other week at the Boilermakers Hall, we had socials all over to raise funds," recalls Jonnie Rankin, a peace activist from the early 1950s who could proudly claim to be a forerunner of the peace movement that would persist throughout the latter half of the century. In Great Britain their activities were popularly known as the "Ban-the-Bomb" movement, and everywhere the focal point was a brief manifesto known as the Stockholm Statement:

> We demand unconditional prohibition of the atomic weapon as a
> weapon of aggression and mass annihilation of people, and that

strict international control for the implementation of the decision be established. We shall consider as a major criminal that Government which first employs the atomic weapons against any country. We call upon all people of good will throughout the world to sign the appeal.[41]

Millions around the world signed the Stockholm Statement, and Jonnie Rankin would recall proudly four decades later that she single-handedly obtained more than one thousand signatures in British Columbia.

One of Claire's contributions to the movement was an article in the *Pacific Tribune* which took strong issue with a plan by the British Columbia Ministry of Education to implement "atomic bomb drills" in the province's schools. "We are not at war," Claire wrote. "No one is threatening to bomb us. We do not intend to have our children dragged into the warmakers' plans of gearing their everyday lives to accept war as an inevitability."[42]

By 1952 Claire's oldest daughter, Roisin, had accompanied Claire to so many demonstrations that she was a veteran peace marcher. She once ventured the opinion that "Dara's really lucky."

"Why do you say that?" Claire inquired of the seven-year-old.

"Because by the time she grows up there won't be any wars—we'll have stopped them all."

Drilling schoolchildren against thermonuclear holocaust as routinely as they were drilled for a school fire was but one of the manifestations of the mounting Cold War hysteria. In the United States anti-communism flourished, fuelled by the discovery that several individuals with connections to the Communist Party U.S.A. and a German-born physicist, Klaus Fuchs, had indeed given the Soviets information on the American wartime nuclear program. A string of early confessions by the spies arrested led eventually to a couple named Julius and Ethel Rosenberg. The Rosenberg case was destined to become a cause célèbre; the story still retains a mythical, mystical quality reminiscent of Greek tragedy and even though it was played out on the stages of New York and Washington, D.C., the intensely emotional involvement of Claire in that drama ensured that it would have a lasting impact on the family of Garry and Kayla Culhane in faraway Vancouver.

The Rosenbergs stoutly maintained their innocence, but their trial jury found the prosecution evidence overwhelming and pronounced both of the defendants guilty of espionage. The federal court sentenced Julius and Ethel Rosenberg to death by electrocution, an extraordinary punishment for a number of reasons. The Rosenbergs were the parents of two boys, seven and three years old; the American government was about to create two orphans. Moreover, the evidence at trial revealed only that the Rosenbergs had spied for the Soviets during the war, when the United States and USSR were allies. The death penalty in espionage cases was generally considered applicable in cases of high treason, that is, spying for an enemy power. Ethel was the first woman in American history to be sentenced to death for espionage, though the evidence against her was much weaker than the proof against her husband. Still more disturbing was the suspicion (since largely confirmed) that the American government was employing a "lever strategy" in its sentencing of Ethel Rosenberg: it hoped to wring an eleventh-hour confession from Julius by holding his wife and the mother of his children hostage to the electric chair.[43]

As the January 1953 execution date approached, Communist parties and other sympathizers around the world suddenly, belatedly, began to rally to the cause.[44] When a branch of the National Committee to Secure Justice in the Rosenberg Case formed in Vancouver, Claire joined, becoming active with her usual fervour. The American consulate in the Marine Building on Burrard Street in downtown Vancouver became a favoured location for rallies and picket lines in support of the Rosenbergs, and Claire was a frequent participant, Roisin beside her, while Dara, still in a pram, experienced her first demonstrations.

∗ ∗ ∗

The January execution date was stayed while the Rosenbergs' lawyers presented a petition for executive clemency to the new president-elect Dwight Eisenhower, and the campaign on their behalf began to gain momentum. By Christmas 1952 the New York Committee was able to fill eight passenger cars in a chartered train to carry supporters to a demonstration outside the walls of Sing Sing Prison where the Rosenbergs were incarcerated. In France, in Great Britain, in Italy, thousands began to demonstrate on the Rosenbergs' behalf, and stories about the couple became daily European newspaper fare. Albert Einstein, Pablo Picasso, Jean-Paul Sartre, and Pope Pius XII joined in the call for a commutation of the death sentence, but none of the appeals influenced President Eisenhower, who denied the Rosenbergs' clemency request on February 11, 1953.

Few events in the Cold War so mobilized—and polarized—international public opinion as the case of Julius and Ethel Rosenberg. Some Rosenberg supporters were, like Claire, sincerely convinced of the couple's innocence, while others advocated a new trial or, at the very least, a commutation of the capital sentence on humanitarian grounds. But the

American establishment and a large sector of American public opinion remained committed to carrying out the death sentence, not least to deter American citizens from spying for the Soviets in the future. This division of opinion, and the fervency with which the conflicting views were held, was apparent even in Vancouver, where someone from the American consulate dropped potentially lethal bags filled with water on the heads of the pro-Rosenberg demonstrators thirteen floors below.

It is perhaps not surprising that Claire came to identify as deeply as she did with Julius and Ethel Rosenberg. Like her, they were the children of Orthodox Jewish parents who had emigrated to North America from eastern Europe early in the century. Their ages were similar (Claire and Julius were born the same year) and the ages of the Rosenberg children were close to those of Roisin and Dara. And, like Claire, the Rosenbergs were highly ideological, and imbued with a deeply rooted commitment to social justice.

But now Claire suddenly encountered opposition to her participation in the Rosenberg marches from an unexpected source: Garry forbade her to take part, for fear that she or the children would be injured by one of the water bombs. Many years later Claire would concede that his concerns for their safety were justified, but at the time she bridled at such male high-handedness. She had always taken the strongest exception when anyone told her what she could or couldn't do, but for Garry to forbid her to continue was absolutely unacceptable. There were ways to protect one's individual safety in such situations, and besides, it would be unthinkable to yield to intimidation. They were both stubborn, wilful individuals, and, on this question as on so many others, the irresistible force had met the immovable object. The Rosenberg case added another level of tension to an increasingly difficult family situation, and there was no doubt the case was becoming a Culhane family affair. It was discussed at the dinner table, and Roisin remembers being fearful that her parents, too, might one day be arrested by the police, carted off to jail, and sentenced to death for their political activities.

Brilliant, and desperate, legal manoeuvres succeeded in delaying the execution several more times, but the decision could not be overturned. June 19, 1953, was the date set for the first husband-and-wife spy execution in American history. Just as a later generation would always remember what they were doing when they first learned that John F. Kennedy was shot, an earlier generation of leftists would never forget where they were when word reached them of Julius and Ethel Rosenberg's execution. Claire and her family were just sitting down to dinner at the table where they had so often discussed the Rosenberg case. The news broke her heart. "I think it was the only time the kids have ever seen me cry." And, indeed, Roisin would always remember Claire's tears at that sombre evening meal.

A year or two later President Eisenhower's name was mentioned on the radio in the Culhane household.

"Eisenhower's a bastard," hissed little Dara.

"You shouldn't use words like that," reproved teenaged Garry Og, who was then living with the family.

"Didn't Eisenhower kill Mummy and Daddy Rosenberg?" Dara asked.

"Well, yes, I guess so, but . . . "

"Then Eisenhower's a bastard," repeated Dara, age three.

The involvement of Claire and her family with the Rosenberg case did not end with the executions. The Rosenbergs' wills had named Emanuel Bloch, their lawyer, as the legal guardian of their sons and the question remained of what would become of Michael and Robert Rosenberg. Offers of adoption came from around the world, and they included one from Claire and Garry. The Culhanes received serious consideration, and Claire remembers that Bloch flew to Vancouver from New York to interview them. But in the end, the boys were placed with a family in New York City, which was probably just as well. Although it was not immediately apparent to an outsider, the Culhane family was in a state of ever-deepening crisis.

They were, by the summer of 1952, ensconced in a large, two-storey house at 3086 Charles Street between Renfrew and Nanaimo in east-end Vancouver. Superficially, it must have seemed an idyllic existence. The house was a commodious ten-room affair, more than ample for the family which now included four children—Garry Og and Paddy had moved in with their father and stepmother shortly after Dara was born. The wood-frame house occupied a triple corner lot, had fruit trees in the backyard, and plenty of room for the Culhane ménage, which included Roisin's dog, Pootchamoo, (the Russian word for "why," Roisin's favourite question when the dog had been acquired several years before). Garry had built an adventure playground in the huge backyard where all the neighbourhood children loved to play. But they had to obey Culhane rules: no toy guns, no saying "nigger," no bullies, no comic books. Dara patrolled the yard and evicted transgressors.

Claire and Garry had purchased the Charles Street house—the second, and last, home Claire would ever own—with the help of Abe and Rose. Claire's parents had continued to make their annual visits to Vancouver, and they quietly despaired over their son-in-law. Garry had parted ways with the drama workshop and was once again drifting in and out of various unrelated jobs, interspersed with long periods of unemployment. His latest passion was cabinetmaking, which he pursued in their basement work-shop. Every time they visited, it seemed, Garry had some new scheme to make money, and each one invariably ended in failure. "If you went into the undertaking business people in Vancouver would stop dying," Abe couldn't resist telling Garry during one of his stays in Vancouver.

Behind closed doors, life was less than ideal in the big house on Charles Street. Claire and Garry argued incessantly now, and the disagreements were becoming more vitriolic than ever. The battle over Claire's participation in the Rosenberg rallies was but one of their political rows. Garry, it seemed to her, was forever analyzing, forever theorizing about a given political question and never getting down to actually doing anything. "You believe in action for action's sake," he would say to her disparagingly. "Yes, but that's better than inaction for inaction's sake," she would retort.

The lack of money was the main sore point; the family was sinking ever deeper into debt, and some weeks there wasn't enough money to put food on the table. At times Claire was forced to resort to shoplifting groceries just to feed her family, and Roisin was with her on the one occasion when she was finally caught. Roisin began to cry as she and Claire were ushered into a back room of the store, certain that her mother was about to be arrested and taken away forever. Fortunately Claire was released after a cautionary lecture.

The shoplifting incident was just one in a series of unhappy childhood memories for Roisin. Even though her parents had left the party, they were still small-c communists, and she was growing up as a typical Red Diaper baby. At least a part of each summer was spent at the party's camp on Lake Hetzeg in the Fraser Valley, and Roisin would always remember what seemed to her then a series of endless meetings, either at their house or someone else's. She was forbidden to read comic books or watch television because both were products of "bourgeois decadence." Certainly, Roisin's upbringing could never be described as normal, a fact of which she was painfully aware. "I always had the sense—in a way it's very Catholic—that our lives were not important, that there was a greater motive for our lives— the advancement of the working class and the working class struggle. Party meetings were far more important than our needs as children." The absence of the normalcy that Roisin was convinced was enjoyed by all of her schoolmates would soon bloom into antipathy for all things political, "because politics was what had destroyed my family."

Perhaps because he was at home so often during her most formative years, Roisin grew extremely attached to her father. She loved to work with him on his various projects. Together they built a chicken coop in the backyard to house the family's small flock of chickens, and a hutch for their pet rabbits. She liked being with him in his carpentry shop, too, where he taught her about the grades and qualities of wood, and how to handle tools. Roisin was clearly her father's daughter. She was tall and big-boned, and she bore a strong facial resemblance to her father.

The hours spent with Roisin were probably among Garry's happiest times on Charles Street, because he was by now a deeply troubled individual. For a man of his abilities, it must have been grievously wounding to be unable to support his family, and yet he was incapable of holding a steady job. As if to compensate, he became more assertive, more emphatic in his views. "There was no sense that he could ever be wrong," Roisin recalls. His black moods became more pronounced—he would sometimes go days without speaking—and his behaviour more erratic. Garry's suspicions that Claire was having love affairs deepened into paranoia fraught with jealous, dangerous rage. At times, overcome by remorse over something he'd said or done to Claire, Garry would go to extraordinary lengths to make up, to please her, but his pride was so great that he could never bring himself to speak the simple words she wanted most to hear. "It used to be a standing joke," Claire remembers, "that the only two words which didn't exist in Garry's vocabulary were 'I'm sorry.'"

Another source of tension was Garry's developing friendship with physicist Arthur Louria and his psychiatrist wife, Risa. Wealthy Viennese Jews who had fled Austria during the early days of Hitler's rise to power, the Lourias had managed to escape Europe with their personal fortunes intact. While Claire rejected religious orthodoxy, her identification as a Jew had remained strong, and she held the Lourias and their ilk in contempt. Like many other secular Jews, Claire believed that being Jewish meant knowing persecution, brutality, and dislocation firsthand; it therefore also meant being committed to the struggle for justice and humanity. But the Lourias, fearing the holocaust that was to come, had chosen to use their ample resources to bring their household furnishings, art collection, musical instruments, and silver and china to the safety of North America, while leaving behind other Jews without the resources to escape the Europe of the 1930s. Claire could never understand nor forgive the Lourias for their actions. More important, she could neither understand nor forgive Garry's ability to ignore or rationalize their behaviour. To Claire, then as now, politics was nothing if it was not lived.

As much as the Lourias' preoccupation with high culture repelled Claire, it was lethally attractive to Garry. Embittered by his rejections by the party and socially ostracized by his former comrades, Garry found familiar comfort discussing music and art in the luxurious surroundings of the Lourias' home, echoing as it did his own childhood and his family's standing among Ireland's intellectual elite.

The Lourias, in turn, admired Garry as much as they derided Claire.

They openly commiserated with Garry about his unfortunate marriage to such an "uncultured creature," born of Eastern European peasants, who padded barefoot around the house and whose children spent their time playing in the yard with other neighbourhood children instead of studying the cello like the Lourias' only daughter, Heidi. Garry held Risa in particular awe and began to insist that her directions on child rearing be followed chapter and verse in his own household. When Risa said nineteen-year-old Garry Og should move out of the Charles Street house, Garry ordered him out, to a downtown rooming house, despite Claire's objections that he still needed and wanted to be at home. The Lourias then proceeded to "rescue" sixteen-year-old Paddy from Claire's influence and offered her a room in their own home, an offer Garry gratefully accepted. When the Lourias' attention began to focus on Roisin and Dara, and when Garry began to support Risa Louria's admonition that as a psychiatrist she could have Claire committed with "only one more signature," Claire became increasingly frightened and desperate.

Claire herself was run ragged during the family's Charles Street period. All of the housekeeping duties fell on her shoulders, along with cooking, and, in season, gardening and canning preserves from the fruit trees out back. The worries of where the next meal was coming from or how they would pay the mortgage were all hers, too; it was clear by now that Garry would never concern himself with such mundane matters. Apart from her children, the one pride and joy in Claire's life in 1953–54 was, improbably, her kitchen stove. It was an Aga, a monstrous affair so heavy that it required special floor bracing to prevent it from crashing into the basement. It was coalfired, ideal for the damp Vancouver winters because it would heat the entire house, and it had enough burners, ovens, and griddles to feed a small army.

Early one Sunday morning Claire decided to make crêpes to try out the stove's griddle. She cooked a stack of the thin French-style pancakes and placed them in the warming oven, serving them to the children when they were ready for breakfast. Covered with butter, icing sugar, and lemon juice and then rolled up into a sweet cylinder, they proved an instant hit, and the children beseeched her to make them the following Sunday. So was born an important family tradition that would outlive her marriage, her stove, and the Charles Street house itself.

But such moments of family warmth as Sunday-morning crêpes were all too rare. Garry's jealousy, which she had once been able to discount, was now becoming so extreme as to alarm her. One night after eleven o'clock when she finally had an hour to herself, Claire decided to type a letter to a friend. She was absorbed in the task when Garry suddenly appeared out of nowhere and pulled the paper from the machine with an air of exultant vindication. It was clear he expected to catch her corresponding with her secret lover. She had, in fact, been writing to Garry's mother. Garry's jealous rages began to seem more menacing, and Claire slept more and more often in the children's room, while Garry paced endlessly back and forth in the hallway outside.

But, worse than all the other pressures, Claire began to fear the effect of the marital tensions on her children. The signs were unmistakable. One night when she went to check on Roisin, Claire found her daughter's pillow was sopping wet, where she had cried herself to sleep as her parents fought. On more than one occasion Roisin remembers hearing arguments so loud they kept her awake, and she would tiptoe to the top of the stairs where she would sit, listening and weeping, as her parents verbally tore one another apart. During the Christmas of 1954 Claire was shocked to see Dara, after breakfast, retreat to the Christmas tree and sit under it for hours, refusing to move. The girls, too, were becoming erratic, moody, and withdrawn.

Little by little Claire arrived at a painful conclusion: she and her children had to leave Garry. Because of Garry's obsessive behaviour there was no one Claire could tell of her decision, and actually escaping with the two children would be difficult. Her husband was in the habit of checking up on her whenever she was out of his sight. There was, however, the narrowest window of opportunity. Once a month she took Dara with her to work on the newsletter for Roisin's school, though Garry had been known to "just happen to drop by" even there. She didn't dare pack anything in advance, but she did take one person into her confidence— the tenant in the basement apartment that Garry had finished downstairs.

Claire left a few things with the tenant, to be forwarded later. But she had to exercise the greatest caution even here, taking only a few items that Garry wouldn't miss, and carefully hiding them in the basement apartment. Then there was the added problem of getting to the train station. Claire asked a trusted friend, an old party comrade, if he would drive them, and he agreed.

Luck was with her on the day in February 1955 that she had selected to put her plan into action. She and Dara left the house with a few shopping bags containing the barest essentials in children's clothes and a few mementoes, and her friend met them as arranged. They caught Roisin just as she was returning to class after recess, and headed for the train station.

When they were settled into their seats on the coach, Claire began to explain to her startled older daughter where they were going.

"Who will feed Pootchamoo?" a tearful Roisin demanded.

"I'm sure your father will."

"Will we still have French pancakes on Sunday?" wailed Dara.

"Yes, we will."

CHAPTER FIVE

Hiatus

> One of the truths about working mothers is that your
> kids pay a price . . . Children are happy if their mother
> is there. Say we give children a choice: your mother in
> the next room on the verge of suicide or in ecstasy in
> Hawaii. My guess is they'd choose suicide in the next
> room every time.
> —Nora Ephron, *The Globe and Mail*, June 14, 1991

A long Canadian winter's night was soon upon them as the train
snaked its way up the Fraser canyon, beginning the long haul toward
the Continental Divide. The children slept fitfully in their seats (Rose had
sent Claire a hundred dollars for the trip; the fare was sixty, leaving them
just enough money for food—a sleeping compartment was an unthinkable
luxury) while Claire studied her fellow passengers, wondering if they were
being followed. She was certain Garry would take some action to stop her
once he realized they were gone.

The night lights were on in the passenger car, and her own face was
reflected in the darkened window. It had undergone a startling transfor-
mation. The most visible change was in her hair, now heavily streaked
with grey. Her eyes, which had always sparkled and flashed above a ready
smile, seemed to have receded and grown darker and more determined.
And the smile was gone, replaced by a distracted, worried look. Here she
was at the age of thirty-six, hurtling through the night toward an uncertain future, with a four-year-old and a nine-year-old totally dependent
upon her. How soon would she find work? Where and how would they
live? Well, she had always supported the family, and she would manage
somehow. The most important thing now, her greatest worry, was to get
away cleanly and safely.

The trip through the mountains and across the Prairies was uneventful, though Dara was tired and cranky and Roisin seemed to miss her father more with every passing mile. But at Winnipeg, before Claire had stepped down on to the platform, they were accosted by a security guard with a telegram in his hand.

"Are you Missus Garry Culhane?"

"Yes."

"I have a telegram from Children's Aid to take your children and return them to their father."

Somehow Claire sensed that he was bluffing, and she fixed the guard with a withering gaze.

"You'll just get out of my way if you know what's good for you."

She grabbed the children's hands and brushed past him, a lioness protecting her cubs. The confrontation had further unhinged the girls. It was an hour until the next train departed, and sitting in the cold station it was all Claire could do to calm them, to keep herself calm.

One of the few advantages to being dogged by the RCMP for nearly twenty years was the sixth sense it had given Claire about undercover cops. She could smell them, and when the train finally left Winnipeg her attention was immediately drawn to a woman sitting across the aisle. She hadn't been on the train before, and she carried no luggage: they were being followed. Claire's mind raced ahead of the eastbound train. Would her pursuer stay with them all the way to Montreal? They didn't dare risk another confrontation with the authorities; the next time it might be more than a bluff.

At Port Arthur, the first city east of Winnipeg with an airport, they slipped away from the train, trudging through the snow to a cheap hotel near the station. Neither Roisin nor Dara had ever experienced the bitter cold of winter on the Cambrian Shield, and none of them owned boots or a heavy coat. They spent the night freezing in a cheerless hotel room, and in the morning Claire called California.

Claire guessed that Garry had figured out her destination. To throw their pursuers off the track, she asked her mother to send enough money for airfare to Toronto, and the ever-dependable Rose complied.

They stayed for a few days with relatives in Toronto. Apart from their grandparents, these were the first members of the Eglin-Briskin clan that Roisin and Dara had ever met. They were made to feel welcome enough, but it was clear that their mother was considered, not entirely unkindly, "crazy Claire." Nor was this such an outrageous conclusion for Claire's kin to draw. Since Claire had left Montreal they had busied themselves with family and business, while Claire, ever the sower of wild oats, had hied off to the west coast with an Irish Communist who was already married to someone else. Now here she was, without even adequate clothing for her children. And then there were her political views, which had already gone a long way to making her the black sheep of the family. Tongues wagged, but fortunately for Claire, blood proved thicker than politics.

In Toronto she contemplated her next move. Montreal was out of the question now; Garry would find them as soon as she registered Roisin in school. She thought of Piedmont. It had always been a childhood refuge, full of happy memories. Best of all, it was her place, somewhere Garry might not think to look.

They travelled to Montreal by bus and took the train north. She hadn't been to the Laurentians in sixteen years, and she was delighted to discover how little the place had changed. She even managed to locate one of the French-Canadian farmers, Monsieur St. Denis, who remembered her parents. He was a godsend, agreeing to rent them a furnished summer cottage, complete with oil stove, for $25 a month. Rose agreed to send her $125 a month, and Claire enrolled Roisin in the local one-room school, where Garry's investigators were far less likely to discover the registration. They spent the rest of the winter in that peaceful haven, and Claire began to put her life back together. Piedmont bought her time, and her instincts proved correct: Garry was having a hard time locating them. In fact, it was the Mounties who got there first.

In late June 1955, RCMP Constable D.Y. Beauséjour, of the Montreal Special Branch, found Claire. "Inquiries . . . have located the subject of this file, who is residing in a small cottage located directly behind the Piedmont, P.Q. post office and general store, operated by Mr. D. St. DENIS," Beauséjour reported to his superiors. Mr. St. Denis "informed the writer that Claire CULHANE was a native of Piedmont, P.Q. and she and her mother and father were well known to old residents of Piedmont . . . Mrs. CULHANE is leading a very sheltered life in Piedmont, and she is afraid that her husband will follow her and cause her harm."[1]

When they first arrived Claire had taken St. Denis into her confidence so far as Garry was concerned. It was a precautionary manoeuvre, in case police or private investigators should land on the old man's doorstep, inquiring about a runaway wife. It had never occurred to Claire that the Red squad would track her down first. As it was, the loyal St. Denis kept the Mountie's visit a secret until just before Claire and the girls left Piedmont in September. "I told them to leave you alone," he confided. "I said you were taking good care of your kids, and that your husband wasn't supporting you."

They were safe enough for the time being, but clearly they couldn't remain in Piedmont forever, depending on Rose and Abe to pay the bills. Besides, Roisin was having a difficult time in the local school—she spoke no French, and most of her fellow students spoke no English. Apart from letting their trail cool somewhat, Claire had another design in remaining in Piedmont until the fall: Dara would be almost five by then, nearly old enough to enrol in school, thereby clearing the decks so Claire could return to work.

She had determined to make a career change to escape the office ghetto to which she had been consigned by secretarial-stenographic work. Claire decided to incorporate her secretarial skills into her nursing background by applying for jobs in Montreal hospitals. She wrote to half a dozen that summer, and several offered her work. She chose to take a position as a medical typist with the Montreal Neurological Institute (MNI), and at the end of August 1955 Claire and her daughters boarded the bus for Montreal. Claire was overjoyed to be back in the city. Montreal had always been, would always be, her favourite city. She loved it for its élan, its vitality, for its memories of the Main and the smoked meat from Schwartz's that had been the Saturday-night treat of her girlhood. She returned bursting with energy, determined to begin life anew. Claire had also made a radical resolution: she would, she promised herself, shun all political activity. She had seen, during her party years, parents who ignored their families in favour of saving the world. Whether conscious of Roisin's resentments or not, Claire here echoed her elder daughter's perception of the impact of party politics upon their own family. Claire knew herself well enough to realize that if she so much as attended one meeting for a political cause she'd end up volunteering for some committee or other, becoming totally committed, and spending too little time with Dara and Roisin. Claire determined to forswear political activity until her familial obligations were discharged, thus beginning the only period in her adult life when she would be absent from the arena of political activism.

Whatever else it may have been, Montreal in the mid-1950s was not the most congenial place for a single mother struggling to raise two children. Though they now had the vote, Quebec women were still discriminated against in law and in fact (not until 1970 would they be allowed to sit on juries, for example) and the province's ubiquitous Catholic institutions perpetuated the inequity in a myriad of ways. The nuclear family was preeminent, and society made few allowances for "broken homes," as single-parent families were then described. The greatest challenge facing Claire in these circumstances was the lack of affordable day care. She lied about Dara's age to get her into school a year early, but responsibility for some of the after-school child care would have to fall on Roisin's shoulders, a demand the older child, just turned ten, understandably resented.

Certainly Claire knew better than to expect day care, or any other kind of progressive social legislation for that matter, from the provincial government. Maurice Duplessis, the old nemesis of communism, was entering his fifteenth year as premier of Quebec and, in tandem with the hierarchy of the Roman Catholic Church and the province's anglo business élite, he ruled with an iron fist. A later generation of Québécois intellectuals would describe this period as *la grande noirceur*, the Great Darkness. Nationalist sentiment had ebbed since the conscription crisis of the Second World War, even though a handful of anglophone businessmen still maintained their stranglehold on the province's economy. When Claire had departed Montreal in 1939, the city was the hub of Canadian finance. Now the sprawling metropolis at the foot of Mount Royal had been supplanted by Toronto as the nation's financial capital. The province seemed to sleepwalk through the 1950s, impervious to the changes sweeping the rest of North America.

Claire had an ulterior motive in choosing the employment offer from the Montreal Neurological Institute over several others: she knew that Rube was there. Dr. Reuben Rabinovitch had had an extraordinary wartime career. He had graduated with his M.D. on the same day that Paris fell to the Nazis, and he was soon interned for being a Jew. He had managed to escape, and began a shadowy, chameleon-like existence, assuming a number of non-Jewish identities to evade capture. He worked with the French underground, providing medical assistance to downed Allied airmen, but on one such mission in the fall of 1943 he was arrested once again. Posing as Sergeant Harry Vozic, an American tail gunner, Rube was shipped to a POW camp in Krems, Austria. He was at considerable pains to conceal both his professional and ethnic identity from his German captors, but he was forced to risk blowing his cover the day a young American airman, newly arrived in the camp, collapsed on the floor, writhing in pain. Rube at once went to his aid, and began barking orders in both French and German. The boy had suffered an attack of appendicitis, Rube told the guards, and needed immediate medical attention. The airman's life was saved, but German suspicions were immediately aroused. How did it happen that an American gunner from New York City spoke German and French fluently and knew so much about medicine?

Rube quickly invented a story about being a medical school drop-out, and spent the rest of the war as an informal "doctor," treating American GIs at Stalag XVII-B, saving countless lives with his medical expertise, his leadership, and the few medicinal aids at his disposal. He organized a handful of his fellow prisoners into a medical corps and during the grim winter of 1943 he led his amateur medics on a "charge" against a neighbouring barracks. The mock raid led to a snowball fight which soon expanded into a brawl that involved the whole camp. "We were boys again, and in that brief inspired moment he had brought many of us back to a realization of our youth and the prospect of a long future," one of his fellow POWs recalled gratefully many years later.[2]

Claire had followed Rube's career through newspaper clippings that a cousin sent to her in Vancouver, and when she saw a story announcing that her old friend had been awarded a fellowship in neurology by McGill, she dashed off a congratulatory letter, noting ironically that the same university which had refused to admit him as a medical student in 1935 because he was a Jew was now welcoming him with open arms, and proclaiming his brilliance to the world. "Now, let's both laugh," was his sardonic reply.

Claire knew when she opted for the job at the Neurological Institute that Rube was happily married with children of his own, but she looked forward to seeing him again as a valued friend. Perhaps they would go for coffee and talk about old times. But things didn't work out quite that way— Claire's tenure at the Institute did not last out the year. She'd heard about a new position that had been created at Grace Dart, a tuberculosis hospital in east-end Montreal which was looking for someone to establish its first medical records department. Claire applied and, to her delight, was offered the position, which carried with it a handsome raise in pay and considerably more responsibility. Her new job started on December 1, 1955.

She had seen Rube over the previous three months, in the corridors or on the elevator, but the hoped-for invitation to lunch or coffee hadn't been forthcoming. In her final week at MNI Claire told Rube she was leaving. "And we haven't even had a cup of coffee."

Rube looked at her for a minute. "C'mere." He motioned her to relative privacy beneath a window at one end of the corridor before uncapping his pen and beginning to sketch something on the back of a prescription pad.

"Remember this?" Claire could see it was the riverbank where they used to go in La Macaza. She remembered.

"And this?" It was the barn on his parents' farm. She remembered that, too.

And then he smiled at her. "With memories like this you don't just go and have a cup of coffee . . ."

While Claire's new job was an undeniable boost to her nascent career in medical administration, it also brought added complications. Grace Dart Hospital was located on Sherbrooke Street, beyond what is today the Olympic Park in east-end Montreal, while Claire and her daughters were living on Western Avenue near Atwater, on the edge of lower Westmount. The Metro had not yet been built, so Claire's daily commute involved three bus transfers and lasted an hour and a half each way. Still, Claire revelled in the challenge afforded by her new position—starting a medical records department from scratch at a major metropolitan hospital; she thrived at Grace Dart. She was allowed to hire her own assistant, and her selection of

Ann Hartley for the position would prove especially felicitous. Hartley eventually succeeded Claire as the head of medical records at the hospital, a position she would hold until her retirement in the 1980s. Claire and her new assistant became fast friends and together they soon established a system for filing and quickly accessing the voluminous records for all the patients at the hospital, no small administrative feat.

Though life as a single parent was far from easy, Claire was well satisfied with family life without Garry. "It was amazing. Here we came from a ten-room house with a yard and cats and dogs and rabbits and family and the kids seemed quite content. The difference between tension and non-tension really convinced me I had done the right thing. And of course I was happy as a lark." Roisin's memories of the period are not so salutary, however. "Our life in Montreal was pretty dismal as children. I don't remember there being too much that was very positive about it. She was working and . . . I used to take care of Dara, and I remember the first place we lived in Montreal was just one room and we used to play in the alley, in the lane behind the house."

Many of Claire's Montreal cousins had successfully pursued careers in business or the professions, and visits to their houses served only to emphasize the social and economic gap that had opened since they had all played together as children in the summers in the Laurentians. "Mummy, why do they live in hotels?" Dara once blurted out as she looked wide-eyed at the spacious mansion of one of Claire's cousins. Only one branch of the family, that of Evelyn and Bill Sperling, struck Roisin as being warm and truly welcoming. Evelyn was the daughter of Claire's aunt Edith (Eglin) and Bill was the first Jewish fireman in the city of Montreal. Their home was far more modest than those of most of the other cousins, and they seemed more inclined to treat Claire and her daughters as equals.

By the spring of 1956 Claire learned that Grace Dart offered bursaries for professional upgrading so she decided to enrol in a two-year correspondence course for certification as a registered record librarian. But the course also required at least one year of post-secondary study in a liberal arts program, so Claire applied for, and was awarded, a scholarship from a Jewish women's organization for tuition to Sir George Williams University in downtown Montreal.

That fall Claire was engaged in an exhausting routine that taxed even her own prodigious capacity for work. Besides her full-time job and being the sole means of support for two children (Garry provided no child support whatsoever), she was taking evening courses two nights a week at Sir George, writing her correspondence course for the record librarian certification, and typing university theses at home to earn a bit of extra money. Her workmates at Grace Dart were amazed by her ability to do so many things at once successfully. A receptionist at the hospital used to tell Claire she got worn out just being around her. "You're mad. You're mad, girl," she'd say. "You're sitting on a million dollars!" But Claire had no intention of turning to any man for support. She was on her own now, and glorying in her freedom.

More than a decade later when she applied to go to Vietnam, Claire listed Ann Hartley as a reference, and her friend and protégé was duly requested to fill out a government questionnaire on Claire's behalf. What started as a simple letter of reference expanded into a fond memoir of Claire during her days at Grace Dart. "Her devotion to her children, even while attempting to carry on her studies, and maintain the responsibility of being head of the department, was something we all admired, and indeed marvelled at," Hartley recalled.

> She combined the roles of bread-winner, housekeeper, mother, and student—and from what we could all see, was doing a first-rate job in all directions. In addition to the cheerfulness and good spirit displayed at work, she was also solely responsible for the rearing of her two daughters . . . She was able to organize her home life in such a way that the girls were able to make their own lunches, and care for themselves during her absence at work. A very close supervision was maintained [with Roisin and the landlady, whom Claire paid a little extra to watch her girls] as the youngsters reported all their movements to her by phone. Needless to say, there were times when things did not go too smoothly, e.g. illness, etc. But she was remarkable in the manner in which she was able to keep things going, as I'm sure she had many problems at that time, but there was never a hint of giving up.

Nor could she refrain from mentioning a standing joke at the hospital—that Claire should dye her prematurely greying hair. It would not be the last time that Claire was urged to make concessions to appearances, and her response was unvarying. "We often tried to persuade her to tint her hair. Needless to say, she consistently refused to resort to any artificialities, for it was too foreign to her nature and anyways, as she also insisted, she never would have the time or patience to waste, for she was always much too busy with her many activities and interests to worry about it."[3]

By the spring of 1957 life was indeed as full as Hartley remembered. Claire had come further faster than she ever dared hope. A less determined person might have faltered under the diverse demands on her time, but Claire thrived. Her children were doing well at school, she was admired and esteemed by her colleagues at work, her own classes were proceeding apace. On top of it all she even managed to have a social life of sorts, sending Roisin and Dara to Evelyn and Bill's the occasional Saturday night so that she and Ann could go out on the town in the city that she loved. It hardly seemed possible that only two years before, the three of them had huddled, penniless, in a freezing hotel room in Port Arthur escaping a life filled with tension and acrimony. No, that spring life was truly unfolding as it should. And then a friend called to tell her the news—Garry was in Montreal, and looking for them.

Assuming that Garry had come to Montreal to gain custody of Roisin and Dara, Claire quickly packed the children off to her parents in California. But when Garry finally found her, Claire was in for a surprise: he had come seeking reconciliation, not custody. He had sold the house on Charles Street, Garry told Claire, and was on his way back to Ireland. He was contrite about his earlier behaviour and now sought to reunite his family. Things would be different this time around, she'd see. He planned to use the proceeds from the sale of the house to start a business and begin life afresh.

Relieved, but not without some misgivings, Claire called her mother and asked her to send the children back to Montreal. Roisin and Dara were overjoyed to see their father and soon fished Claire's wedding ring out of her drawer, leaving it lying around the house as a none-too-subtle signal about their own desire for a return to "normal" family life. At first Claire flatly refused Garry's offer—she had to finish her courses, they were managing well enough on their own, and she had no desire to resurrect the domestic nightmare of their final years together in Vancouver.

But little by little Garry and her daughters eroded Claire's resolve. If it had been only for herself, she insisted later, she would never have considered reconciliation for an instant. But she did feel guilty about depriving the children of their father, though not, certainly, any remorse about depriving him of them.

One night Garry came over to discuss his plans for Ireland, and he stayed after the children were in bed. Why not let him take Roisin and Dara to Ireland while Claire stayed on in Montreal for the three months needed to finish her own studies? There was a freighter sailing in a few weeks, and he could book passage for the three of them. Claire could then follow them over. Dara and Roisin, in bed but not asleep, listened breathlessly to their father's plan, and they burst in on their parents suddenly, excited at the prospect of such a grand adventure and a reunited family. They begged their mother to agree, and at last Claire caved in. All right, they would give it one more try.

On the night before they sailed, Claire went to lie down with Dara and Roisin, as she always did at bedtime.

"Mummy," six-year-old Dara said quietly, "I don't think this is such a good idea."

"What? But you're the ones who hauled my wedding ring out of the drawer and wanted me to wear it. You're the ones who want us all to be together again."

"I just don't think it's such a good idea," Dara insisted.

From the mouths of babes . . .

*   *   *

Garry and the girls set sail from Montreal aboard the *Irish Pine* in May 1957. As the vessel was a freighter and they were the only paying passengers, Garry and his daughters were invited to eat their meals at the captain's table. Perhaps because they missed their own families, the crew doted on Roisin and Dara, and even rigged a rope swing up for Dara on the main deck.

The voyage was uneventful until one night at dinner when the captain made an anti-Semitic remark. Garry took umbrage, proclaiming that his wife was Jewish and so were his daughters and he found such anti-Semitism reprehensible. Dara watched her father stand up to deliver his peroration and then, as if to punctuate his conclusion, dramatically slam his spoon down into a bowl full of tomato soup. Dara would always remember the red soup spreading slowly across her father's white shirt front. The captain was nonplussed by Garry's performance. That was fine, he said evenly. They were on a ship in mid-Atlantic, and it happened to be his ship, and if Garry was so offended by his views then he and his family were welcome to eat their meals in their cabin—which is exactly what they did for the rest of the crossing.

Their first stop was the small town of Cuskinny outside Cobh in county Cork, Ireland's southernmost county. Garry had chosen Cuskinny because his sister Peggy and her husband lived nearby. Unlike Garry, his siblings had chosen the devout Catholicism of the Culhanes over the more secular outlook of the Sheehys (Patricia had become a nun, Frank a priest), and their attitude towards Claire would soon become a sore point within the family.

Claire herself arrived in Ireland in August, and the family moved to a semi-detached row house named Ashdene, on College Road, in a lower middle-class neighbourhood of Cork City. Garry had always loved animals, and the household soon expanded to include a menagerie reminiscent of the one on Charles Street, including Bimbo and Frisky, a pair of cairn terriers, two cats, a budgie, and a special pet for the children, a donkey named Skipper. Skipper was kept in the backyard and allowed to graze in a field at the end of the road, but he also had the irritating habit of barging into the kitchen during the night, and wandering away at the slightest opportunity.

Garry's grand design was to establish a fishing business somewhere on the south coast of Ireland. During his years on Canada's west coast Garry had been intrigued by the fishing camp businesses that thrived there, and he was convinced a similar enterprise would work in Ireland. The Gulf Stream runs past the island's southern coast, carrying with it a variety of game fish, including shark. Garry believed that he could establish a boat rental business that would offer guided tours to sport fishermen from all over Europe. The first challenge was to find the right location, and he spent much of his time during this period visiting coastal villages on the Celtic Sea.

Roisin and Dara, meanwhile, were enrolled in Scoilmuire (Gaelic for "School of Mary"), an élite private girl's school in Cork City. Nationalist and Gaelic first and Catholic second, Scoilmuire was operated by the sisters MacSwiney, who, as the relatives of martyred patriot Terence MacSwiney, boasted impeccable Irish nationalist credentials.[4]

Roisin flourished in Ireland, if not in school. For the first time in her twelve years she felt as if she'd found a genuine home. Every corner, every ruin and wall in the country seemed mystical, enchanted. She loved the people, too, for their down-to-earth and easygoing ways. But school was another matter; Roisin had begun to play hookey every afternoon. Her oldest daughter had always been at or near the top of her class in Montreal, and Claire was not impressed by Roisin's school performance in Ireland.

Garry continued his search for the proper site for his boat business, but by the fall of 1957 living expenses and tuition for Scoilmuire soon depleted his capital. Claire was by now ready, even eager, to return to work as a medical records librarian, but she found her way blocked on two fronts. It soon became apparent that, in Ireland, married women did not work. The few extremely poorly paid jobs open to women were given to widows and single women. A still greater obstacle was the fact that medical records librarians simply did not exist in Irish hospitals. With characteristic determination, Claire set out to create a demand. She phoned several hospitals and made appointments with administrators and doctors to at least listen to her pitch about the invaluable nature of the service she had to offer. The response of the first doctor she met with, one of the most distinguished orthopaedic surgeons in all of Ireland, was disappointing; even he failed to see the need for medical records librarians.

In the end the only option was for Claire to return to Montreal for a few months and work to support the family so that Garry could devote their dwindling savings to setting up his business. She returned to Canada in November, and by early December had landed two jobs. She worked at

Montreal's Royal Victoria Hospital in the Department of Otolaryngology (the treatment of diseases of the ear, nose, and throat) by day, and as a typist in the Medical Records Department of the Neurological Institute at night. She sent money back to Garry to cover household expenses as planned, including the housekeeper Claire had interviewed and hired before she left. But she missed Roisin and Dara terribly and Christmas that year was especially difficult, on both sides of the Atlantic. It was the first time since Roisin's birth that they had been apart during the festive season.

It was not until March 1958, when Garry signalled that he could now cover both home and business expenses, that Claire was able to rejoin the family in Cork City. Garry had by now determined the ideal spot for his boat rental business, the small coastal village of Kinsale, twenty-nine kilometres south of Cork. That summer the family, along with Bimbo, Frisky, the cats, the budgie, and Skipper, was on the move once again, this time to Kinsale. They rented a large house in Summercove, just outside Kinsale, and one of the terms of the lease was that they retain the part-time maid and care for the dog. It was the first and only time in her life that Claire ever had a maid, and it soon became apparent she was not cut out to be a lady of leisure.

Kinsale was a beautiful place, nestled among the hills overlooking the sea, and it still retained something of a Spanish flavour because some of its inhabitants were the descendants of survivors of the Spanish armada. But there was nothing for Claire to do. The girls had returned to Scoilmuire for another year, so they were gone all day. Garry was working long hours at his business. The maid took care of the housework. How much knitting and cooking and reading could one person do? She had always been a breadwinner for her family, usually the primary breadwinner. Now she was reduced to dependency on Garry, prevented from working by social convention and by an utter lack of demand for her professional skills. Indeed, here her profession didn't even exist. Claire was afflicted with increasing dejection; she felt she was going absolutely nowhere. She suffered such intense, unending boredom that she actually began to look forward to Skipper's periodic bolts for freedom—at least wandering the hills in pursuit of the donkey gave her something to do. Sometimes she would climb up above the village and stare wistfully out to sea. On the distant horizon she could see, beneath a smudge of smoke, hull-down freighters just beginning their voyage to America. How she longed to go with them! But then the reality of her situation bore down on her: her marriage was once again rapidly deteriorating; she was trapped, and powerless to do anything about it. She might as well be in jail.

Claire did get one break in the enforced inactivity of Kinsale. The mother of one of Dara's school friends in Cork City happened to be the editor of the women's page of the *Cork Examiner*, and she and Claire became friends. Here at last was some intellectual stimulation. One day her new friend mentioned a weekly women's program broadcast by Radio Éireann and suggested that Claire try to sell them a talk about the difficulties of a Canadian woman living in Ireland. Claire made her proposal, her idea was accepted, and her talk was broadcast over the Irish radio network. She was even paid for her effort—eleven guineas. She and Garry agreed there were three ways to use the windfall: they could do the sensible thing and pay off debts, Claire could take the money and indulge herself with a trip to London, or she could go out of her mind with boredom.

She spent a week in London, staying with Garry's half-brother Ronan Casey and his wife, Louie, both of whom worked in the theatre. The first day she went to the British Museum, in whose reading room Karl Marx had researched and written some of his most famous works. On the way back to Casey's flat, Claire paused at the entrance to the underground. Rush hour was at its peak and she stared, transfixed by the ceaseless flow of humanity around her. Thousands upon thousands of faces which she had never seen before, and would never see again. What a change from Kinsale! It contained barely fifteen hundred souls, and it seemed to her she greeted each of them every morning and every afternoon. With all due respect to them, it was, for her, a life without stimulation, without the surging energy of a city, lacking in the colour and diversity and political involvement that she had loved so much about Montreal.

The London interlude served only to reinforce her feelings of absolute misery upon returning to Kinsale, to remind her what she was missing. She tried to tell Garry how unhappy she was, but his reply was unvarying: "But look how beautiful it is here."

"It's not beautiful if people are shitting on you all the time," she would snap, and, indeed, as a Jew, a Communist, and an atheist Claire was the object of considerable suspicion and resentment from the villagers. The anti-Semitism was overt and unapologetic. Garry's sisters described Claire to Roisin on more than one occasion as a "heathen," who they blamed for leading their brother away from the Church. Baptism, catechism classes, confirmation, these rites of passage were as universal and profound in rural Ireland in the 1950s as birth and death itself. The fact that neither Dara nor Roisin had ever been baptized was a source of particular concern to family and friends, as it meant the children's souls were bound for eternal damnation. There had already been one untoward event before Claire's return from Canada: one of Dara's school friend's mothers had literally "kidnapped" her for a baptism ceremony, so fearful was she of the little Canadian girl's fate throughout eternity. Garry, furious, recovered his daughter before the baptism could take place.

Claire had always attempted to inculcate in Roisin and Dara a respect for the religion of others, while at the same time explaining that it was not necessary to resort to belief in the supernatural to live their own lives by the golden rule of doing unto others what you would have them do unto you. But the influence of Catholicism was everywhere in their daily lives, and its adherents' thirst for the conversion of "lost" souls was unquenchable. Garry and Claire had told the authorities at Scoilmuire that their children were allowed to partake in the classes of religious instruction as a learning experience only, and not in preparation for baptism or confirmation. But Claire, in whose experience the Roman Catholic Church was the very embodiment of reaction—fascism in Spain, virulent anti-Semitism and anti-feminism in Quebec—was becoming ever more concerned about the impact of Irish Catholicism on her children.

And indeed, a schism was opening within her family. As much as Claire detested life in Kinsale, with its languid pace and backwardness, its intellectual sterility, and its bigotry, Roisin was happier than ever before. She shared her father's attachment to Ireland, and his impulsive passion for the place. They might be driving through the countryside and spot some distant ruin. Nothing would do but that Garry stop the car and lead the children through some farmer's fields to explore the remains of the castle or convent, forgetting their original mission while Claire sat in the car, fuming at the delay.

Family life in Kinsale was another attraction for Roisin. Other families always seemed warm and happy, in such contrast to her own, and the Catholic Church was clearly part of the fibre that kept the fabric of family life intact. Roisin was entering adolescence, and the Church was also at the centre of social life in the village. "Meet Saturday night to go to Confession in order to meet your date. Go to Mass on Sunday morning to set up your date for the afternoon," was how Claire would describe the importance of the Church in Roisin's life many years later, and she disliked every aspect of it.[5]

The Culhanes were living proof of the Tolstoian dictum that every unhappy family is unhappy in its own way, and they were courting disaster. The Church influence, the financial situation—still as miserable as ever—the impossibility of Claire's finding work in Kinsale, all contributed to the looming breakup. Claire and Garry hammered out a compromise of sorts: she and the children would move, but only to Dublin. They would maintain, at least publicly, the fiction that they had not split up for good.

And so the fall of 1959 found Claire, Roisin, and Dara in Dublin. Claire had already met Owen Sheehy-Skeffington, Hanna and Francis's only child, on previous trips to the Irish capital. Claire got on famously with this distinguished professor at Dublin's Trinity College and member of the Irish Senate, as well as his family, and Owen was to prove invaluable in the job search she renewed as soon as they arrived in Dublin.

She once again assembled her kit on the subject of medical records, and began making the rounds of the city's hospitals. Medical record keeping had now become a profession of its own, she informed her potential employers, and its practitioners were schooled in anatomy and physiology, medical terminology, hospital administration, statistics, medical audits, research, and the secretarial sciences.

At last her persistence paid off, thanks partly to the good offices of Owen Sheehy-Skeffington. He was on the board of directors of Dublin's Meath Hospital and he prevailed on the administration there to hire Claire as a consultant, at five pounds per week. Claire was reasonably satisfied in her work, and delighted with life in Dublin, after the dull months in Kinsale, but the situation was decidedly less satisfactory on the home front. Roisin was miserable in Dublin. Claire had enrolled her daughters in a private Protestant school, but Roisin hated it; she missed her friends in Kinsale, not to mention her father, and the Dublin school was very much a ruling-class affair. Roisin longed for the easygoing ways and the amiable sociability of Kinsale. And if her parents could no longer be depended upon to maintain the family unit she craved, she would find routine and succour somehow. And where better than the eternal verities and reassuring rituals of the Catholic Church? She had the example of dozens of Kinsale families before her. It was true they were poor, but Roisin had been raised with the notion that possessions and money were not the most important things in life, anyway. More importantly these families seemed happy and hospitable, and who could doubt that the Church, which was so ubiquitous in their lives, was a major element in the domestic accord which was so clearly lacking in her own family? Roisin decided to convert to Catholicism.

Her announcement was anathema to Claire; it was just what she had feared most about their lives in Ireland. One night she confronted Roisin. Catholic dogma had it that unbaptized souls went to hell, but she and Dara had never been baptized. Did that mean they would go to hell, "while you and Daddy would go to heaven?" It was, Claire came to realize, an unfair question to put to a fourteen-year-old searching for meaning, and she bitterly regretted it later. The question upset Roisin tremendously, but failed to shake her new-found faith.

Christmas that year dashed any lingering hopes Claire might have had about making a go of it in Ireland. Garry had been making regular trips to Dublin to visit the children, but he opted to go to Vienna to spend the holidays with friends there, leaving Claire and the girls alone, in a still-unfamiliar city, with little money to celebrate the season. Claire was absolutely furious. And her status in Irish society was brought forcefully home to her by the hospital staff, too. She arrived at work shortly before Christmas to discover there had been a staff party the night before, and that she hadn't been invited. When Claire remonstrated with one of the organizers, pointing out that she worked at the Meath, too, after all, it was made quite clear to her that the affair had been for Christians only.

By the end of 1959 Claire was once again planning her escape, much as she had in Vancouver five years before—they would return to Montreal and resume their far more satisfactory life—but this time there was to be one devastating difference: Roisin demurred. Their previous life in Montreal held few happy memories for her. She was loath to leave her father, her new boyfriend Eltin O'Hea in Kinsale, and the only place she had ever felt she truly belonged. Claire was heartbroken at the thought of breaking up her family, of leaving Roisin behind. She begged Roisin to reconsider, but her oldest daughter was adamant, and Claire realized ruefully that, in the end, all she could do was offer Roisin the choice. Though still only fourteen, she was proving to be as rebellious and as headstrong as both of her parents.

Claire and Dara departed Ireland in February 1960. It was a nightmarish parting at the airport, and each of them knew full well its significance: for the first time in their lives, Dara and Roisin would be separated, and Claire felt that parental failure keenly. The thought of returning to Canada without her firstborn, the child that she had struggled for so long to have, was a shattering prospect. Claire would arrive in Canada physically and emotionally exhausted, her life at its lowest ebb.

*   *   *

They landed at Bill and Evelyn Sperling's doorstep, shunning all of Claire's wealthy relatives in Montreal in favour of the one place Claire and Dara could feel certain of a warm welcome. For Claire it was the start of what would be a six-year healing process. The disastrous attempt at family reunion in Ireland had left her a nervous wreck and sapped her normally remarkable physical stamina—she had lost thirty-five pounds and was suffering from a severe cough.

Money was a concern as always, and she made a beeline for the Montreal Neurological Institute, where she was sure she could find work. Rube took one look at Claire, immediately wrote her a prescription, and referred her to a friend for a thorough physical examination. As always, Claire was delighted to see Rube. The past three years, as she knew from their occasional correspondence, had not been easy for him, either. In the summer of 1958 his secretary had written Claire in Cork to tell her that Rube had suffered a heart attack. Claire promptly sent him a get-well card, and he had dashed off a note in return, reassuring her that his time had not yet come. "I just have to brush up against the old man every so often to test immortality."[6] He was fifty that year.

As she had hoped, Claire was offered a job in the MNI typing pool, and she and Dara settled into a modest two-room apartment on Chesterfield Avenue, in the western suburb of Notre Dame de Grace. There was a fresh beginning in another direction, too: within a few months of her return from Ireland Claire began a relationship with a man who would become an important part of her life over the next seven years.

His name was Ken Andrews, and they met that winter of 1960 at the home of a mutual friend. Andrews, who was employed in the publishing field, was only twenty-nine (she was now forty-one), and he sensed her emotional vulnerability at once. Despite the difference in age, he was immediately drawn to this confident, opinionated woman, whose idealism and fire he found overwhelming. A quiet and gentle man with wavy blond hair and thick spectacles, Andrews still spoke with an unmistakable London working-class accent that revealed his origins. He had never met anyone quite like Claire before, and he would later describe their relationship, the irresistible pull he felt towards Claire, in almost poetic terms. "I was called to her, to bask in the warmth. It was almost as if she were a fire, and I wanted to pick up a chair and sit beside it. But then it gets too hot and you want to get away, and then you discover spring has come."[7]

In Ken, Claire had finally found the right man at the right time. She was attracted to his soft-spokenness, to his unassuming modesty, to the sense he conveyed that here was a man who was comfortable inside his own skin.

In May Claire's cousin Julius Briskin, the lawyer son of her uncle Louis, approached her with a lucrative job offer. Julius was looking for someone to supervise his legal secretaries and to manage the office. Would Claire be interested? The money was much better than at MNI, and the prospect of administrative responsibilities was certainly far more promising than simply being a member of the typing pool. She accepted Julius's offer.

The next year was a quiet, almost idyllic time for Claire. She and Ken went for long walks together, and sometimes attended plays or concerts at the Place des Arts, newly built on the downtown site of the old Office Workers' Union headquarters, where she had first met Garry. On Sundays Claire continued the now well-established family tradition of making crêpes for everyone. In this new relationship there was none of the tumult and tension that had been a constant of her marriage, and it was almost a shock to live with a man who wasn't insanely jealous of her time with other friends. Once she asked Ken whether he'd mind if she went out somewhere without him, and he was almost puzzled by the question—no, he told her, of course not. Why would she even ask? His nonchalance came as such a surprise to her that Claire began to realize the profound impact Garry had had on even her subconscious behaviour.

The year was not such a happy one for Dara, however. She had difficulty accepting the presence of Ken in their lives, she missed her older sister, and she was miserable in her new school, which was located in upper Westmount. The only people she knew there were her wealthy cousins, and they wanted to have little to do with her, a sentiment she heartily reciprocated. It was all very reminiscent of Roisin's unhappiness at the Protestant school in Dublin. Wherever their place in life might be, it was already clear to Claire's daughters, with their keenly developed sense of class consciousness, that it wasn't among the moneyed élites of the world.

The only cloud in Claire's life was Roisin's absence. After Claire and Dara's departure Roisin had returned to Kinsale where she and her father lived together for a time in rooms, but Garry once again proved incapable of handling the day-to-day responsibilities of being a father. Now, for the first time, Roisin began to appreciate some of her mother's difficulties in living with her father. He would sometimes lapse into three- or four-day periods of intense melancholy when he wouldn't speak a word, so self-absorbed was he by his personal demons. Eventually Garry sent Roisin to live with his sister Peggy, and for the next three years Roisin bounced from convent school to Kinsale to London to live with the Ronan Caseys and back to Kinsale again. Her only anchor during this period was the O'Hea family. She had by now fallen deeply in love with Eltin O'Hea, a young man five years her senior, and the O'Heas' Kinsale household, with its roaring fire and mirth and good cheer, was a warm and welcoming haven. In 1961 she and Eltin announced their engagement, which triggered a predictably jealous tirade from Garry. He promised Roisin that he would allow the marriage when she turned eighteen, and not one day before.

In Montreal Ken Andrews watched, and marvelled at, Claire's single-minded determination to win Roisin's return. She wrote letters, which were rarely answered by Roisin, and sent a steady stream of presents and clothes. She telephoned her daughter at the Roscrea Convent School, but the nuns, who considered Claire a wicked, un-Christian influence, refused the call. In 1961 Claire flew to Ireland to visit Roisin, but Garry and his sister Peggy barely let them see one another; the few visits they were allowed were closely supervised.

Taking her father at his word, Roisin and Eltin set a wedding date for September 4, 1963, the day of her eighteenth birthday. But three weeks before the ceremony, Garry reneged on his promise and refused to sign his consent for the posting of the banns. He told Roisin to wait one more year, and then he would give his blessing. Roisin was crushed, and outraged at her father. A month later she placed the trans-Atlantic telephone call that Claire had been longing to receive for three and a half years. Roisin told her mother of Garry's refusal to allow her marriage to Eltin; would Claire help them to elope to Canada? So began yet another furtive leave-taking from Garry. Passports and airline tickets were sent, and arrangements made to have Eltin's brother drive them to the airport, all without Garry's knowledge. By late October Roisin and Eltin were winging their way toward a joyous family reunion at Montreal's Dorval airport. Roisin and Eltin were soon ensconced in a flat just beneath Claire's new, larger apartment on Harvard Avenue in NDG, which she now shared with Ken and Dara.

But there was one final hurdle to the successful completion of the elopement. Quebec's patriarchal laws required an aspiring bride who was under twenty-one to obtain her father's written approval for marriage. Her mother's permission would not suffice. In Ontario either parent's signature was acceptable. So on November 16, 1963, just three weeks after their arrival in Montreal, Roisin and Eltin, along with Claire, Dara, and Ken, squeezed into the latter's Vauxhall Victor for the two-hour drive to a justice of the peace in Ottawa.

A beaming Claire, triumphant in the knowledge that her family was together once again, watched as Ken gave away the bride. ("A supernumerary position, as you know," he would observe with a dry smile years later.) Her joy was truly complete when Rube himself showed up at the reception in Montreal to drink to the bride and groom's health.

It was at about this time that an incident occurred in Claire's life that gave Dara a profound insight into her mother's character. The joints on Claire's hands, feet, and knees began to swell alarmingly, and her doctor returned a swift diagnosis: she had contracted rheumatoid arthritis. This potentially debilitating illness carried especially devastating implications for her mother, the thirteen-year-old Dara realized. "I remember the terror of it. My mother's hands. She typed, she was a secretary, she typed theses on the side, she typed, she typed, she typed. That's how we lived."

It was a single parent's worst nightmare. Claire was, as she had almost always been, the sole source of support for Dara. Although she lived with Ken, the household expenses were split strictly fifty-fifty, and Claire insisted on being responsible for Dara's keep. The spectre that Claire, at the age of forty-five, would now become the victim of a degenerative illness haunted them both. The prognosis was gloomy; the course of the disease would be gradual, Claire's doctor informed her, and in all likelihood irreversible.

The prospect was simply unthinkable to Claire. She took the prescribed medications and was forced to book some time off work, but Dara remembers becoming aware, for the first time, of her mother's "unfathomable will" and inner strength. Against all odds the disease went into permanent remission, never to recur. Dara would remain convinced that it was her mother's sheer willpower, and not the medication, that had defeated the arthritis, just as she had conquered all the other odds when it came to her family.

And a family it was, though a highly unusual one: there were seven now for Sunday crêpes—Eltin's brother Jim had emigrated from Ireland and joined Roisin and Eltin in the downstairs apartment, and Claire, Ken, and Dara had been joined upstairs by Oliver O'Connell, another young Irishman from Kinsale. In June 1964 Roisin announced that the extended family was about to grow yet again: she was pregnant. Claire became a grandmother, at the age of forty-six, on the first day of March the following year, with the birth of Maura Ellen O'Hea. There were now three generations of Culhanes living beneath a single roof on Harvard Avenue.

By the following summer Claire felt her family obligations were easing slightly, and she decided to gratify a lifelong dream—to see Paris. The City of Light had seemed to her the seat of all romance, art, and adventure since the late 1930s when she had seen Rube off at the quay in Montreal, imploring him to let her go with him.

Claire had worked two years at Julius's law office without a holiday for just this purpose, and that spring, her travel plans completed, she made one of her rare calls to Rube to tell him the good news.

"Why don't you come, too?" she asked him, only half-jokingly, even though she knew he couldn't. And she knew too that Rube had never gone back to Paris since the end of the war, though his wife, Denise, a Parisienne, made the trip often enough.

They chatted for a while, and Rube gave her the name of an old friend of his from medical school to look up.

"Of course I can't go. But I'll be with you in spirit. All the time. Don't forget, now." He said it two or three times. "I'll be with you in spirit . . ."

On her first morning she had to suppress the strong urge to dash out of her hotel on the Ile de la Cité, open her arms wide and shout, "I'm here! Claire Culhane is here at last!" And she expected Paris to respond in kind, to sweep her off her feet. When it didn't, a wave of disappointment and loneliness swept over her, even though she always preferred the greater freedom of travelling by herself.

But this *was* Paris, and the feeling lasted only about an hour. By the next day she had met three single men—an artist, a lawyer, and an official in the French Ministry of Finance—and between the three of them her weeks in Paris were every bit as romantic as she could have hoped. She also met

Rube's friend, Dr. Jacques Le Beau, a neurosurgeon, with whom she had a lovely dinner.

When Claire returned to Montreal her desk was piled high with work, and it was a week before she had time to drop Rube a line. "They should change the saying 'See Naples and Die' to 'See Paris and Live,' don't you think? I loved every minute and every cobblestone of it . . . I even brought back a little spot of Paris to rub off on you anytime you can spare fifteen minutes for a cup of coffee . . . for who else can I emote to about Paris who could better appreciate it . . ."[8]

She posted the letter on September 16 from the mail chute outside Julius's office, pausing to glance at her watch after checking the next mail-collection time posted over the slot. It was 1:00 p.m.

That night Rube's secretary called her at home. He had died of a heart attack that afternoon at about one o'clock. In her grief Rube's last words to her came flooding back. "I'll be with you in spirit. All the time. Don't forget, now."

The Montreal dailies, both English and French, carried obituaries for Rube the next day, noting his distinguished medical career and his wartime heroism, and tributes poured in from around the world. But the most remarkable memorial of all, published in the *Montreal Star*, was penned by the Canadian novelist Hugh MacLennan, who had been a patient of Rube's.

> On September 16 Dr. Reuben Rabinovitch, neurologist of this city, died at the age of only 56 at the height of his powers . . . Dr. Rab was a very great, a very rare healer. Whether from his concentration camp experience or from native sensitivity, he had acquired what seemed to me to be a Shakespearean knowledge of men . . .
> When my novel, *The Watch that Ends the Night*, appeared, it was widely believed that its doctor protagonist, Dr. Jerome Martell, was modelled on the famous Dr. Norman Bethune. He wasn't, for I never knew Bethune. But Martell's way of dealing with his patients was Dr. Rab's way. This is not to suggest that Martell was modelled off him; he wasn't. But if I had not known Dr. Rab, I could never have understood Dr. Martell . . .[9]

Claire took Dara with her to the funeral. The synagogue was filled with mourners and tributes. She had, of course, known Rube longer than almost anyone else in the room. She even knew him by a different nickname—everyone else, like Hugh MacLennan, called him "Rab." They had been through so much—together and apart—since the days of the Reel Fren's Club, Claire reflected. She knew that the things Rube had taught her about life and the way it should be lived, and about love, would never leave her. He truly was, Claire realized, with her in spirit.

Even Dara, who was fast becoming a streetwise Montreal hard case, was impressed. "I never knew he was such a great man," she said to her mother as they left the funeral home.

Within six months Claire was to have a second brush with mortality. Her mother died in southern California in March 1966, just short of her seventy-third birthday, and Abe, who had been married to Rose for fifty-two years, was devastated by her loss. Claire, too, mourned her mother's passing. However much she may have disapproved of her daughter's lifestyle, Rose had always been there when Claire needed her, unswerving in her loyalty and steadfast support. It was one family trait that Claire intended to pass down to her own daughters; like Rube's teachings about life, Rose's example of the true meaning of family would outlive her. She, too, would always be with them in spirit.

Certainly Claire now needed every ounce of Rose's motherly commitment when it came to Dara. Claire's younger daughter was proving to be as incorrigible as Claire herself had been as an adolescent—rebellious, unruly, headstrong—and she had never fully accepted Ken Andrews's presence in their lives.

Claire and Ken had been slowly drifting apart, partly over his difficulties with Dara, and partly because they had both come to the realization that he would never share her abiding and passionate interest in politics. In October 1966 Claire's relationship with Ken Andrews ended when she and Dara moved out of the Harvard Avenue apartment. It was an amiable parting, and they were to remain friends for years. It was just that, for Ken and perhaps for Claire, too, spring, in Andrews's words, had come.

Nineteen sixty-seven was a watershed year for Canada, for Quebec, and for Claire. It was the country's centennial, and the nation felt better about itself than it would for the next quarter-century. In Quebec the long years of the *grande noirceur* had ended, and the province had emerged from the shadow of Maurice Duplessis. The populist but authoritarian ruler, who had won an unprecedented five elections, had died of a heart attack in September 1959 and his political machine proved unable to survive without him. Under the Liberal government of Jean Lesage the *revolution tranquille*, the Quiet Revolution, had begun. Hydro Québec nationalized all of the province's electrical utilities, and the Catholic Church's grip on the social infrastructure—schools, hospitals, and the welfare system—had begun to loosen. There were murmurs of disquiet, it is true. A group calling itself the Front de libération du Québec, or FLQ, had begun a campaign of terrorist bombings to highlight its demands for Quebec independence, and in July French president Charles de Gaulle would create a diplomatic row with his famous rallying cry "*Vive le Québec! Vive le Québec libre!*" delivered before ten thousand cheering Québécois from the balcony of Montreal's city hall. But for most Canadians, 1967 would be remembered as the summer of Expo, a halcyon time when Canada showcased its achievements and life-style to an appreciative world.

For Claire, 1967 would prove a turning point, a year of rapid and far-reaching change. Even before the year began she knew this much: it had been twelve years since she had resolved to forgo politics and devote herself full-time to raising and supporting her family. She had kept her resolution, but now her family obligations were rapidly diminishing. Roisin and Eltin, with Maura, had decided to move to North Vancouver, and Dara, too, was becoming less dependent on Claire. She had a boyfriend now, and she planned to find a job and her own place as soon as she finished high school in the summer.

Superficially Claire appeared a typical if somewhat youthful white-haired grandmother. She was a year and a half away from her fiftieth birthday in the spring of 1967, an age when most Canadians would begin contemplating pensions and planning for their retirement. But as Claire anticipated a future free of family responsibilities she found herself still longing for the travel and adventure she had missed during the Spanish and Second World War days. She was careful to consult both Roisin and Dara: would they understand if she worked abroad for a few years? They assured her they would not mind, so Claire contacted the World Health Organization, offering her services as a health care professional to the developing world.

Then, on Saturday, May 27, she came across an article in *Weekend Magazine* that would change her life forever. The story featured a dashing thirty-four-year-old Dutch-born Canadian doctor named Alje Vennema who was working on a Canadian medical-aid project in a place called Quang Ngai, South Vietnam. A Canadian medical aid team, under Vennema's leadership, had been sent to live and work in Quang Ngai province to treat the area's inordinately high number of tuberculosis victims—7 percent of the province's seven hundred thousand residents were estimated to be suffering from the disease. In addition to his other medical duties, Vennema also treated the two thousand prisoners, most of them National Liberation Front (NLF) guerrillas, who were incarcerated in the provincial jail near the hospital. Although they were constantly sniping at jeeps containing American soldiers, the NLF let Dr. Vennema's jeep pass through the countryside unmolested, the article reported. "I treat everyone who needs help, including the Viet Cong. Why should they shoot at me?" Vennema rhetorically asked the *Weekend* reporter.

The Canadian physician was also highly critical of the U.S. war effort, much to the consternation of American officials, the magazine reported. "Dr. Vennema is well-known to many Western journalists in Vietnam for his frank and penetrating insights into the events taking place here. 'Go and see Vennema. He'll tell you the truth,' is a saying among persons who have resided in Vietnam for several years."[10] The story concluded by noting that the Canadians were overseeing the construction of a $250,000 TB sanitorium in Quang Ngai, funded by Canada's External Aid office under the Colombo Plan foreign-aid program. The Canadian medical team in Quang Ngai would train Vietnamese staff to take over the new hospital once it was completed.

It had been two years since the U.S. Marines had waded ashore at Da Nang, marking the first American commitment of combat troops on the ground in Vietnam, and Claire had followed events there with the same keen interest that she brought to bear on other global events, even during her hiatus from active politics. Her views on the ever-deepening conflict in Southeast Asia were unequivocal: she believed the American involvement was wrong, and her sympathies were entirely on the side of the Communist government of North Vietnam, and the National Liberation Front in the south. But, in keeping with her resolution to avoid political commitments to the detriment of her family, she had refrained from joining the anti-war movement, which was then gaining ground in the United States and Canada. Still, Vietnam was clearly where the action was, and the *Weekend* article excited her greatly. Claire was intrigued by this Canadian doctor who was such a forthright critic of the war and she was attracted by the possibility of helping the Vietnamese people on behalf of the Canadian government. Moreover, Vietnam was clearly the focal point of history, just as Spain had been in 1937, or Paris in 1939. It was one of Claire's chief regrets in life that she had been unable to contribute directly, on the ground, in those earlier epoch-making struggles. Perhaps the door of history had opened—just a crack—to her once again.

She wasted no time in putting her foot through the door. She phoned Ottawa on Monday morning after reading the *Weekend* article, and that afternoon drafted a letter to the External Aid Department offering her services in Vietnam. Just two weeks later she was summoned to a personal interview with External Aid official J.A. Arsenault in Montreal. They discussed the political situation in Vietnam, and Claire made no attempt to hide her sympathies. Arsenault replied that they were of no great concern, as Canada was neutral in the war, and its presence there was strictly to provide humanitarian aid for Vietnamese civilians. But he did discuss, at some length, the rigours of life in a developing country.

Claire, for her part, did prudently omit to mention the one obstacle that she feared might prove insuperable to her being posted to such a sensitive part of the world as an official representative of the Canadian government: her political past.

Indeed, even as he was recommending her within the department and arranging for Claire to take a physical examination as a preliminary to an offer of employment abroad, Arsenault was also, on July 6, ordering a routine security clearance of Mrs. Claire Culhane.[11] There now occurred one of the most baffling episodes of the RCMP's long surveillance history of Claire. The Mounties' Security Service had gone to extraordinary lengths to keep track of Claire's whereabouts and political activities over a fifteen-year period. Though it appears to have been inactive since February 1955 when the RCMP tracked her to Piedmont, Claire's file was certainly still in existence somewhere in Ottawa, and it clearly documented her role in the Communist party over a number of years. Presumably the Canadian government maintained files on its citizens for just such an eventuality as this routine yet critical security check. But the public expense and clandestine efforts of a dozen Security Service members, RCMP informers, and the attendant secretaries and file clerks dating back to 1940 would all go for naught. There is no indication that the contents of the file were ever reported to Arsenault in the summer of 1967, while Claire's application lay pending on his desk.[12]

In the absence of a red flag for security reasons, Arsenault and Claire ploughed ahead with the steadily mounting paperwork required by the federal government for any overseas posting. Behind the scenes External Aid had concluded that a person of Claire's qualifications could have real value on the Quang Ngai project, and both Vennema and the South Vietnamese government cabled their willingness to accept her. Just three months after the appearance of the *Weekend* article, it was clear that Claire was heading for Vietnam.

Roisin and Dara accepted their mother's suddenly announced desire to go to Vietnam with considerably less equanimity than the Canadian government. She had mentioned volunteering for service with the World Health Organization or Canadian University Service Overseas (CUSO), and they had given their blessing. But they were apprehensive upon learning that she had signed on for service in the middle of the hottest shooting war since Korea.

Claire, meanwhile, suppressed her mounting excitement and set about enjoying Montreal in the summer of Expo. The pavilion she most wanted to see was the Soviet exhibition, and during her first visit there she met Ruslan Volkov, an attractive Russian geologist who had been assigned to the exhibit for the duration of Expo. Volkov's English was excellent, and before long she invited him home for dinner. It was the start of a valued, strictly platonic, friendship. Ruslan was a Muscovite, and happily married she learned, and he was also, ironically, tubercular. There was an undeniable mutual physical attraction, but they resolved to remain just friends, a resolution they both kept, though it was difficult at times.

As the bureaucratic wheels ground slowly but inexorably toward her departure for Saigon, Claire and Ruslan discussed her impending move with increasing frequency. He, it turned out, was as apprehensive about her future as Dara and Roisin, not least because of its political consequences, and every time they met he would present her with a new list of challenging questions.

Couldn't Claire see that by serving in South Vietnam she was inevitably linking herself with the American aggressors?

But the Canadian program she was destined to serve was "one hundred percent humanitarian aid," she protested. She had been reassured on that score by Arsenault during their first interview. Canada was neutral and its aid efforts on the ground were totally independent of the U.S. war effort, Arsenault had said, though the Canadian aid team in Quang Ngai would be dependent on the Americans for logistical support—flights to and from Saigon, mail, food delivery, and so on.

The next time they met Ruslan had another question: Given the Canadian reliance on the Americans for air transport, what would she do if she found herself in one of the helicopters the GIs used to interrogate their Vietnamese captives? It had long since been authoritatively reported in *Pravda* and elsewhere that the Americans were not averse to throwing uncooperative guerrilla suspects out of airborne helicopters in an effort to get their fellow detainees to talk.

Well, Claire said, she just wouldn't accept a ride on any American helicopters.

The Vietnam adventure—or something like it—was, as she had written to Arsenault, a "particular dream, of many years standing." It was something for which she had been preparing and yearning, consciously or unconsciously, for thirty years, since her nursing-school days and the Spanish civil war. Ruslan's arguments, however well-intentioned, were not going to dissuade her now, any more than Dara and Roisin's worries about her safety. She only knew this was something she had to do, and by August, unbelievably, she received an offer of employment from External Aid. Still more incredible was the salary—$6,000 a year, plus an overseas allowance of $3,264—for a grand total of $9,264 for twelve months' work. In 1967 the figure represented a small fortune, and represented a 100 percent pay increase from what she had been earning at Julius's law office.

Late August found her attending to a myriad of details. She opened a bank account in Dara's name and left $500 with Ann Hartley as a backup, as well as post-dated cheques for a year's rent on their Sherbrooke Street apartment, which her younger daughter had decided to keep. And she agonized over the decision to leave Dara alone in Montreal. She was only sixteen, though she liked to act much older, but she had at least finished school and found work as a typist in the McGill math department. Claire would worry about her daughters throughout her stay in Vietnam but not half so much, as it turned out, as they would worry about her.

Finally, on September 22 Claire received the itinerary, complete with tickets, for her trip to Vietnam: Montreal to Vancouver, Vancouver to Hong Kong, Hong Kong to Saigon.

On September 30 Dara and her boyfriend Donny accompanied Claire on the early-morning cab ride to Dorval. So great was Dara's anxiety about the separation, and about her mother's fate, that she broke down completely as Claire stood in the check-in line, screaming hysterically for all the airport to hear.

But there was no turning back, nor could there be. Cathay Pacific flight 001 Y, which departed Dorval a few minutes late that morning for Vancouver, was to prove, in its way, as fateful as the trip Abe Eglin had sweated through in the streets of Montreal forty-nine years earlier as he struggled to get his Rose to the hospital on time.

Claire was nearly as anxiety ridden as Dara as the jet bumped its way, gathering speed, down the tarmac, until at last it was aloft, landing gear safely retracted, the western suburbs of her beloved Montreal visible above a dipping wing.

Apart from its policy, the Canadian government had just committed its worst mistake of the war in Vietnam.

CHAPTER SIX

In Country

If we can pacify Quang Ngai, we can pacify any province. In three or four years we may not have wiped out all the Charlies, but we will have cut him off from the people and restricted him to the mountains, where he'll be nothing more than a nuisance, like tigers—not a serious threat. Already, Quang Ngai is a bustling beehive of activity. Things are going well.
> —James May, Senior American Adviser
> in Quang Ngai, August 30, 1967[1]

A wave of heat and humidity hit Claire with almost physical force as she stepped down onto the broiling tarmac of Ton Son Hut airport outside Saigon. Once inside the terminal she was quickly swept up in the swirling confusion of what was, by the fall of 1967, one of the world's busiest airfields. Her passage through customs was routine, but bewilderment turned to annoyance when Claire realized that no one from the Canadian mission had come to meet her. She was in a strange country with no local currency. Her concern deepened after she tried to call the mission—the phone books were printed in Vietnamese, a language she could neither read nor speak. Fortunately, the members of a British aid delegation took her under their wing and drove her to their embassy in downtown Saigon. From there they telephoned the Canadian delegation, and four hours after her arrival in Vietnam she was finally met by an apologetic fellow countryman.

As they struggled to cram her luggage into a mini-cab, Gordon Longmuir, a member of Canada's delegation to the International Control Commission (ICC),[2] told Claire shamefacedly that plans for her arrival had gone completely awry. The mission staff had even failed to reserve a hotel room for her. As an interim measure Longmuir had booked her into the Continental-Palace Hotel in the heart of the city. It was one of Saigon's safest hotels, he assured her, because the owners paid taxes to both the South Vietnamese government and the National Liberation Front.

The Continental-Palace was a grand relic of Saigon's French colonial past, and Claire soon found herself ensconced in the largest hotel room she had ever seen. Longmuir, once again apologizing, had more or less dumped her there, explaining that he was off on an urgent tour of the countryside. Bathed in sweat—the tropical heat seemed to have opened every pore in her body—her head spinning from the strangeness and confusion of her chaotic arrival, Claire lay back on the bed and watched the slowly revolving blades of a ceiling fan. It seemed to be fighting a losing battle in its attempt to circulate the heavy, almost liquid, air. Her struggle against drowsiness was equally unavailing.

She awoke refreshed three or four hours later. After checking for messages at the desk (there were none; she felt truly abandoned), Claire began to take her bearings. The lobby of the Continental-Palace was crowded with well-groomed foreigners and Vietnamese; the hotel was obviously a social centre for the city's élite. Her attention was drawn especially to the local women. Impeccably dressed and coiffed, they seemed to glide over the lobby floor on their way to the hotel's outdoor terrace.

But the sidewalk outside revealed a different world altogether. The noise, the humidity, the dense throng of humanity—it was almost overpowering. The streets were jammed with tiny vehicles that seemed like toys: Vespas, Hondas, mini-cabs, all dangerously overloaded and yet darting through the crowded streets at alarming speed, their two-stroke engines whining with an ear-splitting racket. Claire couldn't help but notice the contrast between the poorly dressed, malnourished women she saw on the street and their elegant sisters only a few feet away inside the hotel lobby.

The clamour of commerce was everywhere about her. Impoverished street vendors hawked all manner of American consumer goods; so this was Saigon's notorious black market. American GIs stood out from the crowd, taller and beefier than the Vietnamese, often accompanied by a retinue of imprecating street children. Some of the Americans actually walked through the crush with their arms held at shoulder level to avoid having their rings and watches stripped from their fingers or wrists.

Claire watched with amusement as a GI haggled with a black marketeer over the price of a deck of playing cards. The vendor demanded three hundred piastres. But they were only forty piastres at the PX (the American canteen), the soldier remonstrated. The enterprising Vietnamese responded with a shrug. "So go buy them there."

"But there aren't any at the PX," the GI protested.

"I know," the street merchant replied. "They all here."

It was the sort of confrontation Claire would witness again and again in

this strange war that pitted a Third World country against the most powerful nation on earth. It was a mismatch, certainly; but the struggle was
anything but one-sided.

The Canadian delegation established contact the next morning, and for
the following several days Claire was given a tour of Saigon and through
one of the city's tuberculosis hospitals. Yet, fascinated as she was by life in
the South Vietnamese capital, Claire was eager to take up her posting in
Quang Ngai. On the eve of her departure Gordon Longmuir came to visit
Claire once again. They discussed the unfinished state of the Canadian TB
hospital in Quang Ngai, and the political and military situation there.
Longmuir had spent twenty-four hours in the area about six weeks earlier,
he told Claire, and had witnessed the extreme uncertainty of the war's
progress during a night-time raid. About two hundred National Liberation
Front guerrillas had paraded through the streets of Quang Ngai, and they
had liberated some twelve hundred political prisoners from the local
prison. The American military had basically retreated to barracks, and
South Vietnamese soldiers, members of the Army of the Republic of
Vietnam or ARVN, had gone to ground, quickly removing their uniforms.

The discussion turned to Dr. Vennema. Longmuir described Vennema's
support for the NLF as "naive," although it tended to guarantee the safety
of Canadian personnel in the area. But Vennema was scheduled for eventual rotation out of Vietnam, Claire noted. "What if his successor doesn't
feel the same way?" Her query hung in the air unanswered, but it was to
prove a most prescient question.

The fact was, Claire knew almost nothing about the place to which she
had been assigned, and she had no inkling that Quang Ngai was some of
the most embattled terrain on the planet. Quang Ngai City, the provincial
capital, is 540 kilometres by air northeast of Saigon, and 270 kilometres
south of the 17th parallel, the former dividing line between North and
South Vietnam. Shaped roughly like an inverted triangle, the province is
bordered to the east by the South China Sea and to the west by the
Annamite Mountains. Sandwiched between the mountains and the sea lies
a long, narrow strip of arable flatland eighty kilometres long and ten to
twenty-five kilometres wide. In the fall of 1967 an estimated seven hundred
thousand people lived in Quang Ngai province, 80 percent of them inhabit-
ing the ribbon of fertile coastland. With a concentration of more than 400
people per square kilometre, the area was one of the most densely popul-
ated rural regions on earth.[3]

Although poor peasants for the most part, the people of Quang Ngai
had a long history of rebellion and military prowess. The Nguyen dynasty,
which conquered and then ruled most of southern Vietnam for three
centuries, had its origins in Quang Ngai; when French colonialists

supplanted the Nguyen, the most aggressive armed resistance came from Quang Ngai. The province was also the scene of peasant uprisings in the 1930s; and when the Viet Minh, the predecessor of the NLF, was formed after the Second World War, Quang Ngai was a key centre of its activities. Pham Van Dong, one of North Vietnam's most senior Communist leaders (he would later become the prime minister of the unified Vietnam) was a native of Quang Ngai province, and the area had remained a stronghold of NLF support.[4]

The impoverished but intensely proud peasants of Quang Ngai were proving as intractable to the American and Saigonese military regime as they had been to the French. The NLF controlled most of the province, and in May 1965 the South Vietnamese government had contemplated abandoning Quang Ngai City to the guerrillas. Instead, the United States sent in the marines. The Third Marine Amphibious Force had secured the capital, at least during daylight hours, if not the surrounding countryside. But the military situation remained parlous enough that in the spring of 1967 U.S. commanders decided to step up their efforts to subjugate Quang Ngai. A combined American force composed of light and regular infantry and élite airborne troops was stationed in the province. Their mission was code-named Task Force Oregon.

Just six weeks before Claire's arrival in Saigon a young *New Yorker* reporter named Jonathan Schell had travelled to Quang Ngai to assess the impact of Task Force Oregon. Granted access to American military flights, Schell conducted his own aerial survey of the province, concluding that Quang Ngai's inhabitants were paying a terrible price for their resistance to rule by Saigon and Washington. He discovered to his horror that since the marines had begun their operations, 70 percent of the villages in the province had been destroyed. Roughly 70 percent of the houses in Quang Ngai province had also been razed, Schell estimated, creating an official refugee count of 138,000 people—or about one out of every five residents in the province. In the previous two years, a refugee official told Schell, about 40 percent of the province's total population had passed through refugee camps.[5]

What had been the military impact of such human carnage? Like Gordon Longmuir, Schell had been in Quang Ngai City on the night of August 30, when the NLF attacked. So complete had been their military domination of the city, Schell reported, that U.S. helicopters had been unable to lift off to return fire because mortar shells had zeroed in on the landing pad with pinpoint accuracy from the first moments of the attack.[6]

For thirty years, since the Spanish civil war, Claire Culhane had wanted to serve on the front lines of history, to alleviate human suffering, to somehow make a difference. She was about to get that chance in the crucible of Quang Ngai.

The Air America flight from Saigon to Quang Ngai was something of a milk run, she discovered, with stops at several other provincial capitals, including Nha Trang and Qui Nhon, along the way. Through the airplane window she marvelled at the greenness of the Vietnamese countryside, even more verdant, she thought, than Ireland. But even from the air the scars of war were unmistakable. Bomb craters were everywhere, and like countless other visitors to Vietnam Claire was staggered by their size and number. By war's end, twenty-six million craters would pockmark the country, displacing three billion cubic metres of soil.[7]

She was struck, too, by another form of environmental destruction caused by the war, and Claire would remark on it in her own reportage, long before the green movement became an international cause célèbre. Far below, running die-straight for miles at a stretch, a highway spanned the country—Highway One. To build it, she suddenly realized, the United States Army corps of engineers had bulldozed "buildings and jungles, sugar and rubber plantations, hamlets and villages, to matchstick rubble." What was more, the Americans had used herbicides to defoliate a strip four hundred metres wide on either side of the highway to safeguard military convoys from snipers.

"How is anything ever going to grow here again?" Claire later asked an American officer.

The reply voiced a sentiment she was to hear repeated many times over: "Who cares? We're going to make a parking lot out of this country before we leave." Nor was it an idle threat. In a defoliation campaign dubbed Operation Ranch Hand, the U.S. military forces would eventually spray more than seventy million litres of herbicide over 35 percent of South Vietnam.[8]

When the plane landed at Nha Trang Claire decided to disembark to make sure her own luggage wasn't inadvertently unloaded. She noticed two other Air America planes on the tarmac. They were identical to her own aircraft, but had the usual registration numbers and the words *Air America* painted on the fuselage and wings. The plane she was on had no identifying marks whatsoever. When she reboarded, Claire asked the pilot the reason for the omission. He laughed, and turned to his co-pilot. "Anyone can see she's new around here." Only later would she grasp the full significance of the pilot's derisive response. Air America, which was run by the CIA, specialized in carrying all manner of illicit cargo, especially drugs, throughout Southeast Asia. It was one of the worst-kept secrets of the war.

The flight crew of Claire's unmarked plane were simply following the old New York cabbie's adage: never signal an illegal turn.

North of Nha Trang they followed the coastline, kilometre after kilometre of white sandy beaches rippled by the azure waters of the South China Sea. The coast, Claire understood, offered her plane greater protection from snipers, but inland she could still see reminders of the war on the ground. Long plumes of smoke rose hundreds of metres into the still jungle air above hamlets that had recently been bombed or torched. As they neared Quang Ngai the pilot began a series of evasive manoeuvres designed to minimize their exposure to incoming enemy fire. Instead of taking a long, flat landing approach he corkscrewed the plane steeply downwards in a dizzying spiral, until they were on the ground at last, bumping over the dirt landing strip.

Claire had just deplaned when, to her surprise, she met Dr. Vennema, preparing to board for the return flight to Saigon. A six-man inspection team from Ottawa had just arrived in the capital, he explained hastily, and he was flying south to confer with them. Claire agreed with Vennema that it would have made more sense for her to simply remain in Saigon and take part in the meeting, and they both chalked it up as yet another example of poor planning by the Canadian mission staff.

The airstrip was a five-kilometre drive from the centre of Quang Ngai City, and Claire was keenly interested in this strange new place that was to be her home for the next twelve months. The countryside was just as verdant from the ground as it had looked from the air; rice paddies stretched away to the horizon, bordered by banana palm trees and thatch-roofed huts. Distant sugar cane plantations reminded her of fields of corn. It all looked peaceful enough, but at two sharp turns in the dusty road her driver pointed out "sniper's gulches," places where the high grass and encroaching trees provided excellent cover for Front sharpshooters. Just the week before, he told her, an American captain from the 101st Airborne Division had been killed by sniper fire while driving the same road.

They passed through a small market, crowded with women and children. The surrounding streets were lined with store-front homes, their roofs covered with corrugated tin or flattened Coke and Pepsi signs, "indications that the Americans were not too far away, and [that they] had already made their contribution to the living standards of the local population," Claire noted drily. In many of the store fronts she could see young women bent over whirring sewing machines. The road forked; to the left stood the Canadian hospital, gleaming in the hot sun. The finest building in all of Quang Ngai City, it was a brand-new, two-storey structure clad in whitewashed stucco and set well back from the road. Although it had by

CLAIRE CULHANE

The motto in her high school yearbook said, presciently, that she would be "a helper to Atlas," the mythic Greek hero who was said to carry the world upon his shoulders.

Kayla the "gymnast," at age seven. Though she was small for her age, she later excelled in sports, especially tennis and basketball.

In April 1936 Claire proudly shows off the new uniform of first-year students at the Ottawa Civic Hospital School of Nursing.

A wave of strikes swept across Canada after the Second World War. Here Claire is helping out during the Seamen's Union Strike in Vancouver. Claire and Garry were both active in the Shipyard trade union movement in the 1940s.

Two of the most important influences on Claire's developing political convictions were Thérèse Casgrain, the tireless suffragette and humanist in Quebec (who once helped Claire prepare a high school oration), and Hanna Sheehy-Skeffington (one of Garry's aunts), a feminist, Irish nationalist, and independent thinker.

At Lachine, Quebec, in 1940, Claire reads her leather-bound volume of the speeches of La Pasionaria, one of the leaders of the Republican cause, and another of Claire's idols.

A still happy Garry and Claire (with Roisin, then two years old) in 1948.

Roisin (ten) and Dara (four) with a more sombre Claire after their first ''flight'' from Garry and Vancouver, in 1955.

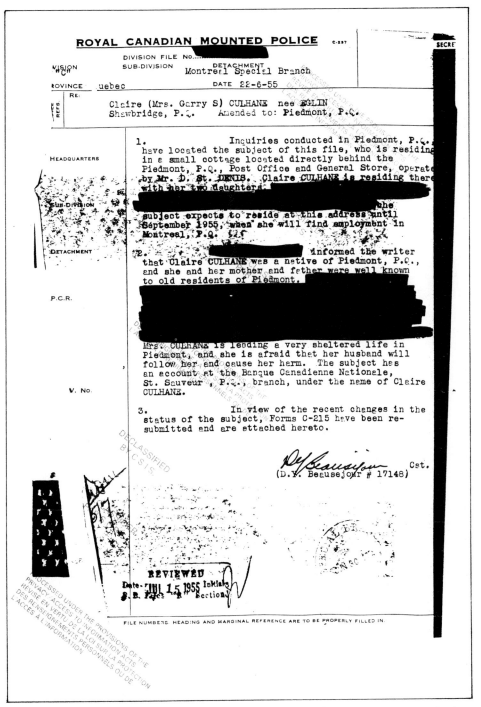

ROYAL CANADIAN MOUNTED POLICE

C-237

DIVISION "C"	SUB-DIVISION	DETACHMENT Montreal Special Branch
PROVINCE uebec		DATE 22-6-55

RE: Claire (Mrs. Garry S) CULHANE nee EGLIN
Shawbridge, P.Q. Amended to: Piedmont, P.Q.

HEADQUARTERS

1. Inquiries conducted in Piedmont, P.Q.
have located the subject of this file, who is residing
in a small cottage located directly behind the
Piedmont, P.Q., Post Office and General Store, operate
by Mr. D. St. DENIS. Claire CULHANE is residing there
with her two daughters.

SUB-DIVISION

subject expects to reside at this address until
September 1955, when she will find employment in
Montreal, P.Q.

DETACHMENT

2. informed the writer
that Claire CULHANE was a native of Piedmont, P.Q.,
and she and her mother and father were well known
to old residents of Piedmont.

P.C.R.

Mrs. CULHANE is leading a very sheltered life in
Piedmont, and she is afraid that her husband will
follow her and cause her harm. The subject has
an account at the Banque Canadienne Nationale,
St. Sauveur, P.Q., branch, under the name of Claire
CULHANE.

V. No.

3. In view of the recent changes in the
status of the subject, Forms C-215 have been re-
submitted and are attached hereto.

(D.Y. Beausejour # 17148) Cst.

REVIEWED
Date JUL 15 1955 Initials
S.B. Files Section

FILE NUMBERS, HEADING AND MARGINAL REFERENCE ARE TO BE PROPERLY FILLED IN.

A heavily censored memo shows that the RCMP special intelligence branch had tracked Claire to the town of Piedmont, Quebec, after she had left her husband. Their specious ''intelligence'' spans almost fifty years of her life.

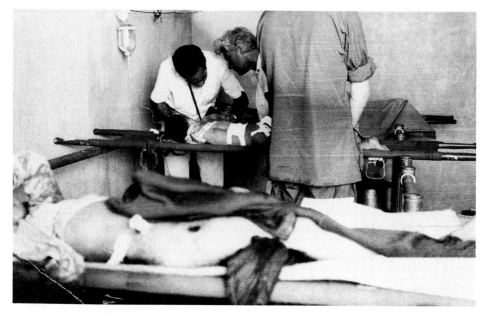

During the Tet Offensive in February 1968, Claire assists Dr. Vennema in emergency surgery at the Quang Ngai Provincial Hospital. The blood was ''splashing on my shoes,'' she would later write.

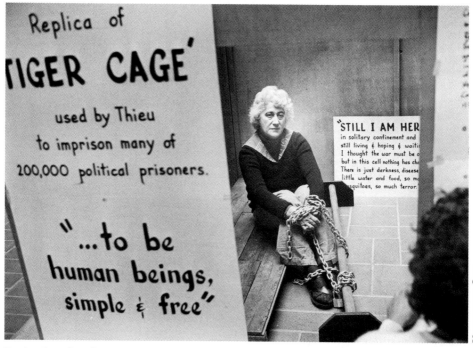

During her first fast on Parliament Hill in 1968, Claire engaged hundreds of passersby, as well as many MPs and several cabinet ministers, in debate on Canada's complicity in Vietnam.

For four years, until it was finally published by a commercial publisher as a full book in 1972, Claire fought to have her critique of Canada's Vietnam policy made public. That same year she joined other anti-war demonstrators to protest U.S. President Nixon's visit to Ottawa.

Four generations together, summer 1992: (front, from left) Dara, Claire, Maura beside her mother, Roisin. (Back row) Roisin's other children, Triona (far left) and Bob (far right), with Dara's children, Lori and Carey, holding Maura's son James.

now absorbed $500,000, the hospital was still of little use to anyone: essential X-ray equipment had yet to arrive.

Minutes later they arrived at their destination, the Canadian House. Unlike most of the other prominent residences she had been shown, that of the provincial chief or of James May, a U.S. Aid official and the chief's principal adviser, the Canadian residence was completely unprotected. This policy, Claire soon learned, was similar to the one adopted by the Quaker mission just down the road: "No guards, no walls, no guns." Most other foreign houses were like fortresses, with high concrete walls, sandbags, barbed wire, and armed guards. Later, Claire would meet many a visiting GI who confessed that he felt safer sitting on the open Canadian patio than he did in the heavily fortified American military compound, which was often the target of incoming NLF mortar rounds fired with deadly accuracy.

Claire was introduced to the other members of the Canadian mission: Dr. Yvon Dupuis, like herself newly arrived from Canada; Dr. Mathias Jerema, a distinguished-looking Polish-Canadian; two young male nurses from Quebec City, Florent and Clement; and the Vietnamese staff: Ba Tao, the housekeeper, a widow with four children; Xuong, the male cook; and Tri, the handyman-gardener. Two other nurses, Louise Piché and Pauline Trudel, were away on holidays.

She was kept awake that first night in Quang Ngai by a host of unfamiliar sounds and smells. Flares lit the sky, amidst the steady thumping of incoming 81 and 60 mm mortar shells; this favoured field artillery of the guerrillas disoriented the local dogs and roosters, who barked and crowed through the night. The air was suffused with the smell of mildew from the damp room, and of vegetables growing in the garden just outside her window. She watched little lizards climb the walls and cross the ceiling, wondering idly if they could remain suspended without falling into bed with her. She thought of Dara in Montreal and Roisin in Vancouver. And then, despite the strangeness of this place half a world from home, she fell asleep.

Claire's first duties in Quang Ngai were to prepare for the opening of the Canadian hospital, conduct an inventory of equipment and supplies, teach English to the Vietnamese staff, administer the hospital's $30,000 monthly budget, and to assist Dr. Vennema in the writing of a final report before his imminent departure. In the absence of the X-ray equipment, however, she spent much of her time volunteering in the provincial hospital located about two kilometres from the Canadian hospital. Claire's years of experience in Canadian and Irish hospitals had done little to prepare her for the horrors of Quang Ngai Provincial Hospital, where conditions were almost inconceivable to a Western practitioner.

The plague of war compounded the curse of poverty, malnutrition, and severe overcrowding. On any given day the four-hundred-bed institution held seven hundred patients, most of them crammed two to a bed seventy-four centimetres wide and less than two metres long. Due to a lack of nurses' aides it fell to family members to care for their ailing relatives, and since they had often walked from distant villages they simply curled up and slept on the floor. Wards containing twenty beds often housed as many as 150 people. Sanitary facilities were rudimentary, and patients (at least those who were ambulatory) and visitors alike relieved themselves outside the perimeter of the ten-building hospital compound.[9]

There were only seven doctors in the whole province of Quang Ngai, or one physician for every 100,000 people.[10] But even this appalling ratio was a misrepresentation. One of the doctors was an Australian missionary who worked primarily with the Montagnard tribespeople in the mountains. Five of the physicians were Vietnamese who charged the sick extortionate fees, and who had little concern for the rural population. Dr. Vennema, therefore, reckoned that he was the only doctor for some 650,000 people. Vennema had long since come to despise his Vietnamese colleagues, who were "busy draining the peasant of his few pennies. It is commonplace for a peasant to spend his life savings in a week on a doctor who does not touch him for he 'stinks.' One visit to a doctor costs the peasant between 500 and 1,000 piastres," or a significant fraction of the average peasant family's 20,000-piastre ($400 Canadian) annual income.[11]

Claire was no stranger to the suffering common to all hospital wards, but she had to steel herself for the charnel house that was the provincial hospital. On the pediatrics ward she watched as children "convulsed and died every day and night when their malnourished little bodies could no longer combat the accumulation of diseases and wounds." On the medical ward she despaired for an eleven-year-old boy "with abnormal blood count, suffering from severe dysentery, [who] used to disappear every weekend to walk fourteen kilometres home to care for his orphaned sister until he could leave her with the neighbours on Sunday night, to return to his bed Monday morning." In the operating room patients were "lifted from blood-soaked litters, still covered with dirt and mud and placed on the operating table for surgery without first being washed" because there was no running water.[12]

New patients presented her with a litany of Third World medical problems—tuberculosis, hookworm, severe anemia, polio, chronic malaria, encephalitis, cholera, and even bubonic plague—in addition to more universal ailments: diphtheria, rheumatoid arthritis, hypertension, influenza, asthma, peptic ulcers, and leukemia. It was all too much for some of the Canadians. Dr. Dupuis who, like Claire, had signed on for twelve months in Quang Ngai, took one look at conditions in the provincial hospital and refused to work there. "I came here as a doctor, not as a missionary," he declared. He remained the minimum three months necessary to receive paid air fare home and promptly returned to Canada.[13] The more Claire saw of the horrors of Quang Ngai Provincial, the more she came to admire Dr. Vennema.

The young Canadian, whose accented English still betrayed traces of his Dutch roots, had been in charge of the provincial hospital since March 1964. Nearly three decades after his graduation from McGill Medical School in 1962, Vennema would recall his life's ambition: "I went to medical school primarily for one purpose. I was not interested in making money. I was interested in being of service to mankind." While serving a one-year stint in Newfoundland Vennema happened across the writings of Dr. Tom Dooley, the legendary American practitioner of jungle medicine. Dooley had died two years earlier, but his example of bringing Western medicine to far-off Indochina inspired Vennema, who contacted CARE-Medico, the American organization that was continuing Dooley's work. Vennema volunteered his services and CARE-Medico assigned him to Kratie, one of two field hospitals in Cambodia founded by Dooley. There was much the idealistic young Canadian doctor did not know: that Dooley had long been a cat's-paw for U.S. intelligence interests in Southeast Asia and that he had collaborated closely with the CIA; that Western aid to the Third World is rarely so altruistic or disinterested as it seems; and that that aid is often intextricably intertwined with foreign policy and the hidden political, economic, military, and intelligence agendas of the donor country. Like Vennema, Claire too would learn these lessons the hard way.

Vennema's first introduction to *realpolitik* came after he had quit his job in Newfoundland and was preparing to depart for Cambodia. CARE-Medico called from New York and abruptly altered his itinerary. Kratie, owing to a deterioration in U.S.-Cambodia relations, was off. Would he accept an alternative posting to a provincial hospital in South Vietnam? "I was aware that there was a war going on and that there were things happening, but I did not know much of the ramifications."

Within months of his arrival, the thirty-one-year-old Vennema found himself in charge of a small CARE-Medico team in Quang Ngai at the provincial hospital, which then had only 250 beds. But just two months later, following the Gulf of Tonkin incident in August 1964, the level of military action rose significantly and CARE-Medico informed Vennema that it was closing the Quang Ngai project because they could no longer guarantee his safety.

The Canadian doctor refused to leave. Instead, during one of his periodic visits to Saigon Vennema approached a member of Canada's delegation on the International Control Commission. Would Canada be interested in sponsoring his work in Quang Ngai under the Colombo Foreign Aid Plan? Unbeknownst to Vennema, his request for support from the Canadian government was most timely because Ottawa was under increasing pressure from Washington to step up Canadian involvement in Vietnam. A Canadian troop commitment was out of the question, Prime Minister Lester Pearson had already told U.S. President Lyndon Johnson, not least because of Canada's role on the ICC. Then how about military aid or a military field hospital? U.S. Secretary of State Dean Rusk asked Canadian External Affairs Minister Paul Martin, Sr. But Martin told Rusk that Canada could not supply military equipment or a medical team for military use.[14]

Perhaps because of American pressure on Ottawa, Vennema's request for Canadian aid fell on receptive ears, and by March 1965 Canada agreed to support Vennema's work in South Vietnam's most embattled province. Vennema's star began to rise steadily, both in country and in Saigon. Under his tutelage the provincial hospital expanded from the original 250 beds to more than 400. Far from becoming a target for assassination, he won the respect of all sides in the fighting because of his physical courage and obvious dedication, and because of his willingness to treat Front captives in Quang Ngai's provincial jail as well as civilian casualties of war.

In Saigon, Ottawa, and Washington, officialdom, too, began to take notice of this intrepid Canadian doctor who had stubbornly refused to abandon his patients. Vennema established a good working relationship with South Vietnam's health ministry, and he was even summoned to a meeting in Saigon with American ambassador Henry Cabot Lodge, Dr. Howard Rusk of the World Rehabilitation Fund, and Howard Schwartz, the U.S. under secretary of state for refugees. The purpose of the meeting was to determine what could be done for civilian war casualties. The first American combat troops had landed at Da Nang on March 8, 1965, and by the end of the year nearly two hundred thousand Americans had joined the conflict in Vietnam. As the war widened, the number of non-combatants killed and maimed in the fighting was increasing alarmingly, Vennema told the American officials.

One of the Canadian doctor's worst experiences of the war had occurred in late May and early June 1965. On the morning of Saturday, May 29, Vennema had been driving northeast of Quang Ngai City when a bus driver heading south had warned him not to proceed any farther "because you will end up in a scene of battle." Earlier that morning, Vennema soon learned, the ARVN outpost at Ba Gia, about five kilometres northeast of

Quang Ngai, had come under heavy attack from NLF forces operating at regimental strength. The fighting intensified throughout the day, until it had become the largest set-piece battle of the war to date. A battalion of ARVN Rangers had been airlifted to Ba Gia in an attempt to relieve the beleaguered garrison. The Thirty-Ninth Rangers included a three-man team of U.S. advisers, and Vennema had had dinner with one of them, Captain Christopher O'Sullivan, the night before the attack on Ba Gia began. The young American officer had been eager to test his élite Ranger battalion in battle.

On Sunday morning Vennema conducted his routine hospital rounds before driving out to the airstrip. From there he could see the air war in progress over Ba Gia. He watched American and ARVN aircraft conduct incessant bombing, napalm, and strafing runs over the besieged outpost. There were still few casualties arriving at the hospital, but that night Vennema received word that the Thirty-Ninth Rangers had been annihilated earlier in the day. The last contact with the ARVN forces had been with U.S. Marine Corps Staff Sergeant Willie Tyrone, who reported that Captain O'Sullivan had been killed. Sergeant Tyrone would himself die at Ba Gia a few hours later.

On Monday the bodies of the Thirty-Ninth began to arrive at the hospital by chopper and truck. Vennema counted up to 250 corpses "and then I stopped counting." The hospital was soon filled with women and children who had come to identify, and then to mourn over, the bodies of their husbands, fathers, and sons. The flow of military casualties stopped only after the provincial government forbade further transport of the war dead to the hospital for fear of panicking the local population. Late Monday the first civilian casualties of the battle started to trickle in, five and ten at a time. But the next day they began to arrive by the hundreds. Vennema had already seen a great deal during his fourteen months in Quang Ngai, but this was different. The most striking thing about the civilian casualties were the napalm victims.

The effects of this American weapon of war were almost too horrible to contemplate. At ground zero a 250-pound napalm bomb generated a temperature of 2,000° C, incinerating everything within a fifty-metre radius. The combustion created carbon monoxide which radiated outward for another fifty metres; anyone breathing within this radius died of suffocation. Anyone within a further fifty metres sustained third-degree burns and severe deformities. The patients who were now streaming into Quang Ngai Provincial were residents of Ba Gia and the surrounding area, victims of the air strikes Vennema had watched from the airstrip on Sunday morning. There was little he could do for the worst napalm casualties; the Vietnamese staff seemed reluctant to treat them, and in many cases their burns were simply too severe for Vennema's rudimentary facilities. He lost two hundred patients within twenty-four hours. Many of these fatalities were the first of the roughly 2,200 napalm burn victims Vennema would treat in his four and a half years in Vietnam. The battle of Ba Gia was the sort of experience endured by few doctors in a lifetime; within a month Vennema's hair had turned prematurely grey. He was just thirty-two.[15]

After Ba Gia and Vennema's meeting with Ambassador Lodge, the Canadian government soon came calling, in the form of a two-man delegation from External Affairs, who flew to Quang Ngai to see Vennema's work. Next Vennema was invited to Ottawa, where he met with External Affairs Minister Martin and with Maurice Strong, the newly appointed director-general of Canada's External Aid Office. The Canadians, like the Americans, wanted to "rehabilitate" Vietnam's shattered citizenry, precisely as Vennema was already doing. Had he any ideas? Vennema took the opportunity to pitch a pet project. Tuberculosis was one of the most widespread fatal diseases he treated in Quang Ngai. He had already set aside a ward for his TB patients, but it would be far better to isolate them altogether, in tandem with a mobile treatment unit that could rove the rural areas of the province, making early diagnoses and preventing the disease in the first place. Such a program was well within Ottawa's scope and budget, and it promised to have a lasting impact on the province, in a way that the day-to-day Band-Aid approach of treating war victims never could. To External it had the added benefit of appearing to be totally unrelated to the war. A TB program would appease the Americans by showing the Canadian flag in a strategic military area. Martin and Strong signed on; they agreed to build and equip a TB hospital in Quang Ngai.

∗ ∗ ∗

Claire learned all of this background in bits and pieces after Vennema returned from Saigon. As she watched Vennema's work in the crowded wards of the provincial hospital by day and listened to his stories by night, Claire's respect for him deepened immeasurably. He seemed the very embodiment of what a physician should be: tireless, courageous, and compassionate. He delivered babies and conducted surgery in operating rooms without running water, often without electricity; sterile technique was out of the question. The operating rooms were totally open to the curious, and to chickens, cats, and dogs. The underfed canines could smell a delivery from afar and they often appeared in the hope they could make a meal of the placenta. Vennema tolerated these conditions over which he had no control. But he had come to despise the war.

There had been no more huge catastrophes since Ba Gia, just a steady increase in the daily inflow of civilian casualties. As Task Force Oregon progressed and the Americans escalated their attempts to "pacify" Quang Ngai, the toll on the rural population grew apace. War injuries had come to represent the greatest cause of death among the young, accounting for nearly 50 percent of fatalities for children under the age of fifteen. In 1965 2,110 war casualties had been admitted to the provincial hospital; in 1966 that number had risen to 3,952; and by the end of 1967 the total would reach 5,219.[16]

By the end of October 1967 the long-awaited X-ray equipment still had not arrived, so Claire settled into the routine of work at the provincial hospital. She had obtained a bicycle, which she rode each day from the Canadian House to work. Already she caught herself hoping that each new day might bring some improvement to the conditions she would find when she reached the hospital. Instead, new horrors awaited. She was learning to match the convoys of young Americans passing through town, waving and scattering coins to the children, to the atrocities she saw the following day in the emergency ward. The soldiers were headed for the countryside to carry out search-and-destroy missions. But this, as Vennema had known since Ba Gia, was no ordinary war. There was evil afoot in the jungles, hamlets, and rice paddies of Quang Ngai. Words—genocide, butchery, barbarism—could never fully convey what Claire saw on the emergency ward. It was evil, malignant, and profound.

A GI had hinted darkly to Jonathan Schell about American conduct in the field in Quang Ngai several months before.

"You wouldn't believe the things that go on in this war," the combat veteran had suddenly blurted out.

"What things?"

"You wouldn't believe it."

"What kind of things, then?"

"You wouldn't believe it, so I'm not going to tell you. No one's ever going to find out about some things, and after this war is over, and we've all gone home, no one is ever going to know."

The observation that "they wouldn't believe it back home" was made to him almost daily in Quang Ngai, Schell reported.[17]

But Claire believed it. She saw the meaning of the war every day on the emergency ward. She helped lift a baby out of a pool of its own blood when it was brought in for treatment. She saw a young girl with her breasts sliced off and a broken bottle rammed up her vagina. She would never forget the child with a hole in its back large enough to put one's fist into, or the dead mother with an infant still suckling at her breast, or an old man with only the top of his face left. She would later term them "unreported, daily mini-massacres. How else to describe 'patients' who had had soapy water and urine forced down their throats and electricity applied to their genitals?"[18]

A first-time visit to Quang Ngai's surgical wards produced a visceral reaction. In August a reporter for the Toronto *Globe and Mail* had accompanied Vennema on his rounds and he was grateful that he was there at night. "The raw, gaping wounds of the Vietnam war, as Dr. Vennema cut away the bandages and soothed shattered men, women, and children, were not unbearable in the low light."[19] Two months later Claire spotted a GI standing on a ward, a horrified expression on his face. She asked him whether he was a new medic assigned to the ward.

"No, I'm a photographer from the air force, but my God, I never thought it was like this," he replied.

Soon afterwards she saw him leaning weakly against the side of the building, vomiting.[20]

But life in Quang Ngai also had its brighter moments. As terrible as the war was, it was, ironically, the Vietnamese themselves who helped Claire overcome the grief and revulsion she felt anew each day at the provincial hospital. If her work there was the low point of her quotidian routine, the high point was her daily language lessons for the Vietnamese student nurses. One of Claire's official duties was to teach them English, and in the process she in turn soon gained a smattering of Vietnamese, particularly from two pupils: Huong, tall, hot tempered, and impetuous; and Kim Nhung, a young war widow with four children.

Claire was at considerable pains to distance herself from the Americans, and the first thing she had the students teach her to say in Vietnamese was "*Toi la nguoi Gia-Na-Dai, Toi khong phai la nguoi My*," meaning "I am a Canadian, I am not an American." Claire also (naively, as she would later realize) took every opportunity to express her own disgust with the endless American bombing, partly to make her own position clear and partly to win the confidence of her Vietnamese co-workers. But her protestations were met only with impassivity. Months after, she came to understand that such guardedness was well-advised in this combat zone where power changed hands with the rising and setting of the sun.

As the weeks passed Claire developed a deepening affection for the Vietnamese with whom she worked on a daily basis. There was not one of these slender, graceful, almost delicate people who had not been touched personally by the tragedy of decades of war, and yet somehow their determination, dignity, and even humour remained largely intact. They were warm and physically demonstrative and they delighted in touching, embracing, or holding hands.

On Sundays when the Vietnamese cook had the day off the Canadian aid workers would take turns preparing meals and it fell to Claire to continue a time-honoured routine—making French pancakes for break-fast. The only difference in the procedure in Quang Ngai was that Claire had to carefully sift the flour three times to remove all the bugs and dirt. Extras were distributed to the neighbourhood children who quickly became as addicted to the sweet pancakes as Roisin and Dara had ever been.

Claire had become especially fond of a young Vietnamese patient who had arrived some weeks before by helicopter with half his chest blown away. Miraculously, he survived, and Claire and the boy became fast friends. She badly wanted to take some of her crêpes to him, but felt guilty that she hadn't enough for everyone else on the crowded ward. As it turned out, she needn't have worried. To her surprise a look of delight lit every face in the room as she tried to slip the boy her two pancakes. Far from feeling embarrassed for showing favouritism, Claire was able to share in the sense of compassion and pleasure that these people so clearly had for one another.

Claire soon developed a friendship with Ba Tao, the housekeeper at the Canadian residence. One of Ba's duties was laundering and ironing the clothes of the Canadian staff, and Claire soon distinguished herself in Ba's eyes because she alone among the *Na Dais* insisted on washing and ironing her own clothes. Besides Ba's delight in finding a Canadian who didn't feel that doing her own laundry was somehow beneath her, Ba was also pleased when Claire offered her the use of the transistor radio she'd bought in Hong Kong. Ba loved to listen to it while performing the tiresome chore of ironing. Claire herself was developing an ear for Vietnamese music, and she often played the radio when she was alone in her bedroom. On more than one occasion Ba would suddenly rush into the room and switch it off. Only later did Claire come to understand why: she had been listening to Radio Hanoi and Ba feared that it might be overheard, and create problems for herself or the other Vietnamese in the household.

The whole concept of a Vietnamese "staff" doing the menial work for a group of North Americans ran strongly counter to Claire's egalitarian grain, as did the patronizing attitudes that inevitably attended such a relationship. Never forgetting her own experiences as a girl in an Orthodox patriarchy or a Jew in a strongly anti-Semitic environment, Claire gravita-ted naturally toward the underdog, the powerless, the oppressed. Nor was she above a bit of larceny when it came to more evenly balancing the scales between the weak and the strong.

Claire and Ba would begin each day by unlocking the supply cup-board. (The Vietnamese staff, Claire's compatriots insisted against her own arguments, couldn't be trusted not to steal supplies.) As soon as they had taken stock and withdrawn the day's rations, and after checking to make sure the coast was clear, Claire and Ba, giggling like errant school-girls, would load Ba's personal basket with all the canned food and other goodies it could hold. Ba, Claire had learned, was a widow and the mother of four small children. They surmounted the language barrier by using Claire's Vietnamese-English dictionary. Claire would make her meaning clear by using the English-to-Vietnamese side to find the right words, and Ba would answer by locating her response in the Vietnamese-to-English section. Their rapport was so complete that one would often understand the other even before all of the words had been translated, and these halting conversations were invariably punctuated with the universal language of laughter.

As Claire had the opportunity to study the Vietnamese she began to grasp how it was that such a poor and, by Western standards, "backward" nation could fight the most powerful industrial country in the world to a standstill. One of the secrets was the astonishing resourcefulness of the Vietnamese people. She saw countless illustrations of their abilities to improvise, but several stood out as metaphors for the differing approaches of the two sides in the war. One was a traffic accident she happened to witness while looking out the window of the Canadian House. Two U.S. military jeeps had side-swiped one another on the badly potholed road out front, and a Vietnamese cyclist had been caught in the middle and was pinned between the vehicles. He was still alive, but he was badly shaken. The American drivers were still in their seats and they seemed totally bewildered. They looked around as if wondering how they could call the American Automobile Association for a towtruck. Instead dozens of Viet-namese immediately poured out of their houses and quickly converged on the vehicle. Working together, they put their shoulders to one jeep and moved it just enough to free the trapped man. It all happened within a few minutes—problem solved.

On another occasion when she was on a foray into the countryside, Claire happened across a U.S. military convoy backed up at a river crossing where the bridge had been blown up by one side or the other. While the Americans, hamstrung by their own complex military technology, waited for still more technology to solve their problems, the Vietnamese civilians on the road were transporting their simpler, lighter goods to the other side. A group of men had managed to salvage a few planks from the old bridge and they stood in the water as human pylons, the planks spanning from shoulder to shoulder. The women and children loaded their baggage on bicycles, and were ferrying their belongings across the crude bridge.

Claire soon became a student of Vietnamese history, and she was partic-ularly impressed by the character of the North Vietnamese leadership—especially Ho Chi Minh and General Vo Nguyen Giap. After his release from prison in China in the early 1940s Ho had returned to his native Vietnam to find Giap drilling a rag-tag military force of twenty-four men, equipped only with wooden rifles. When Ho asked Giap what he was doing the future master strategist of the Vietnam war replied that he was founding an army to drive first the Japanese and then the French out of their homeland.

"But do they know what they're fighting for?" Ho asked Giap.

"To drive the foreigners out of Vietnam."

But Ho, who had read and travelled widely as a young man, demurred. They must understand imperialism, he told Giap gently. They must know that their country is a colony. Then they will know what they are fighting for. He pursuaded Giap to disband his "army" and to turn his energies into politically educating the Vietnamese people. Ten years later, in 1954, Giap stunned the world at the battle of Dien Bien Phu, where his forces encircled and then besieged a force of thousands of French troops near the Laotian border. The French were trapped in a valley surrounded by hills, having abandoned the high ground in the belief that Giap's Viet Minh forces could never bring enough firepower to bear to dislodge them. But they had failed to reckon with the ingenuity of the Vietnamese. The Viet Minh had disassembled their howitzers and carried the heavy field guns piece by piece through the rugged mountains. Once reassembled on the hilltops they turned the valley of Dien Bien Phu into "hell in a very small place," in the words of Vietnam scholar Bernard Fall. The French garrison was forced to surrender and, soon after, France withdrew from its Southeast Asian colony.

The lessons of Vietnamese history and the examples of the Vietnamese people had a profound impact on Claire, inspiring and informing her own practice, and giving rise to what she would later describe as her "grass roots" approach to Canadian political problems.

If the war in Quang Ngai brought out the best in the Vietnamese character, it seemed to do the opposite for the Americans. Claire had, from the outset, resolved to maintain an arm's-length relationship with United States military and aid officials in the provincial capital by holding her own fraternization with them to an absolute minimum. But it was proving to be a difficult resolution to honour. Americans were frequent visitors at the Canadian residence, and on many evenings a GI would poke his head into Claire's room and, in friendly, bluff American fashion, invite her to join him for a drink on the patio. Claire would be busily typing up hospital business or writing letters home, hoping he would take the hint, but finally she had to admit to herself that it was going to be an awfully long year with her sitting there all alone. Gradually she let herself take part in the ongoing socialization between the Canadian staff and their American cousins, and the experience yielded valuable, if disturbing, insights into the attitudes of the average American soldier.

Much of what she heard was doubtless common to all wars—discussions of sex, and why Vietnamese women allegedly preferred Americans, and macho boasts about military prowess. Whenever she could, Claire would steer the conversation in a political direction, using the disarming opening, "How come you're here? Are you a draftee or a career soldier?"

"To keep the Communists from landing on the beaches of San Diego," was the most frequent reply. (It was always San Diego, and she later learned from an American major that such rhetoric was an important part of boot-camp indoctrination for Vietnam-bound recruits. But why San Diego? she asked the officer, who groaned and said, "Damn it, I told them to change that record.")

But if they really wanted to kill Communists, she'd suggest, why not go after them in Russia or China? "There are lots of them there. Why not pick on ones your own size? The people here in Quang Ngai don't even know what the word 'communism' means."

One of the most striking things about these young Americans was their genuine ignorance of the people they'd come to "protect" from commu-nism. "These Orientals don't put the same value on human life that we do," was a commonly repeated American sentiment in Quang Ngai, as it was throughout the United States at the time. One night Claire heard a GI observe that Vietnamese mothers didn't care about their own children, because they tried to leave them behind when they were being evacuated. How had he reached that conclusion, Claire wondered aloud.

"Saw it with my own eyes," he answered. "The other day a woman hopped up on the chopper after setting her baby down on the ground. When I picked it up and handed it to her, she shouted and pointed to the ground and wouldn't accept the baby from me." What the GI did not know was that in Vietnam it was considered bad luck to carry a baby across a threshold. Instead, the mother sets her baby down, steps across, and then reaches back to pick it up, all in one swift motion.

"You can't help these dinks," Claire heard another soldier insist. "They like to live like pigs in hovels, and even when you build them new houses, they won't live in them." But local custom had it that married women must live in houses with cottage-style thatched roofs. The American-built houses had lean-to style sloping roofs, and since most of the women were married they refused to move into them.[21]

Ignorance led to misunderstanding, which in turn bred racism, and then genocide. The Vietnamese were called "gooks," "dinks," or "slopes." Once the adversary had been thus devalued in language, it was easier to kill, maim, and defoliate without remorse, and there was no doubt that the dehumanization in language reflected real events in the field. The coarse boasting of men in groups degenerated easily into obscenity, and then atrocity. "Only you can prevent forests," she heard the GIs say with a laugh. The remark, a variation on the U.S. Forest Service's warning about forest fires, was the slogan of Operation Ranch Hand. "Death is our business, and business is good," was another common GI motto. "I got ten points extra today," boasted an American soldier lounging one evening on the patio. "I lit up a pregnant woman." He grinned between sips of his drink.

One Sunday afternoon an otherwise pleasant GI came to the Canadian House to see if anyone wanted to go on a "turkey shoot" with him. He'd obtained a chopper for a few hours and was eager to find a peasant working his rice field. Once flushed, he would pursue his fleeing quarry with the helicopter, spraying the defenceless peasant with machine-gun fire. "More fun than duck hunting," he assured the Canadians.[22]

These attitudes permeated the entire U.S. command structure in Vietnam. One battalion commander named his helicopter the "Gookmobile," and displayed his kills on the fuselage with a neatly painted row of conical peasants' hats. An American general dubbed his helicopter the "Slopetoter." The Eleventh Armoured Cavalry Regiment, headquartered just south of Quang Ngai, was led by Colonel George S. Patton III, son of the Second World War hero. "Find the bastards and pile on," was the motto of the Eleventh Armoured. "I do like to see the arms and legs fly," Patton would remind his men before sending them into combat. In 1968 Colonel Patton sent special Christmas cards to his friends. "From Colonel and Mrs. George S. Patton III—Peace on Earth," they read. Attached was a colour photograph of dismembered Front soldiers stacked in a neat pile. Despite the fact that a U.S. congressman had read of Patton's deportment and wrote his superiors to complain, the Pentagon promoted him to brigadier general, making him one of the youngest officers to attain that rank.[23]

Twenty-five years later, when the battle over "political correctness"— the notion that North American university curricula overvalued the experience of European males to the exclusion of other cultures, races, and women—raged across campuses and in the news media, Claire would sometimes reflect on American behaviour in Vietnam. The architects of U.S. policy there, the men ultimately in charge, were considered the best and the brightest of their nation. Robert McNamara, Dean Rusk, William and McGeorge Bundy, these appointees of John Kennedy were Ivy Leaguers and Rhodes scholars, and it was said that President Johnson, with his mere teacher's degree from West Texas State Teacher's College, deferred to them, was even intimidated by their intellects.[24] Critics of "political correctness" argue the ineffable superiority of the white European male intellectual tradition. Yet just as their foot soldiers knew nothing of the ways of the Vietnamese peasant, these men, the finest flower of America's Eurocentred academe, knew little of Ho Chi Minh's history, motivation, or methods. And as a result, Claire couldn't help thinking, they had visited ruination upon Vietnam, upon their own nation, and upon themselves. In the end, they never knew what hit them.

*   *   *

Early November brought the monsoon rains to Quang Ngai, but not the X-ray equipment. The members of the Canadian medical team seethed at the delay, none more than Alje Vennema, whose three and a half years in country were nearing an end. The agonizing wait for the essential equipment was just the latest frustration in the short but problem-filled history of the Canadian Anti-Tuberculosis Hospital Quang Ngai, and in letters to Ottawa Vennema raged against External Affairs and External Aid: they had no idea what it was like to practise medicine in a combat zone, nor had the Canadian representatives to the ICC. The latter spent most of their time in Saigon, which "is like heaven compared to the rest of Vietnam."[25]

On November 2 Claire received a pro forma letter from External Affairs Minister Paul Martin welcoming her aboard the Canadian aid team in Vietnam, and she immediately seized the opportunity afforded by Martin's opening to join Vennema's letter-writing campaign. She thanked the external affairs minister for the sentiments expressed in his missive, especially his assurance that "we will give you every possible support and assistance."

> Without wishing to appear presumptuous, should it not be drawn to your attention that the many vital commitments made by the various authorities in your department to Dr. Vennema for the support of this particular project continue to remain unfulfilled—even after the lapse of six months since these numerous personal interviews and absolute assurances were made to him in Ottawa?[26]

After apologizing for any breach of protocol her letter might contain she concluded by urging Martin to "break with the precedent of interminable delays and inexcusable oversights which are blocking the present channels of action between Ottawa and Quang Ngai." It was the opening salvo in what would become a voluminous correspondence between Claire and External Affairs over the Quang Ngai program in particular and Canadian policy in Vietnam in general. The letter was also the first and last time that she would be at all concerned with protocol.

The truth was that the Canadian medical team's position in Quang Ngai was just short of untenable, and the missing X-ray equipment was symptomatic of the overall problem. Support for Canadian aid projects in Vietnam was minimal, and as a result the Canadian medical team found

itself increasingly dependent on the Americans. Even Martin's letter to
Claire was indicative of Ottawa's tenuous links with Quang Ngai. It was
dated October 10, but Claire received it only on November 2. It had taken
twenty-three days for a letter from Canada's most senior diplomat to reach
one of his workers in the field. Still, even that was superior to the telephone
and telex connections between Quang Ngai and Canada, which were non-
existent. Officially, Canada was neutral in the war, but even its humanitarian aid relied on U.S. logistical and transportational support. Aside from
the appearance of a neutral nation forced to piggyback its non-military aid
through the offices of a combatant nation, the relationship could, and did,
founder when Canadians had the temerity to criticize the actions of the
Americans in Vietnam.

The Canadian medical staff were themselves divided over the war. Claire
was an outspoken critic of the U.S. military intervention, as was Vennema,
while other members were sympathetic to the American cause. Vennema,
in particular, had developed into a nettlesome critic of U.S. behaviour in
the field, and he had become a favoured source for Western reporters
seeking the side of the story that was never presented in the daily American
military press briefings back in Saigon. The young doctor with greying hair
and piercing blue eyes was quite willing to show journalists the effects of
napalm on the civilian population of Quang Ngai, and he had even found
evidence of the use of nerve gas—likely CN and CS gases—by the United
States. This accusation brought angry denials from the Pentagon and sent
anxious ripples through Canada's ICC delegation in Saigon, which
advised Vennema to keep quiet.[27] Relations between Vennema and American officials had cooled considerably by 1967, and it was becoming increasingly difficult for the Canadian doctor to move about the country on
U.S.-controlled flights.

Their common views on the war cemented an already strong working
relationship between Claire and Vennema. Although her official title was
"administrative assistant," Claire had, by November, become the administrator of the fledgling hospital in all but name. Vennema came to rely
increasingly on Claire, and he was delighted with her capacity for work, her
competence, and her deep concern for the Vietnamese people.[28] Claire was
also entrusted with all of the hospital's finances, and as there was no bank
in Quang Ngai, she began to make regular monthly trips to Saigon to
personally collect the $30,000 in cash that comprised the Canadian team's
monthly budget. It was on one such trip in November that an incident
occurred which further clarified Claire's understanding of her country's
role in Vietnam.

She was on the way back to Quang Ngai aboard an Air America flight,
the strongbox containing the $30,000 stowed safely in the cargo hold, when

she happened to notice a piece of wire on the floor of the cabin. She picked it up and wondered aloud, to a GI sitting next to her, why the wire was there.

It was probably the remainder of a longer piece that had been used to fasten a VC prisoner's hands, so that he couldn't clutch at the plane as he was being thrown out the door while the aircraft was several thousand feet in the air, the American soldier explained offhandedly. The prisoner's hands were flattened on either side of his face and the wire was run through his hands and cheeks. Claire was horrified, and incredulous.

But you couldn't just open the door of an airplane while it was aloft, could you?

The GI answered by leaving his seat and opening the door on the fuselage. The cabin on the small Beechcraft wasn't pressurized, Claire suddenly realized. The soldier slammed the door closed, returned to his seat, and shrugged.

Remembering her friend Ruslan's grilling about flying on helicopters which might have been used in just this way to torture and murder Vietnamese POWs, Claire had prided herself on refusing all offers of transport on American choppers. But what difference had it made? Despite her noblest intentions, Canada's "humanitarian" aid effort still seemed inextricably associated with the U.S. military. And she was part of that effort.

More soul-searching followed the day she noticed an NLF prisoner staring at her intently from his bed on the recovery ward of the provincial hospital. She knew he was a prisoner because his arm was chained to the bedpost, and as she established eye contact she recoiled from the look of loathing and contempt that flashed from his dark eyes. But how could he not hate her, and what she represented? He was surrounded by the stench and suffering of his own people, and there she was in her freshly laundered white uniform, caring for these civilian casualties of war as if they were ordinary sick patients at the Ottawa Civic. A wave of shame washed over her—shame for her own health, shame for the colour of her skin, shame because she could walk and talk freely, without pain and fear. That she was Canadian and not American seemed faint consolation, suddenly. What was she doing here? What were any of them doing here? The war was the root cause of all this suffering; the fundamental problems were political, not medical.

But Claire had one lapse that was, to her, symptomatic of how easily a moral person can be conditioned to accept amorality when evil becomes banal. That realization came to her the night she was with a group of GIs on the patio of the Canadian residence, listening to the usual boasting about the day's "body count," and her mind began to wander. Normally she would argue with these young Americans, questioning their right to come ten thousand miles from home and count bodies, as if the bodies were not somebody's brothers, sons, and husbands. Claire realized with a start that she was no longer arguing, no longer even paying attention. It was, she wrote later, "the only time I was ever frightened in Vietnam . . . This sudden insight into how a person gives up and accepts the evil around them, as I very nearly had that evening, was terrifying."[29]

For her first leave Claire opted to visit Da Nang, about 120 kilometres up the coast from Quang Ngai. One of only a handful of population centres in all of Vietnam that could aptly be termed a city, Da Nang was also the site of an American naval base, the headquarters of the United States Marine Corps Third Amphibious Force, and home to a sprawling U.S. Air Force base that served as a staging area for the bombing of North Vietnam. About the only useful thing Claire could find in this vast assemblage of American weaponry was a state-of-the-art communications link which allowed her to telephone Dara in Montreal and Roisin in Vancouver. After reassuring herself that things were fine at home, Claire decided to tour as many of the local medical facilities as she could.

Her first stop was the provincial hospital. She had assumed that in a larger centre health care services would be more sophisticated, but she found that medical conditions for Vietnamese civilians in Da Nang were just as appalling as they were back in Quang Ngai. Next she visited the U.S. Naval Hospital, which consisted of rows of Quonset huts perched on a hillside overlooking the harbour. While she waited for the medical director she observed a Medivac chopper unloading wounded personnel. Six GIs, each bleeding from jagged leg wounds, were being gently lowered on to stretchers, and Claire was struck by the tense and angry demeanour of the medical personnel attending to the wounded. "A look of bitter hatred was stamped on every face, expressing their loathing for 'the enemy' who had crippled their buddies," she wrote in her journal.[30]

Once inside the naval hospital she was surprised to find the most advanced medical equipment, in stark contrast to the provincial hospital only a few kilometres away. During the tour she noticed that one ward was sealed off, and she assumed it was some kind of isolation ward to prevent the spread of infectious disease; she knew that the incidence of plague was increasing at an alarming rate among the Vietnamese. She asked her tour guide, an American military doctor, if the isolation ward was in fact a plague ward.

"I wish they were," he answered soberly. "No, they are the psychiatry wards and they are classified."

In Da Nang alone, Claire learned, an average of ten new psychiatric cases per week were admitted to the hospital. Later, she would see similar isolation wards in other American military hospitals she visited in Vietnam. Claire grasped the profound implications of these wards at once: the atrocities being committed daily were also having an effect on U.S. troops. The brutalizer was also brutalized. The presence of American ground troops in Vietnam, which had begun in Da Nang itself, was not yet two years old. But already these classified isolation wards (which were never mentioned on the tours unless she asked) were a disturbing augury for the American public. The patients of these wards, she realized with remarkable prescience, would take their guilt and anger home with them, and the shadow of drug and alcohol abuse and random violence among Vietnam veterans would haunt American life for generations to come.

After the naval hospital Claire was welcomed aboard the USS *Sanctuary*, an American hospital ship anchored eight kilometres out in the harbour. A converted freighter, the *Sanctuary* had been refitted to hold 1,500 hospital beds and boasted the latest medical hardware, some of which was not even in common use back in the States. Once again Claire was struck by the contrast between the medical services available to the Vietnamese and the Americans.

Would Vietnamese civilians be admitted for treatment aboard the *Sanctuary*? Claire wondered aloud.

There were a handful of Vietnamese aboard, the medical director explained carefully, but they had been evacuated to the ship by chance. While they would remain until their treatment was completed, the United States had no set policy of treating Vietnamese civilians in its facilities.

Claire accepted an invitation to stay for dinner, and soon found herself in the *Sanctuary*'s well-appointed state room. The tables were covered in snowy white linen, and the dinner had five courses, with apple pie and a choice of five flavours of ice cream for dessert. Claire was especially bemused by the unintentional black humour of the chaplain's pre-dinner table grace which began, "Forgive us for any harm we may have done to anyone this day."

Contrasts abounded during her stay in Da Nang, and Claire recorded them with an observant eye for detail. She visited the city's French Cultural Centre and noticed a poster which read: *Après la douleur, c'est la sérénité* (After grief comes serenity). She couldn't resist comparing those poetic sentiments with a poster she saw at the United States Marine Corps base just a few hours later. It was the same size, but with a background of red, white, and blue stars and stripes. Vividly displayed in the foreground was a coarse inscription: Fuck Communism.

That evening Claire went to the press club in the city with Eloise Henkel, a stringer for the *Chicago Tribune* whom Claire had first met in Quang Ngai. But even over drinks they were still embroiled over the leading controversy of the day—the American involvement in Vietnam. They wound up arguing with a U.S. general who, after conceding that his country's presence was wrong, nevertheless voiced the oft-heard opinion that "now that we're here, we have to win."

Claire would always remember Eloise's reply. "But if you're driving down a road and come to an unmarked fork, and the one you decide to take leads to a cliff, do you keep right on going to certain suicide, just because you're there, or do you turn back and find a different way?"

They were joined later that evening by Beryl Fox, the documentary filmmaker. Like hundreds of thousands of other Canadians, Claire had been stunned by Fox's film, *The Mills of the Gods*, when it was broadcast on the CBC television program "This Hour Has Seven Days." The documentary had caused a sensation following its first airing in December 1965 because of graphic footage shot from the co-pilot's seat of a bombing run over South Vietnam. Viewers watched and listened as the pilot, a handsome, clean-cut young American, exulted over the plane's intercom as he dropped napalm on a rice paddy. "There you go! Look at it burning! Just short of the treeline. Up we go! Real fine, real fine! That was an outstanding target! We can see the people running everywhere. Fantastic! . . . By Jove, that's really great fun. I really like doing that . . ."[31]

In front of her television in Montreal two years earlier Claire had been torn between disbelief and rejection of the implications of Fox's documentary. But that night in the press club Claire told Fox she no longer had the slightest doubts about the veracity of her film.

On the flight back to Quang Ngai Claire saw more evidence that the war in the northern provinces was intensifying. A hill that had been covered with rain forest on the flight up was now brown and desolate, the earth churned by intensive American bombing. At the Tam Ky airstrip, where they touched down briefly, Claire learned that the hill had been the target of a "Rolling Thunder" operation, the supersaturation bombing conducted by B-52s. One of the huge planes had been shot down during the fighting, she was told. Just three kilometres away heavy fighting was still raging at a district headquarters, which had been attacked, and then held, by the NLF for two weeks. Many Americans were reported killed in the fighting.

That night, her first back in Quang Ngai, the GIs visiting Canadian House had more war news. The outpost at Bin Sohn, fifteen kilometres outside Quang Ngai, had come under five hours of shelling from the NLF just the night before. One American and twenty-eight ARVN had been killed in the barrage. The situation had become so desperate that the garrison's defenders had called air strikes in on their own position to avoid being overrun by their attackers. A camp of South Korean troops based a short distance away had simply watched the fighting and done nothing to relieve Bin Sohn, which outraged the Americans. The crowning irony was that the GIs were angriest at their own division commanders who, they believed, would cover up the results of the attack while refusing to shoulder blame for the disaster.

For all their firepower, Claire concluded, the Americans didn't seem to be winning the war on the ground in Quang Ngai.

By early December the Canadian Anti-Tuberculosis Hospital Quang Ngai was at last ready to admit its first patients, and there was no shortage of clients. As soon as the doors of the new Canadian facility were opened approximately 150 Vietnamese per day flooded into the clinic.

The people of Quang Ngai were intimately acquainted with the spectre of tuberculosis, which they called *ho lao* or *ho ra mau*, meaning "cough of long standing" or "cough of long standing with blood." Unlike North America, where the disease was first introduced to aboriginal people by Europeans, it was not the Western colonizers who had brought tuberculosis to Vietnam, but their Chinese predecessors centuries before. The disease flourished in the close living quarters, large families, and poor diet of the Vietnamese peasantry, exacerbated by wood smoke from the open fires which were typically the only means of cooking in the thatched-roof hut of the average family. The American army's Phoenix project, which uprooted whole hamlets and clustered the population into even denser concentrations in refugee camps, also accelerated the spread of the disease.

The Canadian medical team threw itself into the battle against one of the province's leading killers, apart from the war itself. On the first visit to the clinic each woman, man, and child was given the Mantoux test: a protein derivative of the tubercle bacillus was injected into the skin with a hypodermic needle. The reactions were read after seventy-two hours. If the inflammation around the injection measured more than eight millimetres, the patient was deemed to be tuberculin positive, meaning that they had been or were infected with TB. The initial results were startling: 51.4 percent of those tested over the age of fifteen showed a positive reaction. The positive reactors were subjected to more tests, either sputum examination, X-ray, or both. About 0.7 percent of the people tested were found to be spreading the disease. Treatment varied according to the severity of the symptoms—antibiotics, admission to hospital for a period of bed rest and supervised nutrition, isolation, and, in the most advanced cases, palliative care until death.[32]

Claire faced a formidable challenge for any medical records librarian: starting a medical records library from scratch, drawing up index cards, and filing charts on each patient. Eventually the patients examined at the clinic would number in the tens of thousands. Claire performed the task with a ready will, and she was not without experience. She had, after all, established the medical records library at Grace Dart Hospital in Montreal a decade earlier. Because she was concerned about patient confidentiality, Claire had devised a numbered coding system—hospital patients were assigned a number corresponding to their names and addresses. The latter records were filed safely at the Canadian House. The move was a precaution against the Phoenix program, a CIA intelligence-gathering exercise which involved rounding up often-innocent Vietnamese civilians who could then be classified as "traitors" before being tortured and murdered—drowning was the preferred method. In 1969 alone 6,187 Vietnamese were murdered under the Phoenix program.[33]

The prevalence of TB translated into a crushing workload for all of the members of the Canadian medical team. Twelve- and even sixteen-hour work days were not uncommon. Claire was flabbergasted when Ormond Dier, the head of Canada's ICC delegation in Saigon, asked her during one of his infrequent visits why they worked so hard. It didn't matter if they failed to see a single patient, Dier observed, the important thing was that the hospital was there, a symbol of good intentions.[34]

But medical records were just one of Claire's responsibilities; keeping the hospital supplied with essential medicaments and equipment was another time-consuming task. The logistical exigencies of the situation demanded she become equal parts scrounger, purchasing agent, and expeditor, experience which gave her firsthand insights into South Vietnam's notorious black market. A case in point was the hospital's generator, the delivery of which was several months overdue. There were two RCAF flights a month from Ottawa to various Canadian delegations throughout Southeast Asia but, to Claire's intense frustration, cargo space was taken up with liquor and cigarettes and other personal luxury items that Canadian aid workers abroad couldn't seem to live without. Several sharp letters to Ottawa resulted in the generator finally being shipped aboard a commercial flight. The total value of the generator was only $2,000 Canadian, but the air freight bill, including bribes for South Vietnamese customs, totalled $2,300 Canadian. Conditioned by years of living at or below the poverty line, Claire had long since developed the habit of extreme frugality in her personal life, and she tended to apply the same policy in administering the hospital. Appalled though she was at the waste of taxpayers' money in getting the equipment to Saigon, she had little choice. Claire authorized payment of the bribes and the airfare.

Coincidentally or not, just two weeks after Claire fired off her letter to Paul Martin, word reached Quang Ngai that the X-ray equipment had at last arrived aboard another commercial flight to Saigon. But getting the sixteen-crate shipment delivered to Quang Ngai from Saigon presented another conundrum. Claire accepted the Americans' offer of transport, but when the GI arrived with the shipment there were only fourteen pieces. Aware of the rapidity with which something as valuable as hospital equipment could disappear into the black market, Claire demanded to know where the other two crates were. The GI got defensive, insisting that there were only fourteen pieces in the shipment.

"You better go back," Claire insisted, "because either you left two, or somebody took two. Maybe you can't count, but the Vietnamese can." The driver reluctantly did so, and the two missing crates were found at the airstrip. Nothing was ever simple in Vietnam, Claire was learning, and it paid to be aggressive and to complain loud and long whenever anything disappeared.

But Tri, the hospital carpenter, provided the perfect antidote to the epidemic of theft, corruption, and outright waste that characterized the American war effort. After he had removed the equipment, Claire watched curiously as Tri methodically pulled each nail from the packing crates. He sorted the nails by size into separate jars and then carefully stacked the wooden pieces before busily beginning to hammer and saw. A few days later, to their mutual delight, Tri proudly showed Claire his handiwork: from materials that would have been simply discarded by any other hospital that she had ever worked at, the diminutive carpenter had fashioned forty-six bedside tables for use on the wards.

Early December marked another kind of watershed in the Canadian aid effort to Vietnam—Dr. Vennema's replacement arrived in Quang Ngai. Although at twenty-eight he was only seven years younger than Vennema, Dr. Michel Jutras seemed almost boyish in comparison to his predecessor, who was, after nearly four years in country, a grizzled veteran of wartime medical practice. The new head of the Canadian medical aid team was from Montreal. His father was a prominent physician and his older brother, Claude, was a distinguished filmmaker. Vennema didn't hold Jutras's youth against him—Vennema himself had been only thirty-one when he arrived in Quang Ngai, after all, but he was concerned about his successor's medical qualifications. Jutras had most recently served as a medic at Expo '67 in Montreal, hardly the sort of prior experience with general internal medicine, pediatrics, and infectious diseases that Vennema had hoped to find in Ottawa's selection as his replacement.

Vennema's initial misgivings deepened within a few days of Jutras's arrival. They were sitting around Canadian House one night after supper when a Vietnamese woman knocked at the door. Her child was sick; would one of the *Na Dai* doctors see him? Vennema, accompanied by Jutras, went to examine the sick youngster.

"Why do you let mothers and sick children come to this house?" Jutras asked Vennema.

"I let any patient come to this house," Vennema replied, taken aback at the question. "I'm a physician and that's what we do here. Besides that, to have a good working relationship with the people of this town and this province, that's what we do."

"Oh," the younger man replied. "I think that will have to stop."

Vennema examined the child, and asked the mother a number of questions in Vietnamese: did the child have fever, was he drinking, vomiting, coughing? After a chest examination Vennema concluded that his young patient's symptoms were consistent with pneumonia. He said nothing, but offered his stethoscope to Jutras. "What do you think?"

"Just a little cold," Jutras responded after his own examination.

"So what would you do?"

"Well," Jutras answered with a wave of his hand, "tell her to give him something to drink and an aspirin."

"No," Vennema demurred. "You missed the boat. This child has a serious pneumonia, and needs to be admitted to our ward and prescribed antibiotics and intravenous fluids."[35]

A few days before Vennema's departure Claire confided her own misgivings about Jutras to Vennema—he seemed to lack experience and any genuine concern about his patients. Vennema's own concerns were serious enough that he considered postponing his departure, but Claire insisted that he should take up his studies in tropical disease in Europe as planned.

Life went on in the Canadian House after Vennema's departure, but Claire's unease about Jutras continued to deepen. She remarked a casualness in the attitude of the young physician that seemed at times to be downright cavalier. Jutras had spent little time with Vennema, and indeed in the latter's final week his successor seemed to absent himself altogether. Still more disturbing was that Jutras had wasted no time at all in seeking out and socializing with a special group of American civilians in Quang Ngai. Central Intelligence Agency operatives used any number of official U.S. government agencies as cover, but some vaguely described themselves as "working for the embassy," and were therefore dubbed "the embassy boys." Quang Ngai had such a contingent, and they occupied their own heavily fortified villa. One of their roles was to work with ARVN intelligence in the Security Centre, where important NLF POWs were interned and interrogated. Vennema had treated some of the prisoners at the centre, and he had been sickened by the CIA-ARVN interrogation techniques, which included torture. Vennema made it a policy to shun the embassy boys, but Jutras seemed to feel quite at home with them.

After Vennema's departure in mid-December the relationship between Claire and Jutras steadily deteriorated. Vennema's around-the-clock open door policy to patients was terminated, and regular office hours were strictly enforced, even if it meant turning away patients who had waited all morning. Claire tried to tell Jutras that the frail and elderly would either have to walk ten or fifteen kilometres back to their homes in the scorching sun or stay overnight without food or shelter, but the young doctor was unmoved. Vennema had been idolized by the Vietnamese, who would often smile at members of the Canadian medical team and proclaim "Canada number one. Canada okay." Now Claire found herself turning people away from the hospital, fumbling for an explanation in her broken Vietnamese. She also hated Jutras's attitude towards his patients. More than once she watched him examining a Vietnamese and holding his stethoscope at arm's length as if he could barely tolerate closer physical contact.

Vennema's departure had also shifted the political balance on the aid team. Before, there had been two outspoken critics of the war to offset the pro-U.S. views of the others. Now the head of the team was setting the tone by socializing with the embassy boys, and Claire found herself increasingly isolated. She was marginalized in other ways, too. Where Vennema had asked that Claire assume more and more of the administrative duties at the hospital to free him to see patients, Jutras stripped her of her responsibilities one by one, arrogating the duties to himself. He reduced the number of hours per week that the Canadian staff members spent training the Vietnamese student nurses, a task Claire particularly enjoyed.

Twice Claire had bluntly refused to honour Jutras's claims for out-of-pocket expenses, thus further straining their relationship. The first was when he presented her with a receipt for "a collect telegram." There was no such thing in South Vietnam, and Claire knew it. The amount wasn't large—1,625 piastres, or about $9 U.S.—and Claire guessed it had been paid for by the sender. She took a dim view of a Canadian doctor attempting to pad his expense account at the expense of the public purse. The second time Jutras produced a printer's bill for 6,125 piastres, claiming that the amount was owing. But Claire checked her accounts and discovered that the money had already been paid.

Jutras also seemed strangely reluctant to endorse Claire's get-tough policy when it came to freight shipments that had disappeared aboard Air America flights from Saigon. Claire's method was proven, as in the time when they had arranged for Arthur Ludwick, an X-ray technician newly arrived from Canada, to pick up the monthly $30,000 budget from Saigon. When Ludwick arrived in Quang Ngai, the trunk containing the cash was no longer on the plane. Claire immediately filed a report of the missing funds with James May, the senior American AID officer in Quang Ngai.

May replied that the trunk had simply vanished, but Claire persisted. Each morning for the next three weeks she filed a duplicate complaint. In the end the trunk was found, with the missing money inside. Her guess—and it was only a guess—was that the trunk had been stashed away somewhere in the expectation that the Canadians would give up the search. Only when it became apparent that Claire was not to be put off did the money reappear.

Under Jutras's aegis, however, such punctilious pursuit of missing goods was no longer encouraged. When the hospital generator arrived its gas tank was missing. A few weeks later an eight-crate shipment of Canadian medical supplies from Phu To, a warehouse outside Saigon, disappeared from the U.S. CORDS warehouse in Quang Ngai during the fifteen-minute interval it took Claire to arrive to collect them. Perhaps they had been mistakenly shipped to the Provincial Hospital, she was told, but a quick jeep ride revealed they had not been sent there, either. On both occasions Claire wanted to report the losses to May, but Jutras refused. "We shouldn't make a political football out of this issue," he told her.

But Claire's worst suspicions about Jutras were confirmed early in the new year, when she found him at the Canadian House with one of the embassy boys going through the records of patient names and addresses. The discovery left her outraged and deeply shaken. The confidential medical records that she had so painstakingly amassed were now being shared brazenly with the perpetrators of the Phoenix project! What did that say about Canada's vaunted neutral, humanitarian role in the Vietnam war? What did it say about *her*? From that moment on the administrator and the medical director of the Canadian Anti-Tuberculosis Hospital Quang Ngai were barely on civil speaking terms.

* * *

By January 1, 1968, the Vietnam war was nearing its climax. United States troop commitment had reached nearly half a million men, and the American public was beginning to reckon the grim toll of its government's military policy in far-off Indochina. More than twenty thousand Americans had died in Vietnam by the end of 1967, and another fifty thousand had been wounded. The war was costing U.S. taxpayers $33 billion annually, and attempts by President Johnson to hide the true cost from Congress and from the nation were touching off inflation, a problem that would bedevil Western economies for the next quarter-century.[36] What was more, the war was polarizing American society. The anti-war movement was growing, and in November Lyndon Johnson would face an election. The war had even divided the American establishment, and liberal Democrats like Eugene McCarthy and Robert Kennedy threatened to contest Johnson's nomination on an anti-war platform. As support for the war eroded, the hawks clung to the perennially optimistic assessments from the Pentagon about the course of the war on the ground. But the grand illusion of progress on the battlefield was about to be shattered.

The barrage that literally shook Claire out of her bed in the Canadian House in Quang Ngai early on the morning of January 31, 1968, was part of one of the most audacious military offensives of this or any other war. Across South Vietnam, in a coordinated effort that caught U.S. and ARVN forces completely off guard, the NLF and units of the North Vietnamese army launched simultaneous attacks on all major cities, on 36 of 44 provincial capitals, and on 64 of the country's 242 district towns.[37] Crucial to the element of surprise was that the offensive had begun during Tet, a week-long celebration of the lunar new year that is the Vietnamese equivalent of Christmas, New Year, and Easter combined. Tet had traditionally been a time of cease-fire, an opportunity for family reunions and popular festivities. Many ARVN units had granted leaves to their soldiers, and even Nguyen Van Thieu, the president of South Vietnam, had left Saigon to enjoy the holiday with his family elsewhere.

Claire knew none of this as she walked through the deserted streets of Quang Ngai City in the midst of the Tet Offensive at four o'clock in the morning, alone and utterly exposed, her concentration focused on one narrow objective: to reach the Canadian Hospital. "Though I suspect there were many salvos exploding close by," she would write later, "I couldn't possibly have described them, then or now, with any degree of accuracy. Perhaps it was a subconscious 'turning off' to make it physically possible to complete that short trek with a measure of calm which I was far from feeling."

After what must have seemed an eternity the ARVN sentry post outside the hospital entrance came into view. As she approached, Claire could see to her immense relief that the ARVN guard who had warned her the night before that "VC come tonight" was still on duty. At least he would recognize her and not open fire! The other sentries were so nervous they didn't seem to care who she was. The barbed wire barrier was quickly opened and she was allowed to pass.

"Okay, go," said the sentry from the night before. "Telephone if VC come."

There was in fact no telephone at the hospital so the remark made no sense, except to foreshadow the tragic absurdity of the next twenty-four hours. Once past the sentry point the whitewashed bulk of the hospital soon loomed before her. It was intact, Claire could see through the predawn gloom. She suppressed an urge to run towards it until she was well inside the gates. Then she broke into a sprint and dashed up to the second-floor ward, taking the steps two at a time.

She found the patients and their families awake, many of them gazing out the windows at a sky illumined by flares, flames, and explosions. What astonished her most was the total lack of panic. Claire went to stand beside a young ARVN soldier, whose wife was suffering from very advanced pulmonary tuberculosis. There was a gleam in the soldier's eye and a half smile on his face, as if to say, "Well, we've won this round." At first it struck Claire as odd that a soldier in the South Vietnamese army should draw satisfaction from this tremendous assault, launched by his putative enemy. She later learned he was a conscript, and the expression on his face clearly showed where his real sympathies lay.

While it may have surprised the American military, the offensive was not unexpected among the Vietnamese, Claire concluded. Their calmness in the face of such intense fighting seemed to imply forewarning. Throughout the room she sensed "an odd undercurrent of hope."[38]

Daybreak brought a lull in the battle, and normal breakfast preparations were soon under way at the hospital. When Claire arrived home for her own breakfast, the Canadians around the table seemed remarkably casual about the events of the past few hours. She was mildly chastised by Dr. Jutras for being foolish enough to walk down the road alone in the middle of a battle, but then the subject was changed, as if this were simply another working day. Since it was clear that the Vietnamese staff would be unable to reach work through the myriad roadblocks within the curfew hours that had been declared throughout the area, it was decided that Claire and Pauline Trudel would remain on duty on the wards, while nurse Louise Piché and Tara Dier would take responsibility for the hospital kitchen. Dier, the nineteen-year-old daughter of Canadian delegation head Ormond Dier, was in Quang Ngai as a volunteer with the medical aid team.

On the way back to the hospital Claire noticed that half of the schoolhouse roof had been blown off. She also learned that the post office and girls' secondary school had been occupied by the NLF, which had also released about half of the prisoners in the provincial jail. Fighting was continuing in the prison compound.

Around midday the wife of the young ARVN soldier entered the final, irreversible stages of tuberculosis. She began to hemorrhage, and Claire grabbed every towel and sheet she could find to staunch the flow of blood that was gushing from the young woman's mouth and nose in violent, uncontrollable spasms. As she fought to hold back the spurting pink lung tissue, Claire began to sob with helpless rage. Why was this mother of young children dying, while she, whose own children were fully grown, was being spared? What chance had this young woman ever really had to recover from her illness and live out her life in this country ravaged by war? The criminal waste of it all overwhelmed her. The other patients watched

Claire's ministrations and tears with the detachment born of centuries of suffering. They deferred to Claire's grief, and left her alone.

The woman's parents soon arrived to grieve over the body of their daughter, which led to Claire's first serious row of the day with Dr. Jutras. He wanted the body placed on a stretcher, so that the family could carry the remains home. But Claire wanted to drive them in the hospital jeep. Surely they had suffered enough, without having to carry the body three kilometres beneath the blazing midday sun. Jutras disagreed, arguing that there had been heavy fighting around the sugar refinery, in the family's neighbourhood. But Claire was not to be denied and, accompanied by Chau, the hospital interpreter, she took the family home.

When they arrived Chau disappeared behind the house with the family, leaving Claire alone in the jeep. Normally she would be surrounded with chattering Vietnamese children wherever she went, but this time there was only silence. Soon she heard the rasp of digging in dry ground. The sound and the harsh beating of the sun made her head throb and a half-remembered line from her childhood came flooding back to her in a sorrowing mantra: "Light lie the earth upon her, light lie the earth upon her . . ."

Finally Chau returned and they drove back to the hospital in silence.

Several hours later a young Vietnamese boy arrived at the Canadian residence. His mother had been shot in the leg, he explained, and she was bleeding profusely. Would the *Bac Si* (doctor) come with him, and extract the bullet? Dr. Jerema, Claire knew, was having his daily siesta and he refused to be disturbed before 3:00 p.m. Dr. Jutras instructed the interpreter to tell the pleading boy that the Canadians only treated tuberculosis, and that he should take his mother to the provincial hospital.

But access to the hospital had been cut off because of fighting in the area, the son explained desperately. Jutras was unmoved. Claire thought of going with him herself, but the medical instruments were all locked in Jutras's room. Claire remonstrated with Jutras, but Louise Piché sided with the doctor: it was much too dangerous for him to venture out into the town.

Perhaps sensing the disagreement within the medical team, the young supplicant watched and waited with hopeful patience. This was something new in the Canadian residence, Claire realized—a Vietnamese in desperate need denied care and forced to wait in the hope that something would cause one of the doctors to change his mind.

How had it been possible for Dr. Vennema to make house calls day or night, and never come to any harm, Claire argued. But Jutras was emphatic.

Finally Claire was forced to turn to the boy. "*Bac Si khong,*" she said.

The doctor says no. She went to her own room then, to hide in shame until the boy left. She felt utterly helpless.

It was now 4:30 p.m., according to the clock in her bedroom, twelve hours exactly since she had begun her walk to see if their hospital was still intact. And yet how much had changed! There was an air of unreality to everything that had happened. It was like a waking nightmare. The war had come, suddenly, almost to their doorstep, her relationship with Jutras had ruptured for the Canadian team and even the patients to see, and they were all abrogating their responsibilities as medical professionals. She felt as if she was aboard a ship that had lost its moorings in a storm and was now adrift, rudderless and without power. She was in the midst of the most dangerous and eventful twenty-four hours of her life, and the day was only half over.

Claire decided to cycle to the provincial hospital to see how the patients there were making out. She'd gone only a short distance when an ARVN jeep sped towards her, the soldiers in it waving her off the road. A firefight was raging just ahead, the closest fighting she had yet seen. The target appeared to be the Rural Development Cadre Headquarters, which was just beyond the Canadian House. Claire indicated that she just wanted to go to the hospital, but the ARVN soldiers insisted she turn back.

The road to the Canadian TB hospital was still open, so Claire determined to go there. When she arrived, Hoa, the staff electrician apprentice, was waiting to carry her bicycle up the steps and into the hospital. Usually Claire accepted this courtesy with a mock flourish, but she could see in Hoa's face that something was wrong. He motioned for her to come, and she sensed that this was no time to race Hoa up the wide stone staircase to the veranda, as she so often did.

He led her into an empty section of the ward and motioned to a patient lying motionless on a bed, so heavily wrapped in bandages as to be almost unidentifiable. "Uncle, aunt, cousins, ten . . ." Hoa was trying to tell her something, and at last, thunderstruck, she understood. This man was his uncle, and his wife and ten children had just been killed in a napalm attack. She could smell the nauseating reek of scorched flesh. The family had taken refuge in an underground shelter beneath their hut when a low-flying American plane had let loose a canister of napalm. Only Hoa's uncle had survived.

Pauline Trudel, who had bandaged Hoa's uncle, insisted that the badly burned man must be transferred to the provincial hospital as soon as the Canadian jeep returned. Claire was outraged. That would mean moving him from the relative luxury of a clean bed in an empty part of this ward into an overcrowded and filthy corner of the provincial hospital, where he would doubtless have to share a bed. Worse, it would mean removing him from the watchful and loving care of his only remaining relative.

But Pauline remained obdurate; those were Dr. Jutras's orders. Her voice rising with anger, Claire began to rage at her colleagues. In the span of twelve short hours they had ordered an elderly father to carry his daughter's body home through the blistering sun, they had refused a son's entreaty to remove a bullet from his mother's leg, and now they proposed to send Hoa's uncle off in this pitiable state? What kind of ugly Canadians had they become? Had they been so tainted by the American attitudes toward the Vietnamese that they were unable to show a shred of decency to this one man?

But the hospital's supply of morphine was limited, Pauline argued, and might be needed later on to treat their own patients.

Claire gestured at the sounds of the war outside. But who could know what future there was for anyone at this moment? And who were or were not "their" patients?

But theirs was a TB hospital, Pauline responded, and they were not equipped to treat burn patients.

What supplies did they need? Claire would requisition them from the provincial hospital and go get them herself.

Hoa's uncle might contract TB if he was allowed to stay, Pauline warned.

Good God, Claire exploded, as if the whole country, as well as the provincial hospital, wasn't full of TB! At least in this unused corner of the ward the injured man was isolated from other patients.

And finally came the reply that she would hear *ad nauseam* in the coming weeks, the rejoinder it seemed she'd heard her whole life—but Dr. Jutras is the medical director here, and we must take our orders from him, without questioning.

Claire resolved to await Jutras's arrival in the hope that she could convince him to change his mind.

Night fell, the fighting intensified around the hospital once again, and even Jutras had to concede that moving Hoa's uncle was out of the question, at least until morning. Despite the fact that they had missed the curfew, Jutras ordered Claire to return to the Canadian House with Pauline and Chau. Against her better judgement, but weary from arguing, frustration, and lack of sleep, Claire set off with her companions down the darkened road. But as they approached the sentry post the air around them was suddenly alight with tracer rounds. They heard excited screaming in Vietnamese, and Chau shouted they must return to the hospital *aussitôt que possible*.

They cycled back as fast as they could and arrived gasping for breath, their hearts pounding. When Pauline explained what had happened, Claire was stunned at the nonchalance of Jutras's reply. "I did feel kind of bad sending you off in the dark like that," he said with a shrug.

There was nothing for it but to stay at the hospital for the night. Claire lay down on an empty bed in one of the wards, but she was unable to sleep. She rose again and went to the nursing station where Jutras was sitting up, reading a book. Using hushed tones so as not to awaken the others, she tried to reason with him, suggesting that they really must learn to work together, for the sake of the hospital and the patients. But the young doctor's response was cool: he intended to critically assess each and every one of her recommendations, though she should feel quite free to continue to make them. And he went back to reading his book, a collection of short stories by Art Buchwald.

Claire returned to her bed, but still sleep would not come. She listened to the coughing of the patients around her. Some, she could see, were still awake, listening as the sounds of the fighting grew ever more intense. What must they be thinking? That the war was now raging in their own hamlet? In their own cluster of huts? In their own hut?

Hours passed, but her own dark night of the soul persisted. Of what use were her skills, or anyone's skills, in a situation like this? How inadequate she felt, measured against the overwhelming carnage being wrought in the night around her. Even in this one small hospital, in this one small corner of the war, she had proved unable to instill compassion in her own fellow countrymen. And how many more wounded, sick, and suffering people were out there, unable to even reach a hospital? She wrestled with her situation, and her conscience, until the predawn hours. In the end she decided she must persevere—fight to keep the hospital open, to care for the patients, fight to prevent Hoa's uncle from being evacuated to the provincial hospital. Finally she fell into a restless, fitful slumber, her first in twenty-four hours.

Across the length and breadth of South Vietnam that night fierce fighting continued. From the Mekong Delta in the south to the Demilitarized Zone in the north, American and ARVN forces fought desperately to blunt the Front offensive. The first full day of Tet would prove as significant in the overall course of the war as it would in Claire's life. In Saigon a heavily armed NLF commando unit had blasted its way through the wall around the United States embassy and nearly succeeded in capturing the ultimate symbol of the American presence in the country. U.S. television viewers that night saw news footage of the devastation in and around what should have been the most secure American real estate in all of South Vietnam. They also saw still photos and film footage of General Nguyen Ngoc Loan, the brutish chief of South Vietnam's national police, as he summarily executed a young Vietnamese civilian. Loan pulled out his pistol, stuck the muzzle to his captive's head, and pulled the trigger. The American networks cleaned up the footage slightly to spare their viewers the most gruesome instant as the young man's head flattened against the impact of the bullet. But Loan's outstretched arm and the wince on his victim's face would remain one of the enduring images of the war.

Ellsworth Bunker, the American ambassador, was awakened by marines at the start of the offensive and, still in his pajamas, was removed from his residence in an armoured personnel carrier to a more secure location. No place, and no one, seemed safe in the astounding Communist offensive. The headquarters of General William Westmoreland, the supreme U.S. commander in Vietnam, were under attack. So were the suburban Saigon headquarters of General Fred Weyand, the commander of III Corps. The concussion from a direct hit on a nearby ammunition dump rocked Weyand's command post hard enough to momentarily knock out his communications. On the evening of the thirty-first, military press spokesmen in Saigon tried to put a brave face on the day's events, but back home the American people were watching and wondering. Even after the spilling of so much blood and the expenditure of so much treasure, it was clear the Communists could strike at will anywhere in the country. The day would prove to be the turning point of the Vietnam war.

In Quang Ngai City, meanwhile, Claire and the other members of the Canadian aid team tried to carry on their work the next morning. While Claire was away at lunch Dr. Jutras personally drove Hoa's uncle to the provincial hospital.

For Claire the first week of February 1968 was a kaleidoscope of unforgettable images. She watched an American tank pulling the bodies of two prisoners through the dusty streets. They were eventually tied up and left to rot in the hot sun, as GIs rushed to take snapshots of the spectacle. A Vietnamese neighbour sat in her front yard with her dead husband's head in her lap, weeping hysterically. For two days and a night another man just squatted outside his home, evidently in shock. The roof and one side of his house had been blown away, and there was no sign of his large family. A Vietnamese prisoner was marched through the streets of Quang Ngai followed by a silent crowd of children and adults. The young man harangued his captors and held his fist aloft in a defiant salute as he was led to prison and probable interrogation, torture, and death.

The constant fighting and resulting curfew meant that civilians from the outlying areas were no longer able to reach the TB clinic, so Claire spent part of each day volunteering in the emergency ward and the burns unit at the provincial hospital. The already overcrowded wards were now so overflowing with civilian casualties that some were simply placed on the ground between the buildings of the compound. On one occasion Claire looked in on the tiny provincial hospital jail cell which housed sick or injured prisoners. It held two women. One had just given birth and was still quite radiant from the wonder of it all, while the other, described as *une folle* by her jailers, took one look at Claire and, mistaking her for an American, held up her manacled hands and screamed *"My!"* (American) over and over again. The piercing shriek echoed in Claire's ears. Meeeee, meeeee, meeeeee.

On the afternoon of February 3, the fourth day of the offensive, two ARVN officers came to the hospital to advise the Canadian medical team that they would send soldiers that night to "protect" them. Alarmed at the prospect of having combatants in the building, Claire and Jutras went immediately to lodge a protest with the provincial chief. ARVN troops might remain in the area surrounding the hospital but must not enter, lest the building itself become a legitimate military target. He agreed with the Canadians, but added that if the Front attacked the hospital he would immediately order rockets fired at the building.

Still, that night around midnight a platoon of twenty-four ARVN soldiers came running up the stairs of the hospital's second-floor verandah. They began to set up their guns, but after an hour of heated objection from the Canadians communicated through Chau's translation, they were eventually persuaded to leave.

The next day Jutras went to see the provincial chief again, though this time he insisted on going alone. The Canadians waited anxiously for Jutras's return, their anxiety heightened by the ominous discovery in mid-afternoon that a section of the fencing around the hospital had been ripped up. The breach had been marked with a white flag, presumably so it could be located in the dark. Nightfall brought with it the evening curfew, and still Jutras had not returned. The team decided to beef up its presence in the hospital that night in case the ARVN platoon returned. Arthur Ludwick, Pauline Trudel, and Claire all elected to spend the night in the hospital, as well as Chau and his family. Claire took up a position at the bottom of the stairs to intercept the soldiers, and she spent the whole night there, on sentry duty.

After a nerve-racking but uneventful night Claire returned to the Canadian House for breakfast and found Jutras there. The provincial chief had once again promised that his troops would not come into the hospital, the Canadian doctor assured Claire. But where had he been last night? Claire demanded of Jutras. Surely it would have displayed a greater sense of responsibility on the part of the medical director to bring them this news before the curfew, rather than letting his team spend another jittery, sleepless night at the hospital.

On the strength of the provincial chief's reassurance, the Canadian team relaxed their vigilance that night, but events were about to make the Canadian medical aid effort in Quang Ngai wholly untenable. Only Claire and Hoa Ba, a Vietnamese nurse, were on duty. It was two in the morning when the ARVN platoon ran up the stairs and on to the balcony, pumping tracer rounds into the moonless sky. There was no time for argument. Claire and Hoa Ba helped bundle the patients into their blankets and everyone took refuge under the wardroom beds. The firing continued unabated until six, when the ARVN regulars departed. Fortunately, there had been no return fire, and no one was hurt.

Claire told her fellow team members what had happened over breakfast. Clearly, there was no guarantee that the events of the early morning would not be repeated that night, or the night after. Doubtless because its second-floor verandah offered a superb field of fire the hospital had been turned into a fire base by the South Vietnamese army, inviting retaliation and injury to their patients. Why not evacuate the patients to the provincial hospital, which was relatively secure, Claire suggested. The team could continue to care for them there, while they attempted once again to prevail on the provincial chief to declare the Canadian hospital off-limits to the forces under his command.

This time Claire accompanied Jutras to the chief's compound, but he was unavailable. They communicated their plight to James May, but the chief's response, relayed through his principal U.S. adviser was to "Go and tell it to the VC." They were on their own.

The head of the American military medical team at the provincial hospital was similarly uncooperative. He refused an informal request to admit the Canadian TB patients, arguing that the former TB ward, which was still empty, might be needed for the overflow from other buildings. Claire urged that they make a formal request for a transfer, but Jutras refused. Instead, he ordered that the hospital be closed, and that the patients be given a ten-day supply of medicine and told to go home. Claire took strong exception to Jutras's decision, arguing that it was unsafe for the patients, already weak with TB, to be sent into the embattled country-side, but her protestations were unavailing.

The next day, February 6, brought a heartrending scene to the Canadian hospital: the patients did not want to leave. Their feelings of grief and even despair were unmistakable, and some of them pointed at their chests and shook their heads. Claire was in agony at the sight of this dangerous exodus. How many of them would reach home safely? And what were they likely to find when and if they got there? But there was nothing she could do, and in any event the future of the Canadian medical team in Quang Ngai was now in serious doubt.

The American military had offered to evacuate the Canadians by plane to Da Nang. Dr. Jerema argued that they should accept, observing that the offer could well be a veiled warning that the Americans expected further hostilities in Quang Ngai City, and that the outcome was far from certain. Already the Canadian House, which had never been a direct target, was showing the effects of the nearby fighting. Stray bullets had pockmarked the stucco here and there and a piece of an airplane fuselage had smashed into it the day before. They agreed that everyone on the Canadian team would evacuate, except for Jutras, who elected to move into "Fort May," James May's heavily fortified bunker.

Within hours of the departure of the last patient Claire and her colleagues were preparing their own hasty leavetaking when an American military jeep arrived at the residence. The driver had an urgent cable from Ormond Dier via the British embassy in Saigon: could anyone provide him with information concerning the whereabouts and safety of his daughter Tara? The communiqué struck Claire as tacky and typical of the indifference of the Canadian mission in Saigon to their compatriots in Quang Ngai. Dier's concern for the safety of his own flesh and blood was understandable, but couldn't he at least have added a line inquiring about the well-being of the other Canadians under his nominal command? The nineteen-year-old Tara boarded the flight with the rest of them, bound for Da Nang.

They landed safely at the huge American air base, and only now did Claire begin to appreciate the country-wide significance of the Tet Offensive. Even the personnel in this vast U.S. military complex were on full alert. Her first concern was to place a call to her daughters, to tell them she was safe. That done, Claire was billeted in an apartment building in the city, where all American and Canadian civilian personnel were ordered to stay.

On her second afternoon in Da Nang, everyone in the building was summoned to an emergency meeting with an American general. There were thirty thousand North Vietnamese troops in the immediate area, he told them, and an attack was expected that night. First aid stations would be set up in the stairwells on each floor of the building. The wounded who had little chance of survival should be abandoned, the general continued somberly, and medical attention should be concentrated on those who might recover. If their position was overrun the building's residents were to gather on the roof, where helicopters would be called in to lift them off.

Claire sat up all night, waiting for the attack. As it happened the apartment she was sharing belonged to a secretary from the United States State Department. How ironic, Claire reflected. She doubted if *toi la nguoi Gia-Na-Dai, toi khong phai la nguoi My* could save her now. Still, if her time had finally come, there was no better way to go than watching thirty thousand North Vietnamese overrun Da Nang. But the night passed, and the expected attack never happened. Later Claire learned that the American general who had made the horrific predictions had just received a "Dear John" letter from home, and was considered mentally unstable.

Claire volunteered to work in the hospitals and refugee camps in Da Nang, and she was assigned to assist a variety of American doctors. Most of them had come to Vietnam as part of the American Medical Association's Project Vietnam. In return for a two-month volunteer tour participating doctors received a free trip around the world, two months of tax deductions, short working days, and two weeks of vacation. Her experience with Dr. Pat Moseley was memorable.

The usual practice was to pass through a ward, select a patient, any patient, and proceed to do something, anything. Pat selected a woman whose head had been shaved and bandaged. She assisted in the removal of the sutures, laying back the scalp flap, washing the purulent areas with disinfectant, replacing the flaps and securely binding the head so that the skin edges would make contact and eventually heal.

Claire noticed that Dr. Moseley was keeping careful track of the time, and asked her why. She had a tennis game with a friend scheduled for 12:30, came the reply. Claire was straightening the bedsheets of the patient with the head wound when she discovered a ghastly sight: the woman had been disembowelled. Her lower body was a mass of crushed bone and blood. She was in need of much more work.

But when Claire called this to Pat's attention, she only stopped long enough to laugh. "Don't be silly. Why bother? She'll be dead by morning, anyway. She'll just smell a little sweeter when she dies."[39]

That remark, Claire came to feel, precisely summed up Canada's own medical aid effort in Vietnam. It was calculated to make a few Vietnamese smell a little sweeter before they died.

Claire stayed in daily touch with the Canadian mission in Saigon by telephone, and she asked Gordon Longmuir whether the team should not evacuate to the capital, given the uncertainty of the war, even here in Da Nang.

"Well, all right," Longmuir agreed at last. "Come if you want to."

They were lodged in the usual hotels, and it was apparent at once that Saigon, too, was feeling the impact of Tet. Refugees were streaming into the city from the surrounding countryside, enormous rats were running through the streets, and a dusk-to-dawn curfew was in force. The Canadians soon met other foreign aid workers who had also been forced to abandon their projects in country. The Swiss and Germans, Claire learned, were returning home. Increasingly, she found herself wondering if the

Canadians should not do the same. Certainly they were of little use here in Saigon. Claire volunteered her services to South Vietnam's Ministry of Health, but an official there told her that there were already more volunteers than patients, an answer Claire knew to be specious. The enforced inactivity in the middle of such obvious need weighed heavily on her, and she was critical of the expense to the Canadian taxpayers of keeping the whole team in Saigon for what appeared to be an indefinite period—hotel rooms, meals, they were even receiving a sizeable per diem because they were away from their posts.

On February 14 Dr. Alje Vennema suddenly arrived in Saigon, fearful for the Canadian medical team and certain that his expertise would be urgently needed. But Gordon Longmuir and Jutras accused him of returning to usurp Jutras's position as director of the Canadian team. Internal bickering among the Quang Ngai personnel now flared into the open, and External Affairs decided to physically separate the warring factions. Vennema would undertake a country-wide mission to assess where further Canadian medical aid might best be put to use, Jutras would return to Quang Ngai, while Claire, nurses Trudel and Piché, and X-ray technician Ludwick would be given a week's rest and recreation outside the war zone.

They were flown to Phnom Penh, the capital of Cambodia. Claire found it a serenely beautiful country, as yet untouched by the war. But now it was difficult to sleep at night without the sounds of battle outside. They swam on the beaches of Kep and Kampot and visited the ancient ruins at Angkor Wat, but for once Claire was in no mood for sightseeing. Her thoughts kept straying to Quang Ngai, pulling myriad questions in train: how were their patients, her friends among the hospital's Vietnamese staff, their families? Then, too, everyone they met, after learning that the Canadians had just left Vietnam, wanted to talk about the war. Would the NLF win? Would the Americans withdraw? "If not," they were told over and over by Cambodians, "we know it will spread here, too." "You cannot expect the whole forest not to be destroyed when many trees are burning," one Cambodian observed prophetically.

After returning to Saigon Claire and the other members of the aid team sought to take advantage of a lull in the fighting in Quang Ngai. They asked permission of the Canadian delegation to return north just long enough to pack their belongings. Gordon Longmuir refused, but he was overruled by Ormond Dier on the express condition that they simply pack and return the same day. Claire went to the Air America office to book their tickets, and while she was standing at the wicket a cable with Alje Vennema's name on it happened to catch her eye. The wire advised all Air America stations to refuse passage to Vennema, who, Claire knew, had gone to Hue to inspect the medical conditions there.

Concerned for her friend's safety and outraged at such American high-handedness, Claire went immediately to Longmuir to tell him of her alarming discovery. But the Canadian diplomat showed no concern. Considering Vennema's track record and the fact that his survey might turn up some unsavoury discoveries about American conduct in the war, was it really so surprising that Air America would refuse to carry him?

Claire knew, they both knew, that Hue had become the focal point of some of the heaviest fighting of the Tet Offensive, indeed of the entire war. Suppose Vennema needed to get out in a hurry? Without Air America he would be forced to rely on Air Vietnam, which was as unreliable as it was unsafe. Still more disturbing was Longmuir's bland acceptance of Air America's decision. Canadians in country were completely dependent on United States air support, as he well knew. The implication was that as soon as a Canadian spoke out against the war the Americans had every right to restrict their movements around the country.

Well, Longmuir shrugged, he had already told "Al" not to fly with Air America, but to stick with Air Vietnam, and he just hoped that Vennema would have the sense to do as he was told.

Deeply shaken by Longmuir's indifference, Claire boarded the flight to Quang Ngai, where another unpleasant revelation awaited.

Although the fighting had subsided, little had changed in Quang Ngai City since the team's hasty departure three weeks before. The hospital was still being occupied by ARVN forces each night, the curfew was still in effect, and Jutras was still ensconced in Fort May. Soon after their arrival Claire was astonished to learn that the order banning Vennema from Air America flights had originated in Quang Ngai, over the signature of James May himself. May was Jutras's host, and it was inconceivable that the Canadian doctor had not known of May's order. Jutras, Claire was now convinced, was intriguing with the CIA against a fellow Canadian.

The young Canadian doctor urged the team members to stay, as things were relatively quiet. Pauline and Louise, who had each established relationships with individual embassy boys, were eager to accept Jutras's suggestion. Dr. Jerema was ambivalent. Only Claire was opposed. They had promised Dier they would return to Saigon at once, she argued. Surely they should honour that pledge. Jutras said he would phone Saigon, and clear the change in plans with Dier. When he returned, Jutras told the team members he had reached Longmuir, who agreed that they should remain in Quang Ngai.

Claire was deeply suspicious. Longmuir hadn't even wanted to let them come to Quang Ngai for a few hours. Why would he change his mind now? And what possible good could it do for the team to remain? The hospital was still closed and there was no immediate prospect of its reopening. Even the Quakers down the road had closed up shop and removed to Hong Kong. What was more, Jutras seemed especially insistent that Claire should stay in Quang Ngai.

Every instinct for self-preservation told Claire to get out. She was completely mistrustful of Jutras now, and, for the first time, concerned about her own safety. She agreed to stay for one night, and no more. She had reached another decision, too, Claire announced. So far as she was concerned, the entire medical aid project should be terminated.

The next day Claire paid a farewell visit to the provincial hospital. The TB ward where she had wanted to transfer their patients was still empty, and intact. When she returned to the Canadian House, Claire could sense the attitude of her fellow team members—she was running to Saigon with her tail between her legs while they were the heroic ones, electing to remain in the war zone. The aspersion on her physical courage was obvious, and Claire was tempted to remind them that only she had taken the long walk to the hospital at the height of Tet. But by now she cared little what the other Canadians thought, either of her courage or her decision. The Vietnamese were another matter. She called the staff together to tell them that she was leaving.

"I cannot work with the Americans who are destroying your people and your country. I cannot work with Dr. Jutras who works with the Americans. I think the best way I can help you is to go back home and try to stop the war," Claire told her Vietnamese friends.

Most of them seemed to understand. But Kim Nhung withdrew to the outer edge of the circle. Refusing to look at Claire, the young widow sat cross-legged on the floor and quietly sang a song to herself. Claire had grown to love Kim's singing around the hospital, and one day she told her so. "But I sing because I am sad," Kim had explained. Now Claire found Kim's quiet song a poignant recrimination.

Huong, Claire's other English student, was more voluble in her opposition. She stamped her feet. "You don't go. We very, very sorry you go. YOU DON'T GO!" In a last, desperate ploy Huong, knowing full well Claire's pride in her students' accomplishments, leaned across the counter, her long black hair swaying in rhythm with her pounding fist. "But you come back? We forget our English."

Claire could barely restrain her own tears. It was one of the most painful decisions of her life, leaving these people to the dangers of this slaughter, while she herself was free to return to the safety of Canada. But she had now reached the conclusion that she, and all the Canadians in Vietnam, were doing more harm than good. At best they were the pawns of the

Americans, at worst active collaborators in the war effort. No, far better to change Canadian policy, to bring Canadian pressure to bear on the United States to end this tragic, pointless war.

"I'll come back," Claire promised. "I'll come back when there is peace in your country." She tried to smile back the tears, but her heart was breaking.

And so on the afternoon of February 29, 1968, a stocky, white-haired Canadian woman, almost fifty, fussed impatiently with her baggage on the airstrip outside Quang Ngai City. Just as she was about to board the plane a group of Claire's Vietnamese friends rushed towards her. Ba, Kim, Huong, Nga, all of them were there. They had passed through four military checkpoints to see Claire off, and to present her with a bottle of champagne and a beautiful lacquered painting of a tranquil lake in Hanoi.

Nga, whom Claire had been training to work as a secretary in the hospital office, clung to Claire's arm. "My mother says I go with you," she whispered tearfully, confessing that she was afraid to work with Jutras because he had been making sexual advances towards her.

It was impossible to take her along, Claire explained gently, her heart breaking again even as it was filling with rage against Jutras.

"You come back, you come back," they shouted, smiling and waving as Claire boarded the Beechcraft at last.

Claire's last glimpse through the plexiglass was of her dear friend Ba as she turned away and began the walk home to her four children. Ba lived in an obscure hamlet ten kilometres northeast of Quang Ngai City. They called the place My Lai.

CHAPTER SEVEN

Stopping the Bombs

"But we feel that the bombs must fall on our shoulders. If you want to help, why not return to your country and stop the bombs from coming?"
—North Vietnamese ambassador to
Claire in Paris, March 1968

Claire decided to return to Montreal via the western route—New Delhi, Moscow, Hamburg, Paris, London, Dublin—thus completing her circumnavigation of the globe. It should have been an exhilarating trip, but in the month after her departure from Saigon Claire was tortured by guilt, self-doubt, remorse. Had she done the right thing by leaving? What would happen to her Vietnamese friends? She felt that she had deserted them. What could she do now to best help the Vietnamese people? These questions haunted her waking moments, and she would often discover to her surprise that she had been crying, any time, anywhere, on a plane, a bus, even walking down a city street. It just went on and on, and she gradually became immune to other people's reactions to her behaviour. And then suddenly it stopped, as if scar tissue had covered a deep wound. Vietnam would become to Claire what Spain had been to Norman Bethune—a scar on her heart.

Claire had met with Ormond Dier just before leaving Saigon. The head of the Canadian ICC delegation to Vietnam tried to persuade her to change her mind and stay. But, like it or not, they were in the pocket of the Americans, Claire responded, and the Americans were destroying Vietnam. She had come for humanitarian reasons, to relieve suffering, but the Canadian effort, she was now convinced, was doing more harm than good because it lent credibility and moral support to the American cause.

Besides, in strictly practical terms, the Canadian presence in Quang Ngai was now patently untenable. Because it was occupied by the ARVN each night, the hospital was useless.

Why couldn't she settle for "a 50 percent humanitarian and 50 percent political effort?" the Canadian diplomat asked.

Dier's candid remark suddenly threw everything into focus for Claire. She remembered his surprise at how hard they all worked when the TB clinic had first opened and his observation that it didn't matter if they failed to see a single patient—the important thing was that the hospital was there. Claire reminded Dier that when she had signed on for the Vietnam tour she had been reassured by officials in Ottawa that Canada's effort in the country was 100 percent humanitarian. She was not interested in helping Canada appease the United States by flying the Maple Leaf in a militarily strategic area of South Vietnam. No, the Quang Ngai team should be withdrawn immediately, Claire reiterated.

Her departure from Saigon had been a marked contrast to her arrival at Ton Son Hut five months earlier. Dier himself escorted her to the airport. He seemed concerned about what Claire might say or do on her return to Canada, but she assured him that she would work within channels at External Affairs to change Canada's policy on Vietnam.

Her first stop was New Delhi, where she obtained a visa for the Soviet Union. Claire had kept in close touch with her friend Ruslan Volkov. She had written him in Moscow, asking if she might visit and warning him that she had only a summer wardrobe. Her friend from Expo days met her at the airport with a fur coat and winter boots, and she spent most of the next five days with him, his wife, family, and friends. She had looked forward to seeing Ruslan again, and to finally experiencing firsthand the country she had always looked up to as a socialist model during her party days. But it was March 1968, early in what would come to be known as the Brezhnev era: she found the streets of Moscow especially bleak.

In the sanctuary of the Volkov family apartment Claire was at last able to unburden herself about Vietnam, and Ruslan, who might very well have said, "I told you so," did not. Soon Claire was swept up in political discussions about life in the Soviet Union, and on one memorable evening half a dozen of Ruslan's friends and neighbours gathered in the apartment. They trusted Claire enough to talk openly, and it was clear that these members of the Moscow intelligentsia were deeply alienated from their own political system. They were, in a sense, dissidents, though not in any organized or public way. But their only solution to their plight appeared to be quiet resignation. "What can we do but wait it out? We don't want to go back to the days of the czar, as bad as it is now."

The high point of her visit was meeting Ruslan's mother, Irenée. Claire had learned much of his family's difficult history from Ruslan during their time together the previous summer in Montreal. During the 1930s Ruslan had lived in New York where his father had been a Soviet trade commissioner, and his mother, who spoke four languages, had worked for Aeroflot, the state-owned airline. When Irenée failed to return to New York from a business trip to Moscow, Ruslan's father returned with the two children to the Soviet Union to make sure his wife was safe. Stalin's secret police soon came for him, and Ruslan never saw his father again. Irenée was sentenced to nine years in a Siberian labour camp. At the age of fifty-five she was released, and she promptly took a university refresher course and graduated with a gold medal. Claire was fascinated by the experiences of this still-handsome woman, who was then in her eighties.

Somehow Irenée had managed to obtain an illicit copy of *One Day in the Life of Ivan Denisovich*, the banned novella about life in the Siberian camps by Alexander Solzhenitsyn. Every word in it was true, Ruslan's mother assured Claire. People in the camps really would kill for a crust of bread.

"How did you manage to survive?" Claire asked her one night.

First, Irenée explained, she had never given up hope. At one point she had shared a cell with a strong young Spanish woman who simply turned her face to the wall and died. Irenée resolved that she would never give up her will to live. Second, she had fallen back on her deep love of nature. The stars shone in Siberia just as they did in Moscow, and she kept careful track of astral movements. By mail she would inform Ruslan of what to look for and then he would watch, too. Even though he was in faraway Moscow, knowing her son was watching the same stars at the same moment was a great comfort to both Irenée and Ruslan. The stars, glittering like diamonds in the vast Siberian night, brought them together.

Claire returned Ruslan's winter clothes to him at the airport, and flew off to Hamburg for a brief visit before continuing on to Paris. Even in the City of Light her malaise was overwhelming, and she was unable to summon any of her old excitement about Paris. Instead, she went to the Embassy of the People's Republic of Vietnam to volunteer her services to the people of North Vietnam.

"I won't blame you if you don't believe me, because there's so much CIA activity around," Claire told the ambassador, "but I want to tell you my story." After that preface she recounted her experiences in Quang Ngai. She was filled with a terrible yearning to help her Vietnamese friends. Might she return to Vietnam, but in the service of Hanoi this time? She had her medical training and experience, she was beginning to learn the language, and she had adapted well to the climate, food, and customs. Wasn't there some way she could help his government, his people?

The ambassador listened quietly and when she finished he smiled at her. "Thank you very much for your offer, and yes, I do believe your story. But we feel that the bombs must fall on our shoulders. If you want to help, why not return to your own country and stop the bombs from coming? And then, when the war is over, we will be very grateful for your help in rebuilding our country."

When Claire left the embassy she felt that the weight of the world had been lifted from her shoulders. The ambassador's words had provided her with a focus, a goal, if not yet a strategy: she must return to Canada and stop the bombs from coming. She fired off a letter from Paris to Paul Martin at the Department of External Affairs. She would be back in Canada within a week, she advised the minister, "and available for personal interview at your earliest convenience. At that time I shall present my reasons in detail for requesting permission to withdraw from the Canadian medical team in Vietnam."

Her head was swimming with half-formed ideas, strategies, plans. She felt renewed, re-energized. After sorrow would come not serenity, but action.

Following brief stopovers in London and Dublin Claire boarded a flight for Montreal which touched down at Dorval on the evening of Saturday, April 6, 1968. Dara was there to meet her. The preceding six months had been a time of emotional upheaval for Claire's younger daughter, who had been by turns frightened for her mother's safety, and then angry at Claire for putting herself in harm's way in the first place. They returned together to the apartment on Sherbrooke West, but there was little time for a homecoming celebration. Eager to tell her story in Ottawa, Claire wired Jean Arsenault at External Affairs early the next morning. She was, she informed him, "available for interview as soon as possible. Please advise." Arsenault's response was equally prompt. A meeting with Maurice Strong, head of External Aid, was scheduled for Tuesday afternoon.

Superficially, at least, Strong's debriefing of Claire was cordial. But at a more fundamental level she couldn't escape the feeling that they weren't really communicating at all. She recounted her experiences in Quang Ngai—the conditions of the civilian populace in the war zone, the Tet Offensive, the dubious efficacy of the Canadian aid effort, the unseemly closeness of at least some of the Canadian personnel to the American military and the CIA—much as she had already done to Longmuir and Dier in Saigon. But Strong seemed unable to grasp precisely why Claire had left. Like Dier, he tried to placate her: even if she helped only twenty people, wouldn't that have been worth it?

But what was the point of helping twenty victims if two hundred more were being blown up at a shot by war materials Canada was supplying to the United States at a profit, Claire parried.

She tried a different tack, a cost-benefit argument. Each member of the Canadian medical team was receiving a regular income, plus a twenty-dollar-a-day honorarium, for sitting idly in Saigon. Why should the Canadian taxpayers be burdened with the support of an entire medical team who were unable, because of the war, to do the job they were being paid to perform?

But Strong still seemed baffled by Claire's resignation from the team. In effect, she had thrown half a year's salary—five thousand dollars—away, not to mention a possible career for life in the Canadian civil service. Claire had the distinct impression her words simply weren't getting through. She understood his logic—a position in the civil service was a kind of iron rice bowl, provided one never rocked the boat. But that was not her way. Besides, there were far more urgent issues at stake, chief among them what the war was doing to the people of Vietnam. But before she knew it, she was being ushered out the door, with Strong seeming kind, genial, understanding, but not really understanding at all.

Claire's meeting with Strong was the kind of confrontation that would be repeated again and again with a succession of Ottawa mandarins in the coming years. Strong knew, as Claire did not, the delicate balancing act that his government was performing in its policy on the war in Vietnam. On the one hand Ottawa was anxious to preserve its image as "the helpful fixer" of international affairs. Canada was perceived both globally and domestically as a peacekeeper, a nation concerned with decency and human rights. But on the other hand Ottawa was under pressure from Washington to support its policy in Vietnam. The Quang Ngai hospital was a keystone of Canada's equivocal and essentially deferential policy toward the American tragedy in Vietnam. Its presence, as first Dier and now Strong were signalling, owed as much to the exigencies of Canada's relations with the United States as it did to any noble humanitarian impulse. The domestic side of the equation was also crucial. The Canadian government had, in fact, been under pressure at home to do something for Vietnam's long-suffering civilian populace, and that, too, was a factor in the Quang Ngai project. Indeed, it was the desire to help the Vietnamese people that had impelled Claire to volunteer for Quang Ngai in the first place. Now Claire was charging that Quang Ngai was essentially a form of complicity with the American war effort—not at all the desired domestic image.

The men at External would come to see Claire as naive, simpleminded—and more dangerous than she ever knew. Yet her worldview was at once simpler and more complex than their own. Here was an outsider, female, a grandmother with no scholarly or diplomatic credentials. But she had been there. By sending Claire Culhane to Vietnam, the Canadian government had allowed her to see firsthand both the effects of the war and the impact of Canadian policy on the ground. She had witnessed the suffering and futility of the war, and she had concluded that Canada should withdraw from Vietnam and use its good offices to persuade the United States to do the same. She had experienced the war as had none of the men in External Affairs or External Aid, and her position was unshakable—the war was wrong, and it must be stopped. Canada was a genuinely moral nation only to the extent that its diplomats aided that end.

And, in a way that would forever seem to elude the grasp of her bureaucratic opponents, Claire's understanding of politics was both complex and deeply personal. She now had thirty years of political experience behind her. She had been a member of the Communist Party of Canada at its zenith, when its members fought and died in Spain, when they organized the Congress of Industrial Organizations and led a powerful and spirited trade union movement. The party had taught her how to organize at the grass roots—how to make a speech, how to use the news media to drive a point home to the public. Her political perspective was radical, global, and analytical. Her will had been tempered in a dozen fires, from growing up female and Jewish in Quebec through back-alley abortions and her marriage to Garry, to a long walk down a dark road in the middle of the Tet Offensive.

Claire returned to Montreal to write her official report.

It took her nine days to complete the document that the government would go to such extraordinary lengths to suppress. It was at once reportage, an impassioned *cri de coeur*, and an angry indictment of Canadian policy in Vietnam.

She submitted copies of her report to Strong, Arsenault, and Earl Drake, the director of planning at External Aid. In a covering letter Claire summarized the most urgent recommendations: the immediate withdrawal of the Canadian medical team from Vietnam, the convening of a conference between herself, Drs. Jutras and Vennema, and others "for clarification of issues which should not be left unresolved," and the "cessation of all assistance and supplies to the U.S.A. which are presently being used, or are intended to be used in the prosecution of the war against the peoples of Vietnam, including production which provides substantial financial returns to Canadians."

The report itself was as critical of Dr. Jutras as it was laudatory of Vennema. It detailed Jutras's repeated absences from the Canadian residence, and recapped a number of his controversial decisions: the refusal to treat wounded civilians during the Tet Offensive, the removal of Hoa's badly burned uncle to the provincial hospital, his orders to herself, Pauline, and Chau to return to the Canadian House the second night of Tet and their near-fatal encounter with the hysterical ARVN patrol. The report recounted the overrunning of the hospital by the South Vietnamese forces and the eventual evacuation of the Canadian team, first to Quang Ngai, and then to Saigon. German and Swiss aid teams had withdrawn from the country, Claire noted, as had several religious and humanitarian service groups. Yet Ottawa had left its team marooned in Saigon with no clear signal as to what it should do.

In the body of her report Claire offered six long-term recommendations to improve the calibre of Canada's aid teams in Vietnam. Members should be obliged to learn the local language. They should be encouraged to write brief, individual weekly reports to Ottawa to establish closer contact. There was presently so little communication, she noted, that Ottawa "has no idea if the hospital in Quang Ngai is even functioning." Third, all expenditures of funds should be regularly and frequently examined, with special attention paid to the shipping and storing of essential equipment. All Canadians serving in Vietnam should receive the same privileges—the ICC delegation in Saigon had received special ID cards which gave them shopping privileges at the American PX, while the in-country personnel had no such cards. Moreover, identification cards should be issued to all Canadians serving abroad, as it was "neither safe nor feasible to carry around one's passport." And finally, financial inducements for overseas service should be eliminated. "By raising the initial requirements to a more demanding level, I feel a more responsible and motivated applicant would respond, since the emphasis would be placed on personal contact in the assisted country, and help eliminate those who seek only adventure . . ."

Next Claire tried to illuminate the moral dilemma at the core of her decision to resign from the Quang Ngai team. She had been assured at the outset that she was joining a "100 percent humanitarian effort," but as the months went by it became more and more obvious that the small medical group could not possibly operate without the goodwill and cooperation of the American military forces.

Her very presence in Vietnam on such terms deprived her of her "right to stand aside from some measure of responsibility for all the brutality and horror being inflicted upon innocent human beings." She fully supported the inalienable right of the Vietnamese people to self-determination, Claire wrote, but she had now begun to question whether the Canadian

government did. "I had to weigh for myself the extent to which the mainte-
nance of a medical team in Quang Ngai was becoming an expedient to
compensate for our alleged non-military support and non-participation in
the American war effort," Claire observed pointedly, "at the same time
that Canadian aircraft were flying overhead bearing United States military
insignia. It very soon became impossible for me to reconcile these two
positions."

She had noted a newspaper story that very day which reported that, due
to the Vietnam war, the Canada-U.S.A. Defence Sharing Agreement of
1959 was running a $200 million surplus in Canada's favour. "Are we trying
to justify war profiteering with humanitarian efforts in Vietnam today?"

She concluded her report by meeting head-on the apparently moral
argument proffered by Strong and Dier in favour of Canada's medical aid
to Vietnam, "that even to be able to care for one victim would warrant the
entire effort. As a person still so deeply affected by the sights I have seen,
the victims I have bathed and bandaged . . . I humbly repeat that whatever
meagre help . . . we can give to these ravaged people can no longer be
qualified as righteous when placed in juxtaposition to our participation at
other levels—providing the means to destroy them."

> At this moment in history I do not feel it is sufficient to fervently
> hope and pray for an end to this terrible war. I feel that the time has
> come for a strong stand on the part of every nation in the world, to
> say, "We demand that the slaughter of innocent human beings be
> stopped immediately, and we will withhold and withdraw any and
> every item originating in our country which can in any possible way
> be used for continuing this devastation.

Canadian medical personnel, she concluded, should be withdrawn
immediately because of the real personal danger, and because it was no
longer conscionable to work in tandem with the irreparably corrupt Saigon
government.

> To anyone who may think this is a strange way to help the sick and
> wounded, may I assure them that every day utilized to bring total
> peace will be another step towards the goal of *no more war victims*
> . . . I further submit that the Vietnamese people themselves would
> be the keenest supporters of this action on our part . . . Very
> simply—let us stop making money out of this war—let us withdraw
> our support from the forces which are causing this abundance of
> pain and suffering—let us plan for the day when we can return to
> multiply our facilities to heal and cure, in the secure atmosphere of
> peace.

Claire submitted her report on April 18, 1968, and settled in to await a reply.

The official response reached her three weeks later in a series of letters. The first, from Arsenault, noted that her suggestion that the Canadian team be withdrawn had been made "the subject of a study by the authorities responsible for making this decision." A conference involving Claire, Vennema, and Jutras was out of the question, since Jutras's absence from the TB clinic in Quang Ngai for even a short period of time would jeopardize the whole future of the TB clinic. Finally, Arsenault sidestepped the question of embargoing all Canadian exports to the United States that could be used for military purposes on the basis that such a sweeping decision was "outside our jurisdiction."

In his response Earl Drake, the director of planning at External Aid, praised "the frankness and thought which has gone into the preparation of your report." Claire's recommendations had such wide ramifications that "we want to give them very careful consideration before taking any action, but I can assure you that your efforts in preparing the report have been very much appreciated as has your splendid contribution at Quang Ngai."

Maurice Strong also acknowledged Claire's report in writing, promising a decision about the Quang Ngai medical team "in the near future." He echoed Arsenault's contention that a cessation of all assistance and supplies to the United States which might be used in Vietnam was a matter "outside the jurisdiction of the External Aid Office."[1]

Many people would have let the matter drop there, as the officials at External Aid doubtless hoped Claire would. They had asked for Claire's report, she had submitted it, and her recommendations had been duly deliberated. She had been amply thanked for her contribution in Vietnam, and it was time for her to return quietly to private life. In this expectation the bureaucrats were to be sorely disappointed.

Claire had now been back in Canada for a month, and she was fast losing patience with the bureaucrats at External Aid, but then she had never been the type to simply wait and hope. She had begun to make the rounds in Montreal, renewing old friendships and acquaintances, and the oldest of all was Thérèse Casgrain, whom Claire had first met thirty years before. Casgrain was delighted to see Claire again after so many years, not least because she and a group of supporters were raising money for medical aid to Vietnam. The grande dame of Quebec politics listened with keen interest to Claire's stories about her experiences there.

Claire also shared her observations with Ken Andrews, who remained a close friend. Through Andrews she was introduced to Warren Allmand, the Liberal MP for Notre Dame de Grâce. Both Andrews and Allmand were members of the World Federalists, an organization that advocated the transcendence of national boundaries and prejudices in favour of greater international cooperation. She showed her report to Allmand, and the young MP was scandalized. He promised to investigate and, if necessary, have the document tabled before the Parliamentary Sub-Committee on Foreign Affairs.

Probably through her meeting with Casgrain, Claire soon received her first invitation to speak publicly about Vietnam. The event, sponsored by the Voice of Women (VOW), was scheduled for the evening of May 22, 1968, at Sir George Williams University. Casgrain was the president of the Quebec branch of VOW, the organization that would soon play such a large role in Claire's efforts to expose Canadian policy in Vietnam. Founded in the early 1960s to address peace issues, the Voice of Women had evolved into a national women's organization that was in some ways a forerunner to the National Action Committee on the Status of Women. The organization had become increasingly concerned at the escalation in Vietnam, and, although it could hardly be described as militant, had become the subject of surveillance by the RCMP. Advance press clippings of her speaking engagement duly found their way into Claire's own RCMP file, which had been reactivated for the first time since 1955.

Claire pulled no punches with her audience at Sir George, describing in graphic detail the horrors of the war, especially as it affected women and children. "I saw things which no human being should see. A baby with a hole in its head, a child with his arm blown off, a woman completely burned by napalm, the swelling bands of refugees torn from their homes." Perhaps mindful of the promises of discretion she had given to Dier and that she had since reiterated in her correspondence with External Aid, Claire refrained from specifically criticizing Canadian policy in Vietnam. She did, however, hint at her own conclusions. "This may sound cruel on the surface, but I think that if the regime—which is extremely corrupt— received no outside help, it might fall more quickly . . . We want to save all the children of Vietnam, not just a few. Foreign medical aid is putting a small bandage on a problem which needs a solution cutting to the very core of things."[2]

Eight days after her appearance at Sir George, Maurice Strong sent a confidential letter to the Canadian delegation in Saigon, warning them.

In her correspondence with External Aid Office . . . Mrs. Culhane
has stressed the importance of having the members of the Canadian
Medical Team recalled to Canada . . . This is in accordance with Dr.

Vennema's views as stated in his last report. *You are aware of the decision on this question.* We have endeavoured to explain to Mrs. Culhane the importance of having a Canadian presence in Vietnam, but she has failed to accept our views and has brought this aspect of our program to the attention of a Member of Parliament who has written to the Director General concerning this issue. *We hope it will not develop into an extensive investigation.* However, we thought you should be aware that some pressure is being applied to have the Canadian personnel totally withdrawn from Vietnam.[3]

Claire's report had apparently struck a raw nerve at External, not least because it so precisely echoed the sentiments Dr. Vennema had expressed in his own report. He was, after all, a widely respected professional who had spent nearly four years in country, and who had just been awarded the Order of Canada for his Vietnam service by a grateful Canadian government. Vennema, too, had urged Ormond Dier to withdraw the medical team on the basis that their lives were at risk. Just as he had done with Claire, Dier mentioned the importance of having Canadians in Vietnam. "If it's that important why don't you send a civil servant from the Department of External Affairs who can just sit there and wave a flag?" Let a fancypants diplomat get shot at, Vennema had replied bluntly. Like Claire, Vennema, too, was beginning to piece together the real reason for keeping the Quang Ngai project going. "What was important in Vietnam was Canadian representation—to show we were there. Again, to placate the Americans." The presence of the "neutral" Canadians lent American policy an aura of legitimacy it would otherwise have lacked.[4]

Together, Claire and Vennema represented a potentially explosive combination. Their charges could tumble Ottawa off its Vietnam high wire at a most inopportune time. By mid-May the country was in the midst of a federal election, and a new Liberal leader, Pierre Elliott Trudeau, was seeking to renew the Grit mandate. Canada's Vietnam policy had not become an election issue, and officials at External were anxious to preserve that status quo. Still, Canadian personnel were clearly at some level of risk, even in Saigon, as Claire and Vennema kept reminding Ottawa. On the other hand, External was anxious not to incur American wrath by closing the hospital, and in the end the urge to appease carried the day. The decision Strong alluded to in his confidential letter was in fact a waffle: Canadian personnel would be given the choice to leave or stay, even though there was no immediate prospect of reopening the hospital. Their salaries and per diem would, of course, continue. It was a brilliant, if amoral, strategy. The Americans would not be displeased, and if any Canadians were killed External could wash its hands of the responsibility by pointing out that the medical team members had been aware of the risks, and had made individual choices to remain in Vietnam.

On June 19, 1968, a curious confidential memo crossed the desk of J. A. Arsenault. It was from security officer W. R. Shaw, and it was a reply to Arsenault's year-old request for security clearance for "Mrs. Claire CULHANE. With reference to your request for a security clearance for the above-named individual, please be advised that it would *not* be in the interest of this office to employ her."[5] The Mounties, it seemed, had finally caught up with their woman.

Claire continued what was fast becoming a personal crusade in the face of External's refusal to withdraw the Canadian medical team. (The Quang Ngai hospital reopened in early June, although a number of the personnel, with the notable exception of Dr. Jutras, had followed Claire's lead and returned to Canada.) She peppered Ottawa with letters: to Pierre Trudeau, whose Liberals won the federal election of June 25, 1968; to his newly appointed minister of external affairs, Mitchell Sharp; on down through the ranks of her old adversaries at External Aid. Claire had also begun to accept speaking and interview invitations from around the country, and by August articles by or about her had appeared in a dozen newspapers.

Her strategy was now beginning to find a focus. Many participants in Canada's anti-war movement had concentrated their efforts on criticizing the American role in Vietnam. Claire wanted to shift that orientation, to force Canadians to consider what their own government was doing—the "humanitarian" hypocrisy, the sham of neutrality, the reluctance to criticize the ongoing bombing of the North. Wherever she went she was like a lightning rod, stirring up controversy and often outrage. In Montreal a physician named Kenneth Bowes assured readers of the *Gazette* that during his time in Vietnam he had "found war injuries to be a very small part of my practice," that he had seen "no napalm burns, although I was looking for them," and that "the efforts of the Americans to improve these conditions are visible to all." He dismissed Claire's comments on her experiences in Quang Ngai as "a mixture of propaganda and fantasy."[6]

In July Claire attended an Action-Study Group on Vietnam conference at Toronto's Ryerson Polytechnical Institute, which according to one reporter seemed poorly attended, lethargic, and riven by sectarian feuding. It was Claire, according to an RCMP informant attending the meeting, who took matters in hand, passing a hat to raise money to send telegrams to the participants in the Paris peace talks, which had been under way since May. One telegram urged a halt to the American bombing of North

Vietnam, and another expressed solidarity with the North Vietnamese-NLF delegation.[7]

Drawing some form of positive action, however simple, out of an impossibly fractious meeting of left-wingers was very much Claire's style. To the RCMP and the reporter from the *Globe and Mail*, it seemed inconceivable that such an undisciplined "movement" could actually affect the outcome of the Vietnam war. Derision dripped from their accounts of the Ryerson meeting. But their reports failed to note one salient development—Claire, an old pro at this game, was now meeting, and influencing, an entirely new generation of youthful, enthusiastic social activists who admired her experience, her courage, and her persistence in the face of seemingly overwhelming odds. Claire was beginning to form a new network among a fresh generation, and many of her contacts would outlast RCMP informants, media scepticism, and even the Vietnam war itself.

Nor did Claire ignore the more established venues of political power in that summer of 1968. She wangled a week off work from the Neurological Institute where she had again returned to work and began to haunt the Centre Block on Parliament Hill, copies of her report in hand. To avoid appearing conspicuous she would dress in a blouse and skirt, looking, as she thought, like any other secretary in the building. She knocked on the door of each MP and senator, and made a brief speech: she wasn't asking them to agree with her or support her position on Canada's role in Vietnam, but didn't they at least agree that she should be able to formally table her report before the elected representatives of the Canadian people, as others had on their return from overseas? There were usually one of two reactions. Either they would press a button and summon a security guard to escort her out of their offices, or they would agree with her. But even among those who agreed with her, many shamefacedly confessed their own feelings of powerlessness. The party, the caucus, the layers of bureaucracy severely limited their individual scope. For Claire, the experience was a sobering lesson on the limits to Canada's democratic system. Even the people who were elected to represent the Canadian public felt impotent when it came to influencing the foreign policy of the nation.

Claire's snowballing notoriety in press and political circles came as an embarrassment to both her daughters. Dara, who had yet to turn eighteen and was still in the throes of adolescent rebellion, considered all politics "stupid," and her mother's increasing Vietnam involvement the stupidest of all. Like Roisin before her, Claire's younger daughter blamed her parents' marital breakup and her own bizarre upbringing on politics. Now all she wanted was a "normal" mother, and politics was once again getting in the way. A few months after Claire's return from Vietnam Dara moved out of the Sherbrooke Street apartment and into a place of her own.

In Vancouver, Roisin felt much the same way. Although Roisin had long since given up the expectation that her mother would settle into a respectable life-style for her own sake, she still harboured hopes that Claire would "grow up" and at least be a proper, sedate grandparent. In August 1968 Roisin made Claire a grandmother for a second time, and Claire flew out to see her newest granddaughter. But even then, to Roisin's irritation, her mother could not be content with a simple social visit. She used the trip to the west coast to travel to Vancouver Island where she continued her Vietnam crusade, and then she was off again, this time to a Voice of Women conference in Calgary.

Still, beneath the turbulent surface of the mother-daughter relationships there was an undercurrent of real affection; perhaps, though neither daughter would yet admit it, even a kind of grudging admiration. Knowing how much time her mother spent before her small manual typewriter (Claire was once again typing university theses at night to earn extra income, as well as maintaining her increasingly voluminous correspondence on Vietnam), Dara secretly set aside part of her own income as a secretary at McGill's mathematics department. After six months she proudly presented her mother with a new Smith Corona portable, the first electric machine that Claire had ever owned. And in Vancouver Roisin had named her baby Triona Claire O'Hea.

*   *   *

Claire was an old enough political hand to understand the importance of organization in promoting a political cause, but she was not, and had no intention of being, a member of any political party in Canada. She had, however, been a paper member of the Voice of Women for some time. Partly because of Thérèse Casgrain's prominence in VOW, and partly because of the organization's long-standing concern with peace issues, Claire concluded that VOW might be just the vehicle to help her raise public consciousness about Canada's true role in Vietnam. She attended VOW's national conference in Calgary in September 1968 to lobby the organization to step up its criticism of Canada's Vietnam policy, but, as fate would have it, she would come away with much more.

The Voice of Women was that autumn an organization in flux. Like any other broadly based national political organization in Canada, VOW encompassed many political views and tendencies. Some of its members were content with discreet work behind the scenes on peace issues—fundraising, knitting campaigns, sending telegrams, and conducting petition drives—while others wanted the organization to adopt a more militant stance, especially on Vietnam. The notion of taking its protests to the streets was still an intimidating prospect to many VOW members, who considered such direct action "too political." As the president of the VOW from 1967 to 1971, long-time Halifax peace activist Muriel Duckworth was forced to moderate between the conservatives and the militants. "We were just getting ready to go on the street," Duckworth would recall twenty-five years later of Claire's appearance in Calgary. "We lost membership because of taking political action. Our first demonstration was very controversial, and some of our members said they would leave the organization if we went through with it."

Claire attended the conference as a regular delegate, intending only to quietly lobby on behalf of her Vietnam perspective. But Kay MacPherson of Toronto had just returned from a trip to Hanoi, and she was scheduled to address the conference at a dinner gathering. "Why don't you speak, too?" several women asked Claire. "Kay's just returned from the North, you were in the South . . ." and before Claire knew it, the organizers were prevailed upon to let her address the full conference after MacPherson. To Claire's consternation it was 11:20 p.m. before it was her turn to speak. "Do hurry up, it's very late," MacPherson quietly reminded Claire as she handed her the microphone.

Claire's voice shook with emotion as she began her speech, though whether it was because of her passionate interest in the subject or her repressed rage at being needlessly scheduled for so late a time she could not say. Still, she held the audience spellbound as she linked the horrors of the war in Quang Ngai with Canada's involvement, and when she finished the gathering rose as one and, to Claire's utter astonishment, gave her a standing ovation. The next day she was elected to the National Council of the Voice of Women.

As encouraged as she was by the response to her message, Claire was equally perturbed by an event that had coincided with the Calgary meeting. In New York, Canada's new external affairs minister, Mitchell Sharp, had made his maiden speech to the General Assembly of the United Nations. Claire had expected that Sharp would call for a halt to the American bombing of North Vietnam, especially the devastating B-52 sorties, which Pierre Trudeau himself had condemned during the election campaign in May.[8] Instead, Sharp had attached a quid pro quo: the United States should cease its aerial bombardment if North Vietnam would withdraw its troops from the South. Claire was convinced that Sharp's UN position was but the latest example of Canada knuckling under to its powerful neighbour on the question of Vietnam.

For some time Claire had been mulling over the need for a spectacular public action to call attention to Canada's true role in Vietnam. She knew, too, that in the case of such action it wasn't only the issue that was important, but the timing of the event. Sharp's UN speech afforded the perfect opportunity for a high-profile public response, if it was done quickly. Now yet another series of events was about to fall into place that suited Claire's plan perfectly.

Voice of Women conference participants were planning to hold a vigil at the Suffield Defence Research Establishment, which was located about an hour's drive from Calgary. The purpose of the protest was to heighten public awareness of the chemical weapons testing then under way at Suffield, and the conference broke into small groups to organize the action. Claire was sitting on one such panel, planning the vigil, when Muriel Duckworth came over.

"This panel better break up and rejoin the main group," she advised, "because we've just received an invitation to tour the project and then have lunch with the commanding officers at Suffield."

Before Claire could object another member of her group looked up at Duckworth and very pointedly asked, to Claire's vast amusement and gratification, "Since when do you eat with the enemy?"

A row ensued over whether to accept the luncheon invitation, and the conference almost split apart then and there, but a compromise was arranged. Some members of the executive would take the tour and have lunch, while the others would remain on the lines outside the base gates, conducting a short, silent vigil.

The Voice of Women had rented a bus to take its members to Suffield and it was during the trip that Claire unveiled her audacious plan. Everyone was there—Casgrain, MacPherson, and Duckworth, along with all of the other members of the national executive and national council. Claire lobbied them individually, and because they were on a bus, she had a captive audience.

Ever since her return from Vietnam, Claire explained, she had wanted to do something, well, something spectacular to expose Canada's complicity in the Vietnam War. She had been unable to determine exactly what until now. But with Sharp's about-face at the UN, and with VOW already on record as opposing the bombing, wouldn't it be a perfect time for Claire, as a newly elected member of its national council, to do a fast on Parliament Hill in the name of the Voice of Women to raise consciousness on the Vietnam issue? It was by far the boldest action ever proposed by a member of VOW. "Claire had a tremendous sense of urgency," Duckworth recalled. "She was very courageous. There weren't any other women ready to do that. There was so much emotion around the Vietnam War, and Claire was so far out."

Such an action would require discussion, it would take time, objected a number of the women.

But Claire was not to be denied. Very well, she responded, they could discuss her proposal over the lunch hour and arrive at a decision on the bus on the way back to Calgary. Claire could tell that there was some reluctance to adopt such an audacious tactic, but on the return bus trip she parried the objections one by one.

Her proposed fast might detract from the overall impact of the conference, whose decisions were to be publicized by individual members in their respective cities once they returned home, someone objected. In all likelihood the news media would focus only on Claire's action.

Claire thought fast. All right, then, they would hold off announcing the Parliament Hill protest until the following Monday. Since the VOW delegates were due to return home on Thursday, that would give them four days to publicize the conference outcome.

She had them. There, on a bus rolling through the Alberta foothills, the strategy of Claire's first high-profile protest on the Vietnam war was hammered out. To avoid painting either themselves or the government into a corner the fast would be limited to ten days, and the time frame would be announced at the outset. On the tenth day VOW would organize a march to celebrate the breaking of the fast, and invite the Trudeau cabinet and members of parliament to join.

Claire rushed back to Montreal where she arranged for a leave of absence from the Neurological Institute, and then broke the news to Dara, who did not share her mother's enthusiasm for the fast, which was sure to embroil Claire still more deeply in the anti-Vietnam war movement. Dara was also concerned about the impact of fasting on her mother's health, but Claire brushed her daughter's objections aside. She was perfectly healthy, and while she would consume no solid foods for ten days, she would permit herself to drink fruit juices and take vitamins. In Ottawa VOW stalwart Charlotte MacEwan called a meeting of the group's members to organize logistical support.

The action that would catapult Claire into the national media limelight for the first time began at 9:00 a.m. on Monday, September 30, 1968, four weeks after her fiftieth birthday and one year to the day after she had left Montreal for Vietnam.

The event opened with a bang. At noon, Claire and a dozen VOW members who had joined her in front of the Centre Block had a twenty-minute face-to-face confrontation with one of the key architects of Canada's Vietnam policy. Mitchell Sharp stopped by on his way to lunch and Claire quickly challenged him about the government's about-face on the American bombing.

"We have called for a balanced response," Sharp responded.

"Mr. Trudeau didn't call for a balanced response," Claire snapped, remembering the prime minister's campaign position of total cessation of the bombing.

"Do you support the U.S. in the Czechoslovakian situation?" Sharp shot back. (The Soviet Union had that summer sent its tanks into Prague to repress Czechoslovakia's burgeoning democracy movement.)

But Claire refused to rise to the bait. "That's another problem," she insisted, returning to the subject of Vietnam. "If the government came out with a clear statement calling for an end to the bombing there would be a tremendous response."

"I'm not interested in a response. I'm interested in ending the war," Sharp answered. A crowd had now gathered around to listen.

"Don't talk silly, we don't want any credibility gap here," warned a doughty sixty-seven-year-old VOW stalwart from Belleville named Frances Wilcox. Another VOW member, Goldie Josephy, told Sharp that her son had worked his heart out for Trudeau in the Liberal election campaign. "Now he can't understand why Mr. Trudeau isn't coming out against the bombing. A lot of young people who worked for Trudeau are asking the same question."

If Sharp couldn't make a statement in the House, at least he could take the question to cabinet, Mrs. Josephy urged. "Even if you just told them there was a nut you met on the Hill who says we should stop the bombing."

The last word went to the already diminutive Mrs. Wilcox, who appeared smaller still beneath a large purple hat. Looking squarely into Sharp's eyes she asked, "Do you agree with burning people alive, Mr. Sharp?"

The minister for external affairs turned to answer another question and left for lunch a few minutes later.[9]

Sharp's impromptu encounter with Claire and his other VOW critics appeared to be a classic example of open government, of elected leaders speaking directly to their constituents. But when the *Toronto Star* carried a full report on the confrontation the next day the story was quickly clipped, photocopied, and circulated through the Department of External Affairs under the heading Subversive Activities.[10]

The members of the Parliamentary Press Gallery were clearly captivated by the image of a white-haired grandmother confronting the Canadian government over such a timely issue as the war in Vietnam, and the story was carried coast-to-coast.[11]

VOW groups in Winnipeg and Victoria expressed solidarity with

Claire's vigil and conducted weekend sympathy fasts of their own. Shirley Ball, the president of the Hamilton branch of the VOW, and Mrs. John Anwell, the organization's Ontario president, sent telegrams to Mitchell Sharp endorsing the fast and urging him to support the United Nations proposal "to stop the bombing now."[12]

On the first day, too, Warren Allmand dropped by. The young Liberal MP conceded that he had underestimated the resistance to tabling Claire's report before the Parliamentary Sub-Committee on Foreign Affairs. He still wanted to do something to help, however, and offered Claire the use of his Parliament Hill office. Knowing that public visibility is all-important in a fast, to allay suspicions that the hunger striker is sneaking off to get something to eat, Claire permitted herself only one brief daily absence from the Hill, using Allmand's office to wash and change clothes, and his phones to touch base with Charlotte and Roisin and Dara.

She and a companion slept each night under the portico of the East Block, thus satisfying the authorities that she was not sleeping, strictly speaking, on the grounds of Parliament proper. On Tuesday night she was visited by local VOW members, reporters, members of the Ottawa Committee to End the War in Vietnam, and a twenty-year-old American draft evader. Her voice was so hoarse from constant speaking that she had to resort to strong green tea—though without milk or sugar—as a restorative.

On Thursday it rained steadily, but Claire persevered, though she did seek a brief respite in the Centre Block lobby. "The Vietnamese are out in storms and going to bed hungry every night, not just ten days like me," she told a reporter, who described Claire as "a tanned, young-looking fifty . . . with tousled hair and eyes that sparkled with a determined enthusiasm."[13]

Claire had written to Trudeau, Eric Kierans, Jean Marchand, and Paul Martin, Sr., before the vigil began, urging them to make statements calling for a halt to the bombing, or at least to meet with her. Kierans, the postmaster general, invited Claire to his office, as did Jean Marchand. In an apparent breach of cabinet solidarity which he may not have wanted publicized, Kierans confided that he "was still sticking to earlier statements advocating 100 percent stoppage of American bombing." Claire, however, disclosed the Quebec minister's comments to the *Ottawa Citizen* the following day.[14]

Marchand, who was also a member of the Trudeau cabinet, posed a pointed question in return when Claire asked him why Canada didn't cancel the Defence Sharing Agreement. "Do you want to be the one to tell 150,000 Canadian workers that they're out of work if we discontinue producing war material for the U.S.A. under defence contracts we hold with them?"

Here Marchand candidly touched on the underbelly of Canadian policy on Vietnam. From the nickel mines of Sudbury to the aerospace industry clustered around Toronto and Montreal to dozens of other plants scattered from St. John's to Victoria, Canadian industrialists and Canadian workers were profiting hugely from the war in Vietnam. Later generations of Canadians, seduced by government rhetoric about "neutrality," "balance," and "humanitarian concerns" would pride themselves that their government had "stayed out of Vietnam." But Marchand's candid admission bespoke the limits of both the Canadian conscience and Canadian sovereignty.

Tory MPs George Hees and David MacDonald stopped by to tell Claire that they, too, agreed with her position, and she was invited to meet with eight women senators to discuss Canada's role in Vietnam. But Claire spent much of her time simply chatting with ordinary Canadians who came to Ottawa to visit the seat of their government. If people so much as looked at her she approached them and engaged them in conversation in either English or French. Students on school tours of the Hill stopped to stare and, occasionally, to shake her hand and wish her well. One young girl, who couldn't have been much more than twelve, stepped forward to offer Claire a stick of gum and a peanut butter sandwich. Claire, who suspected she'd been put up to it by her friends, refused the food and told her she was there "to keep her boyfriends and brothers from going to Vietnam." The girl retreated, shamefaced.[15]

The weekend brought still more visitors and supporters, including her old friend and comrade Lea Roback from YCL days, who arrived with a busload of VOW members from Montreal. Claire had now garnered the public support of rank-and-file VOW members in Ottawa, Montreal, Toronto, Hamilton, Winnipeg, and Victoria, as well as the provincial leadership in Ontario. But as her fast entered its second week Claire was becoming restive over one glaring omission: the national leadership of the VOW had yet to release a promised statement endorsing her vigil. She began to press Charlotte MacEwan on the matter during their daily phone conversations, and on Tuesday morning Charlotte told Claire to hold on, she happened to have Muriel Duckworth on the other line.

"Oh, no, oh, no . . ." Claire could hear her friend saying in response to the national VOW president. "I have a message for you from Muriel," Charlotte said to Claire at last. "They've changed their minds. They're not going to come out and make a statement, and Muriel's not going to be able to come to the breaking of the fast. They'll try to get Thérèse Casgrain instead."

"All right, you give Muriel my message," Claire answered evenly. "You tell her I'm going through with it, I'm not stopping, but on the last day I will publicly resign from the Voice of Women and say why."

Then it was Muriel's turn to gasp and say, "Oh, no, oh, no."

In the end, the national VOW leadership did issue a statement, although it was released only after the fast was over. But Duckworth did make good on another promise—Thérèse Casgrain was present for the breaking of the fast on the evening of Wednesday, October 9, 1968. Just before seven o'clock, the appointed hour for her to leave the Hill, a message arrived for Claire from the prime minister's office regretting that he had a prior engagement and would be unable to accept Claire's invitation to attend the fast-breaking dinner, which was already waiting at the Centennial Centre.

Well, couldn't he at least issue a statement that they could read at the dinner? Claire asked.

The prime minister was *very* busy, the aide replied.

Couldn't he just release a one-sentence statement? Claire pressed.

What could the aide say? He agreed to go back and ask his boss.

The aide reappeared moments later. "Actually, he has about fifteen minutes right now. Would you like to go up and meet him?"

"Yes, do," Thérèse urged. "I'll go with you."

Up they went, and as they entered his office Trudeau rose to shake Claire's hand. "I just want to congratulate you on the courage you're showing."

"It doesn't take much courage," Claire replied. "You should be congratulating all the thousands of Canadians who feel the same way I do but who aren't here."

They sat down and began to discuss Canada's policy on Vietnam. Did he agree with Sharp's statements?

Trudeau tried to talk around the issue, suggesting that Claire may have misinterpreted the remarks of the minister for external affairs. But Charlotte had provided Claire with the full text of Sharp's speech, and just as Claire was pulling the paper out to confront Trudeau with Sharp's actual words, a secretary poked his head through the door.

"Excuse me, I don't mean to disturb you, but you really should be leaving . . ."

It was an obvious setup, so well timed that Claire, Trudeau, and Casgrain all had to laugh. But the most revealing moment of the interview came as they were leaving the prime minister's office. Thérèse was already out the door when Trudeau turned suddenly to Claire. For one brief instant it was as if a mask, the veneer of arrogance and Gallic insouciance the Canadian public would come to know so well over the next fifteen years, fell suddenly from Trudeau's face

"You have no idea the pressures I'm under," he said quietly to Claire.

"Of course I do," Claire replied, motioning toward the Hill. "Why do you think I just spent ten days out there, if not to bring on another set of pressures?"

There was no response. The mask went back up, and the interview was over.

Outside, seventy-five people had assembled to accompany Claire on her walk off Parliament Hill. They struggled to light candles, which sputtered in the strong breeze and were in any event outshone by the glare of television floodlights. With Thérèse at her side and still carrying her picket sign, Claire slowly led the procession down off the Hill. She was tired after ten days of constant exposure to brisk autumn weather, and she had lost fifteen pounds, but Claire's vigil was an undoubted triumph.

She had clearly succeeded in her goal, which was, she told the supporters who joined her at the Centennial Centre, "to point up the hypocrisy of profiteering from the sale of war materials while pretending to send aid to the Vietnamese people." Then she broke her 240-hour fast with a slice of homemade bread and a small bowl of clam chowder.

It fell to Gordon Longmuir to attempt to provide a detailed critique of Claire's April report. The Canadian diplomat was now Canada's official ICC representative to Hanoi, and on November 13 he completed a lengthy rejoinder in defence of the Quang Ngai project. It was a revealing document, redolent with sarcasm and arrogance. Claire's report was "highly emotional and erratic," Longmuir wrote, and she had undertaken her destructive crusade "without heed to the possible consequences of her petty slanders."

While he attempted, with varying degrees of success, to refute many of Claire's allegations about specific events in Quang Ngai, Longmuir dismissed the overall thrust of her arguments as those of an overwrought, emotional woman, and derided Claire's "adulation, indeed, worship of 'Saint Alje' [Vennema]. It is clear to me that . . . everything Mrs. Culhane says and does after her traumatic experience in Vietnam is coloured by her political attitude on the war." She was also a woman incapable of drawing her own political conclusions. "Her absolute devotion to Vennema certainly gave her crusade its centre, and I note that many of her views are exactly those expressed in private on many occasions by Vennema. The good doctor, on the other hand, despite occasional slips, has generally had the intelligence and good sense to keep his opinions private."[16]

Longmuir doubtless hoped that he had heard the last of his nettlesome former aid worker, but just six days later he received a rude shock. News of Claire's fast hit the North Vietnamese news media, and she was lionized by the Hanoi press. On November 20 VNA, the official North Vietnamese news agency, moved a story on Claire's protest over its wires. The next day *Nhan Dan* (The People), a Hanoi newspaper, gave the fast feature coverage, including a picture of Claire on Parliament Hill. The Voice of Vietnam, a Hanoi-based radio station, also broadcast news of Claire's protest on the twenty-first. In Longmuir's view, Claire's crusade had "captured the imagination of Hanoi's propaganda makers," and in a restricted memo to his superiors in Saigon he warned of "a renewed onslaught on the subject of arms sales to the United States. Although we have not yet heard from [the Hanoi government], I am reasonably sure that this subject will be brought up at the earliest opportunity. Unless you have any new guidelines for me, I intend to proceed as in the past, and make no reply whatsoever to the allegations."[17] To Longmuir's evident discomfort, Claire's protest had served to hoist Ottawa on the petard of its own Vietnam policy.

The language employed by Canada's permanent ICC representative in Hanoi was a deconstructionist's dream. Canadian aid workers who had the temerity to publicly criticize either American or Canadian policy in Vietnam were committing "slips" beyond the bounds of "intelligence" and "good sense." Claire was "emotional," "political," and "erratic," but the absurdity of Longmuir's own position seems never to have occurred to him. He was the official representative of a putatively "neutral" government, serving on an international control commission mandated to supervise a cease-fire that had never existed and to monitor elections that would never be held. When one side in the conflict complained to Longmuir that the government he represented countenanced massive arms sales to the other side despite its role as a peacemaker, the objections were swept aside as "allegations" worthy of no reply whatsoever, even though Canada had, by the end of 1968, sold nearly half a billion dollars' worth of war material to the United States, a fact that had been widely reported in the press of both countries.

Little wonder, then, that the North Vietnamese considered the Canadians on the ICC as at best extensions of the Pentagon, at worst as American spies, which, indeed, they often were. Vennema, when he was still persona grata with Saigon and Washington, had personally witnessed the circulation of photographs among American intelligence officials of bomb damage in Hanoi taken by Canadian ICC representatives to North Vietnam.[18] From Jutras's sharing his medical files in Quang Ngai with the CIA to covert intelligence-gathering by senior officials within the ICC, Canadians in Vietnam were putting a whole new spin on their old role as "the helpful fixer."

Claire was not privy to External's backchannel communications regarding her charges and activities, but she did receive a congratulatory telegram from the South Vietnam Liberation Women's Union which praised "her noble act and wished her a long life and many successes in her noble activities." And news of her protest had spread to other continents, as well.

At the breaking of the fast she had received a telegram of support from the Swedish Committee on Vietnam, and in November the group invited her to attend a global conference on Vietnam, scheduled for the Swedish capital in mid-December.

Back in Montreal life had resumed a semblance of normalcy. Claire returned to her medical records job at the Neurological Institute, and continued her fencing with External over Jutras, the Quang Ngai project, and Canada's overall role in Vietnam. She had persuaded the local Voice of Women's group to sponsor a silent Vietnam vigil every Saturday morning in Phillips Square, and at the first such demonstration the woman standing next to Claire took a deep breath and said, "You know, Claire, this is the first time in my life I've ever held a picket sign, and I'm doing it just for you."

"Never mind doing it for me, you're doing it for the Vietnamese," Claire said in mild reproof. But as she looked around the square, Claire couldn't help smiling inwardly when she thought how far they had all come. It was the same square, with the same statue of Edward VII, where she had protested against the Spanish civil war as a young woman exactly thirty years before. Then, she and her fellow demonstrators had carried their placards under their coats and counted themselves lucky to make it once around the square before the police came thundering in on their horses to hastily bundle the protesters into paddy wagons. Now, all they had to do was inform the authorities of their plans ahead of time, and they would be assigned a single police officer to watch over the demonstration. That was all. Who could say they hadn't made some progress?

The Stockholm Conference on Vietnam was held from December 15 to 17, 1968, and it afforded Claire, one of two hundred delegates from forty-three countries, the opportunity to contribute to the growing global mobilization against the Vietnam war. She heartily applauded the conference resolution urging that all foreign medical and civilian personnel be withdrawn from South Vietnam, and that governments should then offer the equivalent support in medicine and surgical equipment to both North and South Vietnam through the Liberation Red Cross. The conference also agreed that the Provisional Revolutionary Government (PRG), which had been established by the NLF in South Vietnam in June, should be represented at the Paris peace talks, and that the United States should immediately withdraw all of its military forces from South Vietnam.

From Stockholm Claire travelled to France and England before returning to Montreal. In Paris, even the senior peace negotiators from Hanoi had heard of the extraordinary Canadian grandmother who had spent ten days and nights fasting on the grounds of her country's Parliament buildings. She met privately with Xuan Thuy, the head of the North Vietnamese delegation to the Paris peace talks, and with Madame Nguyen Thi Binh, the foreign minister of the PRG. To her adversaries, Madame Binh seemed a dour and tough negotiator and she was especially despised by Nguyen Van Thieu, the president of South Vietnam.[19] But Claire warmed immediately to Madame Binh who would be, once the PRG was admitted to the talks just a few days later, the only woman at the bargaining table. She had been a political prisoner during the French occupation, and Madame Binh was even then worried about the fate of one of her own daughters, who was missing in the South. In London it was clear that Claire's Parliament Hill protest had also captured the imagination of the British press, and she was the subject of a feature story in the prestigious *Manchester Guardian*.

She barely had time to catch her breath in Montreal before plunging into a nationwide speaking tour, the first of half a dozen such odysseys she would undertake in her eight-year campaign to expose Canadian policy in Vietnam. The tour began on January 7, and took her to scores of Canadian cities and towns. Organized by VOW, the trip established a modus operandi that would stand Claire in good stead for the next quarter-century. She travelled light, except for the ubiquitous tote bag of papers, correspondence, and literature which often outweighed the few items of clothing she considered essential for journeys that might last weeks. She travelled cheap, her fare paid by friends, supporters, or speaking fees, taking buses and trains whenever possible, cadging rides, flying only when the distance between two points was too great to reach efficiently any other way. (She soon reached the conclusion already known to a century of Canadian travellers: "This country is too damned big.") She had friends to stay with wherever she went, arriving early at a resolution she managed to keep for her travels over the next two decades—never use hotels while on the road. Besides being expensive, hotel rooms were lonely places. In private homes she could discuss the issues of the day with her hosts and often meet their friends, thereby adding to her ever-growing list of contacts across Canada. She would refer to herself on these seemingly endless peregrinations during the Vietnam years as a "wandering Jew."

She spoke in church basements and rented halls, on open-line radio shows and through newspaper interviews. She addressed university students and trade unionists, women's groups, and high school classes. No meeting was too small, no media outlet too insignificant to receive less than her full and undivided attention. Often she maintained a punishing schedule that resembled a party leader's itinerary during an election campaign. Her stay in Winnipeg between January 24 and January 26, 1969, was typical. After arriving at the Winnipeg airport from Saskatoon at 7:15

in the morning, over the next sixty hours she attended a meeting of the Winnipeg Committee for Peace in Vietnam, appeared on Bill Treblicoe's open-line program on CKY, was interviewed by the *Tribune*, tape-recorded interviews with CBC AM and FM radio, filmed an interview for CBC television, held a two-hour question-and-answer session with the entire student body of the Canadian Mennonite Bible College, attended a reception for Cheddi Jagan, the Communist party leader of Guyana, had tea with the members of the United Jewish People's Order, attended a reception at the home of Ruth Kottner, spoke at an interdenominational service of the Student Christian Movement at St. John's College before engaging in a spirited two-hour question-and-answer session, attended a public meeting, looked up two Chinese students whose relative she had met in Hong Kong, visited with a young couple who had stood with her on Parliament Hill during the fast, and then boarded a flight for her next destination.[20] Her VOW hosts remarked with a kind of awe on her "terrific stamina," and Claire's almost superhuman capacity for work—often for twenty hours at a stretch—would soon become legendary. She was driven now, running flat out. At the age of fifty Claire Eglin Culhane had reached full stride.

Back in Montreal, Claire continued to bombard the prime minister, the secretary of state for external affairs, and the president of the Canadian International Development Agency (CIDA) with correspondence. (CIDA had replaced the External Aid Office in 1968.) However, the fact of the matter was that despite all of Claire's and the anti-war movement's efforts, Canada's presence in South Vietnam was expanding by the spring of 1969. A new rehabilitation centre, funded by CIDA, had been opened in Qui Nonh the previous fall, and Ottawa had announced that it would spend $535,000 to provide refugee housing in the Saigon suburb of Minh Mang. Knowing full well the corruption that permeated all aspects of life in the South Vietnamese capital, Claire excoriated this use of taxpayers' money, charging that while the housing project might serve a few generals and senior bureaucrats, its very location in the high-rent district of Minh Mang showed that it was never intended to accomodate the genuinely homeless.

Far from withdrawing Canadian personnel from Quang Ngai, External was also digging in on the TB hospital project. In November, officials at CIDA had decided to dispatch two Quebec physicians, Dr. C.W.L. Jeanes, the executive secretary of the Canadian Tuberculosis and Respiratory Disease Association, and Dr. G. Cardinal, director of the Tuberculosis Service of the Quebec Department of Health, to Quang Ngai, to investigate Claire's and Vennema's charges about the project, and about Jutras. The consulting doctors gave the project a clean bill of health, and Jutras's contract with CIDA was renewed for another year. The investigators found that the clinic was no longer occupied by South Vietnamese troops, and that it was once again effectively treating some 17,000 patients per year.[21]

Claire was outraged at these findings, and accused CIDA of a "white-wash." The investigators had not interviewed her or examined her evidence, or that of any of the other Vietnamese with firsthand knowledge of Jutras's alleged professional misconduct.

By the spring of 1969 Claire had determined to take a new tack in her fight to make Canadians aware of their government's policies in Vietnam. Having long since wearied of gaining a fair hearing from External Affairs or CIDA, she moved to pry her official report "out of Maurice Strong's bottom drawer," as she put it, by asking sympathetic MPs to request the release of her report of the previous year. A formal motion in the House to table her report would oblige the responsible minister to release the named document, and on May 12, 1969, David MacDonald, the Tory MP for the Prince Edward Island riding of Egmont, rose in the Commons to introduce just such a motion.

But Maurice Strong had not yet exhausted his repertoire of stonewalling tactics. He assured his superior, Mitchell Sharp, that three different investigations had exonerated Jutras, and Sharp, in turn, tried to convince Mac-Donald to withdraw his motion. Strong raised the possibility of a libel suit if the report were released, hinting that the department itself might be named as a co-defendant. Then, when various MPs responded to Claire's continuing barrage of appeals—among them Ed Schreyer, future premier of Manitoba and governor general of Canada, and Tommy Douglas, then leader of the NDP—Sharp selectively quoted from Vennema's early reports to give the misleading impression that Vennema favoured keeping the team in Quang Ngai.[22] The government strategy was clear: delay, obfuscate, conceal. MacDonald rejected Sharp's personal appeal to withdraw his motion for disclosure, but it languished on the Order Paper as the Commons adjourned for the summer. Temporarily, at least, the government had once again blunted her attack.

But Claire refused to be silenced. In the fall of 1969 she stepped up her work with the Voice of Women, and at the provincial convention on September 25 she was elected Quebec president of the VOW. She promptly organized a series of vigils to be held outside the American consulate in Montreal to protest the impending American underground nuclear test at Amchitka, one of the Aleutian Islands off the coast of Alaska. The turn-outs were small at first, but by October 2, the day of the hydrogen bomb test, about one hundred VOW supporters and their children were gathered outside the consulate in Montreal. Claire had written a letter for the occasion, which she personally presented to United States Consul

Harrison W. Burgess. "It is now abundantly clear to us that no people of the world can consider themselves safe from American terrorism and military aggression," it read. Burgess accepted Claire's letter, but declined to discuss American nuclear policy either with Claire or the news media present.[23]

The tests were carried out despite the continent-wide protests, but history would prove that Claire and a handful of women and children were precursors of a whole new social movement. The Amchitka blasts provided the impetus for a tiny group of protesters in Vancouver to form an environmental organization that would have lasting impact over the next quarter-century and beyond. Greenpeace would come to have global influence long after the Amchitka nuclear tests had been all but forgotten.

Precisely six weeks after Amchitka, the world learned of a shocking example of the "American terrorism and military aggression" that Claire had decried in her letter to the U.S. consul in Montreal. On November 13 more than thirty American newspapers carried a story by an investigative reporter named Seymour Hersh about a U.S. army massacre of Vietnamese civilians in the village of My Lai 4, only a few kilometres outside Quang Ngai City. On the morning of March 16, 1968, according to Hersh's story, Charlie Company, First Battalion, Twentieth Infantry from the American Division had been heli-lifted to the edge of the outwardly peaceful hamlet. Although they encountered no opposition during their sweep of the village, the young American soldiers began to shoot at anyone who moved. As horrified villagers watched the carnage, mothers began to plead for the lives of their babies before both mothers and children were ripped with machine-gun rounds. Young women were raped before being killed, and wailing two-year-olds who attempted to flee were mowed down by laughing GIs. Many of the villagers were herded into a drainage ditch at the east end of the hamlet. "We pushed our seven to eight people in with the big bunch of them. And so I began shooting them all . . . I guess I shot maybe twenty-five or twenty people in the ditch . . . men, women, and children . . . and babies," recalled Paul Meadlo of Terre Haute, Indiana. Private Dennis Conti noticed that "a lot of women had thrown themselves on top of the children to protect them, and the children were alive at first. Then the children who were old enough to walk got up and [First Lieutenant William] Calley began to shoot the children." No one will ever be certain how many civilians were killed that day—estimates would later run as high as five hundred, the overwhelming majority of them women and children.[24] Incredibly, the massacre was documented by army photographer Ronald L. Haeberle of Cleveland, Ohio, whose pictures showing a tangled mass of arms and legs, including those of children and babies, in the drainage ditch, were soon published around the world.

Public reaction in the United States to the My Lai massacre was strongly mixed. Many Americans were outraged, not at the perpetrators but at the American news media for publishing the story and the pictures. "How can I explain these photographs to my children?" complained a Cleveland mother to the editors of the *Plain Dealer*, which had first printed Haeberle's photographs. When the *Washington Star* published the picture taken at the drainage ditch on its front page many readers called to complain that it was obscene, because the corpses had no clothes on.[25]

To Claire, the news about My Lai was a double tragedy. The massacre had happened—and so close to Quang Ngai—just ten days after her own departure from Vietnam. The news reopened her own private wounds— her misgivings about leaving Quang Ngai, her guilt over her own and her nation's complicity—the painful fruit of her own experience which drove her but which she seemed incapable of driving home to the men in Ottawa. The news was also, sadly, a vindication of sorts. Whenever she described American atrocities in Vietnam her critics dismissed her, and quite publicly, as an anti-American propagandist, or as an outright liar. My Lai was proof positive of all that she had witnessed in Quang Ngai. And then there was the dull heartache which would never leave her—the memory of that tearful parting from her Vietnamese friends on the airstrip at Quang Ngai. Three years would pass before Claire learned that in one of three mass graves at My Lai, or in the infamous drainage ditch, lay her beloved friend Ba, along with all four of her children.

The horror of My Lai, combined with the intransigence of the Canadian government, impelled Claire's second audacious action on Parliament Hill, but this time she did not act alone. Her companion was Mike Rubbo, a young expatriate Australian and now filmmaker in Montreal. Rubbo had made a film about Vietnam for the National Film Board but Claire found that while *The Sad Song of Yellow Skin* was sympathetic enough to the plight of the Vietnamese people, it was lacking in political analysis, and she had called Rubbo to tell him so. The filmmaker had, in the end, agreed with Claire's criticism, and asked what he might do to help her work on the Vietnam issue. When in December 1969 Claire felt the time was right for another Ottawa protest Rubbo agreed to join her, and she accepted his offer to finance the action, as well.

Their plan was to camp out on the Hill during the Christmas parliamentary recess. The action would last nineteen days, from Christmas Eve to January 12. During that time she and Rubbo would subsist on a Vietnamese diet of soup, rice, and tea. They would call the campaign Enough/

Assez: enough atrocities, enough bombing, enough defoliation, enough Canadian complicity in all three. Canada had supplied the United States with $370 million worth of war material in 1968 alone, noted one of their leaflets, and Canadian foreign aid to the corrupt regime in Saigon had now reached $8.3 million.[26]

Given the temperatures they would have to endure, sleeping bags under the East Block portico would be inadequate, so Claire and Rubbo attempted to pitch two tents on Parliament Hill on Christmas Eve. They were met by the RCMP, whose officers told them, gently but firmly in the glare of television lights and popping flash bulbs, that the parliamentary grounds were off-limits. The protesters had previously arranged an alternative site in a vacant lot beside the Anglican church at the corner of Elgin and Lewis Streets, just down Wellington Street and around the corner from Parliament Hill, and that was where they repaired to pitch their tents. Claire had met the priest of the church during her ten-day fast, and he offered them the use of toilet facilities in the church basement, as well as the vacant lot. They dubbed their small enclave Enough Village.

They were not greatly put out about being denied access to the Hill—their Christmas Eve confrontation with the Mounties had garnered considerable press coverage, which would continue throughout the nineteen days. Indeed, the camp-out would prove as successful as the fast at focusing national publicity on the Canadian role in Vietnam. A survey by the Canadian Press Clipping Service for the period of December 24, 1969, to January 14, 1970, revealed that Canadian newspapers had printed 175 articles about the protest.[27]

But while the tactic of camping out in the dead of an Ottawa winter would once again provide the media with a novel angle, it also brought real physical discomfort. On Christmas night the temperature dropped to -15° C and it snowed heavily on Boxing Day. Their only escape from the wind was their two small tents, which were lined with two inches of styrofoam insulation, but were heated only with candles. The cold, combined with the spartan diet, represented a formidable challenge. But they carried on, and Claire once again reminded reporters that their own discomfort was nothing as compared to that borne by the people of Vietnam.

At least her daughters were not as hysterical about the camp-out as they had been about the fast, Claire thought. Perhaps they were becoming resigned to their mother's extraordinary protest tactics. Dara even drove over from Montreal to deliver a most welcome Christmas present—a set of thermal-lined long underwear, which Claire lost little time in donning after she had squirmed out of the snowmobile suit, layers of shirts and sweaters, mitts, boots, and toques that had become her round-the-clock attire. Dara's attitude towards her mother's activities was undergoing a subtle change, as was her outlook on the world. She had, that autumn, begun to take courses part-time at Sir George Williams University, and to do volunteer fund-raising work for the American Deserters' Committee in Montreal. As Dara gravitated towards an ever-deepening involvement with Canada's burgeoning anti-war movement, there was no mistaking the universal respect accorded her mother's tireless efforts to end the Vietnam war.

The beauty of "stationary demonstrations" like the fast or the camp-out, Claire would later observe, was the opportunity it offered to leaflet passersby, who would then return and argue after they had read the material. A prime case in point was an Ottawa matron who received a leaflet on one of the first nights of the camp-out. When she returned she was utterly scornful of Claire's position—it turned out her husband was with the ICC in Vietnam. But she kept coming back to discuss the issues, and by the time the camp-out was over she had brought her teenage children down to meet Claire and Mike, and had extended to them a standing invitation to visit her any time they were in Ottawa.

As New Year's approached their tiny tent village was growing. A group of U.S. army deserters pitched their own tent and joined the protest, and so many people were stopping to discuss and argue about Vietnam that they decided to rent a fourth tent, a nine-by-twelve wall tent "furnished" with folding chairs and a heater, to shelter their visitors from the unremitting cold. Someone brought them a charcoal brazier at which passersby could warm their hands while the arguments over Canada's policy in Vietnam raged on and on. They posted a sign outside the wall tent that read: "Come and talk to us, especially if you disagree," and people would be lined up until long after dark, wanting to come in and talk.

On New Year's Day they a had special rice casserole dinner that was attended by a representative of each of the three political parties: Ed Broadbent from the New Democrats, David MacDonald from the Tories, and Warren Allmand from the Liberals. On January 10 they had a special visitor, Dr. Vennema, who was on a national speaking tour of his own to expose Canada's tacit support for the war in Vietnam. Claire was delighted to greet Vennema, whom she had not seen since the Tet Offensive. The Canadian doctor told reporters that he had learned of the My Lai massacre two weeks after it happened, and had even noted it in his diary. When asked why he had not reported it at the time, Vennema replied that atrocities like those committed at My Lai were a daily occurrence in Vietnam, as Claire knew all too well. The only difference was in the number of civilians murdered in one spot, and the fact that attempts to cover up the massacre had failed. Moreover, Vennema added, he had spoken twice "in general terms" to then External Affairs Minister Paul Martin about the killing of civilians, and he had also discussed the subject with former American ambassador Maxwell Taylor in Saigon as early as May 1965.

(In 1976 Vennema's book, *The Viet Cong Massacre at Hue*, was published. Written partially from the viewpoint of poor peasants and townspeople and drawing on his five years of experience in country, Vennema documented in graphic detail the atrocities committed by NLF cadres during their occupation of Hue in the Tet Offensive.

Claire was outraged by Vennema's book—by its title, which used the CIA invented term for the NLF, which both she and Vennema had always eschewed while in Quang Ngai, by Vennema's recurring use of the term "enemy" to describe the NLF in Hue, and by his persistent refusal to let the Hue story drop.

Claire considered Vennema's version of the story one-sided because, while emphasizing the NLF's actions in the battle of Hue in 1968, it made only passing reference to a decade of American atrocities in Vietnam. She found it revolting that Vennema should have ignored these historical facts, which they had so often discussed and agreed upon. By holding only the NLF responsible for the massacre at Hue, Claire considered that Vennema was consciously reinforcing the Pentagon point of view, an unforgivable offence in her eyes. The schism caused by Vennema's book would prove irreparable.)

As she had at the end of the ten-day fast, Claire hoped to have an interview with Prime Minister Trudeau on January 12, 1970, the concluding day of the camp-out. But as she and a handful of supporters were buttonholing returning MPs on the Hill she spied Trudeau's limousine idling nearby, so instead of waiting for an invitation, she walked over to catch the prime minister as he left the building.

After they had waited about twenty minutes in near-zero temperatures, Trudeau finally appeared through the revolving door, looking tanned, jaunty, and relaxed—and warm, "muffled in his $1,500 otter coat," according to the *Globe and Mail*. He greeted Claire warmly, but caught her off guard when he challenged her to tell him what they had learned during the nineteen-day vigil.

Claire recited a series of pointed questions she had prepared in advance. Did he realize that in 1968 alone Canada had sold $370 million worth of weapons and arms to the United States, much of it bound for use in Vietnam, while spending only about $260 million for foreign aid to the entire world? How could Canada claim to be truly neutral in Vietnam?

How much of Canada's 21 percent inflation rate over the previous five years had been caused by U.S. inflation resulting from the Vietnam war?

And how much money had the Liberal party received in the past five years from American and Canadian companies manufacturing war material for use in Vietnam?

Trudeau cited Canada's "repeated" requests to stop the bombing of the North. "You don't seem to have a solution for ending the war tomorrow, beyond appealing to the United States to be more reasonable [at the Paris peace talks]," Trudeau jabbed. "I think President Nixon is very aware of the need to come to a responsible solution to this war."[28]

Claire felt deflated at the end of the confrontation, convinced that for once her media strategy had backfired, and that she had been bested in public by the prime minister. Some of Claire's friends, however, reported that the overwhelming reaction to the telecast confrontation was that Trudeau had simply been putting Claire and Mike down with cold, overweening arrogance. The television audience may also have been intrigued with the improbably contrasting physical appearances of the disputants. Perhaps the average Canadian could identify more closely with two protesters, shivering in the mid-January cold despite their parkas, toques, and snowmobile suits, than they could with a tanned, confident Montreal millionaire wearing a sleek fur coat and hat.

CHAPTER EIGHT

Canada's Pentagon Papers

"Canada's Pentagon Papers should be released. The people have the right to the facts."
—Grace MacInnis, MP Vancouver-Kingsway, on the official suppression of reports on Quang Ngai, June 29, 1972

B y 1970 Claire Culhane had become one of the best known and most persistent critics of Canadian complicity in the Vietnam war. In constant demand as a speaker and conference participant, she now found herself sharing top billing with prominent Canadians, as at the Parliament Hill rally organized by the Vietnam Moratorium Committee on February 28, 1970, where she took the platform with NDP leader Tommy Douglas, former president of the Progressive Conservative party Dalton Camp, and former co-host of "This Hour Has Seven Days," Laurier LaPierre.

Although the event brought out substantially fewer people than antici-pated and was disrupted when members of the Communist Party of Can-ada Marxist-Leninist (ultra leftist Maoists) provoked a fist-throwing mêlée among the demonstrators, Claire was able to deliver her carefully prepared speech denouncing Canada's involvement in Vietnam.[1]

After the Parliament Hill débâcle Claire was off again on another national speaking tour organized by Voice of Women. In mid-March she was in Edmonton, addressing delegates to the city's labour council, and in the first half of April she visited Prince George, Nelson, Castlegar, and Vernon, among other smaller western Canadian cities. While she always kept one eye cocked on the national news media, Claire had also learned not to ignore regional towns and cities across Canada. Because they were visited less frequently by figures with a national profile, public interest was often better, on a per capita basis, than in the larger centres, and the local news media tended to provide greater coverage.

Back in Ottawa, meanwhile, MP David MacDonald had renewed his request for the release of Claire's and Vennema's correspondence with the government, but once again the interest of the government was to override the interest of the governed. "It is our view that the government would stand to gain nothing from either total or even partial compliance with the motion in question," observed Blair Seaborn of External's Far Eastern Division on April 22, 1970, in a confidential intergovernment memo.[2]

Official legerdemain was afoot that week in Washington, too, where the Nixon White House was planning a top-secret invasion of Cambodia by American and South Vietnamese troops. Officially, the Nixon doctrine in Southeast Asia called for a gradual withdrawal of U.S. troops from South Vietnam, "peace with honour" through the Paris peace talks, and "Vietnamization" of the war in the meantime—the South Vietnamese would take over the fighting, backed by massive American military and economic aid. But in practice, as Claire never tired of reminding her audiences, the Americans were trying to make up with technology what they were losing on the ground. The bombing of the South, the use of defoliants, the persecution of political dissidents, all continued apace under the Saigon regime. The killing had spread from combatants to non-combatants to the earth itself, and Claire had begun to use a term she first heard in Stockholm to describe the carnage: biocide.

President Richard Nixon announced the Cambodian invasion in a televised address to the nation on April 30, 1970. The reaction to the widening of the war was as stunning as it was unpredictable. A revivified American anti-war movement closed fully one-third of the nation's colleges and universities in protest, and on a number of campuses the Reserve Officers' Training Corps buildings were burned to the ground; at Ohio's Kent State University National Guardsmen shot fifteen student protesters, killing four; two black students were shot and killed at Jackson State College in Mississippi; between 75,000 and 100,000 protesters converged on the White House, and Richard Nixon, on the verge of a nervous breakdown, hunkered down into the siege mentality that would pave the way to the Watergate break-in and the eventual collapse of his presidency.[3]

But the most tragic impact of the invasion would fall directly on the Cambodian people. Their country would be drawn ever farther into the ambit of American military policy in southeast Asia and ultimately turned into a killing field by Pol Pot and the Khmer Rouge. The dark prophecy Claire had first heard in the streets of Phnom Penh in February 1968, was coming to pass. The flame of war ignited by the Americans in Vietnam had now begun to engulf the Cambodians, too.

After her national tour ended, Claire lingered in the West that summer. Dara had moved to Vancouver in January, and the centre of gravity of Claire's family was shifting from Montreal to the west coast. The trend was further reinforced in early June, when Roisin gave birth to her third child, a boy this time, who was christened Robert Patrick O'Hea. With the exception of her months in Vietnam, Claire had lived no more than a few blocks from at least one of her children since Roisin's birth twenty-five years earlier. Roisin's and Dara's decision to remain in the Vancouver area gave the city a powerful new attraction to Claire, and British Columbia's largest city was, in any event, a magnet for anti-Vietnam war activity.

Claire continued to stump the province, condemning My Lai and Nixon's Cambodian invasion, the Amchitka nuclear tests, and the use of herbicide in the jungles of Vietnam and on the forests of British Columbia. It was a busy summer. In early May she was in Campbell River on Vancouver Island, and in midmonth she travelled to Prince Rupert, speaking to high school students and at public meetings. At the end of May she was back outside the gates of the Defence Research Establishment in Suffield, Alberta, as a featured speaker at a three-day camp-in demonstration to protest chemical and biological research. RCMP agents, indefatigably building their files, reported that eight to nine hundred people took part in the action, and that Claire had played a prominent role.[4]

In August Claire couldn't refuse an invitation to speak at a demonstration organized by the Vancouver Youth International Party, or "Yippies," at the British Columbia Penitentiary in New Westminster. About 150 people joined the protest, which had been called to demonstrate solidarity with a sit-down strike inside the pen, where prisoners claimed that guards had beaten one of their number to death. Claire likened the situation inside Canadian penitentiaries to that of prisoners in South Vietnam.[5]

The comparison was not farfetched. The shooting of student protesters on American campuses the previous spring was but one of the symptoms of an increasing cycle of repression against North America's growing youth rebellion, Claire realized, and a vicious downward spiral was now in play. As governments proved indifferent to peaceful, legal forms of dissent, protesters were driven to more extreme measures at the outer edges of the law. The anti-war and civil rights movements had now discovered the limits of democratic freedoms, and they had learned that a stiff challenge to entrenched ruling authority was often met by sheer brute force. But resort to more extreme methods simply engendered yet more violent repression, and a dangerous and volatile polarization of the society as a whole.

Claire got a good look at the situation in the United States that summer when she made a four-week speaking tour through the northern states, from Chicago to Boston. In the latter city she was invited to speak about Vietnam at the Harvard Medical School, but her hosts advised her to soft-pedal the question of the Black Panther party. She found the very notion antithetical. Like the late black leader Malcolm X, the Black Panthers were exponents of a militant approach to white racism in America. ("Roll on over," warned one famous Panther poster, "or we'll roll on over YOU!") They were also advocates of armed self-defence in black communities, a stance that was anathema to many American whites, including the kind of liberals who were comfortable hearing about racism in Vietnam, but not closer to home. Yet to Claire, the issues were inseparable. How often had she heard American GIs using racial epithets against the Vietnamese people? The killing of babies at My Lai was every bit as racist and genocidal in motivation, though not in scale, as Hitler's "final solution."

But the attitudes that produced My Lai had not started in Vietnam, and would not end there. Their roots lay deep in American society itself. She would never forget her own first exposure to the wounding shame of American racism, and its impact on her young black acquaintance during her first bus trip across the Mason-Dixon line so many years ago. Now the Black Panthers were becoming the target of an increasingly vicious crackdown by the American government. Chicago Panther leader Fred Hampton had been killed in his sleep by police the previous December, and at least forty other Panthers would be gunned down by police between 1967 and the end of 1970.[6] She ignored her Harvard hosts' cautionary urgings and spoke about American racism at home and abroad.

In Rochester, New York, she appeared at an open forum called to discuss recent proposals to ban the use of pesticides. Here, too, there were links to be made. The chemical ban was vigorously opposed by wealthy California fruit growers and by the Dow Chemical Company, the same firm that made napalm. The defoliants were in use in both Vietnam and in North America, but to whose benefit? And with what environmental and human consequences in the years to come?

Claire described her American sojourn in an article in the Voice of Women's British Columbia newsletter *The Voice* in September 1970. She had found, she reported, that American and Canadian women's peace groups had much in common. "The same small core, utterly and tirelessly devoted and involved . . . [but] with the majority . . . content to operate as if it were still the 1960s . . ." She had discovered an alarming, and widening, gulf "between the sincere peace workers and the equally sincere but far less patient young people. Desperate frustrations are being caused by the escalation of wars, by the increase of police brutalities, by the general realization of all sections of the peace movement that violence is no longer a matter of personal choice or philosophy, but like poverty and disease, is here and all about us. That fear and hesitancy to openly support the Panther Defense Fund should exist among any section of peace workers only serves to widen this gulf."

Implicit in Claire's message was her growing impatience with VOW. She was daily in the trenches with the new generation of activists, but the VOW's older, middle-class leadership seemed satisfied to conduct business as usual. "The old life styles of those with the funds and the time to do the conference going and the trips abroad must be replaced by a new life style, using those same funds to speedily react to every relevant situation at home."

Then came a theme she would sound again and again over the next twenty years. The most effective women, she had discovered, were the ones who "deplored their self-defeating, over-structured organizations. The truth of the matter is that . . . spontaneous grass-root, neighbourhood actions are usually the most successful, since they immediately involve the very people concerned and therefore the ones most likely to respond." She sounded a clarion call for action:

Wherever 2,4,5,T is being sprayed is the time and place for women to demonstrate.

Wherever young people are without meaningful work and young Americans [Vietnam-war resisters] in our country are being harassed, and both are being discriminated against, is the time and place for women to demonstrate.

Wherever our national minorities continue to face all the elements of genocide under the guise of brutal paternalism, is the time and place for women to demonstrate.

In this way, the aims of the VOW will develop in scope and influence in Canada as similar peace groups in the U.S.A. are also discovering.

"A sense of urgency is now in order," she concluded. "Abortive acts of violence may well fill the vacuum between the various sections of the peace movement unless new and speedier ways of work are acted upon."[7]

Claire's sense of the times was unerring. One of the most "abortive acts of violence" in Canadian history was only days away, and it would engender a whole new level of government repression, once again riveting Claire's attention on her home province.

On the morning of October 5, 1970, James Cross, the British trade commissioner to Montreal, was abducted from his Westmount home by members of the Front de libération du Québec, thus precipitating the FLQ crisis. The kidnappers demanded the release of detained FLQ members, the public reading of their manifesto over Radio-Canada, the French network of the CBC, and safe passage out of the country. The FLQ manifesto, addressed primarily to the Quebec working class, was read over the network and on October 10 Quebec justice minister Jérôme Choquette guaranteed the kidnappers' exit from Canada, but later that day a second FLQ cell abducted Quebec labour and immigration minister Pierre Laporte. Five days later Quebec premier Robert Bourassa requested the intervention of the federal government, and at 4:00 a.m. on October 16 the War Measures Act was declared by the government of Pierre Trudeau, on the basis that the kidnappings constituted "an apprehended insurrection" in Quebec.

The emergency powers of the act suspended all civil liberties across Canada, banned public demonstrations, and authorized arrest and detention of Canadian citizens without the laying of charges. The Canadian army occupied strategic locations in and around Montreal, more than 450 Québecois were detained without charges, and without the right of habeas corpus, and some 2,000 premises were entered and searched without warrant. Pierre Laporte was strangled by his captors within hours of the imposition of the act, and his body was found in the trunk of a car parked near the St. Hubert air base on October 17.

The Trudeau government's decision to use such draconian powers against its own citizens has become more controversial in hindsight than it was at the time. In the Commons Tommy Douglas was the lone party leader to condemn the action, and in the rest of the country only a handful of courageous souls dared to defy the government. Claire was among them. This was her second War Measures Act, after all, and she knew well the historical tendency of Canadian governments to abuse their civil powers. She helped found the Friends of Quebec in Vancouver, and then to organize a demonstration on the steps of the court house on Georgia Street. Fifty to seventy-five people attended the illegal action and cheered "*Vive le Québec libre*" as the now-banned FLQ manifesto was read through a bullhorn.

In November Montreal civic activist Adele Williams came to Vancouver on a speaking tour to discuss conditions in Quebec under the War Measures Act, and she stayed with Claire. They talked long into the night about what was happening in Claire's native province, and the more they talked, the more Claire felt like an exile. They agreed that if Claire wanted to return to Montreal, she could stay with Adele. By December, Claire had decided to give up her rented room in Vancouver's west end and return east. When she arrived in Montreal Claire was appalled at the lack of public response to the fact that twenty-seven of the more than five hundred individuals detained under the War Measures Act were still in prison, even though they were not charged with any specific crime.

Claire and a half-dozen other women went to meetings of the University of Montreal's Quebec Civil Liberties Union and challenged Professor Guy Vaillancourt to mount a demonstration to protest the detentions. But the detentions and the army presence had had the desired intimidating effect on Quebec activists. "Mayor Drapeau has declared all such public demonstrations illegal," Claire was told time and again. Claire and her supporters received the same response from Dr. Serge Mongeau of the Movement for the Defence of Political Prisoners. But Claire remained determined. Harrowing tales were emerging of psychological and physical torture against detainees.[8] Christmas was approaching, and the holidays were always an ideal occasion to drum up sympathy for people "separated from their families," Claire argued, ever mindful of the necessity for good timing. If the larger organizations wouldn't support the calling of a protest outside the Parthenais Detention Centre in downtown Montreal, Claire warned, she and her little band of supporters would hold an illegal vigil, anyway, accompanied by Madame Rosa Rose, the mother of Paul, Jacques, and Lise (members of the FLQ imprisoned after the kidnapping). They planned to carry roses as a gesture of solidarity. Despite some grumbling, the civil liberties groups voted to hold the protest.

Christmas morning 1970 was bitter cold in Montreal, but nearly one thousand people showed up outside the Parthenais Detention Centre, and many brought their own roses. They marched round and round the base of the grim thirteen-storey building, singing and cheering, and a special shout went up any time one of the twenty-seven detainees above them threw paper out the window or waved towels or T-shirts to show their appreciation for their supporters outside. "I have to say that I've been at many demonstrations in my day, at least a hundred, I'm sure," Claire would write later, "but this had to be the most exciting one, like a bunch of kids let out of school for summer holidays. That kind of jubilance. Who cared how cold it was! Or that they could otherwise be home opening presents Christmas morning. Enough solidarity and good will to toast your toes."

It took more bullying on her part, but Claire also prevailed on the civil liberties groups to hold another demo outside the Tanguay Prison for Women in suburban Bordeaux where Lise Rose was detained. She had been arrested at her classroom at the Beaux Artes on St. Urbain Street on October 19 and subsequently strip-searched by male guards, beaten, and held in isolation for twenty-two days. Lise Rose had begun a hunger strike to protest her plight, and Claire briefly entertained the notion of actually busting Lise out of jail. Posing as architecture students from McGill, Claire and a friend approached the warden at Tanguay. They had been assigned a school project to prepare a blueprint of a proposed prison. Would she be so kind as to allow them a small guided tour of her facility just so they could develop ideas on construction, design, and so forth? The warden complied, and they received their little tour, but soon realized they could never break Lise out of Tanguay. However, about eight hundred people converged on Tanguay on New Year's Day. The weather was just as cold, and the spirit of jubilant defiance was just as high as at the Parthenais the week before.

Twenty years later the legacy of the FLQ would remain a hotly debated subject among Quebec political activists and intellectuals. Claire herself would confess to feeling a certain ambivalence though not perhaps for the usual reasons. Her gut reaction during the crisis had been "Go for it"; perhaps a workers' revolution really was brewing in Quebec. But it was impossible to shrug off the memory of the darker side of Quebec nationalism, of the bigotry and anti-Semitism that had accompanied its rise in the 1930s. The murder of Laporte didn't bother her much. How many Quebec workers had died because of inadequate inspection and enforcement of the province's labour laws while he was minister? How often did the wealthy and powerful enforce policies that enriched themselves while raining death and destruction down upon thousands of others, as she had personally witnessed in Vietnam? And she would always admire Jacques Rose, who accepted responsibility for the decision to kill Laporte but who would also steadfastly refuse to implicate those who had actually carried out the decision.

On the evening of January 21, 1971, Claire scored another major media coup by appearing on CBC television's "Viewpoint," which aired nationally after the nightly news. It was an excellent venue, one which took her message into hundreds of thousands of Canadian living rooms. There had been two major news stories the previous week, Claire told her audience, and they were not entirely unrelated. The first concerned the rising level of unemployment in Canada, the second focused on "the ludicrous role" played by Prime Minister Trudeau in attempting to mediate an end to British arms sales to South Africa. The prime minister's actions were ludicrous "since his own government happens to be the largest arms salesman, per capita, in the world today," with most of the traffic contributing to biocide in Vietnam. The two news stories were related because the arms industry was a notoriously inefficient economic engine which "does not improve the conditions of life," but produces commodities which are "not pumped back into the consumer economy."

She briefly summarized her stock charges of Canadian complicity in Vietnam, including the allegation that participation on the International Control Commission and "humanitarian aid" projects like the one at Quang Ngai were often nothing more than a front for advancing American interests. She outlined the official suppression of her report, and the government's refusal to allow a parliamentary review of its Vietnam aid programs. "If we are supposed to be neutral in Vietnam, why are we violating our status by subsidizing one part of the country [South Vietnam] and not the other?" Claire asked. "And if we are a democracy, why should such relevant questions, officially before the government now for three years, continue to remain unanswered?"[9]

Whatever Claire had been planning to do on Sunday, February 7, 1971, was quickly shelved by a knock on the door of her Laval Avenue room. The caller was a messenger from the telegraph office with a wire for Claire from Paris. The contents of the message were mind-boggling:

> ALERT YOU LAOS INVASION BY TENS THOUSANDS U.S. SAIGON THAI TROOPS BACKED INTENSE U.S. AIR FORCE. EARNESTLY CALL YOU URGENTLY TO MOBILIZE PEACE FORCES IN YOUR COUNTRY. CHECK U.S. DANGEROUS MILITARY VENTURES. INDO-CHINA MILITANT. GREET-INGS.
>
> NGUYEN THI BINH
> HEAD, PRG DELEGATION
> PARIS PEACE TALKS

It was Claire's first contact with Madame Binh since her 1969 Paris visit, but she quickly telephoned her contacts in the peace movement across North America to see if they had received a similar warning: no one had. Claire then turned for advice to Michel Van Schandel, a Montreal university professor and a veteran Quebec activist. The professor, an old friend of Pierre Trudeau's from his days at *Cité Libre* magazine, said they must inform the Canadian government at once. The prime minister and most of his cabinet were in Quebec City at a Liberal convention that weekend, so Claire and Van Schandel jumped into his car and drove to Quebec City. They saw Trudeau briefly and he turned them over to Marc Lalonde. Lalonde suggested that they take the matter up with Mitchell Sharp in Ottawa. "You go straight there, and I'll phone him and let him know you're coming," Lalonde assured them.

They drove to Ottawa only to discover that Sharp had left the capital for Toronto, but on Monday, February 8, they were received by A.E. Ritchie, the deputy minister of external affairs. Meanwhile, the invasion of Laos by units of the South Vietnamese army backed by intense U.S. air support had begun that morning. The operation was code-named Lamson 719 and its purpose was twofold: to root out the Laotian section of the Ho Chi Minh Trail supply route used by the North Vietnamese to supply its fighting forces in the south; and, because the troops deployed were exclusively South Vietnamese (the United States Congress had barred American ground troops from entering either Laos or Cambodia after the latter country was invaded in May 1970), the Laotian incursion was also to serve as an important test of the "Vietnamization" strategy.[10]

Claire and Van Schandel urged Ritchie to add Canada's voice to the worldwide condemnation of the Laotian invasion by calling on the United States to halt its activity there and by reconvening the Geneva Convention on Laos. Ritchie replied by pointing out that Hanoi's use of the Ho Chi Minh Trail through both Cambodia and Laos violated the neutrality of both nations, inviting American bombing and invasion. And as he also noted, Claire and Van Schandel refused to "equate the use of the Ho Chi Minh trail system by the North Vietnamese with the [American] military invasion of South Vietnam and the B-52 bombing raids, which were 'equal to two Hiroshimas a week.'"[11]

Still frustrated in her attempts to have her report released to the Commons, Claire had, by early March, determined to hold yet another militant protest on the Hill. But this time she planned to take the action directly to the parliamentary chambers by chaining herself to a chair in the visitors' gallery of the House of Commons. She tried to find other members of VOW who would join her in the protest, which would mean almost certain arrest and public ridicule. But there were no takers. Only one person volunteered to accompany her—though not to chain herself—a young woman named Mimi Taylor, a curator at the National Gallery. Claire rehearsed the action carefully three days in advance. She had planned to conceal a bundle of leaflets under her coat, but she discovered that visitors were asked to hang up their coats before entering the gallery. She wore an apron with deep pockets to hold leaflets instead. Charlotte MacEwan's husband, Gavin, was pressed into service to make her a chain out of tempered steel with a heavy-duty lock so that it would take security guards some time to cut through the shackles.

On Thursday, March 4, 1971, Claire and Mimi Taylor entered the gallery without incident, the chain and leaflets safely hidden under Claire's clothing. Question period was just getting under way, and Mitchell Sharp was the acting prime minister in Trudeau's absence. The first thing Claire noticed after she was settled in her chair was that she was perched directly above the external affairs minister. Why, if she chose to leap over the railing she could land right on top of him, but she resisted the impulse. As the Honourable E.J. Benson, minister of finance, droned on in answer to a question from Tommy Douglas about Canada-U.S. relations, Claire quietly chained her ankle to the leg of her chair.

Douglas had just risen to ask a supplementary concerning the continuation of Canadian exemption from the U.S. Interest Equalization Tax when Claire began to rain leaflets down on the startled honourable members. "Why is Canada building another hospital in South Vietnam while still supplying the United States with war material under the Defence Sharing Agreement?" Claire demanded at the top of her voice.

"Mr. Speaker, I am used to—" Douglas stopped in midsentence.

"Will the honourable member kindly ask his question?" the Speaker replied. "The Chair is able to hear him."

"Mr. Speaker, I am used to being interrupted. I have been married for a long time," Douglas wisecracked after hearing Claire's voice, and the remark was met by a gale of appreciative laughter from the denizens of the male bastion that was the House of Commons. "In view of the fact that when Canada was granted this exemption . . ."[12]

Security guards, meanwhile, scuttled back and forth, trying to find bolt cutters with enough leverage to cut the chains, while Claire made all the commotion she could.

It was all over in about fifteen minutes. Claire was then hustled to the police station, charged with creating a disturbance, and released on her own recognizance. But once again she made headlines across the country, successfully directing public attention to Canada's role in Vietnam.

Her court date was set for April 19, giving Claire time to accept several speaking invitations in the West. On March 22 she attended an anti-war conference at the University of Alberta in Edmonton, and four days later she spoke to a small anti-war demonstration in Vancouver. She used those appearances to tackle the question of Canadian complicity in Vietnam from yet another angle. At issue was the participation of Canadian citizens in the American armed services. Claire well remembered how hard the Canadian government had made life for the volunteers of the Mackenzie-Papineau Battalion, and how the application of the Foreign Enlistment Act to the Spanish civil war had thwarted her own desire to serve in Spain. Claire did some checking, and discovered that the Enlistment Act, complete with its maximum penalties of a $2,000 fine and up to two years imprisonment, was still in effect, and that the act's wording was unchanged. The law still expressly forbade any Canadian from enlisting in the armed forces "of any foreign state at war with any friendly foreign state." Yet Ottawa was allowing Canadian boys to enlist in the American army, and to serve in Vietnam, and thousands of young Canadian men were doing just that.[13]

Ottawa had conjured up the Enlistment Act in 1937 to prevent Canadians from serving in the Spanish civil war, a conflict in which the government had claimed to be neutral, Claire reminded an audience of one thousand demonstrators at Toronto City Hall on April 29. It had never rescinded the act, and today, in 1971, Ottawa claimed to be neutral in Vietnam. Certainly Canada was not at war with Vietnam, nor had the Provisional Revolutionary Government of South Vietnam or the government of North Vietnam ever been declared unfriendly states. So why wasn't the federal government enforcing its own laws, and prosecuting Canadian citizens who were openly serving in the armed forces of a foreign state at war?[14]

It was a telling point, and one she would hammer repeatedly in the coming months. The fact was that thousands (estimates run as high as ten thousand) of Canadian youths served in the American armed forces during the Vietnam era, and many of them saw combat duty in Vietnam. Special recruitment offices for Canadians had been set up in the border cities of Bellingham, Washington, and Plattsburgh, New York. Canadian volunteers would receive a "letter of acceptability" from the American recruiters before returning to Canada. When he re-entered the United States the Canadian recruit would exchange the letter of acceptability for an American visa and a promise of American citizenship before being officially inducted into the U.S. military. All of this was going on under the noses of Canadian border officials, but Ottawa turned a blind eye to this traffic, unlike the active steps it had taken to discourage service in the Mac-Paps. In 1937, of course, the left had been waging a war against fascism, and the Canadian government had actively enforced its neutrality. Indeed, in one of the cruellest ironies of all, Canadian recruiters actually rejected a number of Mac-Pap veterans when they volunteered for service against Hitler because they were suspected of Communist sympathies. In Vietnam the United States was fighting communism, and Ottawa tacitly accepted the fact that its citizens were enlisting. The situation was one of the clearest examples of Canada's sham neutrality in Vietnam. "It would have been more honest if Canada had just sent a brigade," observed one Canadian Vietnam-era veteran of the United States Air Force. When Canada's own Vietnam veterans returned home with all of the physical and psychological difficulties experienced by American vets, Ottawa cruelly compounded its hypocrisy by washing its hands of these young men.[15]

On April 19, 1971, Claire appeared in an Ottawa courtroom before Judge Thomas Swabey to answer the charge that she had caused a disturbance by shouting in the House of Commons. In her own defence, she offered an impassioned statement on the Canadian role in Vietnam. She had, she noted, repeatedly attempted to have her official report tabled in the

Commons, and her lawful actions had been, and were still being, stymied by the actions of the government.

> With a clear and determined conscience I decided to take the matter directly to the House of Commons since all other methods to rouse its sense of humanity seemed to have failed. I felt obliged, as a responsible citizen, to protest our participation in this mass murder. These are some of the reasons why I went to the House of Commons on the fourth day of March to raise before the elected representatives the question: *Why are we supplying the U.S.A. with war materiel which creates the patients for the hospitals we are building and maintaining in Vietnam?*
>
> I went before Parliament to object to a crime, not to commit a crime.[16]

The charge against her was dismissed, though not, as she might have wished, on political grounds. Judge Swabey ruled on a narrow legal basis that there was insufficient evidence to prove beyond a reasonable doubt that Claire had actually created a disturbance.[17]

A month later Claire had decided to seek an entirely new venue to air her allegations about Canada's role in Vietnam—the United States Congress. She was in Washington by June 12, presenting her documentation to a series of congressional aides, and on Monday, June 14, Bella Abzug, the pioneering feminist congresswomen from New York City, read into the Congressional Record the criticisms of Canadian conduct which had yet to appear in Hansard. Mrs. Claire Culhane, Abzug noted, "is a courageous Canadian woman" who had worked on a supposedly humanitarian Canadian aid program in Vietnam. "The implication which one draws from her disclosures is that not even a medical unit functions in Vietnam without having American political interest as their foremost consideration. The reports made by Mrs. Culhane demonstrate clearly how the most humanitarian of programs can become distorted and diverted to warmaking purposes. I respect Mrs. Culhane for her undeterred efforts to make these facts public . . ."

Ironically, Claire had now accomplished in American leglislative circles what she had so far failed to do in Canada.

Her achievement, while it was noted in the Canadian press, was overshadowed by another media event which had occurred just the day before. On Sunday, June 13, the *New York Times* had begun publication of a classified Pentagon study of the Vietnam war. The multivolume document, soon dubbed the Pentagon Papers, included a number of high-level interoffice memoranda which were still considered classified by the United States government. The *Times*'s breach of U.S. national security created a furor, and Canadian reporters searching the documents for a Canadian angle on the story were not long in finding it. The Pentagon Papers revealed that Blair Seaborn, the former head of Canada's ICC delegation in Saigon (the same Seaborn to whom Vennema had turned for aid in funding in Quang Ngai, the same Seaborn who would later advise against the release of Claire's and Vennema's official reports), had in fact acted as Washington's messenger boy to Hanoi in 1964 and 1965. (One wonders if he was also the source of the intelligence photos of bomb damage in the North that Vennema reported having seen in Saigon in 1965.) He had borne the Americans' "carrot and stick" message to the North: either surrender, or face an escalation of the war in the South.

The revelation created a storm of controversy in Canada, and one pundit likened Ottawa's role in Vietnam to serving as "chore-boy for Moloch," the Semitic deity whose worship required the sacrifice of one's first-born child. This latest example of Canadian complicity in American Vietnam policy triggered a new round of questions in the Commons, and on June 17 Mitchell Sharp rose wearily to defend his government's role in Vietnam yet again. It was true that Seaborn had travelled to Hanoi six times in 1964 and 1965, Sharp conceded. But he defended Canada against accusations of conveying messages of American threats to bomb Hanoi. Sharp went on to deny the validity of such charges, and reaffirm the integrity of his government's actions.[18]

Claire had no sooner returned to Montreal from Washington than she received a call from American peace activist Frank Browning. Browning explained that a friend of his had been organizing American Vietnam vets to testify at the impending International Commission of Enquiry into United States Crimes in Indochina to be held in Oslo, Norway, and at the last minute one of the five veterans scheduled to participate had cancelled. Since there was now a ticket left over, Browning had given his friend Claire's name—perhaps she would want to offer testimony from a Canadian perspective? A few minutes later Browning's friend did indeed call: if Claire could be at New York City's Kennedy airport by six o'clock the following evening, she was welcome to come along.

Claire jumped at the chance. Fortunately her passport was in order, and she managed to scrounge the airfare from Montreal to New York. Less than twenty-four hours later she was in the terminal at Kennedy, searching for Browning's friend and the American vets. But getting to New York was the only easy part.

When Claire arrived in Oslo she was told that the conference organizers had not received her report, and so she had not been placed on the agenda; and when she did finally wangle a spot on the schedule she was slotted for just before noon, so there would be no time for questions from the tribunal. But Claire was not to be bested. After learning that her report was missing, she stayed up all night to retype it from memory. The next day she refused to accept her allotted spot on the agenda, insisting that she be allowed to speak after lunch, and not before.

Despite the deadline pressure, or perhaps because of it, Claire's testimony before the tribunal was some of her best writing to date. She took her audience to Vietnam, describing in graphic detail the effects of the war on the Vietnamese people.

> While making rounds in the wards of many hospitals in South Vietnam I gradually began to realize that there were some wounds and conditions that did not correspond to the usual categories of bomb splinters, artillery, cannon fire . . . Examples included: a peppering of the skin which did not always penetrate deeply into the organs and therefore could not have resulted from gunfire, and which was later explained to be from antipersonnel bombs calculated to penetrate only flesh and not metal or wood; or a girl with her breasts closely sliced off; or a baby with a hole in its back the size of a small orange; or a buffalo boy castrated; or the pattern of tracer bullets across a two-year-old's face, extending from the lobe of one ear across the cheeks, under the nostrils, and across to the lobe of the other ear; an old man with literally no distinguishable features on his face, only the sockets where his eyes, nose, and mouth once were; or a young girl with clear evidence of vaginal passage destruction by sharp and jagged objects . . . The shrill hysteria of very young babies when approached by a non-Vietnamese person whether in the hospital or in the countryside became a consistent pattern.
>
> In the burn ward I have seen patients so disfigured from napalm as to make it impossible to verify whether they were men or women. I have seen skin and bone sizzling on a child's hand . . . I have heard a doctor assure visiting journalists and doctors that the victims in the burn wards were mostly the result of gasoline explosions, as he was sure the patients would confirm through an interpreter. However, on many occasions, when a second question was placed asking, "Where did the gasoline come from?" the patient would point to the sky.[19]

Claire titled her testimony "Canada: The Butcher's Helper."

In spite of all the hassles, the Oslo tribunal proved one of the most memorable and useful of the international gatherings on Vietnam that Claire would attend over the years. It was thanks to Oslo that she met

F. Barton Osborn. One of the Vietnam vets who had come to give testimony, Osborn had served as an "agent handler" for United States Army Intelligence in Vietnam from September 1967 until December 1968. Osborn explained to Claire how the American intelligence apparatus used foreign-aid projects of other nations to its advantage in Vietnam. Such operations were either called "stay-behind" or "sleeper" operations, and they involved maintaining contact with agents in the field even after the military or CIA presence had been withdrawn. Sometimes, Barton added, the nationals of the third country were not even aware they were being used. They could thus be described as "witting or unwitting support agents"[20] Barton's information added to Claire's suspicions about the Canadian aid projects in South Vietnam.

∗   ∗   ∗

Perhaps because they hoped to avoid public scrutiny of their Vietnam policy, the bureaucrats at External and CIDA rarely responded openly to Claire's allegations about Canadian complicity in Vietnam. Instead, they attempted to fight her by proxy in public, and by the circulation of derisive, poisonous memos in private. The best example of the first government stratagem was a cover story on Claire that appeared in the September 1971 issue of *Canada Month*, an arch-conservative self-styled "Magazine for Freedom," under the title "The Great Galloping Granny of Canada's Far Left." The article was written by Peter Clark, a retired Canadian army officer who had served two and a half years on the ICC delegation in Saigon. "Mrs. Culhane," wrote Clark, "who was returned to Canada after less than three months employment as a clerk at the Canada-built tuberculosis hospital in Quang Ngai, South Vietnam, gives herself the role of an expert, experienced authority on this complex situation and presumes to speak as an eye-witness to events she has never seen."

The hospital had never been requisitioned as a military base by the South Vietnamese forces during the Tet offensive, Peter Clark insisted, but had "come under Viet Cong attack during the February 1968 . . . offensive and the patients as well as the Canadian staff were evacuated to safety." Most of what Claire claimed to have seen with her own eyes was a fabrication, Clark suggested, because she had been evacuated to Saigon at the outset of Tet. "Unless this gremlinesque granny were a flying nun and managed to sneak out of Saigon unobserved, it is inconceivable she could be an eye-witness to events which happened some five hundred miles away."[21]

Sometimes the government would actually originate letters and articles critical of Claire, while at the same time being careful to maintain an arm's-length distance from their authors. On September 22, D.B. Rheault, a project officer with CIDA's Asia Division, wrote Dr. C.W.L. Jeanes, medical director of the Canadian Tuberculosis and Respiratory Disease Association in Montreal who had been one of two "independent" consultants sent to Quang Ngai in the wake of Claire's allegations about Jutras. Rheault remarked that he was "incensed at the webb [sic] of mis-truths, half-truths, outright lies and misinformation which Mrs. Culhane has succeeded in getting published . . . I wonder if we might speak about the basis for some sort of a 'reply' . . ."[22] Within a month Jeanes's obliging response, having been submitted to CIDA in draft form, was published in the *Globe and Mail*.

Jeanes wrote that he fervently hoped that "Mrs. Culhane [would] return to her grandmotherly duties in Montreal and leave our dedicated Canadian medical team overseas to get on with their humanitarian work for the suffering peoples of the world."[23]

Sexism became an increasingly ubiquitous part of the internal record as Claire, and women like her, stubbornly refused to give up their fight against the Canadian diplomatic establishment. One candid disclosure about attitudes towards Claire and VOW at the most senior levels of the Canadian government was revealed in a secret memo from Henry Alain Lawless, the correspondence secretary of Prime Minister Trudeau. "You have no doubt noticed," Lawless wrote D. Beavis in the Privy Council office,

> that there has been something of an upsurge in the correspondence being addressed to the Prime Minister by the Voice of Women and more particularly by Claire Culhane.
>
> My own reading of this correspondence is that it has reached new heights of irrationality, of stridency, and sometimes even of hysteria; my impression is also that the prose is more and more of the standard dialectic common to those who are motivated to an excessive degree by propagandists from the other side.
>
> I think the stuff stinks and I state without reservation that this idiotic group, which is allowing itself to be stupidly manipulated, scares me a hell of a lot more than do [sic] the Communist Party of Canada . . ."[24]

The implication of Lawless's remark—that women, because of their tendency to be "irrational," "strident," and "hysterical" should leave the exercise of public policy to male professionals—was always just beneath the surface in the private record left by officials at CIDA and External.

By the spring of 1972 Claire had been drawn into yet another political struggle—one that was raging literally on her doorstep. She had, since returning to Montreal from Vancouver in 1970, lived in a room on Laval Avenue, in the Milton-Park area, a neighbourhood just east of the McGill University campus. Because of its central location and aging housing stock, Milton-Park had become a prime target for downtown redevelopment. The scheme was all too familiar. A private developer had, between 1958 and 1968, acquired 96 percent of the property in a twenty-five-acre expanse of Milton-Park at a cost of $18 million. The developer, Concordia Estates, planned to demolish most of the existing housing in the area and in its place build a $250-million complex that would include high-rise apartment units, offices, and luxury shops for a planned population of six thousand people. Milton-Park's traditional residents—seniors, students, and low-income families—would be forced to seek affordable housing elsewhere.[25]

But Concordia Estates had failed to reckon with the determination of the neighbourhood's tenants. Led by community organizers from McGill's School of Social Work, area residents formed the Milton-Park Citizens' Committee (MPCC) to oppose the urban renewal scheme, and by the end of 1968 the largest citizen-developer confrontation in Canadian history had begun.

For a number of reasons it was natural that Claire would gravitate towards such a struggle. She favoured ordinary people over wealthy developers and their well-heeled clientele, and she wholeheartedly endorsed the sense of empowerment that the community struggle in Milton-Park was imparting to the residents there.

But there were other, more personal reasons, for her involvement, as well. Milton-Park epitomized the city of her birth and her youth, the Montreal that Claire had come to love above all other cities in the world. The neighbourhood included the site of her birth—Montreal Maternity Hospital, at the corner of St. Urbain and Prince Arthur, which had since been renamed Hôpital Ste-Jeanne d'Arc. The area teemed with memories—there, on St. Urbain Street near Prince Arthur, was a house that she had lived in for a time with her parents. Just a few blocks to the north up St. Lawrence was the Main, the home ground for so many Jewish immigrants newly arrived in the city early in the century. While Claire had never actually lived on the Main, it had still played a large part in her childhood—the Colonial Steam Baths, where her father had gone every Saturday night; Schwartz's, the home of the delicious smoked meat they had every Saturday night as a treat; and the St. Louis Bakery where her mother had shopped for *challah* and bagels.

The streets of Milton-Park seemed to whisper with history, lined as they were with two- and three-storey houses in the Victorian Picturesque style of the late nineteenth century: graceful ornate greystone facades, carved dormers, stained glass windows and wrought-iron balconies. Here was the craftsmanship of the very workers who had marched in that Labour Day parade which had so frustrated her father on the day of Claire's birth more than half a century ago. The marchers were now long gone, but their handiwork lived, it survived. Some of the buildings had begun to decay, it was true, but how much better to repair them, to preserve this visible legacy from the past, than to consign it, and so much of what made Montreal unique, to the wrecker's ball!

There was one other personal twist to the Milton-Park struggle for Claire: the owners of Concordia Estates were former comrades of hers. Norman Nerenberg and Arnold Issenman had been active in the Quebec wing of the Labour Progressive Party, and Claire had known them both in her YCL days. Now, like so many other erstwhile comrades, both Nerenberg and Issenman had dropped their socialist ideals and turned instead to making money. Claire privately disdained this selling out, but she was also pragmatic enough to accept offers from old comrades of money to fund her trips out of and around the country on issues like Vietnam. Her involvement with the MPCC obviously precluded such an appeal to Nerenberg and Issenman, however. Instead, she found herself confronting them across picket lines.[26]

Claire soon became a fixture at meetings and demonstrations of the MPCC. Her favourite placard read No More Craters in Vietnam, No More Demolition in Milton-Park. The slogan perfectly summarized her approach whenever she was involved in campaigns around a single issue—contextualize the struggle in question, draw out the linkages, show the people involved in one issue how their concerns related to other, seemingly separate, struggles. In this case, the people of Vietnam were fighting for survival in their own land and being bombed for their efforts, while in Milton-Park people were battling to preserve their homes and their neighbourhood. Why shouldn't people control their own countries, their own destinies, their own homes?

MPCC activists, including Claire, had illegally occupied some of the doomed units on Prince Arthur Street, to physically prevent their demolition. Events reached a climax on May 23. When the police surrounded a crowd of demonstrators who had gathered to support the occupation, Claire was one of fifty-nine people arrested and charged with private mischief. She and thirty others entered not guilty pleas, and opted for trial by jury, in French. They hoped to turn the proceeding into a political trial when they finally received their day in court.

Shortly after her arrest in Milton-Park, it appeared that Claire had lost a critical battle on another front, as well. On June 29, 1972, the tabling of her four-year-old official report was debated for the last time in the House of Commons. David MacDonald had agreed to withdraw his private member's motion to produce Claire's papers and to throw his support behind a similar motion from Grace MacInnis, the NDP member for Vancouver-Kingsway. The debate was lively and protracted, with MacInnis calling Claire's and Vennema's official reports "Canada's Pentagon Papers." The government continued to stonewall—repeating its assertion that all such reports from its employees were considered confidential, and that the release of these reports would make government employees reticent about writing similar documents in the future.[27]

MacInnis was especially laudatory of Dr. Vennema, referring repeatedly to his membership in the Order of Canada, and as the debate continued it soon became apparent that she was pursuing the release of his reports only. Although the Vancouver MP praised Claire as well, it was clear that her motion did not call for the release of Claire's April 1968 report. Claire felt betrayed by both MacDonald and MacInnis, the former for not renewing his motion for the production of Claire's papers, the latter for excluding her report in favour of Vennema's.

But MacInnis's efforts were unavailing. Claire's long campaign for parliamentary scrutiny of her official report and, through it, Canadian policy in Vietnam ended with a whimper when a government member sought, and received, the unanimous consent of the House to return to routine proceedings, ending the debate over MacInnis's motion without a vote. "Four years of writing, speaking, fasting, demonstrating, vigiling, civil disobedience—all brushed aside by a point of order," a bitter Claire would write shortly afterward.[28]

It was certainly a nadir of sorts, that summer of 1972. For all her efforts, Claire was no closer to winning public exposure for her Vietnam report, and the demolitions in Milton-Park were increasing, despite all of the protests. But from somewhere deep inside herself, perhaps from the searing experience of Quang Ngai, which was never far from her conscious thoughts, Claire somehow summoned new reservoirs of energy and hope. If the elected representatives of the Canadian people were not to see and debate her findings on Vietnam, then she would exploit another means of taking her report directly to the Canadian people.

Claire had for some months been searching for an English-Canadian publisher for an expanded and updated form of her report, and she had found some interest in Toronto publishing circles. Anna Porter at McClelland and Stewart asked to see the manuscript, but Claire was suspicious that Porter wanted to pass a copy on to officials at External or

CIDA. There was no apparent basis for this mistrust of Porter, except that Claire's paranoia had gotten the best of her, as Claire herself would later concede.[29]

In the end Claire signed on with NC Press, then a small left-wing ultra-Canadian nationalist publisher in Toronto. The title of the book was to be *Why Is Canada in Vietnam?: The Truth about Our Foreign Aid*. Wilfred Burchett, the veteran Australian foreign correspondent, wrote the introduction, and he was an unabashed fan. "Doubtless there is no other single person in Canada who has done so much to alert public opinion there to what is really going on in South Vietnam," Burchett wrote of Claire. "In charging ahead as she has done to blast public indifference with some highly imaginative forms of shock treatment, Claire Culhane has rendered invaluable service not only to the Vietnamese people, but to her own people and to humanity at large."

The preparation of her manuscript was not without its difficulties for Claire. Her editors wanted her to adopt a more stridently nationalistic tone and, grudgingly, she complied. *Why Is Canada in Vietnam?* was launched on Thursday, November 2, 1972, in Toronto, and the event was certainly one of the prouder moments in Claire's life. She likened holding the finished book in her hand to cradling one's newborn infant for the first time. "It's the closest you'll ever get to knowing the sensation of having a baby," Claire confided to a neophyte male author fifteen years later.[30]

Why Is Canada in Vietnam? was a modest enough effort—127 pages, published only in mass market paperback, with a cover price of $1.50—and yet it would stand the test of time. Now sadly out of print (though it may still be found in libraries and the occasional used book store), the book remains a minor classic of Canadian reportage. Part memoir, part journalism, part polemic, the book tells the story, in Claire's serviceable prose, of her months in Quang Ngai, of the conditions there, and of Canada's complicity in Vietnam.

Ottawa had hoped that by suppressing Claire's original report the charges in it would evaporate into thin air. In the event, however, the opposite was true. The report had taken on a life all its own, and had grown in length and scope over the years. What had begun as an eighteen-page typewritten document consisting of an original and three carbon copies had gradually evolved into a full-blown manuscript that would be published in press runs of thousands in both official languages, and that would sell seven thousand copies in the English-language edition alone.

Claire was now a full-fledged author, which further heightened her credibility. Publishing the book also meant touring to sell it, and for the final two months of 1972 she was on the road again, embarked on yet another trip across Canada to discuss the war in Vietnam and Canada's complicity in it.

Christmas that year was not an auspicious season for the anti-war movement. The Paris peace talks broke off in early December, and on the eighteenth, President Nixon ordered an intensive aerial bombardment of Hanoi and Haiphong by B-52s—the notorious "Christmas carpet bombing" of North Vietnam. The bombing raids lasted for eleven days, and to peace activists it seemed there was no limit to the American appetite for destruction. Even with the bombing, it was proving ever more difficult to arouse public opinion in North America about Vietnam. People were sick of hearing about the war. Most American troops had been withdrawn from the conflict, but the United States continued to wreak havoc in the country by proxy—through the ARVN—and by the use of superior technology. On January 27, 1973, the Paris Peace Accords were signed by the United States, the governments of North and South Vietnam, and the PRG. The bombing of the North was halted, but the war in the South continued, despite the peace accord. Ever mindful of the plight of the Vietnamese people, Claire soldiered on, stubbornly resisting the twin undertows of public apathy and private despair.

On February 8, 1973, Claire was in court in Montreal to stand trial for the Milton-Park occupation. The MPCC had made elaborate preparations to turn the proceeding into a political trial, and their option, as anglophones, to request a jury trial in French was unprecedented in Quebec legal history.[31] Still, the news media were indifferent to the story, and the trial passed largely unnoticed. Claire made an impassioned speech from the prisoner's dock linking Milton-Park to other global issues, including Vietnam, and several other defendants attempted to use their trials as a bully pulpit, but the outcome was something of a disappointment. Claire and her codefendants were acquitted, but on a legal technicality rather than on the larger issues they had hoped the trial would address. Claire's only consolation was that several of the jury members approached her after the trial and congratulated her on her speech.[32]

By the summer of 1973 it appeared that Claire and the MPCC had been defeated, but such a view underscores the risks of drawing premature conclusions from history. A combination of factors—the poor Quebec economy of the day, the paucity of foreign investment thanks largely to the FLQ crisis, and the delays and public outcry against the Milton-Park development engendered by the MPCC militated against further demolition in the neighbourhood after the completion of phase one. By the early 1980s area residents, with the help of architectural preservationist Phyllis Lambert, heiress to the Seagram whisky fortune, had turned Milton-Park into the largest cooperative housing project in Canada. In the end, much of the neighbourhood was saved from the wrecker's ball, and part of Montreal's architectural heritage was preserved.[33]

As part of her involvement with the Voice of Women and the anti-Vietnam War movement, Claire had helped to organize visits of Vietnamese women for national speaking tours across Canada. In 1973 it was Claire's turn to enjoy a reciprocal visit to North Vietnam as a guest of the Vietnamese Women's Union. She was determined to use the trip to the North as a springboard for visiting the South, too, especially the Canadian aid programs there.

Claire arrived in Hanoi on October 6, 1973, six years after she first touched down in Saigon. She was immediately struck by the startling differences between the capitals of the two Vietnams. In Saigon the street life had been frenetic, noisy, and polluted. Hanoi was like an old silent movie—everyone glided past on bicycles that were noiseless and odourless. On their second day in the city Claire ventured into a downtown park to play ping-pong with a group of Vietnamese children. A crowd of fifty or so soon gathered to watch the action, and Claire left her purse with her money and passport on a bench, and promptly forgot all about it. As it turned out there was no need to worry; no one even looked at her purse. What a contrast with Saigon, where American GIs had risked having their valuables stripped right off their bodies in a crowd. Unlike the South, where Claire had experienced so much hostility towards Westerners, the people of the North all seemed friendly and curious, and they either smiled as Claire approached them, or responded gaily as soon as she smiled at them. Only three or four times during her entire two-week visit did Claire experience people turning away grim-faced.[34]

Bomb damage was everywhere in and around Hanoi and Haiphong, and the destruction left by the Christmas carpet bombing of the year before was especially in evidence. Bach Mai hospital in Hanoi, the country's largest medical facility, had been bombed repeatedly on December 19 and again on December 22, killing twenty-eight patients and staff and wounding another twenty-two, even though American officials had insisted that the Christmas bombing had been directed at purely military targets.

Claire and her group were introduced to Bruce Woodberry, the Australian ambassador to Hanoi, and their interview with him was quite instructive. Australia had recognized North Vietnam the previous February and opened its embassy in Hanoi just two months earlier. The Australian government, moreover, had just voted $3 million (Australian) in aid for the Democratic Republic of Vietnam. Canada had yet to either recognize the

DRV or send it any aid, though Ottawa had been funding aid projects in South Vietnam for more than a decade. Woodberry told Claire that unlike Canada, Australia had elected not to deliver aid under the Colombo Plan because such aid had clearly military implications. Canada, he concluded, "is more conservative than us" in its Vietnam policy.[35]

Because their tour was sponsored by the women's union, Claire and her cohorts were introduced to Vietnamese women, whose stories they heard, wherever they went. The most memorable of such encounters took place in the city of Hon Gai, across Ha Long Bay from Haiphong. There a woman named Minh told them how a group of local women had organized and taken over one shift of the ferry operation between Hon Gai and Haiphong. From the captain down, everyone in the crew was a woman. The ferry service was a critical operation in wartime, and, as a result, it had come under severe American bombardment, especially betweeen July 8, and September 7, 1972, Minh explained. Despite several direct hits, the women had kept the ferry running and even, Minh added with a proud smile, increased the number of crossings from forty-eight to fifty-two per shift. Minh's was just one of dozens of such inspirational stories told by the Vietnamese women.

"All of these stories were told by simply dressed, ordinary women of all ages," Claire noted in her journal, "sitting in the huge dining room of the Ha Long hotel overlooking the bay. Each one started off shyly, almost as if they could hardly go on. But once into their personal story (very personal—always starting with family life, work, studies, and then into what they did when the bombs fell) their speech quickened and there was no stopping them." Often the women recounted their experiences as militia members serving in anti-aircraft batteries, and it soon became apparent that more than a few of the American planes downed during the air war over North Vietnam had been shot out of the sky by women.[36]

Claire was mightily impressed by everything she saw and heard in the North, and she left Hanoi on October 20 more convinced than ever that the Vietnamese would win the conflict they had been fighting for so long.

It was out of the question to fly directly from Hanoi to Saigon, so Claire travelled to Vientiane, Laos, and Bangkok, Thailand, before attempting to enter South Vietnam. Dara and Roisin had expressed considerable trepidation about this leg of their mother's trip—from the moment she set foot on South Vietnamese soil Claire would be at the mercy of the Thieu regime. Claire herself had doubts that she would even be admitted to the country. She half expected the worst and had taken the precaution of tucking a bilingual message into the top of her bra: "Take this to the Canadian delegation in Saigon" it read, in Vietnamese, on one side. On the other an

English message read "I'm a Canadian being detained at the airport, and I'm going to go on a hunger strike if I don't get out of here."

However, in the event, Claire's worst-case preparations weren't needed. The customs official at Ton Son Hut smiled warmly when he saw the colour of Claire's passport. "Blue—ah, so you're a Canadian. I saw one of these just last week—a doctor," the functionary observed in French.

"With blue eyes and short grey hair?" Claire had heard that Vennema was planning a trip to Vietnam. Yes, yes, that was the one. Claire took advantage of his congenial attitude to quickly pick up her passport, smile, and leave with a parting "*Bonjour, monsieur*," before he had time to check the "black list" in his hand. The customs officer nodded and merely waved the pleasant-seeming grey-haired lady through . . .

Saigon was more of a hell-hole than ever, doubly so after her two weeks in Hanoi. She paid a thousand piastres that first night to stay in a crummy hotel in a poor district. Two drunken kids kept trying to get in through the window, and Claire barricaded herself in by pushing the dresser and two chairs up against the door. She left the light on all night, and watched as a small lake formed in the centre of the room, fed by a water leak of some sort out in the hall. She was reading Koestler's *Darkness at Noon*, "not the most nerve-soothing material. Here it was Neon Light at Midnight," she noted drily in her journal. The next day, Sunday, she checked into another hotel "1,200 piastres, but safe and clean," before dropping into the Continental-Palace. The scene there, like life in Saigon generally, seemed to have deteriorated. The streets had been overrun by cripples, child prostitutes, beggars, and hawkers. Inflation had reached runaway proportions, and everyone, it seemed, was on the make, hustling frantically just to earn enough money to survive.

On Monday morning she went straightaway to the offices of the Canadian delegation in the Metropole Hotel. A lone Canadian official was seated at his desk as she entered. When he looked up, diplomat André Gingras stared at her in amazement.

"How did you get in?"

"Whaddaya mean?" Claire replied ingenuously. "I have a Canadian passport, I'm not a criminal. Why shouldn't I get in?"

"I read your book."

He had no choice but to invite her in, and Claire declared her intention of visiting not only Quang Ngai, but also the newest Canadian medical aid project in the Mekong Delta, which Jutras was directing.

"I have to admit my kids were a little worried when I told them that I was going to try to get into the South, but I told them they didn't have to worry, that I'd go straight to the Canadian delegation and report. They don't have anything to worry about, do they?"

She caught the first available Air Vietnam flight to Quang Ngai. After dropping her luggage off at the Quakers', who were now living in the former Canadian House, Claire walked down the street toward the hospital, and old acquaintances began pouring out of their houses to greet her. She was hailed by Dao, who had worked as a Vietnamese-French interpreter, by Huong and her husband, Huyhn, and right next door, by Nga. They couldn't believe that she had actually returned, and Claire couldn't believe how her old friends had changed. Huong, the impetuous, strong nursing student with the beautiful black hair, was now a listless, wizened mother of three. Nga, the pretty young secretary who had been fearful of Jutras's sexual advances was nine months pregnant with her third child and her face and body were so bloated and fat that Claire failed to recognize her at first. But Nga remembered Claire's promise at the airstrip. "Does the fact that you're back mean now we have peace?"

Everyone invited her for dinner but, sensing the hunger all around her and knowing they would insist on sharing what little rice they had, Claire lied, claiming she had already accepted another invitation. It was excruciatingly painful to see how poverty, famine, and war had aged her young women friends prematurely. The old physical warmth was still there—they would sit so close to her, holding hands and sometimes pinching her arm, as if they couldn't believe Claire was actually sitting next to them, or that a human being could have so much flesh on her body—but the laughter and gaiety were gone.

"Much grimness and hostility in evidence in the streets," Claire noted of Quang Ngai in her journal, "open jeering at Westerners, 'Ba My' (Mrs. American), children almost dangerous, not just curious and crowding but shoving, pinching, kicking and stone throwing—sense of feverishness in their attitudes, which gnawing, nagging hunger pangs and disease produce."

She forged on to the hospital, and what she found there was equally heartbreaking. One of the old Vietnamese staff—Ba, an electrician—was still there, and he recognized Claire immediately which he indicated by mimicking her sitting at a desk and typing. He escorted her upstairs, and she was at once engulfed in a flood of memories. But the old ward room where she had watched the Tet Offensive with the patients and their families had changed beyond recognition. All forty beds had been removed, and in their place a conference room had been established with a long table and chairs, and with slogans on the walls. On the other side of the floor was a series of empty offices. Claire knew that the facility had been given over to the South Vietnamese Ministry of Health and that the hospital had been officially downgraded to a clinic, but it was still sad to see that the old TB hospital, which had begun with so much hope, and which had absorbed so many thousands of Canadian dollars, had come to this. The whole building was like an empty, mocking shell haunted by memories of what might have been.

Still, some medical records were being kept and she discovered that the clinic had investigated about three hundred TB cases a month in 1973, a far cry from the number they would have seen in the old days, but enough to allow the Canadian government to defend its continued financial support of the Quang Ngai project. Next Claire went to visit the provincial hospital where, she learned, acute TB patients were once again being accommodated in the old TB ward. She found about twenty listless patients, and was later told they were actually starving as no relatives were allowed in the highly contagious ward, and no provisions had been made to provide food to the patients of the provincial hospital. She found the whole place, which had always been squalid at the best of times, "bleak and miserable." It made her angry to think that Ottawa was billing the conditions here and at the TB hospital as any kind of successful program for the tuberculosis victims of Quang Ngai.

And there were other unpleasant surprises. When the Quakers had moved into the Canadian residence after Jutras had left a year earlier, they discovered that the house had been turned into a mini-fortress. One room had been converted into a bunker, with its windows and doors cemented closed, except for small openings that had been left to serve as gun ports. Jutras had surrounded himself with two German-made submachine guns, a case of hand grenades, and even Claymore mines, with which to defend himself in the event of an NLF attack, he had boasted to the Quakers. It was all a far cry from the "no guns, no guards, no walls," policy of the Canadian aid project in its heyday. The Quakers had quickly filled in the gun ports as soon as they occupied the house, lest the local people think they might ever be used.

Because of Jutras's known CIA associations, Claire learned, the Quakers' patients were reluctant to go to the Canadian hospital for X-rays or tests—why let one's name and location be registered for possible checkup later? When Claire asked how she could prove that Jutras had worked with the CIA the answer was simple: "Just ask anybody why he armed and protected himself this way? Against whom?"

The streets of Quang Ngai City were like a waking nightmare. People were so hungry, Claire was told, they were eating bark. The city was crowded with refugees because a major evacuation of civilians from the northern areas of South Vietnam was under way. Helicopters flew overhead incessantly, huge tanks rumbled through the streets on their way to the airstrip, and the roar of cannon and artillery fire (outgoing) was unceasing. Ambulances sped by with bloodied legs sticking out the rear doors. Claire had been informed at a briefing in Hanoi that the PRG now controlled the countryside to within a three-kilometre radius of Quang Ngai City, and the report seemed accurate enough. It had been eight and a half years since the battle of Ba Gia, almost six years since Tet and now it seemed that Saigon's control of Quang Ngai was nearing an end at last. Whenever Claire mentioned to her Vietnamese friends that she had just been in Hanoi, their eyes brightened and they took a keen interest in conditions there, a considerable change from pre-Tet days when absolutely no one would register that they even heard her talking anti-war.

Claire saw many of the former Vietnamese staff from the hospital, but after four days in Quang Ngai it was time for one more leavetaking at the airstrip. Once again a small group of her Vietnamese friends assembled for the departure, and once again they brought her presents—a lovely woven basket and a precious tablecloth, made by a woman prisoner.

"When will you come back?" they asked her.

"When there is one hundred percent peace, not just fifty percent . . . "

"You will never come back again . . . Take me with you instead . . . "

After Quang Ngai Claire concluded her one-woman inspection tour of Canadian aid projects in South Vietnam. All pretext of neutrality had now been abandoned, she discovered. The projects flew the South Vietnamese, not the Canadian flag, they had each been turned over to Saigon's Ministry of Health, and they were guarded by ARVN soldiers. She found the standards lax, the attitudes lackadaisical, and the first-rate facilities underused (if they were in use at all), much as she had found the hospital at Quang Ngai.

Before departing Saigon Claire reported her findings to Gingras at the Canadian delegation. Gingras telexed Ottawa and circulated statistics about the number of sputum tests done at the Quang Ngai clinic over the previous ten months to buttress CIDA's contention that Canadian aid money was really accomplishing something worthwhile. Moreover, Gingras reassured Ottawa, Dr. Halet, director of the World Health Organization's anti-TB campaign, had pronounced the Quang Ngai project satisfactory. Besides, it was always possible to find small things wrong in projects of this kind in an underdeveloped country, and direct comparisons with the way things might be done in a more advanced nation were invidious.[37] There was no mention of the patients starving in the provincial hospital, no mention of the children stoning Caucasians on the streets, no mention of people eating bark. The gap between Quang Ngai and Saigon was still as vast as ever.

Claire returned to Canada from her visit to the two Vietnams with a greater sense of urgency than ever before. Her success in visiting both sides was in itself a remarkable accomplishment—few Westerners had managed to do such a thing—and it gave her added credibility in the remaining months of the Vietnam struggle. As the Americans had withdrawn from Vietnam and the Paris Peace Accords had been signed, the irritants that had given rise to the anti-war movement were removed one by one. Conscription was abolished in the United States, the number of American casualties was reduced to a trickle, the U.S. news media shifted its attention to another corner of the world—the Middle East and the Arab oil embargo. One by one leading anti-war campaigners in North America—Jane Fonda, Tom Hayden, Joan Baez, to name a few—rolled up their maps of Vietnam and turned to other issues, other struggles. But not Claire. Instead, she continued her old work methods and habits—touring, speaking, writing letters and articles—never ceasing to remind the public of the suffering of the Vietnamese people and of Canadian involvement in the war. It was at just such an appearance in Vancouver in November 1974 that poet Pat Lowther heard Claire speak, despite a balky projector, and wrote "This Movie Is Not Over." She was still at it the following spring, on April 30, 1975, when the forces of the NLF and the North Vietnamese army finally liberated Saigon.

Claire would later evince a certain dissatisfaction with her own performance during the Vietnam years, complaining of a lack of "concrete" results, and feeling guilty that she had perhaps ignored subsequent events in Indochina like the Chinese invasion of Vietnam (which she opposed), Vietnam's own invasion of Cambodia (which she supported), and the U.S. economic embargo of the Republic of Vietnam, which attempted to grind the economy of the new socialist republic into dust.

But how is an impartial observer, indeed, how is history itself, to gauge the behaviour of this one woman around the question of the Vietnam war? Certainly, concrete, measurable results of her individual actions are hard to come by. There is no proof, for example, that all of Claire's efforts on Vietnam shortened the war by one day or even one hour. And yet she made herself an important and effective part of a global movement that, combined with the decisive determination of the Vietnamese people, brought the Vietnam war to an end. The domestic opposition to that war, and the defeat of the United States military, would have far-reaching repercussions. Until the end of the century American presidents would shrink from once again committing U.S. troops to protracted ground wars on foreign soil. Even before the start of the Persian Gulf war President George Bush would find it necessary to reassure the American public that the impending conflict would "not be another Vietnam," and he withdrew American forces rather than have them fight their way through to Baghdad to overthrow Saddam Hussein. Claire, and the hundreds of thousands of anti-war activists like her, can take some of the credit for American reluctance to use even more force than it has.

And what about closer to home? Can it be said that Claire influenced Canada's policy in Vietnam? Certainly we now know that her adversaries at External Affairs and CIDA followed her activities and scanned her public utterances far more than she herself could have imagined at the time. This in itself was no mean feat. She had started, after all, from a position of absolute weakness, or so it seemed. She had no cachet in the male-dominated worlds of Canadian politics or diplomacy, no credentials and no pedigree. And yet through sheer determination and force of will, combined with political savvy, courage, and compassion, she managed to impinge on Canada's national conscience, to help mobilize opposition to the country's complicity, to give Canadian policymakers pause, at the very least.

The war in Vietnam lasted too long, and took too many lives. Yet how much longer might it have lasted without the efforts of tireless anti-war campaigners like Claire Culhane? Perhaps, in the end, that is their aggregate accomplishment: that it might, without them, have been worse. And there is one other concrete lesson to be drawn from all this, a lesson that Claire had learned from the Vietnamese and which ought never to be forgotten by future generations wishing to make change: the race is won not only by the swift, the rich, the powerful, but also, on occasion, by those who *endure*.

CHAPTER NINE

The Best Fight in Town

We can't change prisons without changing society. We know that this is a long and dangerous struggle. But the more who are involved in it, the less dangerous and the more possible it will be.

        —Motto of the Prisoners' Rights Group[1]

Let the prison door open and the real dragon will fly out.

        —Ho Chi Minh, Prison diary

"Get to the gym, get to the gym," the warden accompanying Claire ordered the prisoners in a harsh, dictatorial voice.

"Aw, t'hell with you both!"

The words were mumbled, barely audible in the cacophony of slamming doors, blaring radios, and shouting female convicts that filled the corridor of the Oakalla Women's Correction Centre. The insult was aimed at the matron who was at Claire's side as they strode down the range together.

It was April 1975, and Claire was at the women's prison in Burnaby, British Columbia, to teach a women's studies course as part of an extension program offered by a local community college. The first class this Friday night was scheduled for the gym, but the warden's attempt to drum up students for Claire was proving a dismal failure. Friday evening was *their* time, several of the women informed Claire, and besides, no one was terribly eager to study with some white-haired straight broad who was obviously part of the system. And no, no one wanted to watch the movie Claire had brought to animate her first class.

It was a rude introduction to life behind bars, and Claire beat a quiet retreat from Oakalla that first night. But she was not about to give up; she returned the following week with a copy of *Our Bodies, Ourselves*, by the Boston Women's Health Book Collective. The book, which is an illustrated guide to female physiology, sexuality (including lesbianism), and reproductive issues, elicited some interest from a few potential students. Slowly Claire began to recruit a handful of registrants for her women's studies course.

Claire had moved back to the west coast early in 1974, and this time the move would be permanent. The desire to be nearer her daughters and grandchildren had proved irresistible, and the lure of Quebec politics had dimmed somewhat. Parti Québécois-style nationalism was gathering momentum in the province, and it featured a nativism that reminded Claire too much of the Duplessis years.

The last straw had come while she was working at the University Settlement House on St. Urbain Street. She'd been involved in an argument with a young co-worker about the future of the province. *"C'est notre Québec, pas la vôtre!"* he had shouted in exasperation. ("It's *our* Quebec, not *yours.*") They were standing directly across the street from L'Hôpital Ste-Jeanne d'Arc, the former Montreal Maternity Hospital where Claire had been born. She tried to tell him that she had been demonstrating, fighting the cops to create a better Quebec before he was even born, but it was all profoundly disheartening. Somehow, because she was an anglophone, or because she was Jewish, it always seemed that the *indépendantistes* never considered her to be a Québécoise, too, despite the fact that Quebec was her native province. Like thousands of other Anglo-Quebeckers in the mid-1970s, Claire had grown weary of fighting for her own place in the province's political sun.

By early March 1974 she had settled into a small attic apartment at 3965 Pandora Street in the northwest corner of Burnaby, just three blocks east of Boundary Road, which divides east-end Vancouver from suburban Burnaby. The following year she had applied to be an instructor at several Vancouver community colleges where degrees were not essential, offering four areas of expertise: Southeast Asia, Canadian foreign policy, women's studies, and Quebec. Again, it seemed as if her whole life had, unintentionally, been a preparation for what would now become an all-encompassing struggle, and add another badly neglected area—penology and the situation in Canada's prisons—to her expertise. Capilano College in North Vancouver offered her a "Quebec in Canada" course, Vancouver City College invited her to teach "Women in Politics." It was the latter course that had taken Claire into the Oakalla women's prison for the first time.

The event that would begin to draw Claire into prison issues began on Monday, June 9, 1975, just six weeks after the liberation of Saigon. Upon learning that they were about to be returned to solitary confinement, a trio of male prisoners at the maximum security British Columbia Penitentiary took fifteen staff members hostage, sparking a standoff with authorities that lasted forty-one hours. The incident ended when a prison Emergency Response Team (ERT) stormed the hostage takers against the warden's orders. Mary Steinhauser, a young classifications officer loved and respected by many of the prisoners because she had initiated a course for prisoners in segregation, was the only one of the eight hostages killed in a hail of bullets fired by the ERT. Prisoner Andy Bruce was shot through the chin but survived. The hostage taking and its tragic conclusion drew national publicity, and Claire, who was then teaching her weekly course at the Oakalla women's prison, followed the incident with keen interest.

The following month Claire heard a radio news account about a demonstration outside the Lower Mainland Regional Correctional Centre or LMRCC—the provincial men's prison that was known locally simply as Oakalla. The prisoners had gone on a sit-down strike in the prison yard to protest conditions inside the provincial institution, and a citizens' group calling itself the Prisoners' Union Committee had camped just outside the walls to monitor the protest and ensure that the Steinhauser tragedy was not repeated. Intrigued, Claire went to visit with the PUC protesters. The group included a number of young lawyers concerned about prisoners' rights and prison conditions, she discovered, and a handful of prisoners' rights activists. Claire joined the protest and when, on July 23, the PUC gathered at the front gate of the British Columbia Penitentiary to show solidarity with a week-long prisoners' strike, she attended that demonstration, as well.

A number of factors contributed to Claire's incipient interest in prison issues. There was, first of all, her teaching at the women's correctional centre—although it had gotten off to a rocky start, Claire had soon grown to like many of the women she met behind bars, and the affection was reciprocal. Claire could relate to these women prisoners because at times in her life Claire, too, had operated outside the legal system, and she had seen the inside of more than one lock-up and a few prisoner's docks, though she herself had never spent a night in jail. From Duplessis's Padlock Law through the first and second War Measures Acts, Claire was acutely aware of the state's propensity for repression and control through the use of physical force. And what was a prison but the locus of final, absolute state power over its citizens? Then too, the lower mainland of British Columbia was the site of one very special prison.

The British Columbia Penitentiary in New Westminster was destined to consume much of Claire's energy over the next two years. Much as Quang Ngai had done, the grim old structure overlooking the Fraser River would prove a turning point in her life. Antiquated and overcrowded, the maximum security institution was, by the summer of 1975, nearly a century old, and conditions behind its grey walls had turned the Pen into a powder keg. The worst conditions in the Pen were in the notorious Penthouse, a solitary-confinement unit perched atop B-7 cell block where some of Canada's most hardened prisoners were locked away for special punishment. There were forty-four cells in the Penthouse, each three metres long by two metres wide, or about the size of an apartment bathroom. For twenty-three and a half hours a day a prisoner was confined in a space so small he could almost reach out and touch the walls. The cell had a solid steel door with a tiny window in it, and no bed—just a concrete slab on the floor. Each night prisoners were given a foam sleeping pad and bedding, but the light bulb was left on. Prisoners had to sleep with their heads visible to the window, which meant sleeping beside the toilet bowl. There were no hobby crafts in the Penthouse, no access to the prison library or gym. The only exercise consisted of a half an hour a day out on the tier in front of the cells. Men would spend months, even years in the Penthouse, until they repented or went mad.

By the time they were returned to the general prison population many denizens of the Penthouse emerged with an even more smouldering hatred for the society that had subjected them to such inhumane conditions. Life in the Penthouse—indeed, in the penitentiary as a whole—resembled Thomas Hobbes's famous description of humanity's existence in a state of nature: nasty, brutish, violent, and short.

In December 1975 even a federal court judge, Darryl Heald, ruled that the Penthouse constituted cruel and unusual punishment, but instead of closing the place the authorities in New Westminster merely enlarged the window in the door, agreed to turn the lights off at night, and installed proper beds.[2] For Claire, the Penthouse was to the British Columbia Penitentiary what the provincial hospital had been to Quang Ngai. What kind of society countenanced such a place? To be aware of such inhumanity and to simply walk away would be an act of unthinkable complicity.

In the eighteen months after the Oakalla demonstration Claire took a number of the small steps which would eventually turn her into Canada's foremost prisoners' rights advocate. One of the first was that she began to visit a prisoner in the B.C. Pen who never received visits from anyone else. His name was Jack Pettipeace. "It was typical," Claire would recall years later of her first visit to a Canadian prisoner. "I got the application for a visit, and went through all the red tape, and finally I was approved for a visit. I phoned and made an appointment and arrived at the Pen, and the guard in the visitors' area said, 'Don't have anybody by that name.'

"I said, 'C'mon, I filled out a form. Look it up.'

"'Well, he's not here.'

" 'What, has he gone home?' I asked.

"I get these games all the time, you know—and still do. So I was off to a good start."

Through sheer pertinacity Claire finally had her visit with Pettipeace, but a more serious confrontation with prison authorities was in the offing. Within a few days of her attendance at the B.C. Pen demonstration calling for a public investigation into the Steinhauser killing, Claire's course at the Oakalla women's prison was cancelled because of her participation in protests at both Oakalla and the B.C. Pen. Although she was forced to stop teaching her women's studies course, Claire continued to correspond with and visit the young women she had met there.

Claire's eye for detail was as keen as ever, and on her visits to Pettipeace she spotted a seemingly insignificant item that revealed a great deal about Canada's penitentiary system. It was a sign on the way to the visitors' parking area that read Do Not Enter. But the only way in to the Pen was past the sign, which was clearly intended to confuse, rather than direct, the public. The sign, she concluded, was a symbol of something far more important and much more sinister about the way Canada's prisons worked: they were designed not just to keep convicts *in*, but also to keep the public *out*. The last thing in the world Ottawa and its regional and local minions wanted was public scrutiny of what went on behind the bars and walls and wire of Canada's prisons. Like Canada's policy in Vietnam, the official attitude seemed to be that Corrections should be paid for by the citizens, who ought then to be discouraged from asking too many questions about what was actually done with their tax dollars.

But in the spring of 1976 Claire found a crack in the forbidding exterior of the Canadian Penitentiary Service (CPS). In an effort to improve its community relations the CPS had recently encouraged the establishment of citizens advisory committees (CACs) at each of its institutions. Claire accepted an invitation to become a permanent member of the CAC at the B.C. Pen, even though some of her fellow activists worried that the committee would be too much a part of the system, and that Claire would be "selling out" by joining. Certainly, the CAC for the B.C. Pen was a prestigious group, including prominent lawyers, professors of law and criminology, journalists, and other professionals. But Claire stood her ground on joining the CAC, arguing that anything which got her in to meet with prisoners was worth doing.

At its first meeting with staff and prisoners in July, the committee began to gain some insights into the sordid conditions in the sprawling penitentiary. The Protective Custody unit or PC, for example, housed eighty or ninety prisoners at any one time, even though it was built to accommodate just over twenty. The men were literally "stacked like cordwood," the acting director, Ken Peterson, admitted. In theory protective custody prisoners (suspected informers, and "skinners" or sex offenders who were at risk in the general population) had the same rights as other prisoners. In practice, their opportunities were far fewer, as their unit had no separate staff or kitchen facilities.[3] Overall, due to shortages of staff and equipment, the prison's general population spent significantly more time locked in their cells than their counterparts at Canada's other maximum security institutions, a fact that did little to relieve mounting tensions.

The second half of the CAC's orientation meeting provided an opportunity for the group to meet with representatives of the prison guards, and of the prisoners' committee. The B.C. Pen's mildly reform-minded warden, Dragan Cernetic, had sanctioned the election of an Inmate Committee (the IC, as it was called) to represent inmate opinions to the administration. Its chairman was Ivan "J. J." Horvat, whom Claire knew well from her two years of prison visits.

Once the citizens' committee and the IC had settled into the conference room Horvat expressed his pleasure at the opportunity for the meeting. "But there are two things you should know. First, this is the first time that we, as an Inmate Committee, have had a place to sit down and meet. We have been getting together . . . in the gymnasium toilet until now." Second, Horvat continued, the IC had decided that they could not meet with the CAC as long as RCMP Staff Sergeant Paul Starek "who has personally booked several of us" remained on the advisory committee.

A joust over Starek's and Claire's membership on the CAC ensued. The other half of the CAC was at that moment meeting with the guards' union, a member of the advisory committee told Horvat. It was quite likely that the guards were objecting to the presence of a prisoner's advocate like Claire on the CAC, just as the prisoners were objecting to Starek. "Are you suggesting that we accept your recommendation to exclude Sergeant Starek and to accept their recommendation to exclude Ms Culhane?"

But the IC members rejected the parallel, pointing out that Claire had never personally mistreated any member of the guards' union, whereas Sergeant Starek had a "personal record of actual mistreatment of prisoners . . ." Burnaby detachment, which he commanded, had, the IC members claimed, harassed not only offenders but their families, as well. It was clear that the CAC and IC had reached an impasse that threatened to jeopardize all future relations before the two groups could even begin their stated task of "reducing tensions."

A number of compromises were suggested, but the Inmate Committee was adamantly opposed to sitting down with an outside committee "as long as the police make up a part of its membership. Any other organization would have been fine. Judges, probation officers, and so forth, but not the one group who continually and publicly refer to us as animals and advocate shooting us down in the street like dogs." The Pen's prisoners' committee newsletter warned that the "only thing that the RCMP can accomplish with such a group is to get clearer access to B.C. Pen files, and the Committee will not be the vehicle used to accomplish that."[4]

When parts of Claire's RCMP file were declassified by the Canadian Security and Intelligence Service thirteen years later, they revealed that the prisoners' suspicions were not unfounded. A "secret" RCMP memo dated August 10, 1976, contained information about impending activities of the Prisoners' Union Committee, the United Prisoners Rights Movement, and about Claire Culhane. The RCMP informant was "S/Sgt P. Starek, RCMP Burnaby."[5] Within a few days of Starek's surreptitiously providing information about a fellow CAC member to his RCMP superiors, the prisoners' hard-nosed bargaining position had prevailed, and Starek voluntarily resigned from the Citizens' Advisory Committee.

Few rebellions in the annals of the Canadian prison system have been as thoroughly presaged as the riot that was now about to rock the British Columbia Penitentiary. Dragan Cernetic's attempts to ameliorate prison conditions had been thwarted by the implacable hostility of the local leadership of the Public Service Alliance of Canada, the prison guards' union. By September 1976 tensions at the Pen had reached the breaking point, as control of the institution slipped away from Cernetic and toward local union president John Lakusta. To further exacerbate matters Lakusta's union members were attempting to negotiate a new contract. Lakusta notified Cernetic that his members would henceforth refuse to work overtime, perforce reducing the number of hours prisoners could spend outside their cells, hours which were already shorter than in other maximum security prisons in Canada. Prisoner resentment against the guards' union spilled over into more violence, which left three prisoners dead. A series of hostage takings and other incidents had produced six violent deaths among the prison population in as many months. The time bomb that was the B.C. Pen was about to explode, precipitating one of the worst crises in the Canadian prison system in at least half a century.

Claire watched these events with a growing sense of alarm, and her fears were hardly allayed when, during a September 25 visit, Ivan Horvat asked Claire if she was going to be around for the next little while "or whether she might be planning a vacation." Claire assured him that she would be around for a long time. Their conversation took place in a "closed visit" where the prisoner and visitor are separated by a thick sheet of plexiglass and must talk through a telephone system which is closely monitored by prison security officials. The question was Horvat's signal to Claire that she might soon be needed.

Two days later, while visiting Paul Leister, Claire could see that the IC secretary was also upset. Leister urged Claire to contact C. G. Rutter, the Ottawa-based director of inmate welfare for the Canadian penitentiary system, without delay and to discuss Pen conditions with him. Claire did so, explaining to Rutter that Cernetic was no longer in even nominal control (he had taken a leave of absence for health reasons) and "that unless someone in authority from Ottawa came out immediately, a grim situation looked as if it were going to get much grimmer." Rutter reacted with surprise and bland reassurance, a response which came as no surprise to Claire. "I would have been amazed had he reacted any other way, for the hallmark of the penitentiary bureaucracy appears to be to postpone any decision until the situation explodes into someone else's jurisdiction."[6]

It happened that Claire had placed her call to Rutter from the office of lawyer Ron Stern, who had himself telephoned warnings to the commissioner of penitentiaries, André Therrien, the senior civil servant in charge of Canada's federal prison system. Claire's warning, like all the others, went unheeded. After almost a century, the day of reckoning at the British Columbia Penitentiary had finally arrived. Four hours after Claire called Rutter the Pen came down.

The riot began at 6:40 p.m. on Monday, September 27. Claire first got wind of it from a 7:00 p.m. radio news report. She immediately phoned some of her fellow CAC members, suggesting that they should go to the Pen at once, but they had decided to wait until morning. It was 1:00 a.m. on the twenty-eighth when Claire's phone rang.

"Get over here as quickly as you can."

The caller was lawyer Mary McGrath. She and other members of the CAC were already at the Pen, meeting with the IC.

Twenty minutes later Claire was turning off Columbia Street and into the driveway of the B.C. Pen. A drizzling rain was falling and a thick fog had rolled in off the Fraser, giving the scene an air of sombre foreboding. Claire drove past the Do Not Enter sign, cursing it under her breath as she always did, parked in the first empty Staff Only spot she could find, and hurried to the board room, where she was kept waiting for about thirty minutes. The other members of the CAC were already behind the lines in areas controlled by the prisoners, she was informed. Her demands to be taken to join the others were met with indifference by prison authorities. "There'll be lots of time," she was told, as she fumed and worried.

At last Don Sorochan of the CAC arrived to collect Claire. As they climbed up the hill toward the cell blocks the young lawyer briefly outlined the situation. The prisoners, under the nominal leadership of the Inmate Committee, now controlled all of the B.C. Pen with the exception of the Penthouse and Protective Custody. Two hostages were being held in the kitchen, and property damage inside the North and B-7 wings and East block was said to be extensive. As they neared the cell blocks Claire could hear clanging noises and shouting coming from East block, where the windows had been smashed out. Ten bedsheets had been unfurled through the gaping holes where the windows used to be. Each sheet bore a single letter and they bannered the theme of the riot: SOLIDARITY.

The Inmate Committee had set up shop in the commissary, Sorochan continued, and five CAC members were meeting with Horvat and the others there. The first IC demand—that the CAC be called in as observers to prevent another Mary Steinhauser tragedy—had obviously been acceded to by the authorities.

Seven members of the IC were in the commissary, and Claire found the atmosphere tense, the air thick with invective, as the prisoners denounced the administration. Sensing that Claire was being intentionally excluded from the meeting, the IC had at first refused to proceed until she was called in, and yet again while she had been left cooling her heels in the board room. At last they were able to get down to business, and Claire and Horvat struggled to calm things down so the group could formulate some concrete recommendations.

They decided to focus on two immediate demands: a news conference in the prisoner-controlled gymnasium with the forty or so media representatives who had been waiting outside the walls of the Pen since early evening; and the installation of two telephones—the first to communicate with the hostage takers in the kitchen and the second for maintaining contact with prison authorities. In return, as a gesture of good faith, the IC would authorize the release of one of the hostages at the press conference. Either Walter Day, a fifty-year-old food service worker, or Wayne Culbert, twenty-one, a guard, would be free to go.

At 5:50 in the morning three CAC members went down the hill to the front gate to read a press release from the IC to the media. "The Inmate Committee wants it made public how this incident came about and to expose the corruption of this institution," the news release began. The rioting had begun on Friday night when all of the toilets in empty cells were destroyed. On Saturday all of the furniture in the empty cells had been destroyed, and "on Sunday the railings along the tiers went." The East wing had been destroyed sufficiently that "it will never be used again." No escape demands had been made, even among the hostage takers in the kitchen, and the cause of the unrest lay not with the prisoners but with the "grotesque justice and court system. Prisoners are being used as political pawns by selfishly motivated politicians who don't really care about the consequences," the release concluded.

As grey dawn broke over the Fraser, the full scale of the disturbance became apparent to prisoners, guards, and reporters alike. Fifty armed combat troops from Canadian Forces Base Chilliwack had been rushed to the prison to patrol the perimeter grounds, and a busload of RCMP were now present inside the walls. The Mounties included a tactical unit and a thirty-eight-man riot squad. In the bleak light of early morning Claire and a few of the IC members watched as police weapons were brought through the gates and unloaded. The vehicle used to transport them, Claire noted, savouring the irony, was an ambulance!

Like the members of the Inmate Committee, Claire had had little sleep the night before, but she plunged ahead with the day's urgent work. The CAC had agreed that at least one of their members should be with the IC around the clock for as long as the standoff lasted, but by the wee hours of Tuesday morning many in the citizens' group had begun to feel the strain of tension and exhaustion. Claire quickly volunteered to stay on in the commissary that first night so that the others could get some sleep, and she remained with the prisoners for the duration of the crisis. Apart from the lone hostage who remained in the kitchen, she was the only non-inmate present in the prisoner-controlled part of the Pen for the full eighty hours of the occupation.

It was an improbable scenario: a fifty-eight-year-old grandmother surrounded by a small male band of hardened prisoners. And yet her presence during those long, tension-filled hours was indispensable. The desperate young men attempting to keep the volatile situation under control trusted her implicitly. She was calm, knowledgeable, and utterly fearless, and her life had prepared her magnificently for this moment. She had been inured to physical hardship by life in Vietnam and by camp-outs on Parliament Hill in the middle of an Ottawa winter, and her remarkable stamina gave Claire an unusually high tolerance for sleep deprivation.

For part of that first night they had all tried to snatch a few hours' sleep on the floor of the commissary. When they should have been resting Claire and Ivan Horvat huddled on the floor, talking. For Claire, it was a welcome opportunity to chat with the prisoner leader without the electronic surveillance and physical control that were always part of closed visits. They chatted and laughed together instead of sleeping. Some day, they promised one another, they would collaborate on a book about the Pen.

The members of the Citizens Advisory and Inmate Committees spent Tuesday formulating the eight prisoner demands that would be presented to a news conference that night.

While awaiting the installation of the telephone lines to the kitchen and to the CPS officials near the front gate, one of the CAC members returned from outside with a confidential message from Jim Murphy, the Pacific regional director of the Canadian Penitentiary Service who was heading up the penitentiary service end of the bargaining. Security could no longer accept responsibility for the safety of the CAC members inside, Murphy had warned. If any of the advisory committee members wanted to leave, they should sit by the door in the gym during the news conference, and then leave with the media. Claire could see that the proposition appealed to some of her fellow committee members, but in the end none of them accepted Murphy's offer.

"Thank you for being here, but where were you yesterday? Where were you last week?" Horvat asked the reporters pointedly as the news conference finally got under way. True to its word, the IC now prepared to free Walter Day, one of the two hostages. The fifty-year-old food service worker appeared nervous and pale, but Day told reporters he had been treated "with courtesy" by his captors before Horvat intervened to shut down the questioning. Clearly Day had been through an ordeal, the chair of the IC told the press. He should be reunited with his family, and the media could interview him another time. With that the former hostage was led to the door by members of the IC.

After Day's exit Horvat went on to spell out the prisoners' demands. Over the short term the IC wanted the RCMP brought in to oversee the Pen's return to normal; a guarantee of no reprisals, physical punishment, or double jeopardy; and permission for prisoners being transferred to take their personal effects with them. Over the longer term and most importantly, the prisoners wanted a public inquiry into conditions at the B.C. Pen.

At the conclusion of the news conference the press corps was taken on a tour of the Pen—or what was left of it. The damage to the prison had been thorough and systematic. Twenty-five of the 95 cells in North wing were trashed, and 50 of the 110 cells in B-7 wing were no longer fit for habitation. The worst damage was in East block, which had been totally destroyed. After smashing up the toilets, doors, and tier railings in their two hundred cells the occupants of East block had gone on to tear down the brick-and-plaster walls between cells so that it was possible to walk from one end of the range to the other through gaping holes in the cell walls. The prisoners had organized themselves into wrecking crews, complete with foremen, to ensure that East block could never again be used to house inmates. The floor of East wing was knee-deep in torn mattresses, splintered bookcases and cupboards, and smashed sinks and toilets. Reporters were greeted with a sheet hung from one of the upper tiers proclaiming that the area was "Under New Management."

"We did in twelve hours what the government couldn't do in fifty years," the prisoners boasted. "If you ever need a demolition crew, come and see us," shouted another. Indeed, the prisoners had accomplished in a twenty-four-hour rampage what the penitentiary service had been unable to do—begin the phasing out of the century-old Pen, a move which successive federal governments had been recommending for decades. Later estimates would put the total cost of the damage at $1.6 million.[7]

Nor was that all. Just two hours before the B.C. Pen riot started, a similar disturbance had broken out at another hundred-year-old federal prison on the other side of the country. At Laval Institution in Quebec (formerly St. Vincent de Paul) prisoners had sacked and burned their cells, causing an estimated $700,000 in damage. Like the British Columbia Penitentiary, St. Vincent de Paul had been declared unfit for use on several occasions, but it had been reopened as Laval in 1973 owing to an increase in the Quebec prison population. Within a week the unrest would spread to another maximum security prison in yet a third region, when rioting broke out at Millhaven Institution outside Kingston, Ontario.

Claire spent the second night of the B.C. Pen riot in the projection room overlooking the gym, where the Inmate Committee had moved so that the commissary could be used to resume serving meals. Horvat roamed the ranges that second night, reassuring, explaining, ensuring that the IC's demands were reflective of its rank and file. The prisoners had not, however, gained control of the Penthouse, and they feared the guards would take out their frustrations on the prisoners who had had the misfortune to be locked up there when the riot started. Their fears were fully justified. The guards turned firehoses on the luckless Penthouse residents, leaving their cell floors several inches under water and the prisoners dripping wet, before removing all of their clothing and bedding. The heat was turned off, and the windows opened. The prisoners were left cold, wet, and hungry. Not surprisingly, a number of them fell ill.

Negotiations dragged on through Wednesday and Thursday, and there were several more attempts to persuade the CAC members to leave the prison interior, with the clear implication that some sort of action by the authorities to regain control of the prison was imminent. Tensions rose but the CAC members refused to leave, and nothing happened, although the daily newspaper in New Westminster reported later in the day that staff at the nearby Royal Columbian Hospital had been placed on alert and told to stand by to treat possible tear gas victims from the Pen.

"There was never a moment in the eighty hours that we weren't aware of the possibility of police storming the prison," Claire wrote later. The memory of Attica—the New York state prison where a September 1971 riot and hostage-taking had ended with the deaths of twenty-nine prisoners and ten hostages after police and national guardsmen stormed the prison on orders from then governor Nelson Rockefeller—was very much on everyone's minds. During one of the IC meetings Claire asked prisoner Jack Dow whether her presence made an attack by the authorities more or less likely.

"If they're going to come down, they'll come down anyway—whether you're here or not," came the reply.

Claire was left to make her own decision about leaving or staying, and, characteristically indifferent to her own safety, she decided to remain with the prisoners.[8]

By late Thursday the negotiations were finally beginning to produce results. A tentative memorandum of understanding was hammered out between the Inmate Committee and the Canadian Penitentiary Service, with the CAC acting as observers and mediators. Claire personally typed up the final agreement. The memorandum defined the responsibilities of the RCMP in reinstituting order at the B.C. Pen; called for transfers from uninhabitable areas to habitable areas, or to other institutions; ensured there would be no physical reprisals or double jeopardy against prisoners taking part in the riot; guaranteed permission for transferred prisoners to take their personal belongings with them; and urged that a public inquiry be held. The CAC had been closely involved in formulating this latter point, and the inquiry was supposed to be "full and open with broad terms of reference to enquire into the particular and general causes of the disturbances at the B.C. Penitentiary, the resolution of the demands made by the inmates, the implementation of the settlement, and the future role of the B.C. Penitentiary in the prison system."[9]

Taken as a whole, the document could be regarded as a signal victory for the prisoners. It provoked a predictable barrage of criticism from the guards' union, which immediately decried the agreement as "very dangerous to the public." The union also claimed that the agreement, in effect, allowed the prisoners and the advisory committee to run the B.C. Pen and to oversee the RCMP. Wayne Culbert was released unharmed by "the kitchen people" early on the morning of October 2. Culbert's captors were hailed as heroes by the rest of the Pen's population as they gave themselves up to the Burnaby detachment of the RCMP. "You guys won the war for us," one denizen of the battered cell blocks shouted as the hostage takers walked by.

While the media packed up and the RCMP prepared to enter the prison to act as a buffer between the guards and the prisoners, the IC members held one last meeting with the CAC in the corner of the gym. "We just want to thank every one of you for what you've done," began IC member Gordie Duck. "But there is still one thing more . . . You know as well as we do that when this is over we're marked men . . . So, we're asking you, would you please stick around? Not twenty-four hours at a stretch as you've been doing, but will some of you come in every day to see us? Don't lose touch. We're really going to need you for what's going to happen next."

It was Duck who had earlier explained the apparently ironical request to have the Burnaby detachment of the RCMP—commanded by the same Starek whom the Inmate Committee had earlier refused to accept on the citizens' committee—enter the prison as soon as the agreement was signed. Duck had offered to introduce the Mounties to a pair of prisoners who had survived a riot at Millhaven the year before. "You'll find when you talk to them that their brains are scrambled. They had to run the gauntlet of two rows of guards with clubs as they were moved—naked and on their hands and knees—from the yard back to their cells. We just figured we would try and avoid that if we could. That's why we asked you here instead of the guards, when it ends." An official government inquiry into the Millhaven riot and its aftermath confirmed Duck's allegations of staff brutality.[10]

The CAC members promised that they would indeed remain frequent visitors to the Pen in the weeks to come, and with that they departed. It was early on the morning of Friday, October 2, and it had been three and a half days since Claire had been outside the walls of the B.C. Pen.

The role played by Claire and the other members of the CAC during the B.C. Pen riot of 1976 was both remarkable and controversial. Despite the severe property damage and the almost total control of the institution by its inmates, there were no fatalities and no serious injuries to either hostages or prisoners. Credit for the positive outcome of the riot must go partly to the level-headed leadership of the Inmate Committee, and partly to the presence of the Citizens Advisory Committee. The former group kept the lid on the explosive forces which were constantly simmering within the prison population, and, in so doing, they did not force the administration's hand into ordering an all-out Attica-like attack. At the same time the population as a whole demonstrated extraordinary restraint, living up to their bannered goal of "Solidarity." The "kitchen people," too, by holding but not harming the hostages played their trump card well, deterring precipitate action by the authorities while at the same time not leaving themselves open to criminal charges at the end of the conflict. The presence of Claire and other CAC members throughout the disturbance was unprecedented and won high praise from a parliamentary sub-committee which subsequently examined the unrest in the Canadian prison system.

"The Citizens Advisory Committee, which was invited to get involved in negotiations, made an outstanding contribution to the settlement of the problem. The authorities were fortunate in finding such negotiating talent in this Committee, which was not chosen for that purpose," concluded the MacGuigan Report in 1977. However, the sub-committee hastily added, such a negotiating role was not appropriate for a CAC, negotiations should not be carried on with hostage takers, and full-blown agreements like the one negotiated at the B.C. Pen were even less desirable.[11]

But prison authorities took a much dimmer view of the CAC's actions in general and Claire's role in particular than the MacGuigan committee and payback time was fast approaching.

For the first three days after the hostage taking ended Claire continued to make daily visits to the Pen to monitor the situation, as the IC had asked the citizen's advisory members to do. On Wednesday, October 6 she arrived at the Pen to begin a shift at 8:00 a.m.

The attitude of the guards toward the resolution of the riot was reflected in a conversation with her escort that morning.

"Guess you're satisfied now you've given the inmates everything they've asked for," he said belligerently as they walked toward the gym where some two hundred prisoners were now being housed.

"Not exactly everything. But anyway, you have your two hostages safe and unharmed, haven't you?"

"We should've been allowed to do what we wanted to do in the first place."

"And what was that?"

"Gas 'em."

"And then what, after that?"

"There would've been no after that!"[12]

At the gym Claire met with half a dozen prisoners to discuss their grievances and she was given six or seven letters for mailing to their families. Claire knew well the official prison policy on letters: all prisoner correspondence in or out of a federal institution must first pass through Visitors & Correspondence for inspection. Letters which circumvented V&C, known as "kites," were considered contraband and were a serious offence against prison regulations. Claire turned to a group of RCMP and a prison guard and asked them what the current procedure was for letters. When they merely shrugged, she accepted the letters and showed the guard in charge that she was placing them in her outside jacket pocket until she could reach the mail drop at V&C, which was near the front gate. He made no reply.

The meeting she had come to the Pen to attend had just started when a guard suddenly asked Claire to accompany him. He led her to the office of Ev Berkey, the prison's acting director of security. In the presence of another officer Berkey asked Claire if she was in possession of any prisoners' letters, which were still stuffed, clearly visible, in her pocket. Claire gave the letters to the security chief and started to explain the circumstances when he cut her off. The letters were contraband, Berkey declared, and Claire was clearly in violation of pentitentiary rules. She would be escorted off the premises immediately, and she could never come back.

Claire was stunned. Her first inclination was to simply refuse to move— to stage a sit-in in Berkey's office right then and there. But she hesitated, not wanting to jeopardize the CAC's working relationship with the prison administration. Deeply humiliated, Claire allowed herself to be escorted out of the Pen. She drove immediately to the Legal Aid office of fellow CAC member Mary McGrath, who telephoned Berkey at once.

She herself had delivered letters to V&C just the day before, McGrath explained, because a letter drop had yet to be established in the gymnasium in the wake of the riot.

"Claire will return now," McGrath insisted, "as she is our representative at the Transfer Board meeting this morning."

But Berkey was adamant: Claire was persona non grata at the B.C. Pen. She would never again be allowed access to the institution.

Claire's barring became the subject of intense news media coverage in the lower mainland, but its significance can best be understood in relationship to another, less well publicized development the day before. After coming under increasing pressure from the guards' union, Commissioner of Penitentiaries André Therrien had decided to abrogate the memorandum of understanding which had ended the hostage-taking incident just four days earlier. Since the Inmate Committee was not a legal entity, Therrien concluded, the agreement was not legally binding. "It is entirely a matter of CPS discretion as to whether the so-called Agreement is to be honoured in full or in part, or not at all."[13] Seen against this backdrop, Claire's banning may be regarded as part of a hardball strategy by penitentiary officials to regain control of their system, and it was a strategy in which the CAC ultimately acquiesced. It didn't help Claire's position that Scott Wallace, a Conservative MLA and fellow CAC member, was pressing for Claire's resignation because of her overt pro-prisoner attitude. When the CAC finally met again, Chairman Edwin Lipinski asked for Claire's resignation. Faced with the possibility that the entire CAC might have to abandon its work at the Pen, Claire reluctantly agreed to resign. The RCMP had begun withdrawing from the Pen, leaving the CAC as the only outside group monitoring developments behind the walls. For the good of the prisoners, the CAC must continue its work, and Claire did not want to jeopardize that role.

Having now disposed of the Memorandum of Agreement and the most troublesome member of the CAC, prison officials settled down to the business of punishing the rioters. Despite the fact that they had promised to transfer 250 prisoners into habitable areas of the Pen or to other institutions altogether, for two months the authorities left about two hundred prisoners, including the Inmate Committee members, to languish in the gym. They were denied fresh air and exercise and visitors, and provided only with substandard food and medical care. They were completely deprived of that rarest of all prison privileges—privacy—by being forced to camp out on the gymnasium floor. As December neared, the B.C. Pen time bomb was once again ready to detonate—this time literally. On November 22 a pipe bomb exploded in the shower room adjacent to the gym, prompting authorities to announce that the fifty or so prisoners remaining in the gym would be transferred back into cell blocks. But the prisoners' destination was astonishing. Despite the fact that it still lacked running water, heat, windows, and even proper cell blocks, East wing was to be returned to service.

On November 23 as the prisoners, with their few possessions, were waiting to finally leave the gym a fire broke out in the rear of the large room, further adding to the chaotic shambles. When journalists were shown the gym a day or two later one of them described the place as "a cesspool." The sharp-eyed reporter for the *New Westminster Columbian* noted a few lines of prison graffito that had been scrawled on the gym wall by one of its former residents: WE GET OUR WISDOM FROM OUR EXPERIENCE. WE GET OUR EXPERIENCE FROM OUR FOOLISHNESS.

Claire kept in close touch with some members of the CAC, and as Christmas neared it became apparent that conditions inside the Pen had reached a new low, and that East wing was the worst.

"The conditions [in East wing] were truly appalling," the CAC reported. "The cells had no facilities whatsoever, although chemical toilets were available. There was no running water, and most depressing of all, most of the cells did not have any light. The members visited every inmate . . . and their responses ranged from open hostility to complete and utter despair."[14]

In vain Claire urged her contacts on the CAC to bring conditions in East wing to public attention, by whatever means necessary. The message being sent would-be prison rebels by the authorities was unmistakable: do not resist, do not question, do not stand up; it will only make matters worse.

To resist authority, to struggle for one's dignity, to respect every human being, no matter how poor or benighted, these were the themes of Claire's life, the wisdom distilled from fifty-eight years of experience, even though many considered her foolish. She could no longer stand by and do nothing about the worsening situation at the B.C. Pen. As a last resort it was once again time to put her own body on the line.

On the morning of Wednesday, December 15, Claire and another member of the Prisoners' Rights Group entered the office of Robert Swan, the acting director of the British Columbia Penitentiary. She had come with eight demands, Claire announced, and until they were met she intended to stay in his office, offering herself up as "a voluntary hostage" to the prison system. Her demands: that all prisoners be moved out of the East wing immediately; that visiting periods be reinstated at once; that Penthouse prisoners should be allowed into the general population for brief periods to offset the sensory deprivation of solitary confinement; that Inmate Affairs Director C. G. Rutter or Correctional Investigator Inger Hansen be dispatched from Ottawa to talk personally with the prisoners at the penitentiary; that a press conference be called with the Inmate Committee and representatives from the Penthouse; that the CPS word for prisoners' meal time—"feeding"—be changed to "meals"; that one or more members of the CAC be called in to witness her discussions with Swan (this latter as a guarantee of reliable reporting); and also that a press release regarding Claire's activities be delivered to the Inmate Committee to offset any false rumours.

Having already succeeded in gaining Claire's removal from the CAC, Swan was in no mood to negotiate with her now. So, while Claire's friend left the office and went out to Columbia Street to begin picketing the Pen, Claire prepared to occupy Swan's office. In answer to his threat to call the police, Claire replied calmly that it would be far better for her to become a voluntary hostage of the prison authorities—whether they wanted her or not—than to have the prisoners seize hostages once again, which they were clearly being driven to do by the conditions inside.

A few minutes later Claire was bodily removed from B.C. Pen property and taken to the New Westminster police station. After her identity was established she was subjected to an interrogation by two of New West's finest.

"Nationality?"

"Canadian."

"Religion?"

"Do unto others as you would have them do unto you."

"What! You mean 'no religion'?"

"I didn't say that. You asked me what my religion was and I answered: Do unto others as you would have them do unto you."

"Racial origin?"

"Canadian."

"Are you Irish?"

"No, I'm not Irish. Just because I have an Irish name doesn't mean I'm Irish."

"Racial origin?"

"Canadian."

"Racial origin?" This time the question was shrieked and the police officer had brought his face to within an inch of Claire's.

"Well, if you must know, my mother came from Kiev and my father came from Vilna."

With that the cop turned triumphantly to his partner. "That's Irish!"

Several hours later Claire was back on the Columbia Street picket line. A few reporters had come out to see what the fuss was all about and Claire announced her intention to fast and picket every day until Christmas to call attention to conditions in the Pen. Even the SPCA should be called in to inspect the East wing, she added, "because it is not fit for the rats that inhabit it, much less the people."[15]

For the next ten days Claire maintained her vigil during daylight hours, walking back and forth in front of the penitentiary entrance carrying signs that read Restore Open Xmas Visits, Only The Rich Can Afford Justice, Abandon Supermax Everywhere (referring to super-maximum security and its greater isolation), and No More Solitary Confinement.

As in her earlier "stationary demonstrations," Claire proffered her opinions to passersby, often learning from them in the process. The venomous reaction of the public, either to her presence or to the conditions she was protesting, was quite startling. Many motorists whizzing past on Columbia Street reacted with pure hatred of her cause, making obscene or violent gestures, while pedestrians often stopped to chat. A former member of the Pen's "goon squad" told her how he had cautioned his fellow tactical squad members to restrain themselves from making cruel reprisals against prisoners. Some of the ones who had ignored his warning had paid the price, he noted, perhaps thinking of one guard who had had his hands blown off by a mail bomb thought to have been sent by a former convict. He himself had resigned from his job before descending into barbarism, the former guard confided.

And there were always the prisoners to lift her spirits. Even though she was unable to enter the Pen, they knew she was out there, and whenever a busload of prisoners from Matsqui, a medium security prison in the Fraser Valley, passed by on their way to the New Westminster courthouse, they would cheer and wave clenched fists. If the driver happened to be sympathetic, he'd even slow down as they passed.

But the retribution continued, both inside and outside the walls. The handmade Christmas cards she had sent in to the prisoners were returned by V&C and, when a group of prisoners, led by Native inmate Clarence Johns, attempted to send her money for legal fees, the funds were returned to them, without explanation, by the Pen's accounting office. Behind the thirty-foot prison wall the grim cycle of reprisals continued unabated, despite her presence. All Christmas visits were suspended as were all festive activities. In the bombed-out shell that was now the B.C. Pen, prisoners gave themselves over to despair in record numbers that Christmas of 1976. In the East wing alone, sixteen men "slashed up" on Christmas Eve, after they received special "gifts" from the guards: razor blades had been embedded in apples with a note attached wishing the men "A Merry Christmas and a Slashing New Year."[16]

$$* \quad * \quad *$$

Rarely in her long years as a social activist had Claire Culhane faced such insurmountable odds. She was now challenging one of the most tightly controlled and inaccessible aspects of Canadian society: its prisons. Claire had come to see prisons within a societal context, and to understand that their role was indispensable in the perpetuation of the status quo. The prison system was the sharp end of the stick (which included the courts, the police, and the army) that kept unruly social elements in check. By challenging the nation's prison system Claire believed she was also challenging the social system as a whole. "As I see it, by trying to abolish the present prison system we challenge a social/political/economic order which must preserve and expand its prisons to confine anyone who dares resist it— trade unionists, nuclear protestors, and political activists all qualify as potential 'criminals,'" she observed.[17]

But how could she prosecute her case against the system? Prison wardens and administrators throughout British Columbia had followed the B.C. Pen's lead and barred her from their premises, too. Throughout 1977 Claire fought a losing battle to regain her access to federal prisons in the province. Despite her sit-in and despite a petition signed by 128 prisoners at the B.C. Pen requesting "a reinstatement of visiting privileges for Mrs. Claire Culhane," she remained barred from federal institutions in the Pacific region. For the most part the wardens, bureaucrats, and guards who controlled Canadian prisons had enjoyed absolute authority in their domain, and their response to Claire's challenge was predictable. They would deny her access, interfere with her correspondence, and allege in internal security reports that "almost everywhere she has appeared, she has been a most disruptive influence—both with the inmates and the administration."[18]

Being barred from prison redoubled Claire's resolve. She found ways to communicate: through friends who visited prisoners, through letters to and from prisoners which were allowed by V&C, and, having been barred from federal institutions in British Columbia, she broadened the scope of her interest to provincially controlled facilities. The destruction of the B.C. Pen had resulted in scores of prisoner transfers to other maximum security prisons, and she kept in close touch with a number of her friends from New Westminster. This diaspora spread her influence and knowledge beyond the Rocky Mountains. She gradually became knowledgeable of conditions in prisons across the country as former Pen prisoners told their rangemates about the sixty-year-old lady in Vancouver who could be counted on to speak out or write a letter to the authorities when no one else would listen.

As she had done with External Affairs during the Vietnam War days, Claire began to bombard correctional officials at all levels with correspondence. Prisoner grievances, prison conditions, arbitrary decisions by the authorities, all became grist to her prodigious epistolary mill. Although she could no longer visit prisoners at the B.C. Pen, she was still able to correspond with them and receive the occasional phone call. In this way she was able to compile what she called her "grievance list," and in Dragan Cernetic's successor as warden at the B.C. Pen she found a sympathetic ear. Herb Reynett was an easy-going career corrections officer who was willing to at least listen to Claire's prisoner-generated list of grievances. Because his office was located outside the wall around the Pen and accessible from the street, Claire was able to pay periodic visits to Reynett without having to physically enter the grounds, which she was forbidden to do.

Claire would run through her grievance list and Reynett would listen and then give her an answer. "No way," he'd say, or "There'd be too much heat on me." But once in a while the response was positive. "Okay, I'll try this . . ." And Claire found that Reynett kept his word.

On June 9, 1977, Claire appeared before Judge F. K. Shaw of the New Westminster Provincial Court on the charge of trespassing on penitentiary land as the result of her December 15 sit-in on the warden's office. As she had in the previous court appearances resulting from her acts of civil disobedience, Claire seized the opportunity to make an impassioned speech from the prisoner's dock. She considered herself innocent of any wrongdoing, Claire told the court, but she charged the CPS and the B.C. Pen administration in particular, "with gross mismanagement, unbelievable callousness and a less than human attitude in its dealings with prisoners, and friends and families of prisoners."[19] Judge Shaw found her guilty of trespassing, however, and ordered Claire to pay a $25 fine, an order she promptly refused. At the B.C. Pen Claire received a remarkable show of support on the day of her trial. The prisoners there went on a peaceful one-day strike, refusing to take their meals or perform their normal work.

A scant seven weeks after her first trespass conviction, Claire sat in Reynett's office once again. The issue this time was the fate of Clarence Johns, the native prisoner who had attempted to raise money for Claire's legal defence before his transfer to Dorchester, the maximum security federal penitentiary in New Brunswick. After spending three months at Dorchester, Johns had been suddenly returned to the B.C. Pen. So hasty had been his departure from the New Brunswick prison that he hadn't even been allowed time to gather his few personal possessions together. In late July Claire received a letter from Johns. He was in the Penthouse, his personal belongings were God knows where, and Johns beseeched Claire to have a native court worker visit him. She could tell from the tone of his letter that after four months of solitary confinement Johns was *in extremis*.

Convinced that Johns's plight was truly a matter of life and death, Claire went to see Herb Reynett in his office on July 29. She urged the warden to send a court worker in to check on Johns's condition. Reynett refused. Then at least the warden could allow Johns to be brought to his office so that she could see the man herself, Claire pleaded, even for just ten minutes. Once again, Reynett refused. Then she had no choice, Claire declared, but to sit-in at his office until someone outside the CPS verified Johns's condition. Reynett called the police and summoned one of his deputy wardens as a witness.

"Aw, Mizz Culhane, you're not going to do that again," Reynett's underling, a short roly-poly fellow said sadly. "I hate to see you carried out. It hurts."

"How do you think *I* feel?" Claire retorted. By that time the police had arrived. Besides charging her with trespassing, the officer told the warden that Claire could also be charged with assault, a far more serious matter, if there were physical contact between herself and Reynett. At this prompting Reynett reached out to touch Claire on the shoulder, as she leaned away. The ridiculous pas de deux was repeated several times before the warden finally succeeded in actually touching Claire, who was loudly denouncing the absurdity of it all. In the end, the Crown attorney must have agreed, because she wasn't charged with assault over the incident, just simple trespass once again.

A week or two after her sit-in Claire called Reynett; she had another grievance list she wanted to discuss with him. Not surprisingly, the warden was leery.

"I can't let you come by anymore, you'll just sit-in on me again."

"But when I make an appointment with a grievance list, I won't sit-in on you."

"Give me your word," Reynett demanded.

"No, that's not what I'm saying. Whenever I have an appointment I promise I won't be sitting-in on you. That doesn't mean I'm promising I'll never sit-in on you again."

Reynett agreed, and Claire's working relationship with the B.C. Pen warden resumed once again.

Claire was scheduled to make her first court appearance on the second trespass charge on October 5, and in the meantime she went to work tracking down Clarence Johns's missing belongings. The authorities at Dorchester produced proof that they had been shipped by CN Express, and the waybill further showed they had arrived safely in New Westminster. Some of Johns's things, including a family photograph album belonging to his mother, had turned up in the garbage at the B.C. Pen, with all the pictures removed. After pleading not guilty to the trespass charge Claire read all of this into the record. The fate of Johns's belongings might seem trivial, she told the court, "but I would draw attention to the fact that prisoners have very little else to call their own but the few personal items such as photographs of family and friends which are irreplaceable for the most part." Johns's treatment was clearly an example of the penitentiary system's attempt to "break" some prisoners, to literally destroy their individuality, their identity.

Johns's case also raised another problem, "the discriminatory treatment of native Indian prisoners," an issue to which she would devote special attention over the next fifteen years. Her trial date was set for December 30.

A week or so before her court appearance Claire drove out to the penitentiary to pay one of her periodic visits to Reynett. She had a special purpose, which she explained to the warden. Tommy Shand's birthday was approaching, and she wondered if Reynett might not "happen" to have him in his office that day so that Claire could "happen" by and wish Shand, one of the "kitchen people" who had helped prevent bloodshed during the riot by holding hostages in the kitchen area, a happy birthday.

"No, we never have them in our office, but I'll take your birthday present to him," Reynett promised.

While Claire had carried out an extensive correspondence with Shand since October 1976, she had never actually met him, but she had once asked him what he would do first if and when he was released from prison. The thing he missed most, Shand replied, was Kentucky Fried Chicken.

On December 28, 1977, Claire arrived at the Pen with a yellow plastic shopping bag filled with three still-hot orders of Kentucky Fried Chicken, and crackers, cheese, pancakes, and small jars of jam that she had rustled up out of her own kitchen, as well as her own crêpes. Reynett carefully pored through the contents of the three bags. He rejected the marmalade because the glass jars posed a security hazard, but the warden approved everything else. True to his word, Reynett then hurried up the hill towards the cell blocks to deliver the bag to Shand "before it gets cold." Claire would still chortle at the scene years later. How she wished she'd had a helicopter shot of Reynett, warden of the toughest joint in the country, hustling Kentucky Fried to Tommy Shand on his birthday.

A few days later Claire received a thank-you note from Shand. "It nearly blew my mind to see Reynett standing there with that shopping bag," he wrote. "We're all lifers and we added up all the time we've done, and it was the first time any warden had showed any of us a single humane act. We'll go easy on The Man from here on."

Claire couldn't resist reading the passage to Reynett the next time she went to see him. "You see," she proclaimed, her eyes sparkling, "I've saved you a million-dollar riot with three pieces of chicken."

Reynett had to agree.

But the story didn't end there. The next time she saw Reynett, the warden told her he'd had to fly to Ottawa to attend a disciplinary hearing for his decision to deliver Tommy Shand her birthday present. The guards' union at the Pen had charged Reynett with bringing in contraband!

"Don't look for street signs in the jungle," she would later advise prisoners who complained about the arbitrariness and inhumanity of Canada's prison system, and the story of Tommy Shand's Kentucky Fried was a prime illustration. The simplest act of kindness, something that might genuinely help to defuse tensions or restore one's faith in humanity could become the focus of grievances and disciplinary hearings, even when it was carried out by a warden.

Two days after Tommy Shand's birthday Claire went on trial for her second trespass charge of 1977. Judge W. S. Selbie admonished Claire that the court was not a political platform, but she made her points, anyway. In the end, Judge Selbie was no more sympathetic than Judge Shaw had been five months earlier. In view of the fact that this was her second trespass, Judge Selbie ruled, he was imposing a $150 fine. Once again, Claire promptly refused to pay the fine. After all, what was Selbie going to do— send her to one of the jails from which she had already been barred by the authorities? As Judge Shaw had done earlier, Selbie decreed "No default," and Claire went home.

By 1978 Claire's tireless efforts to improve prison conditions, her court cases, media stories, letters to the editor and burgeoning private correspondence with prisoners had begun to cement her national reputation as a prisoners' rights advocate. Increasingly, prisoners came to her with their problems, usually through letters or telephone calls. Claire had become a lifeline, someone who cared, even about Canada's most abject offenders. Letters began to arrive at her Pandora Street apartment from isolation cells and special handling units across Canada. Often the letters were a last, desperate cry for help from men and women who felt forgotten and alone. A typical example was the letter Claire received in December 1977 from one Polly Chernoff, a Doukhobor* jailed in Kingston's Prison for Women.

Dear Claire—
I hope you could give me some information & hope, as I am very much concerned about a sister whom I will have to leave behind in a couple of months under these unbearable conditions in womens jail in Kingston. We are two Doukhobor Sons of Freedom women who try to defend our principles. Mary was in Kingston over a year, in segregation & I joined her in April of 77.

We are not only not allowed to excersize, we are not see each other, just when passing the cells on the way to take a bath . . . we were forced into long fasts, in fact most of the time we are fasting we get no time to pick up strength enough to feel normal. In protest we set fires in our cells six times for which we were severely punished . . . We are watered with buckets of water and fire hoses & left on a slab with not a stitch of clothes or bedding, with windows wide open till you do not feel any more . . . then 30 days are added to our terms. We are very cheap to keep, we do not waste by habit. We eat just the cheapest food vegetables & fruit. No meat, no deserts & baked stuff, no coffee or sugar. So instead of helping us get out, they extend our stay.

I am concerned about Mary, she is 63 yrs. old & in very poor health which is a big problem with the diet. There is so much prejudice against us being vegetarians. Mental cruelty is endless. Our religion is considered setting fires & not the other way around our religion is being prosecuted which brings us to be human sacrifices for our religion. I would like to know what right Mary has being

---

*A religious sect that had emigrated to western Canada from czarist Russia, the Doukhobors refused to acknowledge the primacy of any government over their lives. They were also prone to radical protest—nude marches and burning their homes in extreme cases.

locked in her cell till sept. day & night is beyond human endrance with nothing but the walls to stare at.

In addition to listen to disturbed girls downstairs slashing & hanging themselves swearing & nervewrecking radios blaring day & night. Well I know for an elderly woman that is too much. Three thousand miles from family & friends. I would appreciate if you could let me know how I could help her. With your knowledge of prisons, I'm sure you could help. So thank you ever so much in advance.

Admiring your spirit,

Polly Chernoff

And what could the Polly Chernoffs of the world expect from Claire in return? First would come a prompt acknowledgement of their letter containing a warm, if measured, response. Claire had, by now, been led down the garden path by enough prisoners that she had established three cardinal rules which she stated up front when undertaking a grievance.

Don't bullshit me—tell me the 100 percent truth.

Don't expect anything, and don't get your hopes up. I have no special clout. I can only promise that I will stay with your case.

Don't maintain further contact if you can't take the extra heat of corresponding with me.

Next Claire would dash off a letter to the relevant authority: a warden, the regional office of the CPS, the commissioner's office in Ottawa, the solicitor general, or a sympathetic MP. Often she would target one of the above and send copies to the higher-ups in the chain of command. The recipient of this opening salvo ignored her at his or her peril. Every thirty days the cases which had not evoked a response from the appropriate authority would receive a follow-up letter. In every federal prison, in every region, bureaucrats learned that Claire would not simply go away.

If Claire found the initial response unsatisfactory she would lob in another barrage, picking holes in the official position and asking a set of follow-up questions, backed up by another brace of carbons to more senior officials or politicians. "Win some, lose some," Claire was fond of saying, and in the early years there were far more losses than victories. But at the very least her interventions served a minimal purpose, providing the prisoner with the reassurance that someone on the outside was listening and caring, and warning the CPS that the grievance was known beyond the walls and wire where their authority was absolute.

In the most urgent and outrageous of cases she carried other arrows in her quiver, and the officials in charge of CPS knew that, too. She might threaten to picket the institution in question, or engage in some act of civil disobedience, raising the spectre of unwanted publicity or yet another trial, which she would turn into yet another political/propaganda platform. It was little wonder that John Drummond, a prisoner at Millhaven, came to dub Claire "The one-woman army from the West."

In Polly Chernoff's case, the Prisoners' Rights Group circulated a petition and made a big enough fuss to get Mary's release date moved up so that she and Polly could travel west together. Claire's efforts on Chernoff's behalf produced a spate of correspondence from other Doukhobor women prisoners. In the women's section of Oakalla they had received brutal treatment similar to that in Kingston. Because of their incendiary habits as a means of protest—an admittedly dangerous practice in any jail—they had been held in isolation, stripped of their clothing, hosed down, and subjected to vaginal inspections by a male doctor who used toothpaste as a lubricant while searching for matches. When they demanded a meeting with warden Marie Peacock she refused to meet with them, engendering more protests and fire-setting and still more heavy-handed reprisals from the authorities. Claire wrote Peacock, and found her to be no more tractable than many of her male counterparts. On Monday, June 19, 1978, Claire spent the day outside Oakalla in an unsuccessful attempt to hand deliver a letter to Peacock. She was finally physically removed from the premises by police late in the evening. Next Claire turned to the news media, and she returned to Oakalla on Wednesday, accompanied by a clutch of reporters and television news cameras. This time Peacock deigned to stop her car just long enough to accept Claire's letter through a rolled-down window.[20]

The publicity around the Doukhobor women sparked an investigation by Dennis Kent, the inspector for British Columbia's corrections branch. By the end of August Kent announced that the (unnamed) doctor who had used toothpaste as a vaginal lubricant had been fired by the prison system, and he conceded that the Doukhobor women had been held "in rather an unpleasant situation."[21]

Claire's prison activities were now beginning to win her admiring notices in the news media, much as her Vietnam protests had done a decade before. When Lisa Hobbs, a Vancouver newspaperwoman and friend of then Liberal MP Simma Holt, was appointed to a $50,000-a-year, ten-year position on the National Parole Board, *Vancouver Province* columnist James Barber suggested the position should have gone to Claire, "the woman who knows more about prison systems than anybody in Canada, the woman who actively campaigns for basic human rights for inmates, who clashes head-on with the system . . ."[22]

But even as she chalked up some victories in her campaign to increase public awareness about prisons, there were also some serious defeats. A particularly heavy blow befell Claire in March 1978. She was about to appear before the British Columbia Royal Commission on Female Offenders at Oakalla, an inquiry that had been established to investigate allegations of sexual misconduct by male guards against female prisoners at the Oakalla Women's Correction Centre. An anonymous letter to Claire from an Oakalla staffer had helped to prod the provincial government into appointing the commission, chaired by British Columbia Supreme Court Justice Patricia Proudfoot. On March 10, as Claire was preparing to give her own evidence, a number of guards and prisoners who had testified before Madame Justice Proudfoot announced publicly that they could not cooperate with her inquiry any further because they had been threatened with reprisals. Both Proudfoot and commission chief counsel Jon Hall insisted witnesses had nothing to fear, as they would make sure there would be no such reprisals. Before reading her own report, Claire took a few minutes to inform Proudfoot and Hall that, while she understood they meant well, there was absolutely no way they could enforce such a guarantee.

During the noon break Claire placed a call to a prisoner at the Oakalla women's centre, only to be told that the woman would not be allowed to speak with her and that she would no longer be allowed to visit anyone there, either. Claire went straight to Proudfoot with the news, and the Supreme Court justice was furious. She immediately called Oakalla warden Henry Bjarnasson who firmly told her that: Claire had been barred from his institution. A call to Bjarnasson's boss, British Columbia Regional Corrections Director E.W. Harrison, produced even worse news: Claire had been barred from all provincial prisons.

When Harrison's superior, British Columbia Corrections Commissioner John Eckstedt, appeared before her, Proudfoot grilled him concerning the decision to bar Claire.

"Why is Mrs. Culhane barred from the prison? People like Mrs. Culhane are helpful, and they don't have any reason to feel they shouldn't be allowed in institutions," Proudfoot observed.

"Yes, yes. We are looking at it, as I say, we are going to be discussing it with the attorney general," Eckstedt responded.

But on April 17, 1978, British Columbia Attorney General Garde Gordom informed Claire that "this recommendation is made by both Management and supported by the Union and after having the file examined . . . I am not able to justify my interference with their decision."[23]

The number of prisons to which Claire had now been denied access was growing as wardens and administrators attempted to break her links with the prisoners in their care. Claire was "a disruptive influence" and a "threat to the good order of the institution." Claire challenged her barring in a succession of court cases, and lost every round. The wardens were deemed by the courts to be the omnipotent masters of their domains. It was all more than a little reminiscent of the suppression of her Vietnam report by Maurice Strong and Mitchell Sharp. A careful study of Claire's government and RCMP files from Vietnam days might have forewarned Canada's correctional authorities what was about to happen next. But, while they had learned nothing from history, Claire had forgotten nothing. As her sixtieth birthday approached Claire prepared to once again practise her own unique brand of political jujitsu. The Japanese martial art of self-defence without weapons, which allows a weaker fighter to disarm her opponent by turning his superior strength and size against him, had served her well during the war in Vietnam, and it was about to do so again.

By the fall of 1978 Claire had corresponded with hundreds of prisoners, but J. J. Horvat still occupied a special place in her heart. The charismatic leader of the B.C. Pen riot had been transferred to Archambault, a Quebec maximum security prison, in the wake of the riot, but he maintained a steady if somewhat intermittent correspondence with Claire. In September 1978 Claire was able to confide to Horvat that she was carrying through the resolution they had made while lying on the floor during the first night of the B.C. Pen riot. She was contemplating a book "to include everything. Title will be BARRED FROM PRISON." She hoped to have it published, Claire predicted confidently, by the end of the year.[24]

In the event, her timetable proved overly optimistic. Although a prodigious writer of letters to prisoners, bureaucrats, and newspaper editors, Claire nevertheless agonized when writing for publication. She found the work painstaking and time-consuming, and the temptation to put off serious writing in the face of the endless day-to-day demands on her time was, all too often, irresistible. *Barred from Prison: A Personal Account* was not published until August 1979, and even then it was a near thing. The launch party held in her honour on August 15 by Vancouver publishers Pulp Press was well under way before the first cases of books, still wet from the printers, were delivered. A month later she was off on an extensive national book promotion tour that would mark a turning point in her career as a prisoners' rights advocate.

Her itinerary had not escaped the nervous notice of CPS officials in Ottawa, not least because Claire had applied to visit a number of prisoners throughout the Atlantic, Quebec, Ontario, and Prairie regions. It was her first real foray as a prison critic into the political and media hub of central Canada, and it posed a crucial question for the managers of Canada's federal prison system: should the ban on Claire's prison visits in the B.C. region be extended to include the whole country?

Claire's first stop on the tour was Prince Edward Island where she received a cordial enough greeting from Keith Fairbanks, the warden of Sleepy Hollow Correctional Centre, the province's only penitentiary. Fairbanks invited Claire for lunch, allowed her to tour his facility, and graciously accepted a copy of *Barred from Prison* for the Sleepy Hollow library. But Sleepy Hollow was a provincial institution. The first acid test of the federal response would come at Dorchester, a maximum security prison located outside Moncton, New Brunswick. Claire had already applied to visit prisoners there, but Gil Rhodes, the warden at Dorchester, had rejected her application. "The agitation for reform on the part of the Prisoners' Rights Group, in my opinion, is generally unrealistic, biased, and tends only to raise the expectations of inmates to unattainable levels. This in turn serves only to increase the level of tension between inmates and staff," Rhodes had written to Claire.

"While I do not quarrel with the overall purpose of your organization and feel some of its goals are laudable . . . a side effect of your group's efforts has been the subversion of institutional management and the creation of a poor institutional environment characterized by hostility between staff and inmates," Rhodes had continued, echoing the overall CPS attitude towards Claire and the PRG. "Since relations between staff and in particular, the security staff, are quite good, I cannot in good conscience sanction a visit . . ."[25]

Claire, however, was undeterred. She told the Maritimes news media repeatedly that she had every intention of visiting Dorchester, even though she had been officially barred. The looming confrontation at Dorchester was, in any event, a "nice feed in to my publicity . . ." Claire wrote her publishers from Charlottetown.[26] In his office at Dorchester Rhodes monitored Claire's approach through the media. Her barring had now become the subject of discussion on open-line radio shows in the region and "there seemed to be a fair measure of public support for her activities," Rhodes would concede years later. To Dorchester's warden, Claire's progress through the Maritimes must have felt like the approach of a besieging army toward some medieval fortress, a structure to which Dorchester had often been compared. He had every desire to express solidarity with Herb Reynett and his "sister institution," the B.C. Pen, Rhodes recalled, but in the face of Claire's offensive, he began to waver. Her methods had been well documented in CPS internal security memoranda, after all. "I knew it usually meant her sitting on the doorstep with a coterie of reporters." Besides that, the media began to call, asking Rhodes why he wouldn't let Claire visit. To continue barring her now threatened to turn the whole affair into "a media circus." The warden at Dorchester began to second-guess his original decision. "I asked myself 'What if and why not?' I figured to let her in would mean some short term pain and then she's going to go away. I mean, it wasn't as if she lived anywhere close by. What harm could she do?"[27] On September 27 Rhodes allowed Claire into Dorchester for a series of visits with a handful of prisoners. His last-minute reversal set a precedent for the rest of the tour.

Over the next ten weeks, Claire gained admission to every maximum security federal prison outside the B.C. region, and to a goodly number of lower-security institutions as well. Her book and her meetings with prisoners outside British Columbia further solidified her reputation and provided her with a national base of contacts both inside and outside Canada's so-called "correctional" facilities. But one prison visit stood out. On October 16 she was reunited with Ivan Horvat, who had been transferred out of maximum to the medium security Leclerc Institution just three days earlier. She found Horvat in good spirits, and both of them were overjoyed that he had, after seven years in maximum, cleared the hurdle to medium. They reminisced about the B.C. Pen riot and its key players, many of whom had been scattered to prisons across Canada. For Claire, Horvat's presence in medium and the completion of "their" book, which they had dreamed about writing that first long night of the B.C. Pen riot, was like a dream come true. When it was time to take her leave, Claire had no inkling that this would be the last time she would see Horvat alive.

Another triumph was awaiting Claire in Ottawa a few days later. Donald Yeomans, André Therrien's successor as the top bureaucrat in Canadian corrections, invited her to a private meeting in his office. When her visit with Yeomans ran over time and she was late for her next appointment, the commissioner of corrections offered Claire his car and driver to speed her on her way. It was the beginning of a reasonably close working relationship that would last until the end of Yeomans's tenure as commissioner. On October 29 Yeomans circulated a memo, entitled "Notes of a meeting with Claire Culhane" to top CPS brass, and its contents represented yet another breakthrough for Claire. Their discussion had been "most agreeable," Yeomans noted, and he had concluded that Claire "is clearly a person with an extremely sensitive social conscience who cannot tolerate seeing her fellow human beings mistreated . . ."

Yeomans also put "paid" to the prevailing CPS notion that Claire was at the very least a disruptive influence and troublemaker, if not a downright dangerous threat to prison security. "I got the impression that while she would use vigorous political protest, she would never resort to any illegal act, including smuggling contraband . . . Would Deputy Commissioner, Security, please tell me whether she has ever been accused of or strongly suspected of any illegal activity?" The answer, handwritten on Yeoman's memo, was a simple "No."[28]

The commissioner then went on to list several questions and grievances posed by Claire, and he referred them down the ladder, leaving no doubt that he wanted prompt replies. Her meeting with Yeomans represented a signal change in CPS thinking towards Claire, though it was by no means unanimous. While Claire was not privy to Yeomans's memo, there was also a public acknowledgement that official attitudes towards her work were shifting. While in Ottawa she had consented to an interview with *Liaison*, the monthly house organ of the federal solicitor general's department. When it appeared in November, the article, entitled "Persona Non Grata?" was surprisingly favourable. Describing Claire as "the self-appointed conscience of the penitentiary system," *Liaison* added that "prisoners put their faith in her; officials respect her influence."

From Ottawa Claire continued her tour through Ontario and the West. She returned home to Vancouver in early December suffering from acute laryngitis and utterly spent. Even for a veteran of gruelling national tours like Claire, it had been an exhausting trip. Over the previous two and a half months she had visited twenty-three towns and cities. She had given forty-nine radio interviews, she tallied later, twenty-six television interviews, spoken to the print media thirty-five times, had lectured before twenty-five university classes and three church groups, participated in eighteen community events, and attended eight bookstore autographing sessions. Her efforts had also translated into book sales. Pulp was already considering a second printing. The tour would yield other lasting benefits, as well. She was now firmly ensconced as a national authority on the state of Canadian prisons, and she had extended her network of contacts into every city in Canada. This informal network, which would eventually number in the many hundreds, included cons and ex-cons, lawyers, professors, women's and native activists, journalists, and social and correctional workers and officials.

She had earned a well-deserved rest after the tour, but it was not to be. On the night of December 9, 1979, just four days after her return home, Claire received devastating news from Quebec: Ivan Horvat had been murdered. Not since the loss of Rube fourteen years before (not even the death of her father, which she had learned of while on the tour in Regina in November—she had resolutely carried on) had a death hit her with such emotional force.

Things had begun to unravel for Horvat within hours of Claire's visit with him in Leclerc. The same evening prison security had searched Horvat and found twenty-two hits of acid. He was promptly thrown into "the hole" for a week. Upon her return home to Vancouver Claire had discovered, in the usual mountain of mail that accumulated during her absence, a letter from Horvat written on November 5, his twenty-sixth birthday.

> The day I saw you, that night I got thrown into the hole for seven days. Strange trip. I think a set-up, but doesn't matter—won't be repeated . . . Coming to this institution is like awakening from a long sleep—that's what Archambault was—a waste. I'm bursting with creative energy and am on the move—very important month for me, this one, feeling very involved and it feels good. Am together for a change.
>
> I'm being paged—I think the boys got a surprise birthday party waiting (but I already heard about it)—so I'm gone for the night. Take care my friend—be good to yourself.
> Much love,
> J.J.

Despite his claims that he had been set up (Horvat insisted the drugs had been shoved into his hand by a fellow prisoner just moments before he was accosted by the guards), Horvat had been involuntarily transferred or "scooped," in prison parlance, back to maximum security at Archambault on November 21. A few days later Horvat told his wife, Dorothy, during a visit that Archambault was "a madhouse, where nobody's life is worth anything." Concerned for his safety, Horvat holed up in his own cell, coming out only to take his meals. But on the evening of December 9 Horvat inexplicably left his cell to watch television in the relatively unsupervised recreation room. Horvat's behaviour was strange because a friend of his had been beaten in the same rec room just three days before, and another prisoner had been murdered there earlier in the year. Horvat's body was found beneath a table in the room shortly after 7:00 p.m. It was marked by hammer blows to the back of the head and stab wounds from the front. Horvat's was the fifth homicide of the year at Archambault, where twenty-five prisoners had died unnatural deaths in the previous twenty-four months.

Many years later Claire would reconcile herself to what she eventually came to believe was the true cause of Horvat's death: a prison drug deal turned sour. But in the days that followed her friend's murder she worked like a woman possessed to expose "the last of the reprisals for [Horvat's] attempts to improve the conditions of his fellow prisoners." She prepared a one-page memoriam to Horvat which would be included in all subsequent printings of *Barred from Prison*; she spoke with Don Yeomans himself on the phone and demanded an independent investigation (which was never forthcoming) into Horvat's murder; she meticulously assembled every scrap of available information about his death; and, most of all, she wrote and wrote and wrote.

By Christmas week of 1979 she had dashed off explanatory letters and her memoriam to Horvat to more than 150 of her contacts across the country. The ostensible purpose of her letters was to raise money for a film about Horvat. But the correspondence was also a poignant outpouring of grief—and guilt. "Well, here's one tangible result of my visit—I now torture myself into realizing—that Ivan Horvat was set up exactly the day I visited him, and on the eve of my book-trip, which identified him so closely," she wrote one correspondent. "It will forever be a burden to me, personally, wondering how much of it was triggered by my visit to him that same day he was set up, and the month my book got rolling, since it was very much 'our' book," she confessed to another. "What will, of course, haunt me forever, is the 'coincidence' of it all starting the day I visited him—given the publicity around the book too at that time (which renewed attention about his role in the 1976 affair)," she wrote a third.

Christmas Eve and Christmas Day found her still at the typewriter, still composing letters. (The mailing had now mushroomed to 350.) Claire had never really had time to recover from what even she had been forced to admit was an enervating national tour, and still she plunged on, nearing physical and emotional exhaustion. In *Barred from Prison* Claire had managed to humanize the men of the B.C. Pen, especially the members of the Inmate Committee, and none more so than J.J. Horvat. Instead of hardened criminals or desperate inmates, thousands of readers had come to see Horvat and his fellow prisoners as people, struggling for dignity and empowerment in the most abject surroundings. The killing of someone so young, so able, and so well respected came as a shock to many of Claire's readers and supporters, too.

And yet despite the grief and exhaustion Claire managed, just barely, to avoid giving herself over to despair. It was as if she had tapped some last well of inner strength. In every note she wrote that Christmas she let the reader know that she had come through the emotional slaughter with beliefs and determination intact. "Anyway, nothing else to do now but try and ensure that others don't die the same senseless way." "And so it goes—but still very much worth it all, as life sure has meaning." "As Joe Hill said, 'DON'T MOURN: ORGANIZE.' "[29]

*   *   *

By the early 1980s Claire's modus operandi was well established. She early on christened her prison work "the best fight in town," for prisons are "the Achilles heel of this whole rotten system." Flowing from Claire's opposition to the Canadian prison system and to the Vietnam war was her growing understanding of the political philosophy of anarchism: that government is essentially a mechanism for imposing the will of the powerful multinational minority on the powerless majority of ordinary people, and is therefore intrinsically evil. Contrary to the prevailing and well-cultivated popular misconception, anarchism does not advocate chaos or terrorism but espouses meaningful cooperation and coexistence. The attempt by the United States to annihilate Vietnam was the ultimate example of a powerful nation using its military force to control a weaker one. The impervious front the Canadian government had presented through all her efforts to have her Vietnam report accepted, strengthened Claire's own convictions. Later her understanding of the prison's relationship to society further confirmed those beliefs—the status quo's historical need to control the populace by every possible means. Faced with the formidable power of one's enemy survival becomes the reality, and never more so than in the prison scene.

Like the NLF guerrillas she had watched in Vietnam who contented themselves with lightning strikes against limited military objectives, Claire's unremitting attacks on Canada's prison system had the impact, as an interviewer once noted, "of water on stone."[30] Although she is often referred to as "a prison reformer," Claire bristled at the description, preferring the more accurate term "prison abolitionist." Prison abolition does not mean opening the gates and releasing everyone tomorrow. It does mean dismantling a system where approximately 80 percent of the incarcerated, who have not committed a violent crime and who are not considered dangerous, would be better off working to make restitution to their victims and supporting their families. An additional 15 percent who are not yet ready to return to work should receive the appropriate medical, economic, and social care to prepare them for a return to the community. The less than 5 percent of the prison population who are a genuine danger to society might have to remain incarcerated.

Given the high level of unemployment and the stigma attached to being an ex-con, Claire conceded, the first goal might seem unattainable. But that is an economic shortcoming. "The question that must be faced," she wrote in 1985, "is—are too many people being held in prison for too long because of tough economic times, and if so, is it practical to house this surplus of 'hostages to the economy' in prisons?"[31]

Prisons, Claire was convinced, had become a sinkhole for taxpayers' dollars on a colossal scale. The total cost for Canada's "criminal justice system" (legal fees, courts, police, jails and prisons) soared to $7.7 billion by 1991. Almost $1 billion of that was spent each year on the federal correctional system, which had wasted tens of millions of dollars in construction costs alone.

The longer she stayed on her prison beat, the more Claire became the recipient of anonymous tips and insider information from all levels of the Correctional Service Canada bureaucracy. (The Canadian Penitentiary Service was renamed the CSC in the early 1980s.) As a frequent visitor to prisons across the land Claire was often able to confirm these reports firsthand. She learned, for example, that the $40-million foundation that had been laid outside Drummondville, Quebec, for the extension of a medium security federal institution had been abandoned when the government decided to build a new $68-million prison in Port Cartier, in the home riding of Prime Minister Brian Mulroney. At Millhaven, Ontario's maximum security federal penitentiary, she learned that more than $40 million had been expended to start building a special handling unit or SHU, which was never used. The SHU was built in Prince Albert, Saskatchewan, instead. Outside Archambault in Quebec expensive ground preparation and foundation work had been completed for four separate new institutions—a maximum, medium, and minimum security unit and a health care facility—which were instead located elsewhere: at Donnacona, Drummondville, and Port Cartier. She was told that the cost for each aborted project (officially they were "postponed") could conceivably reach $40 million each, for an estimated total of $160 million. CSC bureaucrats would never offically confirm these figures, but they would never deny them, either.[32]

More and more it became obvious that the Canadian "correctional" system was not committed to corrections at all. Instead, the system was often a pork-barrelling make-work scheme for less developed regions of the country. In a score of cases—Kingston, Ontario, Prince Albert, Saskatchewan, and Springhill, Nova Scotia, to name but three—whole cities had become financially dependent on federal prisons, which comprised a vital component of the community's annual payroll. Like the Canadian military or the Department of Indian Affairs, the CSC had become a bloated institutional juggernaut, unstoppable, and answerable to no one, not even the elected politicians who are supposed to be in at least nominal control. In 1976 then Solicitor General Jean-Jacques Blais declared that his goal was to reduce the federal prison population, which then totalled 9,400 men and women. But by 1991 that number had risen to 13,819.[33]

At the outset Claire's message was not popular with the Canadian public. As "victims of violence" groups sprang up across the country in the 1980s Claire often seemed a minority of one. Predictable accusations were hurled at her: she was "a bleeding heart" or she wanted to "coddle" dangerous criminals who deserved harsh punishment. But she carried resolutely on, unshakable in her convictions, unstoppable in her efforts. As she had attempted to demolish the myth that Canada was neutral during the Vietnam war, so too did Claire now campaign to pierce the bubble of yet another great Canadian conceit: that the nation's "justice" system was indeed just. Too often, prisons were simply an instrument for class, racial, and national oppression. The numbers alone told the story, she explained to interviewers over and over again. At the provincial level fully 27 percent of the jail and penitentiary population consisted of people who had failed to pay fines. What was that but a form of debtors' prison that penalized the poor? In the CSC's Prairie region 36.4 percent of male prisoners and 47.2 percent of female prisoners were native Canadians, even though aboriginals constituted less than 8 percent of the Prairies' population. That was evidence of racial discrimination, surely.[34]

She strived to undermine complacency and the smug belief that law-abiding Canadians are "us" and law-breaking Canadians are "them." Prisoners are not subhuman animals; they are people, and Canadians ignore what happens to them behind bars at their peril. The vast majority of prisoners, after all, will eventually be released and return to society. Neglect and brutality in the nation's jails will return to haunt everyone just down the road. The "us" versus "them" formulation is, in any event, a chimera. By 1991 2.5 million Canadians had criminal records, almost one out of every ten people in the country.[35] Given that each offender had a mother or father, brothers or sisters, or a family of his or her own, 40 or 50 percent of Canadians were intimately related to someone who has been convicted of a criminal offence. The "us" was perilously close to becoming "them."

As she watched the number of prisons and cells expand and the incarceration rate rise precipitously, Claire also brought a darker warning to her fellow citizens. In times of economic deterioration and mounting civil unrest, many law-abiding Canadians might find themselves jailed for political offences. The charge sounded outlandish, but Claire had seen mass internment before, during the War Measures Act of the Second World War, and during the FLQ crisis in Quebec.

To anyone who still entertained any doubt whether the prison system was a part of the political structure, calculated to control dissidents of any stripe, Claire would point to the Emergency Powers Order (EPO) passed in 1981 by Order in Council, which granted special powers to the solicitor general's department, which includes the Correctional Services of Canada, the National Parole Board, and the RCMP. A state of emergency would be declared when the nation was faced with natural disaster such as floods, earthquakes, etc., war, *or a breakdown of law and order*. This non-debatable order (1981-1305) empowers the government, among other things, to *establish, administer, and operate civilian internment camps*.

Occasionally conditions behind the prison walls became so desperate that Claire felt obliged to personally intervene in any way she could. One such occasion arose in the fall of 1980 at Dorchester. It had been a year since her precedent-setting visit to New Brunswick's maximum security penitentiary, but the prisoners there hadn't forgotten about her. One of the first inklings Claire received that something was wrong inside Dorchester had come from a letter that had been kited out to her. It was dated September 20, 1980.

> Dorchester is about to riot any time now. Prisoners are being put in the hole for no other reason but suspicion. Over half the general population is in segregation now. They are handcuffed, taken off the range, thrown or pushed downstairs, and once in the hole they are beat by four, five or six pigs, then gassed and shackled and left that way for days on end.
>
> The brutality here is unreal. One guy was taken out of his cell, stripped, had his hands cuffed behind his back and was told to lay face down on the cold cement while guards spent an hour searching his cell. Another was gassed in the hole because he told guards to lay off when they were beating another guy. Guards refused to take cuffs off another guy so he could eat his meal. He had to put his face in the tray so he could eat. Finally, he broke his handcuffs somehow after three or four days of pissing himself. Guards told him they run this prison now and they can do what they want with us.[36]

Tensions rose still further in early October when three convicted murderers took a guard hostage. When the guard was shot and killed by a member of the prison's Emergency Response Team during a botched rescue attempt, Dorchester was ready to explode. A newly released prisoner from Dorchester phoned Claire and reported that gassings and beatings had become commonplace as the guards took revenge for the death of their fellow officer. Worst of all, half a dozen prisoners had been handcuffed to the bars of their cells. They were still there, naked, forced to lie in their own urine and excrement in conditions that would outrage any animal rights activist. Claire borrowed a thousand dollars and flew to Moncton.

With the closing of the B.C. Pen the previous May, Dorchester had become the oldest prison still in service in the federal correctional system. Like the B.C. Pen, Dorchester was ringed by metre-thick cement walls and it had the forbidding aspect of a fortress. Like the Pen, too, Dorchester's current crisis had been presaged by a cycle of spiralling violence—escape attempts, hostage takings, and the death of a prison employee at the hands of his erstwhile rescuers—reminiscent of the shooting of Mary Steinhauser.

During her layover in Toronto Claire phoned New Democrat MP Svend Robinson and CBC radio's "As It Happens" to tell them she was heading for Dorchester, and the reasons why. It was a tactic she had employed successfully in the past—using the news media to raise a public alarm so that an outside, independent authority might be brought to bear to defuse tensions and air prisoner grievances. The technique was, of course, anathema to prison officials, who might be forced to admit that they had completely lost control of the bitter enmity between guards and prisoners.

Once on the ground in Moncton she called the local news media, as well. But then she hit an unexpected snag. As had been her custom throughout her public career, Claire relied on her own contacts for accommodation and transport rather than on commercial sources—it saved her money, and kept her in touch with the people who mattered to her. But her Moncton host's car was in the garage for repairs, and renting a car was prohibitively expensive on Claire's budget. She promptly set out to hitch-hike to Dorchester. The motorist who finally picked her up happened to have his radio on, and Claire interrupted their conversation when she heard her name on a Moncton newscast.

"Claire Culhane and her Prisoners' Rights Group have arrived from Vancouver to investigate conditions at Dorchester prison," the announcer intoned.

"You wanna know something?" Claire winked at the driver. "That's me."

She could see him looking at the back seat in the mirror, as if wondering where the rest of "the group" was. Instead, the impressive-sounding delegation to Dorchester consisted of this one unassuming-looking senior citizen dressed in a duffle coat and black beret to ward off the fall chill. She appeared an improbable challenger to the supposedly omnipotent authority which was struggling to maintain control of Atlantic Canada's only maximum security federal prison.

"Don't get stuck out here after dark," the motorist warned as they pulled up to the prison walls. He gestured towards Dorchester's imposing gun towers. "They're likely to shoot you."

This time there was no way that Dorchester's authorities (Gil Rhodes was no longer warden) were going to let Claire through the gates, so for two days she maintained her one-woman vigil outside the prison. She spoke to reporters from the Moncton news media who came out to cover her activities, and provoked an angry statement from a CSC spokesman. It didn't look like much, but she knew that word would soon reach the ranges that she was outside. Her very physical presence might reassure and hearten the prisoners whom she could not see, though she was too late for one of them, who committed suicide even as she walked back and forth outside the prison gate. To know that there was at least one person in the outside world who knew, and cared, what was happening to these otherwise forgotten men might make a difference. And it did. Within forty-eight hours Svend Robinson, accompanied by a local member of Parliament, arrived at Dorchester. Prison authorities could not bar elected representatives of the Canadian people. Eventually the acting warden at Dorchester resigned, citing "health reasons," and the inspector general of the CSC conducted an investigation into conditions at the New Brunswick prison. It wasn't the public, judicial inquiry that Claire had demanded, but the inspector general's report was ultimately leaked to Svend Robinson, and it confirmed many of the atrocities Claire had been at pains to expose.

And Claire's efforts in the Dorchester case had one other footnote. About five years later she was attending a party in Kingston when she unexpectedly found herself enclosed in a warm bear hug from a complete stranger. He introduced himself as Brian Gough, one of the prisoners who had been handcuffed to his cell door at Dorchester. As soon as word spread that she was outside the gates of Dorchester that day, prison officials had ordered that he and the others be unchained. The hug was his way of saying thank you.

As Claire came to know the individual histories of more and more Canadian prisoners she reached the conclusion that the country's criminal justice system was far from infallible. The more she talked to and corresponded with prisoners across Canada, the more she became convinced that there were an alarming number of wrongfully convicted prisoners rotting in Canadian jails. In the early 1980s her claim was met with a good measure of scepticism, but that was before Donald Marshall. The young Micmac Indian from Cape Breton, Nova Scotia, who served eleven years in prison for a murder he did not commit, came to public notice only slowly, but when he did, Claire was quick to react, spurred to action by a letter from Mike Platko, a prisoner at the Prince George (B.C.) Regional Correctional Centre. Acting on his own initiative Platko had passed the hat among his fellow prisoners to raise money for Marshall's legal defence. The local Inmate Committee had then matched the amount raised. Could Claire ensure that the funds reached Marshall's Halifax lawyer? Claire agreed, and then sent copies of Platko's letter and cheque on, through about fifty wardens, to Inmate Committees across the country. She sought the wardens' permission for similar fund-raising activities among prison populations in their own institutions and was pleasantly surprised when about half of them agreed. In all, $1,600 was added to Marshall's defence fund by his fellow prisoners across Canada.

As Marshall's wrongful conviction became public knowledge Claire used it in her own interviews. "Come with me to every prison in this country and I guarantee I'll find one Donald Marshall each month," she repeatedly challenged journalists. "And call my bluff." But few investigative reporters were prepared to commit the time and resources to ferret out more Donald Marshalls. Finally, by 1982, Claire was determined to expose British Columbia's own version of Donald Marshall through her involvement with the Norman Fox Defence Committee. Claire had come to know Fox through her visits to the medium security Mountain Institution in Agassiz, British Columbia.

The Fox case had begun on the night of January 16, 1976, when a thirty-eight-year-old woman agreed to accompany an older man to Room 307 in a seedy hotel in Vancouver's downtown Granville Mall. Once in the room, however, the expected routine sexual transaction quickly turned ugly, and for two hours the woman was assaulted, tortured, and brutally raped by her customer. She finally managed to escape her assailant and ran naked into the lobby of the King's Castle Hotel. After receiving assistance from hotel staff, the woman went to hospital for treatment and contacted police. Her attacker had vanished.

Two months later, on the evening of March 24, 1976, Kenneth Norman Warwick and his girlfriend Trudy Harkness were in the dining room of their North Vancouver apartment when police burst through the doors of their home. They placed Warwick under arrest, leaving the shaken Harkness behind. Warwick (who would later change his name to Norman Fox) had served twelve years of a life sentence for a 1960 rape conviction. He had taken university courses while in jail and after his release had become a successful businessman. Harkness, who was in the shoe business, knew of Warwick's criminal record, but she had also come to know him as "a kind and gentle man." When she called police to determine her lover's whereabouts, Harkness was told that he was a suspect in "The Highway Murders," a series of grisly killings along British Columbia highways. But twenty-four hours later she learned that Warwick had been charged with rape and wounding in the King's Castle assault.

Harkness never doubted Warwick's innocence. She had been with him in North Vancouver on the night of the assault, and one of her co-workers also remembered seeing Warwick and Harkness together in North Van, many miles from Vancouver's Granville Street, on the night in question. Warwick, who was still on parole from his earlier conviction, was held without bail and ordered to stand trial in late June. The King's Castle victim had been shown a photo array by police, but Warwick's picture was larger and a sepia-coloured Polaroid, while the ten other photographs were in black and white. The other ten "suspects" were scruffy, while Warwick, in a suit and tie resembled the "clean-shaven businessman" type the victim had earlier described to police. The victim immediately selected Warwick's photograph, and she also picked Warwick out of a police line-up, but again the other "suspects" were far seedier looking than Warwick. The victim also positively identified him as her attacker in court. "I spent two hours looking at that face and I won't forget it," she testified, pointing at Warwick.

Besides the woman's identification, however, there were strange incongruities in the evidence. She remembered that her attacker had a four-inch appendectomy scar and Warwick had no such scar; her attacker had "perfect teeth as far as I could see" and Warwick's teeth were poor; police had discovered that cigarette butts found in the hotel room were a special type of the Belvedere brand which were then being test marketed only in Ontario and there was nothing to link Warwick to the East in the weeks prior to the attack. Trudy Harkness and her co-worker also provided alibi evidence for the defence. But county court judge Raymond Paris believed the victim's eyewitness identification and sentenced the thirty-nine-year-old Warwick to ten years concurrent on each charge.[37]

As a convicted repeat sex offender, or "skinner" in prison parlance, Warwick was eventually placed in Protective Custody away from the general prison population. Even so, his life was a living hell, he would say later, and the knowledge that he had been convicted of a crime which he had not committed surely made matters even worse. But Warwick (now Fox) never stopped protesting his innocence, and Trudy Harkness stood by him. Together they wrote letters to MPs, approached a succession of lawyers and reporters for help, and searched for new evidence. In 1977 their hopes were raised when an investigative reporter from the *Vancouver Province* wrote a story on the case, but it was spiked by the paper's editors, who may have been wary of taking up the cause of a convict who had one legitimate rape conviction on his record.

Claire, however, had no such compunctions. She had long made it a policy of her prison work to assist all prisoners, regardless of the reason for their incarceration. Her willingness to fight for the rights of sex offenders was controversial both within the prison population and without, but she stubbornly refused to yield to what she called "groupism." "There are also many wrongful convictions in Protective Custody," she reminded her critics. As she visited Fox more and more often in the early 1980s she became convinced that he really had been wrongfully convicted. She was also impressed with Trudy Harkness, who continued to struggle against all odds to somehow win Fox's release. Claire began to help Harkness in her dealings with lawyers and the federal Justice Department, and the ranks of Fox supporters grew still larger when David Blake, a paralegal social worker with the British Columbia Legal Aid Society also began to work on the case. Claire had been leading a seminar on prison issues under the auspices of Vancouver's Unitarian Church and when the series was over some members of the group had asked her what they might do to become involved in prisoners' rights. Claire was then in the thick of her work on behalf of Fox; why not join the effort to prove a prisoner's innocence? And so the Norman Fox Defence Committee was born.

One of the greatest frustrations of the Fox campaign was the succession of lawyers who had agreed to take up the case and then, to Claire's mind at least, did nothing. Her relationship with the legal community was ambivalent at the best of times, and when it came to lawyers she was not above a little groupism of her own. "There should be a special place in hell for 95 percent of lawyers," was one of Claire's most oft-repeated observations. Twice Claire advised Trudy to change lawyers, after the new advocate would simply sit on the case just as the old one had. While searching for yet another solicitor who would take on the difficult case *pro bono*, Claire and Trudy met with David Gibbons, a prominent Vancouver criminal lawyer, who levelled with them: Fox had exhausted his appeals, the federal Justice Department had refused a 1979 request to reopen the case, the media had turned a deaf ear. He suggested the Fox committee try a new approach. They knew that Norm Fox had not committed the King's Castle rape. Why not try to find the man who had?

The group pondered this new strategy. The rapist had left few clues at the crime scene, and the physical description of him by the hotel staff had been extremely vague. Apart from the victim's description, a four-inch appendectomy scar, and an odd type of cigarette, the committee had very little to go on. Then someone thought of the hotel registration book. The rapist had scrawled something on the blotter but police investigators had reported at the time that the signature was illegible. Perhaps the book was worth one more look. The group secured a court order allowing for the unsealing of the physical evidence from the trial, and then obtained a photocopy of the signature. Next they approached a local handwriting analyst with the registration book and a sample of Fox's own handwriting. She concluded that the registration signature was clearly not from Fox's hand. Moreover, she was able to decipher the screed. The signature was that of one H.A. Porter.

The news was greeted with jubilation by the little band, but then came the sobering realization that the analysis really proved very little. The police, after all, would argue that Fox had used a pseudonym since he had clearly intended to commit a crime within minutes of signing the registration book. The same was true, even highly likely, of the real rapist. But now at least they had a name to go on. Trudy had discovered in the course of her own legwork that a union loggers' convention had been under way in Vancouver on the night of January 16, 1976, and the group approached the union with the name of H.A. Porter. Union officials opened up their records to the Fox committee, but the search proved a dead-end. No H.A. Porter had attended the convention. Other attempts, like poring through every Canadian phone book they could find, proved equally unavailing. It was as if H. A. Porter had vanished into thin air or, more probably, that he had never existed in the first place.

Finally the group hit on one last long shot. Why not place a classified ad in newspapers across Canada intimating that H.A. Porter had come into some kind of financial windfall if only he or his heirs would step forward? The committee bought space in Personals columns from one end of the country to the other, and a few weeks later, to their utter amazement, one of their ads received a response. It was from a woman in Ontario, from one of the communities where the specially filtered Belvederes had been test marketed. The woman said she was related to an H.A. Porter, but that he had committed suicide the year before (in 1982). His widow and children were still living on Vancouver Island. David Blake caught the next ferry to the Island. Porter's widow agreed to see him, and it was all he could do to contain his excitement. Yes, her husband had had a noticeable appendectomy scar, Mrs. Porter confirmed, and he had been in Vancouver on the weekend of the King's Castle rape. She also agreed to give the amateur investigators a business document bearing Porter's original signature. The document was turned over to two handwriting experts this time, one of whom often worked for the RCMP. The results were conclusive: the late H.A. Porter had signed his real name on the hotel registry for Room 307 on the night of January 16, 1976.

Armed with this astonishing new evidence, the Fox committee presented a new brief to the justice ministry in Ottawa in August 1983. With agonizing slowness the Fox case was reviewed and reinvestigated. A federal report was finally presented to then British Columbia Attorney General Brian "Bud" Smith. On October 11, 1984, the federal cabinet passed Order in Council PC 1984-3324, "hereby granting a free pardon to WARWICK, Kenneth Norman."

Claire was at Mountain prison that morning, but Fox's release was slow in coming, interminably so for Claire. It seemed the prison system relinquished a convict, even a totally innocent one, only grudgingly. Finally, late in the morning, Norman Fox emerged from Mountain prison a free man, after spending eight and a half years in prison for a crime he hadn't committed. In a life brimming with both triumph and tragedy, that morning was surely one of Claire's proudest moments.

When word of Fox's release reached the news media it created a flurry of headlines and the same question was asked over and over: how could such a gross miscarriage of justice have happened, and in Canada? Judge Ray Paris, the man who convicted Fox, had since been promoted to the British Columbia Supreme Court. He refused to be interviewed about the case but a spokesman described him as "upset" by the Fox revelations. David Gibbons, who was then Fox's lawyer, described the case as "a classic example of the weakness of eyewitness testimony." Attorney General Smith acknowledged "that the man was wrongfully convicted, that the system is not infallible. The system is a good one, but it's a human system . . . And in this case a mistake was made."

"I'm absolutely delighted that Ken is out, but I'm not happy about the others I know who should be out and who might not be so lucky," Claire told the press. Her sentiments were echoed in an editorial in the *Vancouver Province*, which wondered "if other mistakes have been made without coming to light." The paper's editors were silent, however, about their own decision not to run Fox's story seven years earlier.

Inevitably, questions soon arose about the irregular if not highly improper procedures used in the police investigation.[38] In December 1984 British Columbia Ombudsman Karl Friedmann filed a writ with the provincial supreme court seeking an order that the Vancouver Police Department be forced to cooperate with his investigation into the police tactics that led to Fox's conviction. Vancouver police officials refused to comply with Friedmann's order, and the facts surrounding the police investigation that resulted in Fox's conviction remain a closely guarded secret to this day. Six months after Fox's release Attorney General Smith appointed a royal commission, but only on the narrow issue of how much Fox should be compensated for his eight-year ordeal. Once again Friedmann was unsuccessful in prying the relevant files out of the Vancouver Police Department when Commissioner Meredith McFarlane ruled that police conduct was not relevant to his proceeding.

In the end, the British Columbia and federal governments split the cost of a $275,000 payment to Norman Fox. Much of the money went for legal fees, and Commissioner McFarlane ordered that $100,000 be paid to Fox's 1960 rape victim. Norman Fox slipped quietly back into private life in British Columbia, as did Trudy Harkness. The pair went their separate ways, but Claire remained in touch with them both.

Six years later Trudy Harkness would recall Claire's role in the extraordinary tale of Norman Fox.

Claire was fantastic. She's the one who said, "Don't believe the lawyers." She's the one who made us sit on them, she's the one who made us go. She's the one who gave us hope. She was the guide, she directed us on the path, the highway through the system. She knows the way. Otherwise it's just a maze. We had lots of people who believed in his innocence, our group was strong in that belief, but where we were getting was nowhere. So she plotted the path.[39]

$$* \quad * \quad *$$

By the time of Norman Fox's release Claire had just turned sixty-six, an age, convention has it, at which a person should begin to slow down, enjoy retirement, and contemplate at least partial disengagement from the cut and thrust of daily affairs. But as Claire approached seventy her life became even busier. With the Fox case, her name became a byword in Canadian prisons, and her daily correspondence assumed mountainous proportions. Each day's mail brought five to ten letters from prisoners seeking her help, many hoping that she could somehow expose their perceived victimization at the hands of the justice system. As always in such cases she strove to dampen expectations. "I don't get to collect them at the gates very often," she reminded her prison correspondents, referring to Norm Fox's release.

Claire challenged mortality by working still harder. She began each day, after as little as four hours' sleep, at five in the morning British Columbia time because she had long ago learned that the best time to reach the bureaucrats at CSC headquarters in Ottawa was before 9:00 a.m. in the East. The days were full of letter-writing, telephone calls, media interviews, speaking engagements, trips to all points of the country, and always, on Sunday mornings when she was at home, cooking crêpes for friends and family which would, on December 5, 1986, grow to include Claire's first great-grandchild, James Arthur Liam O'Hea, the son of Maura.

Turning sixty-five brought with it one not inconsiderable advantage. Claire was able to collect her old age and Canada pensions and qualify for "seniors" discounts and subsidies. When she was invited to speak at a university or conference in the East, she would extend her trip into a two- or three-week stay, visiting Quebec and Ontario region prisons, as well as CSC headquarters when passing through Ottawa. With a briefcase full of files and grievances she was greeted with respect, if no little trepidation, by the most senior officials in the CSC.

"You're looking well," men twenty years her junior would say with a smile as they ushered her into their offices.

"You're damned right." Claire would smile back just as sweetly. "I intend to outlive all you bastards!"

And indeed, in an institutional sense, she has. Wardens, CSC commissioners and their deputies, and solicitors general came and went, but Claire and her endless stream of letters, questions, phone calls, and media agitation would become an enduring aspect of Canada's prison administration.

"You know you have us terrified," a member of the CSC's top brass confided to Claire during one of her Ottawa visits.

"But why? I'm just a grey-haired old grandmother. I don't pack bombs around."

"Oh, but we have to be afraid of anyone who knows as much as you do about what goes on inside, who writes books, gives lectures, and can't be fired!" Or, he might well have added, retired, either.

Barred from Prison had by 1985 become a modest publishing success, and it had entered the reading lists of many criminology and sociology university classes in Canada, where Claire's name has become almost as well known as it is in the country's prisons.

Even as the Norman Fox case was winding down, Claire decided to write a sequel. *Still Barred from Prison: Social Injustice in Canada* was launched on April 13, 1985. Once again she was off on a three-week national book promotion tour, and she seized on the media opportunity to promote yet another project, an impending twenty-five-day protest against the length of the twenty-five-year sentence for first degree murder.

The campaign ran from May 13 to June 6 at the site of so many of Claire's previous protests—Parliament Hill. Each day focused on a particular prison issue—solitary confinement, special handling units, physical and psychological abuse, forced and involuntary transfers, overcrowding and double-bunking, discrimination against native prisoners, and the status of women prisoners, among others.

Claire was accompanied for the duration of the campaign by Liz Elliott, a young criminologist from Kingston. As she had during the Vietnam War era, Claire had by now come to inspire members of a whole new generation of people concerned with Canadian prisons. Elliott, who was then working with the Elizabeth Fry Society in Kingston, had first met Claire in 1981. Elliott was demoralized at that time and wrote to Claire about the censorship of the Odyssey Group (a lifers' organization) newsletter at Millhaven. In reply she received a three-page single-spaced letter full of strategy and tactics. "It was so nice to hear from a person who had persevered the way she had. Claire Culhane is the one who inspires you to keep going, who gives you more energy," Elliott later recalled. Elliott and Claire demonstrated on Parliament Hill from nine in the morning until five at night for the full twenty-five days, handing out more than five thousand leaflets and talking to hundreds of people, including a number of ministerial aides.

It was a memorable experience for Elliott, who came to define Claire's style as one of "self-empowerment." She was present at a Parliament Hill confrontation between Claire and then Solicitor General Elmer MacKay, who had stopped by for a visit. Elliott's attention focused on MacKay as the dialogue grew sharper and she was astonished to see, in the bright Ottawa sunshine, that MacKay was literally shaking from nervousness beneath his white shirt and tie. Claire talked to him as if he were a prisoner or any other acquaintance. "She talks to everyone the same, and never seems to be flustered or overawed by the powerful—that's what I mean by self-empowerment."

Elliott also witnessed a second verbal sparring match, this time with an Ottawa taxi driver who averred that the solution to Canada's justice problems was a return to the death penalty.

But what if society hanged the wrong person? Claire asked.

It would be all right to execute the odd innocent person, the driver replied. It might, after all, act as a deterrent to violent crime.

"Yeah," Claire shot back, "but what if that innocent person was *you*?"

Elliott came to see Claire's life and political style as of piece. "What Claire is all about is *living your politics.*"[40]

The choice of *Still Barred from Prison* as the title for Claire's third book bespoke her continuing status in all of British Columbia's provincial penitentiaries and all but two federal correctional institutions in the Pacific region: she was still persona non grata in her home province, and it rankled. Nearly a decade after being barred from provincial jails and all but two federal institutions in British Columbia, Claire decided to take the province and the federal government to court. She had attempted to overturn the provincial ban in 1980, but the British Columbia Court of Appeals had ruled two to one against her case, upholding the right of prison authorities to regulate entry to their institutions, adding that the wardens did not have to give a reason for their actions.

Early in 1987, however, Claire decided to try again. She sought legal advice from Vancouver lawyers Ann Cameron and John Steeves, but she was determined to argue her own case in court. The trio decided to sue under the Canadian Charter of Rights and Freedoms. On May 19, 1987, Claire filed her petition against British Columbia Attorney General Brian Smith. Her barring from provincial jails violated three sections of the charter, the petition claimed: Claire's freedom of expression and association as guaranteed in Section 2, her legal right to due process and fundamental justice in Section 7, and her equality rights under Section 15. A trial date was set for September 10, 1987. In the meantime she served notice on federal correctional officials of her intent to sue them before the Federal Court of Canada.

Like so much else about Canada's prison system, the CSC visitor policy can be described as arbitrary if not downright quirky. Individual Canadians are restricted to visiting one prisoner per institution per region, with the exception of volunteer agencies such as the John Howard and Elizabeth Fry societies. Outside British Columbia, Claire had, by 1987, a well-established track record of visiting as many prisoners as wanted to see her within a single institution. She had also been admitted on a regular basis to federal prisons of all security classifications east of the Rockies. Even in British Columbia two federal prison wardens—Tom Crozier at Elbow Lake and Al Bender at William Head—allowed Claire to visit their institutions. Claire's lawyers sought to exploit this crack in administrative solidarity by soliciting letters from wardens in other regions confirming that she had visited as many prisoners as she liked within their respective institutions. The inference that would then be drawn was clear: the prison walls had not shattered, riots had not ensued in the wake of this self-avowed prison activist's visits.

This divide-and-conquer strategy and the threat of legal action produced the predictable flurry of memos at the British Columbia Correction headquarters in Victoria. On September 1, just nine days before her court date, Claire received word from British Columbia Ombudsman Stephen Owen that the ban against her in the province's correctional facilities would be lifted unconditionally—provided she agreed to drop her lawsuit against Attorney General Smith. She agreed.

Heartened by her victory at the provincial level Claire rejected any conditions for her unbarring in the Pacific region, and on March 2, 1988, she filed a Statement of Claim under the Charter of Rights and Freedoms against six federal Pacific region wardens. A trial date before the Federal Court of Canada Trial Division was set for November 7. Still Arthur Trono, deputy commissioner for the Pacific region, and his wardens attempted to maintain their hard line vis-à-vis Claire's visits. Claire might be permitted to visit the maximum-security Kent Institution, wrote Warden P. H. de Vink, "on the understanding that you would be willing to abide by the regulations as they apply to our visiting program." "One per institution per region per country," Claire scribbled on de Vink's letter, "No way!" In an internal confidential memo Trono mulled yet another fall-back position. "If you decide to admit [Claire] to your institution, it is my hope that you establish an agreement as to what is acceptable and what will happen if the agreement is abrogated. Ms. Culhane should sign as agreeing and as understanding . . . Would it be sensible," Trono inquired wistfully, "to suggest to her that she may be admitted on the understanding that she not work through the press?"

But Trono's steady retreat before Claire's implacable advance soon turned into an all-out rout. The federal government was no more eager to defend its actions before the courts than had been the provincial government the year before. Once again, just days before the trial was scheduled to begin, Claire was called to negotiate the terms of Trono's surrender. And once again she dropped the court case in return for complete victory—unconditional multiple visits to every federal prison in the region.

Claire acknowledged her victory by retitling a revised 1991 edition of *Still Barred from Prison*. The new title was *No Longer Barred from Prison*. "I cannot let the moment pass without encouraging anyone who has been unjustly deprived of their visiting rights to also try to confront the authorities and have them restored," she wrote in the preface. "To the best of my knowledge (except for the agencies such as the John Howard Society and the Elizabeth Fry Society) while other people are restricted to visiting one prisoner per institution and per region, I am the only private individual who is allowed to visit at every prison in this country. There should be others."[41]

In 1982 investigator Thierry Maleville had filed a damning report about Canada's prisons to the International Federation of Human Rights in Paris, France, and a decade later Claire would still see his recommendations as encapsulating her years of struggle on behalf of Canada's prisoners. The rule of law must prevail inside Canadian penitentiaries, Maleville warned. The correctional investigator must be responsible to Parliament, not the solicitor general; the penitentiary system must be administered openly and be subject to control of the citizenry, and Canada must immediately cease its violation of international agreements by prison procedures which constitute denials of basic human rights and dignity as defined by the United Nations Charter, and its internal legislation.[42]

It was one of the grand themes of her life, this plea that Canada's offenders should not be unnecessarily isolated from and abused by the greater society, and it was a refrain that had echoed through the decades. From bringing light into the dungeons to exposing a genocidal war half a world away to fighting McCarthyism to bettering the lives of working people to opposing fascism in Spain, it was a call that had been on her lips as a romantic young student at Strathcona Academy fifty-six years before, where a prescient yearbook editor had noted, for posterity, her favourite saying as a high-school student: "Open the windows!"

EPILOGUE

This Movie Is Still Not Over

On September 2, 1988, Claire Culhane celebrated her seventieth birthday at Dara's home, surrounded by family and friends. Congratulatory greetings flooded in from hundreds of prisoners at dozens of institutions across Canada. The messages varied, but the sentiments expressed were similar: we admire your courage and compassion on our behalf, we are grateful that you have never forgotten us, *you have given us hope*. Thank you.

The esteem in which Claire is held by prisoners and ex-cons and her fellow social activists is in marked contrast to the chilly reception she is still accorded by much of the Canadian establishment. After fifty-five years of tugging at the national conscience she has yet to receive a single honorary degree or civic award. (A notable exception is the University of Windsor Faculty of Law, which invited her to deliver the George M. Duck Memorial Lecture in October 1989. Among the other Canadians so honoured: former Supreme Court chief justice Bora Laskin and former prime minister and Liberal leader John Turner. The title of her address: "Decriminalization of the Prison System—A Citizen's View.")

Even at the age of seventy-four, it seems, Claire is too radical and too controversial to receive recognition from the nation's élite, and as the unremitting foe of the wealthy, the powerful, of those who oppress others, she wouldn't have it any other way.

So how are we to take our leave of this remarkable woman? For, truly, this movie is not yet over. She moves among us still, tireless, unyielding, uncompromising, like a film projector casting a powerful beam of light into the shadows of our national morality, into the dark corners and recesses that most of us would prefer to deny or forget. We cannot, even now, foresee the end of this movie, for the images are still flashing past. But we can freeze some of the most recently projected frames.

August 28, 1990. The standoff at Oka finds her demonstrating on the streets of Montreal. "Not only was I in my element, walking the streets of Old Montreal with a thousand others in support of the First Nation people, but finally, as I just knew would happen, I bumped into five or six old, old friends, in every sense of the word. Even from the old YCL days. Often we'd recognize each other, and both laugh, knowing we were thinking the same thing: wow, how *old* you look . . . as if *we* were each still in our own eighteen-year-old body."

March 25, 1991. The aftermath of the Gulf War brings a moody reflection on the future of our species, as if even Claire's unquenchable fighting spirit has been sorely tested. "Grim realist that I am, there's no way I can ignore the ten-year sentence the environmentalists fear has been laid on the planet. It adds up to the fact that, accepting all this grim reality, one has two choices: jump out the window or live with it. Obviously we're living with it. In which case one has another two options. Sit back and let it happen, or find a corner to fight back from, again for two reasons. It's the only way to keep one's sanity, to keep the adrenalin pumping, which is an essential physiological function, and it's the last straw of hope (one cannot live without hope) that maybe, maybe, if enough people everywhere are fighting back, just maybe, maybe, we *don't* go down. Once I get my head into that space I can keep going, since my prime drive is how to smash the system, my corner being the prison system, which is the Achilles heel of the whole rotten system."

June 1991. Roisin, Dara, and two of their daughters are visiting Garry in Dublin. He has been committed to a nursing home for Alzheimer patients. The women have come to say goodbye to their father and grandfather while he still can occasionally recognize them.

Garry and Dara are walking in the park next to the home and Garry begins a rambling anecdote about his childhood. He is confused and mistakes Dara for his sister.

"No, Dad," Dara says, "I'm your daughter, not your sister. I'm Dara, the youngest. Remember?"

A flash of recognition sweeps across the old man's face. He winces with pain. "Oh, my god!" he exclaims, "what a fool I am. What a bloody eejit I've been . . . You are my daughter and I denied you. I am a bloody fool."

"It's okay, Dad," Dara soothes. "You forgot for a moment. That's all."

"No," Garry says, his pale blue eyes fixing on his daughter with a piercing clarity rarely achieved now that age and senility have taken their toll on the man who never apologized to anyone, for anything. "This time I am a foolish old man and I can be forgiven. But this is the second time I have denied you. You are my flesh and blood and I denied you. I denied you at birth. I denied you when you were a child. That was unforgivable. Tell your mother if she wants to slit my throat, I'll give her the knife. She took you kids away from me . . . It almost killed me . . . but she did the only thing she could . . . It would have gotten worse . . . I was a fool . . . I just didn't . . . I couldn't . . . Don't forgive me . . . It will do you no good to forgive me."

"Dad," Dara answers, "I'm forty years old now. I know life is hard. We do things sometimes . . . Of course I forgive you. It would do me no good not to."

But the old man's eyes have clouded over again and his mind is wandering. He resumes his rambling. It's 1916 . . . The Black and Tans are marauding through his beloved Dublin. Aunt Hanna's husband has been shot. The children are being hidden from the troops. The Republican forces are standing their ground . . .

July 1991. Back in Vancouver, Dara tells her mother the story. Claire's eyes fill with tears. "Well, at least he apologized to you," she says. "Thank God he made it right with you. He never acknowledged you to me. He never said he was sorry to me."

"You know," she says, gazing wistfully out her window. "There's not much I'm envious of in my life. I've lived a full life. But you know, to this day, when I see a pregnant women and her husband is there with her and making a fuss over her, I get a lump in my throat. It still nearly kills me. I never had that and I wanted it so much. It's one thing I never had."

There are some wounds time does not heal.

January 9, 1992. Time and her own inevitable mortality are the enemy now, too, and Claire's solution is to work harder. She begins this typical day by talking with a University of British Columbia professor who has put her book on his required reading list. Would she give a lecture in March when they'd had time to read and discuss it? "Of course." Then a Vancouver halfway house for women invites her to speak. "Of course." Next she receives a call from the native liaison department at Mountain prison. Since they're interested in prisoners' rights they'd like to have a few workshops on the subject, and would she start them off? "Of course." The next call is from a stranger, John somebody in Vermont who receives Canadian television and who saw an eight-minute profile on her aired by CBC's "Newsmagazine" in November. He has been doing similar work in

American prisons for some years. Would she exchange information with him, and maybe even consider organizing a prisoner network in Canada as he had been trying to do with American prisoners? Although she first insists that he agree it's a pretty tall order, it ends in another "of course"— but he has to do the first mailing.

Now it is midmorning, and time to collect the mail. Today's is typically voluminous, and it will take Claire an hour to simply read it all before sorting through it to determine what absolutely *has* to be answered today. She's due to fly to Saskatoon in two days to attend a parole hearing for a prisoner at Prince Albert Penitentiary, so next she's off downtown to pick up her airline tickets, which she's already booked by phone. But the reservation agent now has her flying out tomorrow, *not* the day after tomorrow as she'd already confirmed by phone. The grade eleven student at Strathcona Academy whose pet aversion was "Waiting" has mellowed not one whit over the intervening fifty-seven years. Five precious minutes are wasted as Claire waits, not graciously, while the ticket agent pounds her computer keyboard. When she finally receives the ticket with the correct departure date Claire steams out of the airline office, leaving her purse on the counter.

"Hey, Claire Culhane," yells the ticket agent at the next wicket over, "you forgot your purse."

After returning to pick it up she asks him how he knew who she was, as her name hadn't been mentioned.

He just laughs. "I know who you are. You're doing a great job. Keep it up."

Then it's back home where there are the usual day's calls to take from half a dozen prisoners with various problems, as well as a couple from reporters. The days of humping news releases around Vancouver newsrooms for a bit of media coverage are long since over. Now Claire's number is in the Rolodex of newsrooms all across the country, and they call her for reactions to a multitude of criminal justice stories.

Next she settles in for a long night at the word processor, answering the most urgent letters of the day's mail, and following up on unanswered queries to prison bureaucrats in the "Thirty days and still no answer" file. Even here she's devised a system to maximize her efficiency, placing the plastic front of the diskette box in such a way that she can see the day's news and current affairs programs reflected on the clear Lucite case. Even with her back to the television she can listen to the program, keep one eye on the visuals, and still type her letters, all at the same time.

It will be after midnight before this typical "day in the life" is over, and it will resume long before dawn. Claire's house guests or her hosts on the road will long since have gone to bed, exhausted by the pace even though they may be many years younger. And when they arise in the morning she will be exactly where they left her, still writing or reading, refreshed from a few hours' sleep, eager to resume the struggle.

The struggles, too, flash past with the speed of film streaming through a projector. There is the March 1991 killing of two Prince Albert prison hostage takers by the prison's Emergency Response Team. CSC officials maintain to this day that the killings were a "righteous shoot" to protect the lives of hostages, but Claire's own investigations have revealed serious flaws in the CSC story. She is pushing for a royal commission on prison violence. There is her painstakingly documented case, soon to be argued before the courts, concerning racial discrimination against native prisoners applying for escorted passes from federal institutions, especially on com-passionate grounds. Time and again native applicants have been denied passes for funerals, for example, while non-native applicants have far higher success rates. Then there are the more mundane cases: helping prisoners oppose involuntary transfers from one prison region to another, or helping others gain transfers that the CSC has opposed; appearing at parole board hearings on a prisoner's behalf; pushing for full investiga-tions of prison and jail suicides. The frames flash past, never slowing, never losing focus.

So how are we to take our leave, in the end, of this remarkable woman?

It is Sunday morning in her cramped, one-bedroom, co-op apartment made smaller still by the floor-to-ceiling bookshelf crammed with hun-dreds of books—about, among other topics, Vietnam, prisons, aboriginal peoples, women, and politics—by her desk and computer and copier, by files and clippings and boxes full of letters to and from prisoners. She has made the crêpe batter the night before; the tradition begun on Charles Street forty years before has continued in Montreal, in Ireland, in Vietnam, in Montreal again, and now back in Vancouver, and her family arrives singly and in bunches, to partake in the ritual that is older than most of them—eating mother's, grandmother's, great-grandmother's crêpes on Sunday.

Roisin is here. Claire's first-born daughter separated from Eltin years ago, and has long since abandoned her animus against political activism. She is now an executive with the British Columbia Human Rights Coali-tion and a leader in the Canadian movement for support of a free, united, and democratic Ireland. Dara, a respected anthropologist, author, and activist, is here, too, along with her two children, Lori and Carey. Roisin's children arrive: Maura, Triona, and Bob, and Maura's son, James.

The five grandchildren are all tall and strikingly handsome, and the room is soon full of conversation and laughter. Roisin and Dara inspect their children with a piercing maternal gaze: you look tired, you're not taking care of yourself, what have you been up to? The grandchildren exchange glances and feign exasperation. Claire smirks and contributes an anecdote about her daughters' own youthful extravagances. Their children look smug. "Nanny" is always an ally. "You didn't laugh then," her daughters remind Claire.

Young James is the apple of everyone's eye. He is the first-born of the next generation. Sunday mornings are his time to shine. He moves from lap to lap, basking in the doting affection that greets his every utterance of five-year-old wisdom.

These gatherings are rarely limited exclusively to family. Everyone is free to bring a friend, and the generations—old friends of Claire's, middle-aged friends of Dara and Roisin, youthful friends of the grandchildren—mingle and take turns at the table, devouring Claire's crêpes. The room is full of conversation and laughter. But these are the Culhanes: politics come with the pancakes and everyone has an opinion on the latest news, whether it is the co-op's landscaping policy or the breakup of the Soviet Union. Vociferous arguments punctuate the joking and teasing.

"In most families," Dara says, "the rule is to be silent and avoid conflict. In our family, it's a crime not to speak your mind and fight for your position."

Claire passes a seemingly endless flow of crêpes back and forth through a window hatch that divides the kitchen from a small dining alcove, kibitzing, proudly surveying her family. In a sense, this is what her life has been about: family and children, happy, healthy children, unafraid, living life with dignity. It is all that she has ever wanted for herself, and for every other parent on the planet. She has realized her own dream, but how can she forget the millions of other parents and children whose lives have been devastated by hunger, by war, by exploitation?

It is Sunday afternoon now. The dishes have been tidied up, the confectioner's sugar wiped off the dinner table. As always, time is of the essence. She has some urgent errand to run—letters to mail, a social at one of the nearby prisons to attend, a meeting. Claire hurries around the apartment, unplugs her transistor radio, the same one she had in Vietnam—she had refused to pay two hundred dollars to have one installed in her Toyota and takes it with her now in the car—and she never grabs the radio without thinking of Ba, and how she loved to listen to that radio while she did the ironing, and she never forgets Ba and her children in that ditch in My Lai. Claire surveys her apartment one more time before leaving—the imposing bookcase, the picture on the wall brought to her by Ba and the others at the airstrip on that gut-wrenching day she left Quang Ngai, at the paintings and cards and crafts on the walls sent to her by prisoners across Canada, mementoes of a lifetime of struggle and of the thousands of lives she has touched. Then she turns off the lights, sets the lock on the door, and is gone.

Endnotes

A Note on Sources

After Claire's own recollections, far and away the most valuable source material for this book was provided through Freedom of Information and Privacy Act applications. By monitoring Claire's movements, actions, and utterances over a fifty-plus-year period (doubtless for "security" reasons) the Canadian government turned out to be her biographer's best friend.

A surprising amount of the material turned out to be simply newspaper clippings of articles by or about Claire. Yet by so painstakingly clipping and preserving primary source material from 1940 to the present, the RCMP Security Service and other government agencies unwittingly created a priceless record about Claire (and, no doubt, about thousands of other Canadians), which it would have taken a researcher months, even years to replicate, if, indeed it could have been duplicated at all.

A cautionary note must, however, be addressed to future researchers wishing to dip into this federally funded treasure trove. While police intelligence is not quite an oxymoron, historians and biographers are urged to beware of taking everything they find in such files at face value. Errors in fact and interpretation within Claire's files are as legion as the gaffes in spelling, grammar, and syntax. In some instances (as, for example, when the Mounties tracked down Claire and her daughters in the Laurentians where they were hiding from Garry in 1955) the police work is positively sterling. At other times, as in the government's inexplicable lapse of sending Claire to Vietnam despite her voluminous RCMP files, police efforts appear to be more of the Keystone Cops variety. Perhaps the ultimate moral here is that the RCMP Security Service and its successor, CSIS, are human, like the rest of us, and no stronger than their weakest source or dimmest employee.

Unless otherwise noted by footnotes within the text, the main source for this book is Claire's own memory. While it has become collective wisdom among professional historians that oral history is to be regarded sceptically, I found Claire's memory both vivid and amazingly accurate in detail. Her accounts were confirmed time and time again by independent sources.

The Freedom of Information and Privacy Act material on Claire arrived in a welter of files from a number of government agencies. I reorganized all of it chronologically, by date of document. These files, along with all other research materials for this book, including tape recordings, clippings, notebooks, files, correspondence, and manuscripts, can be found in the Claire Culhane Collection at the University of British Columbia Library's Special Collections.

One final note: for the record, Claire's oldest daughter was actually christened Sandra Rosheen Sheehy-Culhane. She later opted for the more traditional Irish spelling of her name—Roisin—and to avoid confusion, and by mutual agreement, I have used the latter spelling throughout.

Abbreviations used
CC: Claire Culhane
G&M: Toronto *Globe and Mail*
ML: Mick Lowe
MG: *Montreal Gazette*
MS: *Montreal Star*
NAC: National Archives of Canada
OC: *Ottawa Citizen*
OJ: *Ottawa Journal*
PT: *Pacific Tribune*
RR: Reuben Rabinovitch
TC: The New Westminster, B.C., *Columbian*
TMD: The *Main Deck*
TS: *Toronto Star*
TT: *Toronto Telegram*
VDC: *Victoria Daily Colonist*
VDT: *Victoria Daily Times*
VP: *Vancouver Province*
VS: *Vancouver Sun*

Chapter One: Now We Begin

[1]Bruno Ramirez, "Brief Encounters: Italian Immigrant Workers and the CPR, 1900-30," *Labour/Le Travail* 17 (Spring 1986): 13.

[2]MS, September 2, 1918.

[3]CC, June 1, 1987.

[4]Louis Rosenberg, "Canada's Jewish Community: A Brief Survey of Its History, Growth and Characteristics," Canadian Jewish Population Studies, Canadian Jewish Community Series #1 (Montreal: Canadian Jewish Congress, Bureau of Social and Economic Research, undated): 3.

[5]Louis Rosenberg, "A Study of the Growth and Changes in the Distribution of the Jewish Population in Montreal," Canadian Jewish Population Studies, Canadian Jewish Community Series #4, (Montreal: Canadian Jewish Congress, Bureau of Social and Economic Research, 1955): 2, and Rosenberg, "Canada's Jewish Community": 2-3.

[6]Erna Paris, *Jews: An Account of Their Experience in Canada* (Toronto: Macmillan, 1980), 50, and Lita-Rose Betcherman, *The Swastika and the Maple Leaf: Fascist Movements in Canada in the Thirties* (Toronto: Fitzhenry & Whiteside, 1978), 23-24.

[7]Terry Copp, *The Anatomy of Poverty: The Conditions of the Working Class in Montreal, 1897-1929* (Toronto: McClelland and Stewart, 1974), 25-26.

[8]CC, June 1, 1987. In October 1990 Claire happened across the following description in the *Edmonton Journal* of a Muscovite attending a dedication of a monument to victims of Stalin's political terror: "Isaac Strelchik had one curt and wordless comment on the KGB on Tuesday. With as much force as he could muster, the eighty-year-old former political prisoner spit on the ground across from the secret police headquarters." "EXACTLY how my Grandmother EGLIN would react," Claire scrawled across the top of the page.

[9]Rosenberg, "A Study of the Growth and Changes," 8.

[10]Thérèse Casgrain, *A Woman in a Man's World* (Toronto: McClelland and Stewart, 1972), 61.

[11]Catherine L. Cleverdon, *The Woman Suffrage Movement in Canada* (Toronto: University of Toronto Press, 1950), 232.

[12]Ibid., 229.

[13]Ibid., 240.

[14]Ibid., 246 and Casgrain, *A Woman in a Man's World*, 82.

[15]*The Oracle*, Yearbook of Strathcona Academy, vol. 6 (Montreal, 1935): 15.

[16]Casgrain, *A Woman in a Man's World*, 74.

[17]Cleverdon, *The Woman Suffrage Movement*, 247.

[18]*The Oracle*, 16.

Chapter Two: This Is the World We Live In

[1]Brian Young and John A. Dickinson, *A Short History of Quebec: A Socio-Economic Perspective* (Mississauga: Copp Clark Pitman, 1988), 226.

[2]Ibid., 197.

[3]Lita-Rose Betcherman, *The Swastika and the Maple Leaf: Fascist Movements in Canada in the Thirties* (Toronto: Fitzhenry and Whiteside, 1978), 24.

[4]Lea Roback, interview, October 7, 1989.

[5]Margaret Henricks, telephone interview, January 16, 1991.

[6]For Bennett's authoritarian style see Valerie Knowles, *Leaving with a Red Rose: A History of the Ottawa Civic Hospital School of Nursing* (Ottawa: Ottawa Civic Hospital School of Nursing Alumnae Association, 1981), 35 and 52; for Bennett as a power in Ottawa, *see* 35; for Rogers' reputation, *see* 59.

[7]Ibid., 24.

[8]Ibid., 32.

[9]Ibid., 24.

[10]Hugh Thomas, *The Spanish Civil War* (Harmondsworth: Penguin, 1961), 537-538.

[11]Ibid., 39-42.

[12]Betcherman, *The Swastika and the Maple Leaf*, 23-24.

[13]Evelyn Dumas, *The Bitter Thirties in Quebec* (Montreal: Black Rose Books, 1975), 60.

[14]Elizabeth H. Armstrong, *The Crisis of Quebec, 1914-1918* (Toronto: McClelland and Stewart, 1937, 1974), 257-258.

[15]Ted Allan and Sydney Gordon, *The Scalpel and the Sword: The Story of Doctor Norman Bethune* (Toronto: McClelland and Stewart, 1952), 163.

[16]Paris, *Jews*, 94.

[17]Ibid., 96.

[18]Bourassa, paraphrased in Betcherman, *The Swastika and the Maple Leaf*, 131.

[19]Tim Buck, *Yours in the Struggle: Reminiscences of Tim Buck* (Toronto: NC Press, 1977), 285.

[20]Victor Hoar and Mac Reynolds, *The Mackenzie-Papineau Battalion: Canadian Participation in the Spanish Civil War* (Toronto: Copp Clark, 1969), 238.

Chapter Three: Underground

[1]Buck, *Yours in the Struggle*, 285.

[2]Ibid., 286-289.

[3]Leah Levenson and Jerry H. Natterstad, *Hanna Sheehy-Skeffington: Irish Feminist* (Syracuse: Syracuse University Press, 1986), 4.

[4]Ibid., 9.

[5]Ibid., 165.

[6]R. Sheehy-Culhane, interview, December 15, 1990.

[7]"Vote Garry Culhane" and "LPP standard bearers for B.C.," campaign leaflets published before the June 11, 1945, federal general election.

[8]Letter from CC to ML, August 13-14, 1989.

[9]Levenson and Natterstad, *Hanna Sheehy-Skeffington*, 46.

[10]Ibid., 19.

[11]Quoted in Reg Whitaker, "Official Repression of Communism During World War II," *Labour/Le Travail* 17 (Spring 1986): 138.

[12]Ibid., 145.

[13]Ibid., 139.

[14]Joan Sangster, *Dreams of Equality: Women on the Canadian Left, 1920-1950* (Toronto: McClelland and Stewart, 1989), 166.

[15]All references to documents obtained under the Freedom of Information and Privacy acts are hereafter denoted FOIA/PA. For detail on their provenance, see comments at beginning of endnotes.

[16]Cleverdon, *The Woman Suffrage Movement*, 259-260.

[17]Letters: J.J. Hearne to O.D. Skelton, January 10, 1941, O.D. Skelton to S.T. Wood, January 13, 1941, and O.D. Skelton to J.J. Hearne, January 16, 1941, all in NAC MG 30, vol. 14, File 170.

[18]Irving Abella, *Nationalism, Communism and Canadian Labour: The CIO, the Communist Party and the Canadian Congress of Labour 1935-1956* (Toronto: University of Toronto Press, 1973), 70.

Chapter Four: Kayla

[1]Dominion Bureau of Statistics, *Canada 1945: Official Handbook of Present Conditions and Recent Progress* (Ottawa: Department of Trade and Commerce, 1946), 127.

[2]Ibid., 6-7.

[3]Howard White, *A Hard Man to Beat: The Story of Bill White, Labour Leader, Historian, Shipyard Worker, Ranconteur* (Vancouver: Pulp Press, 1983), 20.

[4]RCMP memos November 27, 1942 and December 29, 42, FOIA/PA.

[5]Letter from CC to ML, September 1988.

[6]Edith Iglauer, *Fishing with John* (Madeira Park, B.C.: Harbour Publishing, 1988). The excerpt appeared in *Saturday Night* magazine, August 1988.

[7]Letter from CC to ML, September 1988.

[8]Letter from CC to ML, December 2, 1989. It is one of the small ironies of history that Garry and Claire may well have unknowingly shared the lounge of the Empress—long a favourite meeting place of Victoria's expatriate British community—with the murderer of Garry's uncle. After spending eighteen months in Broadmoor, an English asylum for the criminally insane, Captain J.C. Bowen-Colthurst, who gave the order to "lock and fire" at Francis Sheehy-Skeffington's execution, retired to Victoria, where he died in 1965 at the age of eighty. See Levenson and Natterstad, *Hanna Sheehy-Skeffington*, 90.

[9]Letter from CC to ML, September 1988.

[10]Whitaker, "Official Repression of Communism," 146.

[11]Merrily Weisbord, *The Strangest Dream: Canadian Communists, the Spy Trials, and the Cold War* (Toronto: Lester and Orpen Dennys, 1982), 112.

[12]Ibid., 120.

[13]Donald Creighton, *The Forked Road: Canada 1939-1957* (Toronto: McClelland and Stewart, 1976), 80.

[14]Abella, *Nationalism, Communism and Canadian Labour*, 80.

[15]Ibid., 84-85.

[16]Ibid., 4.

[17]John Swettenham, *McNaughton* (Toronto: Ryerson Press, 1969), vol. 3: 72.

[18]Ibid., 74. Italics are mine.

[19]Vote results in Swettenham, *McNaughton*, vol. 3: 77. For Godfrey's split of the anti-Tory vote see Mason Wade, *The French Canadians 1760-1967* (Toronto: Macmillan, 1968), 1082.

[20]David Lewis, *The Good Fight: Political Memoirs, 1909-1958* (Toronto: Macmillan, 1981), 263.

[21]TMD, February 2, 1945, 5.

[22]VS, January 25, 1945, 3.

[23]White, *A Hard Man to Beat*, 42.

[24]VDT, June 9, 1945, 8.

[25]Lewis, *The Good Fight*, 268-269.

[26]*The Future of Women in Employment*, Conference Report (Vancouver, January 20, 1945), 1.

[27]Ibid., 1.

[28]Ibid., 2.

[29]PT, March 8, 1946, 2.

[30]Sangster, *Dreams of Equality*, 228-229.

[31]Letter from CC to ML, September 1988.

[32]VDC, October 20, 1946, 7.

[33]White, *A Hard Man to Beat*, 86-87.

[34]Abella, *Nationalism, Communism and Canadian Labour*, 138.

[35]Ibid., 136.

[36]Ibid., 35-37.

[37]Ibid., 162-163.

[38]White, *A Hard Man to Beat*, 172.

[39]Ibid., 174-175.

[40]Details on the York from Sylvia Friedman. *Tribune* review extract from FOIA/PA, RCMP HQ File, April 28, 1950.

[41]Quoted in John Cox, *Overkill: The Story of Modern Weapons* (Markham: Penguin, 1981), 192.

[42]PT, FOIA/PA, undated.

[43]A contention documented repeatedly in Ronald Radosh and Joyce Milton, *The Rosenberg File: A Search for the Truth* (New York: Holt, Rinehart and Winston, 1983).

[44]Ibid., 347-351.

Chapter Five: Hiatus

[1]FOIA/PA "C" Division Montreal Special Branch memo, June 22, 1955.

[2]Reuben Rabinovitch, "In Memoriam" (Montreal: published privately, 1965), unpaged.

[3]FOIA/PA, Hartley to External Aid, July 5, 1967.

[4]A poet, dramatist, IRA member, and lord mayor of Cork, MacSwiney died in an English jail in fall 1920 after a seventy-four-day hunger strike. Levenson and Natterstad, *Hanna Sheehy-Skeffington*, 135.

[5]Letter from CC to ML, August 1988.

[6]Letter from RR to CC, July 22, 1958.

[7]Ken Andrews, interview, August 14, 1989.

[8]Letter from CC to RR, September 16, 1965.

[9]Rabinovitch, "In Memoriam."

[10]*Weekend Magazine*, May 27, 1967, 6.

[11]External Aid Office, "Roster of Experts and Teachers," Action and Routing Sheet, FOIA/PA, September 18, 1967.

[12]Claire always believed that the Mounties had searched their files under S for Sheehy-Culhane, the name on her passport, rather than under C for Culhane, where they would almost certainly have discovered her political past.

Chapter Six: In Country

[1]Jonathan Schell, *The Military Half: An Account of Destruction in Quang Ngai and Quang Tin* (New York: Vintage Books, 1968), 207.

[2]Canada had been a charter member of the ICC at its founding in 1954. The commission's mandate was to oversee the reunification of North and South Vietnam and the holding of democratic elections. Neither goal was ever achieved under ICC supervision.

[3]Schell, *The Military Half*, 5; Duncan McLeod, "A Doctor's View of Viet Nam," *McGill News*, October 6, 1966: 6.

[4]Schell, *The Military Half*, 7-8; Neil Sheehan, *A Bright Shining Lie: John Paul Vann and America in Vietnam* (New York: Random House, 1988), 536.

[5]Schell, *The Military Half*, 10.

[6]Ibid., 212.

[7]CBC, "Vietnam: After the Fire," *The Nature of Things*, aired November 28, 1990.

[8]Ibid.; Claire Culhane, *Why Is Canada in Vietnam?* (Toronto: NC Press, 1972), 17.

[9]McLeod, "A Doctor's View," 6; Alje Vennema, *The Viet Cong Massacre at Hue* (New York: Vantage Press, 1976), 70.

[10]There is approximately one doctor for every one thousand people in Canada today.

[11]McLeod, "A Doctor's View," 6.

[12]Culhane, *Why Is Canada in Vietnam?*, 34.

[13]Ibid., 33.

[14]Paul Martin Sr.'s memoirs, as quoted in G&M, July 3, 1986.

[15]Vennema, *The Viet Cong Massacre at Hue*, 72; and interview, September 27, 1991.

[16]Ibid., 77.

[17]Schell, *The Military Half*, 43.

[18]Culhane, *Why Is Canada in Vietnam?*, 36.

[19]David van Praagh, "In the Wake of a War Machine," *Globe Magazine*, August 26, 1967.

[20]Culhane, *Why Is Canada in Vietnam?*, 37.

[21]Seymour M. Hersh, *My Lai 4: A Report on the Massacre and its Aftermath* (New York: Vintage Books, 1970), 7-8.

[22]Culhane, *Why Is Canada in Vietnam?*, 44 and 48.

[23]Hersh, *My Lai 4*, 8-11.

[24]PBS, "LBJ," parts 3 and 4, *The American Experience*, aired October 2, 1991.

[25]Letter from Alje Vennema to Maurice Strong, August 30, 1966.

[26]Letter from CC to Paul Martin Sr., October 2, 1967, FOIA/PA. Emphasis in original.

[27]G&M, January 6, 1968; Alje Vennema, "Why Didn't We Speak Out?" *Canadian Commentator*, July-August 1971: 6.

[28]Alje Vennema, interview, December 16, 1990.

[29]Culhane, *Why Is Canada in Vietnam?*, 53.

[30]Ibid., 46.

[31]Eric Koch, *Inside Seven Days* (Scarborough: Prentice Hall, 1976), 100.

[32]Alje Vennema, "Tuberculosis in Rural Vietnam," *Tubercle*, 1971: 49-55.

[33]Stanley Karnow, *Vietnam: A History* (New York: Viking, 1985), 602.

[34]Culhane, *Why Is Canada in Vietnam?*, 54.

[35]Alje Vennema, interview, December 16, 1990.

[36]Sheehan, *A Bright Shining Lie*, 717; David Halberstam, *The Best and the Brightest* (Greenwich, Conn.: Fawcett Crest, 1973), 732-741.

[37]Gabriel Kolko, *Anatomy of a War* (New York: Pantheon, 1985), 308.

[38]Ibid., 67.

[39]Ibid., 82-83.

Chapter Seven: Stopping the Bombs

[1]Letters from Jean Arsenault to CC, May 6, 1968; from Earl Drake to CC, May 7, 1968; from Maurice Strong to CC, May 9, 1968, FOIA/PA.

[2]MS, May 25, 1968, FOIA/PA.

[3]Letter from Maurice Strong to the Canadian Delegation in Saigon, May 30, 1968, FOIA/PA. Emphasis added.

[4]Alje Vennema, "Why Didn't We Speak Out?", 6.

[5]Letter from W.R. Shaw to Jean Arsenault, June 19, 1968, FOIA/PA. Emphasis in original.

[6]MG, August 16, 1968.

[7]G&M, June 8, 1968; FOIA/PA, RCMP report July 18, 1968.

[8]Culhane, *Why Is Canada in Vietnam?*, 10.

[9]TS, October 1, 1968.

[10]FOIA/PA, October 1, 1968.

[11]Ibid., September 30, 1968 to October 10, 1968.

[12]Ibid., October 2, 1968.

[13]OC, October 4, 1968.

[14]OC, October 8, 1968.

[15]Ibid.

[16]Gordon Longmuir, "Comments on a report submitted by Mrs. C. Culhane, April 18, 1968, concerning the Canadian Colombo Plan Project at Quang Ngai," Hanoi, Vietnam, November 13, 1968, FOIA/PA.

[17]Restricted memo from Gordon Longmuir to the Canadian Commissioner, ISCS Saigon, November 21, 1968, FOIA/PA.

[18]Vennema, "Why Didn't We Speak Out?", 7.

[19]Nguyen Tien Hung and Jerrold L. Schecter, *The Palace File* (New York: Harper and Row, 1986), 163.

[20]*Voice of Women/La Voix des Femmes* newsletter, Winnipeg, Manitoba, February 1969.

[21]Letter from Dr. C.W.L. Jeanes to Bruno Gerussi, January 17, 1969, FOIA/PA.

[22]Memo from the office of the Secretary of State for External Affairs, May 13, 1969; confidential memo from Maurice Strong to Mitchell Sharp, May 27, 1969, FOIA/PA; from Tommy Douglas to Mitchell Sharp, July 31, 1969, FOIA/PA; from Mitchell Sharp to Tommy Douglas, August 20, 1969, FOIA/PA.

[23]MS, October 3, 1969, FOIA/PA.

[24]Hersh, *My Lai 4*, 44-75.

[25]Ibid., 152.

[26]Enough/Assez leaflet, December 15, 1969, Ottawa, FOIA/PA.

[27]TT, letter to the editor from CC, February 21, 1970, FOIA/PA.

[28]OC, January 13, 1979, FOIA/PA, G&M quoted in *The Canadian Annual Review for 1970*, 325.

Chapter Eight: Canada's Pentagon Papers

[1]RCMP report, February 24, 1970, FOIA/PA, and MS, March 2, 1970, FOIA/PA.

[2]Confidential memo from Blair Seaborn to McGill (no initial on document), April 22, 1970, FOIA/PA.

[3]William Shawcross, *Sideshow: Kissinger, Nixon, and the Destruction of Cambodia* (New York: Washington Square Press, 1979), 154-158.

[4]"K" Division Report, Edmonton S.I.B., July 13, 1970, FOIA/PA.

[5]"E" Division Report, Vancouver, B.C., August 24, 1970, FOIA/PA.

[6]At least eighty-five party members were wounded by police gunfire as well, even though "not one cop was ever conclusively shown to have been killed or even badly wounded by a Panther." Saxifrage Group, "Huey p. Newton: Tribute to a Fallen Warrior," *New Studies on the Left*, vol. 14, nos. 1 and 2, Spring/Summer 1989: 133.

[7]*Voice of Women/La Voix des Femmes* newsletter, British Columbia, September 1970, FOIA/PA.

[8]This sordid chapter in Quebec history would later be dramatized by Montreal director Michel Brault in his moving film *Les Ordres*.

[9]Transcription of CC's full address, January 21, 1991, FOIA/PA.

[10]Karnow, *Vietnam: A History*, 629-631.

[11]A.E. Ritchie to Mitchell Sharp, memo, February 9, 1971, FOIA/PA

[12]Parliament, *Hansard*, May 4, 1971, vol. 4, 3940. The casual reader of Parliament's official record would receive no inkling as to what transpired that day, except for the cryptic notation, "Whereupon there was an interruption from the gallery." Like the modern-day television coverage of Parliament, which remains narrowly focused on the speaker to the exclusion of any reaction from the

honorable members, *Hansard* is frustratingly oblivious to the nuance of history.

[13]Victor Levant, *Quiet Complicity: Canadian Involvement in the Vietnam War,* (Toronto: Between the Lines, 1986), 210-211.

[14]TS, April 29, 1971, FOIA/PA.

[15]Estimates of the number of Canadian volunteers in Levant, *Quiet Complicity*, 210; Mac-Paps refused enlistment: *see* Hoar and Reynolds, *The Mackenzie-Papineau Battalion*, 239; confirmed by ML's telephone interview with Vietnam-era vet Mike O'Brien, Aurora, Ontario, October 7, 1991. *See also* Culhane, *Why Is Canada in Vietnam?*, 101-104.

[16]*Voice of Women/La Voix des Femmes* newsletter, July 1991, FOIA/PA.

[17]TS, April 29, 1971, FOIA/PA.

[18]"Canadian Contact with Hanoi," *Historical Abstracts 1972*, 19-B: 233-237. Sharp would continue to defend Canada's "integrity" in Vietnam long after the fact, even while retrospectively describing the ICC in Vietnam as "a farce" (a descriptor frequently used by Claire at the time) and conceding that Canada should never again join such a mission outside UN auspices. See Mitchell Sharp, "Review of Canada-U.S.A. Relations During Tenure as Minister of External Affairs," lecture delivered at Laurentian University, *Laurentian Gazette*, Special Report, December 16, 1987.

[19]Frank Browning and Dorothy Forman, eds., *The Wasted Nations: Report of the International Commission of Enquiry into United States Crimes in Indochina* (New York: Harper and Row, 1972), 52-55.

[20]CC, presentation to the Department of External Affairs, August 7, 1971, FOIA/PA. See also CC, *Why Is Canada in Vietnam?*, 113-114.

[21]Much of the piece by Clark had first appeared in CIDA files in February 1970 over the signature of A.J. Noel, an employee of the Atomic Energy Control Board. Noel had confided in a letter that he was enclosing "the article that I have prepared in answer to our so-called 'Apôtre de la Paix' (Claire Culhane)." Many of the key paragraphs in Noel's article, which was rejected by *Weekend Maga-zine*, were identical word for word with the *Canada Month* story supposedly authored by Clark eighteen months later. CIDA officials followed the progress of both articles with interest, and when Claire wrote a mild rebuke to the editor of Canada Month, a copy of her letter was circulated at CIDA even before it was published in the magazine.

[22]Letter from D.B. Rheault to Dr. C.W.L. Jeanes, September 22, 1971, FOIA/PA.

[23]Memo from D.B. Rheault to file, January 10, 1971.

[24]Memo from Henry Alain Lawless to D. Beavis, February 5, 1971, FOIA/PA.

[25]Claire Helman, *The Milton-Park Affair: Canada's Largest Citizen-Developer Confrontation* (Montreal: Véhicule Press, 1987), 25-26.

[26]Ibid., 86.

[27]Parliament, *Hansard*, June 29, 1972, 3056-3063, FOIA/PA.

[28]CC, *Why Is Canada in Vietnam?*, 100.

[29]Letter from CC to ML, January 8, 1990.

[30]Letter from CC to ML, December 14, 1987.

[31]*Montreal Sunday Express*, July 22, 1973, FOIA/PA.

[32]Helman, *The Milton-Park Affair*, 90-91.

[33]Ibid., 164-173.

[34]Journal, CC, 4 and 8-9.

[35]Ibid., 7.

[36]Ibid., 13. Claire was not the only North American woman to be inspired by the fighting spirit of her Vietnamese sisters during the war. Exchanges between American, Canadian, and Vietnamese women's groups had a galvanizing impact on the North American women's movement in the early 1970s. The story of such sharing has been captured in books such as Arlene Eisen Bergman, editor, *Women of Vietnam*, (San Francisco: People's Press, 1974).

[37]Restricted telex, Saigon-Ottawa, re Quang Ngai visit of Culhane, November 22, 1973, FOIA/PA. Original in French. See also telex of October 29, 1973.

Chapter Nine: The Best Fight in Town

[1]Originally used by Coalition for Prisoners' Rights newsletter, Santa Fe, New Mexico.

[2]Robert Sarti, *Bandit at Three O'Clock* (Vancouver: unpublished, 1985), 83-4; 182-3.

[3]Claire Culhane, *Barred from Prison: A Personal Account* (Vancouver: Pulp Press, 1979), 20.

[4]Ibid., 24-25.

[5]RCMP memo, classified "Secret," August 10, 1976, FOIA/PA.

[6]Culhane, *Barred from Prison*, 9-10.

[7]Parliamentary Sub-Committee on the Penitentiary System in Canada, Report to Parliament, 25; Culhane, *Barred from Prison*, 36.

[8]Culhane, *Barred from Prison*, 46.

[9]Culhane, *Barred from Prison*, 47.

[10]Parliamentary Sub-Committee on the Penitentiary System in Canada, Report to Parliament, 32.

[11]Ibid., 28.

[12]Culhane, *Barred from Prison*, 130.

[13]Quoted in Culhane, *Barred from Prison*, 116.

[14]B.C. Pen Citizens Advisory Committee submission to the Parliamentary Sub-Committee on the Penitentiary System in Canada (Ottawa, 1977), quoted in Culhane, *Barred from Prison*, 142-143.

[15]TC, December 16, 1976.

[16]Parliamentary Sub-Committee, Report to Parliament, 44; Culhane, *Barred from Prison*, 149.

[17]Culhane, *Barred from Prison*, 218.

[18]Memorandum from Deputy of Preventive Security to Senior Preventive Security Officer, January 26, 1977, FOIA/PA.

[19]Statement of Claire Culhane, Provincial Court, New Westminster, B.C., June 9, 1977, FOIA/PA.

[20]VS, June 21, 1978, FOIA/PA.

[21]VS, August 25, 1978, FOIA/PA.

[22]VP, January 21, 1978, FOIA/PA.

[23]Culhane, *Barred from Prison*, 166-167; Claire Culhane, *Still Barred from Prison* (Montreal: Black Rose, 1985), 6; letter from CC to ML, October 7, 1989.

[24]Letter from CC to Ivan Horvat, September 5, 1978, FOIA/PA.

[25]Letter from Gil Rhodes to CC, August 1, 1979, FOIA/PA.

[26]Letter from CC to Pulp Press, September 25, 1979, UBC, Box 23, File X-23.

[27]Letter from Gil Rhodes to ML, March 26, 1992.

[28]Memo from Donald Yeomans to Senior CPS administrators, "Notes on a meeting with Claire Culhane," October 29, 1979, FOIA/PA.

[29]Ivan Horvat correspondence, UBC, Box 28, File X-23.

[30]Janine Mitchell, "Woman as Revolutionary: An Interview with Claire Culhane," *Makara*, 1978: 2. FOIA/PA.

[31]Culhane, *Still Barred from Prison*, 145.

[32]Letter from CC to ML, March 18, 1992.

[33]TC, August 11, 1978, 2, FOIA/PA; Correctional Services Canada, *Basic Facts About Corrections in Canada 1991* (Ottawa: Ministry of Supply and Services, 1991), 22.

[34]Statistics Canada, 1991; Correctional Services Canada, *Basic Facts 1991*, 27.

[35]Correctional Services Canada, *Basic Facts 1991*, 11.

[36]Culhane, *Still Barred from Prison*, 51-52.

[37]VS, October 17-18, 1984.

[38]Wilson Napoose and David Milgaard come to mind, as does the case of Gary Comeau and Rick Sauvé. For a detailed account of the latter pair's case and the remarkable parallels with the Fox police investigation see Mick Lowe, *Conspiracy of Brothers: A True Story of Bikers, Murder and the Law* (Toronto: Seal Books, 1989).

[39]Trudy Harkness, interview, December 8, 1990.

[40]Liz Elliott, interview, December 9, 1990.

[41]*Canadian Human Rights Advocate*, November 1977, 11; VS September 3, 1987; letter from P.H. de Vink to CC, November 23, 1987, FOIA/PA; memo from Arthur Trono to distribution list, October 20, 1987, FOIA/PA; letter from Arthur Trono to Deputy Commissioners December 24, 1987, FOIA/PA; letter from Arthur Trono to E. McIsaac, March 14, 1988, FOIA/PA; Culhane, *No Longer Barred* (Montreal: Black Rose Books, 1991), 5-8.

[42]Culhane, *Still Barred from Prison*, 87.

Bibliography

Articles, Monographs, Leaflets, and Media and Government Reports

Correctional Services Canada. Ministry of Supply and Services, *Basic Facts About Corrections in Canada 1991*, August 1991.

Culhane, Claire. "Report on Project of Anti-Tuberculosis Hospital Quang Ngai, Vietnam, Canadian Colombo Plan." Prepared for the Department of External Aid, Government of Canada, submitted April 18, 1968.

_____. Journal of "Tour Through Hanoi, Haiphong, and South Vietnam." 1973, unpublished.

Victoria, British Columbia, Labour Progressive Party. "The LPP is Right!" Campaign leaflet issued June 1945.

CBC. "Vietnam: After the Fire." *The Nature of Things*. Aired November 28, 1990.

Hannant, Larry. "Using the Privacy Act As a Research Tool." *Labour/Le Travail* Fall 1989: 181-185.

Mitchell, Janine. "Woman As Revolutionary. An Interview With Claire Culhane." *Makara* 1978: 2-9.

PBS. "LBJ, Parts 3 and 4." *The American Experience*. Aired October 2, 1991.

McLeod, Duncan. "A Doctor's View of Viet Nam." *McGill News*, October 6, 1966.

Praagh, David van. "In the Wake of a War Machine" *Globe Magazine*, August 26, 1967.

Rabinovitch, Dr. Reuben. "In Memoriam." Published privately, Montreal 1965.

Ramirez, Bruno. "Brief Encounters: Italian Immigrant Workers and the CPR, 1900-1930." *Labour/Le Travail* 17 (Spring 1986): 9-27.

"Report of the Conference on The Future of Women in Employment." Vancouver, January 20, 1945.

Rosenberg, Louis. "Canada's Jewish Community: A Brief Survey of Its History, Growth and Characteristics." Canadian Jewish Population Studies, Canadian Jewish Community Series #1. Montreal: Canadian Jewish Congress, Bureau of Social and Economic Research, undated.

_____. "A Study of the Growth and Changes in the Distribution of the Jewish Population in Montreal." Canadian Jewish Population Studies, Canadian Jewish Community Series #4. Montreal: Canadian Jewish Congress, Bureau of Social and Economic Research, 1955.

Saxifrage Group, "Huey P. Newton: Tribute to a Fallen Warrior." *New Studies on the Left* Vol. 14, nos. 1 and 2 (Spring-Summer 1989): 129-135.

Shipyard and General Workers' Federation. "Statement to all Members of the Boilermakers and Iron Shipbuilders Union Local No. 2." in Victoria, British Columbia, August 1945.

Sharp, Mitchell, "Review of Canada-U.S.A. Relations during tenure as Minister of External Affairs." Special Report from lecture delivered at Laurentian University, Sudbury, Ont., October 14, 1987. *Laurentian Gazette.* December 16, 1987.

Sub-Committee on the Penitentiary System in Canada: Mark MacGuigan, Chairman. "Report to Parliament." Minister of Supply and Services Canada, 1977.

Vennema, Alje, M.D. "Tuberculosis in Rural Vietnam." *Tubercle* 1971: 49-59.

_____. "Morbidity and Mortality in Children Under 16 at the Provincial Hospital of Quang Ngai, South Vietnam, 1965 to 1968." *Public Health* Vol. 84, no. 6 (1970): 291-298.

_____. "Malnutrition as seen at the Provincial Hospital of Quang Ngai, South Vietnam, 1965 to 1971." *Environmental Child Health* December 1973: 388-395.

_____. "Perinatal Mortality and Maternal Mortality at the Provincial Hospital, Quang Ngai, South Vietnam, 1967 to 1970. *Tropical and Geographical Medicine*, no. 27 (1975): 34-38.

_____. "Why didnt we speak out?" *Canadian Commentator* July-August 1971: 6.

Whitaker, Reg. "Official Repression of Communism During World War II." *Labour/Le Travail* 17 (Spring 1986): 135-166.

Books

Abella, Irving M. *Nationalism, Communism, and Canadian Labour: The CIO, the Communist Party and the Canadian Congress of Labour 1935-1956.* Toronto: University of Toronto Press, 1973.

Allan, Ted and Gordon, Sydney. *The Scalpel and the Sword: The Story of Doctor Norman Bethune.* Toronto: McClelland and Stewart, 1952.

Armstrong, Elizabeth H. *The Crisis of Quebec, 1914-1918.* Toronto: McClelland and Stewart, 1937, 1974.

Bernstein, Carl. *Loyalties: A Son's Memoir.* New York: Simon and Schuster, 1989.

Betcherman, Lita-Rose. *The Swastika and the Maple Leaf: Fascist Movements in Canada in the Thirties.* Toronto: Fitzhenry & Whiteside, 1978.

_____. *The Little Band: The Clashes Between the Communists and the Canadian Establishment 1928-1932.* Ottawa: Deneau Publishers, 1982.

Boston Women's Health Book Collective. *Our Bodies, Ourselves: A Book by and for Women.* Second Edition. New York: Simon and Schuster, 1979.

Bothwell, Robert and Kilbourn, William. *C.D. Howe: A Biography.* Toronto: McClelland and Stewart, 1979.

Brooke-Shepherd, Gordon. *November 1918.* Boston: Little, Brown and Co., 1981.

Browning, Frank, and Forman, Dorothy, eds. *The Wasted Nations: Report of the International Commission of Enquiry into United States Crimes in Indochina.* New York: Harper and Row, 1972.

Buck, Tim. *Thirty Years: The Story of the Communist Movement in Canada 1922-1952.* Toronto: Progress Books, 1952.

_____. *Yours in the Struggle: Reminiscences of Tim Buck.* Toronto: NC Press, 1977.

Casgrain, Thérèse. *A Woman in a Man's World.* Toronto: McClelland and Stewart, 1972.

Cleverdon, Catherine L. *The Woman Suffrage Movement in Canada.* Toronto: University of Toronto Press, 1950.

Copp, Terry. *The Anatomy of Poverty: The Conditions of the Working Class in Montreal, 1897-1929.* Toronto: McClelland and Stewart, 1974.

Cox, John. Overkill: *The Story of Modern Weapons.* Markham: Penguin, 1981.

Creighton, Donald. *The Forked Road: Canada, 1939-1957.* Toronto: McClelland and Stewart, 1976.

Culhane, Claire. *Barred from Prison: A Personal Account.* Vancouver: Pulp Press, 1979.

_____. *No Longer Barred From Prison.* Montreal: Black Rose, 1991.

_____. *Still Barred from Prison.* Montreal: Black Rose, 1985.

_____. *Why Is Canada in Vietnam?* Toronto: NC Press, 1972.

Dominion Bureau of Statistics. *Canada 1945: Official Handbook of Present Conditions and Recent Progress.* Ottawa: Department of Trade and Commerce, 1946.

Dumas, Evelyn. *The Bitter Thirties in Quebec.* Montreal: Black Rose, 1975.

Gouzenko, Igor. *This Was My Choice.* Toronto: J. M. Dent & Sons, 1948.

Greaves, Desmond C. *The Life and Times of James Connolly.* New York: International Publishers, 1971.

Halberstam, David. *The Best and the Brightest.* Greenwich, Conn.: Fawcett Crest Books, 1973.

Harbron, John D. *C.D. Howe.* Toronto: Fitzhenry & Whiteside, 1980.

Harris, Michael. *Justice Denied: The Law versus Donald Marshall.* Toronto: Macmillan, 1986.

Helman, Claire. *The Milton-Park Affair: Canadas Largest Citizen-Developer Confrontation.* Montreal: Véhicule Press, 1987.

Hersh, Seymour M. *My Lai 4: A Report on the Massacre and Its Aftermath.* New York: Vintage Books, 1970.

Hoar, Victor and Mac Reynolds. *The Mackenzie-Papineau Battalion: Canadian Participation in the Spanish Civil War.* Toronto: Copp Clark, 1969.

Hung, Nguyen Tien and Schecter, Jerrold L. *The Palace File.* New York: Harper and Row, 1986.

Karnow, Stanley. *Vietnam: A History.* New York: Viking, 1983.

Knowles, Valerie. *Leaving with a Red Rose: A History of the Ottawa Civic Hospital School of Nursing.* Ottawa: Ottawa Civic Hospital School of Nursing Alumnae Association, 1981.

Koch, Eric. *Inside Seven Days.* Scarborough, Ont.: Prentice-Hall, 1976.

Kolko, Gabriel. *Anatomy of a War.* New York: Pantheon, 1985.

Krepon, Michael. *Strategic Stalemate: Nuclear Weapons and Arms Control in American Politics.* New York: St. Martin's Press, 1984.

Levant, Victor. *Quiet Complicity: Canadian Involvement in the Vietnam War.* Toronto: Between the Lines, 1986.

Levenson, Leah and Natterstad, Jerry H. *Hanna Sheehy-Skeffington: Irish Feminist.* Syracuse: Syracuse University Press, 1986.

Lewis, David. *The Good Fight: Political Memoirs, 1909-1958.* Toronto: Macmillan, 1981.

Linteau, Paul André, Durocher, René, and Robert, Jean-Claude. *Quebec: A History 1867-1929* (Robert Chods, Trans.). Toronto: James Lorimer and Co., 1983.

Lowe, Mick. *Conspiracy of Brothers: A True Story of Bikers, Murder and the Law.* Toronto: Seal Books, 1989.

Meeropol, Robert and Michael. *We Are Your Sons: The Legacy of Ethel and Julius Rosenberg.* Boston: Houghton Mifflin Co., 1975.

Mitford, Jessica. *A Fine Old Conflict.* New York: Vintage Books, 1978.

——————. *Kind and Usual Punishment: The Prison Business.* New York: Vintage Books, 1974.

The Oracle, vol. 6, Yearbook of Strathcona Academy. Montreal, 1935.

Paris, Erna. *Jews: An Account of Their Experience in Canada.* Toronto: Macmillan, 1980.

Penner, Norman. *The Canadian Left: A Critical Analysis.* Scarborough, Ont.: Prentice-Hall, 1977.

Radosh, Ronald, and Milton, Joyce. *The Rosenberg File: A Search for the Truth.* New York: Holt, Rinehart and Winston, 1983.

Richler, Mordecai. *The Street.* Toronto: McClelland and Stewart, 1979.

Robertson, Heather. *Igor: A Novel of Intrigue* (Vol. 3 of the King Years). Toronto: James Lorimer and Co., 1989.

Rosten, Leo. *The Joys of Yiddish.* Toronto: Pocket Books, 1968.

Salutin, Rick. *The Organizer: A Canadian Union Life.* Toronto: James Lorimer and Co., 1980.

Salisbury, Harrison E. *Behind the Lines-Hanoi*. New York: Bantam, 1967.

Sangster, Joan. *Dreams of Equality: Women on the Canadian Left, 1920-1950*. Toronto: McClelland and Stewart, 1989.

Sarti, Robert. *Bandit at Three O'Clock*. Vancouver, unpublished, 1985.

Sawatsky, John. *Gouzenko: The Untold Story*. Toronto: Macmillan, 1984.

Saywell, John, ed. *Canadian Annual Review for 1970*. Toronto: University of Toronto Press, 1971.

Schell, Jonathan. *The Military Half: An Account of Destruction in Quang Ngai and Quang Tin*. New York: Vintage Books, 1968.

Schneir, Walter and Schneir, Miriam. *Invitation to an Inquest: Reopening the Rosenberg "Atom Spy" Case*. Baltimore: Penguin, 1974.

Shawcross, William. *Sideshow: Kissinger, Nixon and the Destruction of Cambodia*. New York: Washington Square Press, 1979.

Sheehan, Neil. *A Bright Shining Lie: John Paul Vann and America in Vietnam*. New York: Random House, 1988.

Smith, Cameron. *Unfinished Journey: The Lewis Family*. Toronto: Summerhill Press, 1989.

Swettenham, John. *McNaughton*, 3 vols. Toronto: The Ryerson Press, 1969.

Thomas, Hugh. *The Spanish Civil War*. Harmondsworth: Penguin, 1961.

Vennema, Alje. *The Viet Cong Massacre at Hue*. New York: Vantage Press, 1976.

Wade, Mason. *The French Canadians 1760-1967*. Toronto: Macmillan, 1968.

Watson, Louise. *She Never Was Afraid: The Biography of Annie Buller*. Toronto: Progress Books, 1976.

Webster, Jack. *Webster! An Autobiography*. Vancouver: Douglas & McIntyre, 1990.

Weinrich, Peter. *Social Protest from the Left in Canada 1870-1970: A Bibliography*. Toronto: University of Toronto Press, 1982.

Weisbord, Merrily. *The Strangest Dream: Canadian Communists, the Spy Trials, and the Cold War*. Toronto: Lester and Orpen Dennys, 1983.

White, Howard. *A Hard Man to Beat: The Story of Bill White, Labour Leader, Historian, Shipyard Worker, Raconteur*. Vancouver: Pulp Press, 1983.

Wicker, Tom. *A Time to Die*. New York: Ballantine Books, 1976.

Young, Brian and Dickinson, John A. *A Short History of Quebec: A Socio-Economic Perspective*. Mississauga, Ont.: Copp Clark Pitman, 1988.

Index